Delicious Mirth

DELICIOUS MIRTH

The Life and Times
of James McCarroll

Michael Peterman

MICHAEL A. PETERMAN

McGill-Queen's University Press

Montreal & Kingston • London • Chicago

© McGill-Queen's University Press 2018

ISBN 978-0-7735-5467-2 (cloth)
ISBN 978-0-7735-5565-5 (ePDF)
ISBN 978-0-7735-5566-2 (ePUB)

Legal deposit third quarter 2018
Bibliothèque nationale du Québec

Printed in Canada on acid-free paper that is 100% ancient forest free (100% post-consumer recycled), processed chlorine free

This book has been published with the help of a grant from the Canadian Federation for the Humanities and Social Sciences, through the Awards to Scholarly Publications Program, using funds provided by the Social Sciences and Humanities Research Council of Canada. Funding has also been received from the Symons Trust Fund for Canadian Studies of Trent University.

Funded by the Government of Canada | Financé par le gouvernement du Canada | Canada | Canada Council for the Arts | Conseil des arts du Canada

We acknowledge the support of the Canada Council for the Arts, which last year invested $153 million to bring the arts to Canadians throughout the country.

Nous remercions le Conseil des arts du Canada de son soutien. L'an dernier, le Conseil a investi 153 millions de dollars pour mettre de l'art dans la vie des Canadiennes et des Canadiens de tout le pays.

Library and Archives Canada Cataloguing in Publication

Peterman, Michael A., 1942–, author
    Delicious mirth : the life and times of James McCarroll / Michael A. Peterman.

Includes bibliographical references and index.
Issued in print and electronic formats.
ISBN 978-0-7735-5467-2 (cloth). – ISBN 978-0-7735-5565-5 (ePDF). –
ISBN 978-0-7735-5566-2 (ePUB)

    1. McCarroll, James, 1814 or 1815–1892. 2. Authors, Canadian – 19th century – Biography. 3. Biographies. I. Title.

PS8475.C37P48 2018   C811'.4   C2018-905708-4
                                                               C2018-905709-2

This book was designed and typeset by Peggy & Co. Design Inc.
in 11/14 Garamond.

Contents

Illustrations

Acknowledgments

I DEDICATE THIS STUDY TO JANET FRISKNEY, now a research officer of York University. She did much of the hard spadework in helping me to rescue James McCarroll from the faded and hard-to-read columns of old newspapers and magazines. She believed in the project and took a lively interest in gathering the fragments from many different places, including the Customs Department Papers in Ottawa and the microfilm reels of the *Toronto Daily Leader*. She was – and is – a model researcher with remarkable staying power and resiliency. I couldn't have completed this book without her help and support, and I thank her profusely.

I owe many thanks to two Irish-Canadian historians. I am deeply indebted to David Wilson, now the head of the *Dictionary of Canadian Biography* and the author of the two-volume biography of Thomas D'Arcy McGee, for his help and encouragement over many years. I thank William Jenkins of York University for his insights into "Stanly Street" (Lombard Street) in Toronto and his knowledge of the Irish communities of Toronto and Buffalo in the latter half of the nineteenth century.

Jonathan Crago, my very considerate editor at McGill-Queen's University Press, has steadily supported my McCarroll project over the last ten years. He was always there when I needed him and he kept me on track as we settled on matters of structure, emphasis, and detail. To him as well I owe the title, which so nicely unifies McCarroll's literary life. I would also like to thank the two readers who assessed the unedited manuscript for MQUP; their praise and critical reactions buoyed me as I strove to complete the book. My copy editor Kate Merriman has been wonderfully patient with me in all textual and bibliographical matters. Thanks also to Ryan Van Huijstee for his guidance through the publication process.

Close friends have been loyal and good humoured in their support of my obsessive project. I especially thank my long-time friend Michael Levine, Toronto entertainment lawyer extraordinaire, who knows the story well; Robert Thacker of St Lawrence University who, among many other kindnesses, drove me around County Leitrim while I checked out McCarroll sites; fellow scholar Leonard Conolly, now associated with the Shaw Festival in Niagara-on-the-Lake; and Jim Forrester of Lakefield, Ontario, who has helped me with both research challenges and power-point presentations. I thank them all for their continuing fellowship and good counsel.

Many others have helped me over a period exceeding thirty years, sometimes with specific help and sometimes with empathetic interest and scholarly support. The list is long and my gratitude is large: I include Christl Verduyn and Robert Campbell, Carole Gerson, Gwen Davies, Len Early, David Bentley, Judy Donnelly, Chris Raible, Charlotte Gray, Jane Urquhart, Charles Foran, Jack Hodgins, Yvan Lamonde, Patricia Lockhart Fleming, Fiona A. Black, James Doyle, Anne Goddard, William Toye, Bruce Elliott, Germaine Warkentin, Heather Murray, Tom Vincent, George Parker, Katrin Urschel, Michele Holmgren, Sean O' Suilleabhain (Sullivan), Thomas G. Murray, Riana O'Dwyer, Elizabeth Tilley, Helen O'Neill, Maeve Conrick, Vera Regan, Isabelle Lemée, Paul Hutchinson, Lynne Prunskus, Dennis Gagnon, Brendan Edwards, Jean Cole, Lucille Strath, Jodi Aoki, Gordon Johnston, Don Willcock, Patricia Life, Claire Senior, Elwood Jones, Dale Standen, Dennis Carter-Edwards, Richard Plant, Ken Brown, Lewis Macleod, Alistair MacLeod and his son Lewis, Margaret Steffler, Mark Finnan, Sharon Keogh, Charmaine Lindsay, Cheryl Barlow, Gerald Lynch, Andrew Titus, Carl Ballenas, Helen O'Day, John Logan, Marion R. Casey, David R. Beasley, Donna Harrington-Lueker, Joshua Brown, Peter Vronsky, Tom Behr, Timothy Bohen, Madeleine B. Stern, Kathleen Garay, and Sophie Dupré.

Finally, I am greatly indebted to my wife, Cara, for her untiring and often humorous support and to our son, Rob, and daughter, Jessie. They all endured occasional disjunctions and black moods as I pursued James McCarroll over more than three decades.

Delicious Mirth

Introduction

JAMES MCCARROLL IS FORGOTTEN TODAY. However, at the peak of his powers he was a highly regarded literary figure and musician. While his parental roots were Irish Protestant, the imaginative lens he chose for himself was Irish-Catholic, Gaelic, and integrative. By the time he left Canada – in the year before Confederation – he had established himself as one of Canada West's outstanding lyric poets and had earned a strong reputation as an editor, musician, entertainer, and humorist, especially in the then-popular mode of the Irish brogue. In all he did he was "an Irishman to the core" and "an able champion" of his native land.[1] To those attributes should be added his lesser-recognized enthusiasms as a pioneer critic of theatre and music in Canada West and an amateur scientist and would-be engineer, keenly at work on projects but without scientific credentials.

Given his range of interests and skills, his invisibility and the absence of concern for that neglect among contemporary scholars – even of Irish-Canadian life in the nineteenth century – are puzzling. One can find many references to him in biographical dictionaries, anthologies, newspapers, magazines, and archival collections; but to this point they have led nowhere. Since his death in New York City in April 1892, he has slipped through the cracks of "official" cultural memory in Canada. Little has been done to gather up and assess the many fragments that make up the story of his energetic, multifaceted, and productive literary life.

This cultural amnesia calls out for the restoration of James McCarroll's life and literary achievements. The challenge is to gather and reassemble the many fragments of his public life and to see them as a whole. Indeed, there is a plethora of cultural and historical information that can be unearthed in pursuing the i.1 The only extant photograph of James McCarroll, likely taken in New York for inclusion in *Madeline and Other Poems* (New York: Belford, Clark, and Company, 1889). The signature is McCarroll's.

path of a poet-journalist and musician like McCarroll. Furthermore, his busy, sometimes volatile life runs alongside and just below the surface of Canada's uneasy movement from colony to nation just as it moves in parallel to the lives of friends and colleagues like Francis Hincks, Thomas D'Arcy McGee, and John A. Macdonald. His personal experiences, his ventures into publishing, his pursuit of anonymity and use of pseudonyms, and his evolving cultural and political views provide a fresh perspective on the slow emergence of Canada as a political (and cultural) entity over those decades even as they show the extent to which his deeply rooted Irish identity always informed his point of view and general outlook.

Two studies in which we might have expected to find more about McCarroll are noteworthy for this omission. He is totally absent from Nicholas Flood Davin's vanity history *The Irishman in Canada* (1878).[2] Rather conspicuously, Davin includes McCarroll's long-time Peterborough friend William Cluxton, but he seems to have deliberately erased McCarroll because he had become notorious by opting to leave Canada in 1866 and supporting the Fenians in Buffalo. Militant Irish nationalism that threatened Canada did not sit well with Davin and many other Irish citizens in the new nation: McCarroll's pursuit of Fenianism not only ran counter to Canada's evolution as a nineteenth-century democracy but was viewed by some observers as an outrageous, even a traitorous, act. In 1878, nationalist sensibilities were overly sensitive and protective – the timing was too close to the struggle for Confederation for the dispassionate consideration of alternative views of how Canada might have evolved and developed.

Over a century later, in an apparently comprehensive study of the many Canadian writers who moved to New York City in the last half of the nineteenth century, Nick Mount similarly neglected McCarroll, despite the fact that he had been among the first Canadians to move to the city in search of literary and journalistic work after the Civil War. In 1869 McCarroll took up employment there as a journalist and editor at *Watson's Art Journal*; overall, he spent twenty-three years as a writer and editor in New York City. However, he is nowhere mentioned in *When Canadian Literature Moved to New York* (2005). Mount argues that "In the peak years of the exodus, Canadian writers figured prominently in the literary journalism of New York";[3] hence, it is surprising that he overlooks McCarroll's presence there even as he fails to register his involvement with popular magazines like *Watson's Art Journal, Frank Leslie's Chimney Corner*, and *Belford's Monthly Magazine*. Likely the fragmentary nature of the evidence affecting McCarroll's long literary career in Canada – for example, the short-lived runs of many journals and newspapers – was a significant factor in his work as a journalist in New York being overlooked.

Mount's omission has served to amplify my interest in McCarroll. He needs to be retrieved and given place among both notable nineteenth-century Irish Canadians and the leading Canadian poets of his century. Having pursued him and the details of his life for over three decades, I am all the more convinced that attention must be paid to his achievements as well as his errors of judgment. His is a life in fragments to be sure, but once those disparate biographical and literary details are gathered up and pieced together, an important Canadian life emerges. In fact, a close look at the intricacies of his life allows us to see the nineteenth century in Canada in a much more personalized and intricate way, particularly as we focus on the experiences of the Irish during its early decades.

McCarroll's intriguing story comprises three distinct national experiences – his upbringing in the hills and towns of County Leitrim in southwestern Ireland (1814–31); the thirty-five years he spent making his journalistic life and literary reputation in Canada West (1831–66); and his final twenty-five years as a journalist and poet in the United States. His brief respite in the Buffalo camp of the Fenians (1866–68) and his busy autumnal years in New York City make up the third part of his story. McCarroll achieved considerable success in both Canada and the United States, but his shift southward in 1866 meant a change of allegiance and citizenship; those changes cost him a good deal of his earlier fame in Canada.

James McCarroll led a thoroughly nineteenth-century life. His is a classic immigrant's story; it begins with his arrival in Canada with his family in 1831 and his personal struggles as a talented teenager who, starting out as a lowly shoemaker, sought to forge his way upward as a musician, poet, journalist, performer, and scientist. Indeed, his story opens a new path by which to track the lives of writers and musicians like himself in early Canada. He was a professional first as a journalist and then as a Canadian custom's officer, but his life was always a struggle to make ends meet and a personal saga involving numerous relocations and readjustments. He married Ann Davis, who also lived in Peterborough, in 1837. But his financial circumstances and relocations meant living separately in the early years of their marriage and in the last year of Ann's life. From his Canadian beginnings in the village of Peterborough to his years of greatest fame and influence in Toronto in the 1860s, he was a cultural force on the make, a whirlwind of energy, and a man of many talents. He lacked personal wealth and family connections, and he was occasionally intemperate and pugnacious, but he had many musical and literary skills and a notable affability; moreover, he was by temperament and inclination an artist, or, at least, a large part of him insistently was. He was, in the words of the *Irish Canadian*, "a born wit, as he was a born poet, musician and *litterateur*."[4]

McCarroll enjoyed contacts with many of the prominent individuals of his time – politicians like Francis Hincks, John A. Macdonald, Thomas D'Arcy McGee, and William McDougall; businessmen like William Cluxton, William Weller, J. Hamilton Merritt, James Beaty, and the Belford brothers; journalists like Charles Lindsey, James Lamb, Henry J. Ruttan, James Moylan, Ogle Gowan, Patrick Boyle, Henry Cood Watson, and Frank Leslie; musicians like Jenny Lind, Ole Bull, Frederick Griebel, Kate Hayes, Lucca, Henri Vieuxtemps, Maurice Strakosch, and Anna Bishop; and fellow writers like Thomas Moore, Susanna Moodie, Catharine Parr Traill, Isabella Valancy Crawford, Henry Morgan, William A. Foster, Charles Dickens, Henry Wadsworth Longfellow, and Oliver Wendell Holmes. When reconstituted, his experiences offer revealing glimpses into the lives of many of his acquaintances even as they provide insights into his own aspirations and the ways in which he conducted his life.

But, at heart, James McCarroll was an Irishman of charm, warm humour, and good will. He was genial and open – a friend to many, a congenial drinking companion, and a sociable fellow at ease in a variety of social situations. The *Irish Canadian* remembered him "brimful of the sparkling wit proverbial of his country [who] talked and wrote in a vein of delicious mirth."[5] At the same time he could be a combative journalist and writer, "fearless and incisive, yet manly in combat and generous to the vanquished."[6] He could not abide snobbery, pretentiousness, or social airs, and he believed in the opportunities open to worthy individuals in a democratic society. In that regard he was always poised to fight for recognition of his own worth in a world where public notices and newspaper puffs were too often the superficial badges of worth and merit. Schooled to issue a quick and unyielding response to a challenge, he never hesitated to attack his enemies with ad hominem fervour when faced with personal or political challenges. As a creative writer and poet he could be similarly prickly when matters of reputation and relative merit were involved. He was particularly sensitive to being undervalued in relation to other poets and writers.

McCarroll took his genial Irish spirit and rich bank of memories wherever he went. Those who knew him in New York City in his later years recalled that he still spoke with a distinctive Connaught accent and proudly promoted his Irish identity; it was evident in his bearing and his creative grasp of the vernacular. One observer, likely Robert Belford, defined him glowingly as "a true Irishman of the old school": he was "the last of the genuine Bards of Inisfodhla, the latest of the Seannachas of Eirinne, who held in their grasp the learning and the poetry of their nation."[7] Not surprisingly, his writings occasionally celebrated his deep affection for his beautiful, beleaguered home. "He loved his native land, and sung its praises in his own inimitable verse. He loved its legends and its lore; and its music breathed from his soul with the pathos and passion of a master."[8] Always an attentive reader, he attached himself in Canada to the brogue of the stage-Irish tradition as developed by such popular nineteenth-century novelists as Samuel Lover, William Carleton, Clarence Mangan, and the Banin brothers, as well as the playwright Dion Boucicault. That legacy, which he often drew on for creative purposes, can be found throughout his oeuvre – in the poetry belonging to what he called his "Irish Anthology," in the comedic letters written to Thomas D'Arcy McGee by his "lovin cousin" Terry Finnegan, and in his serialized novel "The New Gauger" (1856). So popular were his Finnegan letters that many Canadian readers in the 1860s came to know him simply as Terry Finnegan. He was a talented, light-hearted Irish humorist, "a man of mirth," but he was also a close observer of political matters and what was an acceptable public image in Canada West.

One of McCarroll's abiding habits as a writer was to practise anonymity. He did so almost as a matter of course, since most journalistic writing prior to Confederation was unsigned. Once he became an employee of the Customs Department in 1849 he was concerned, for professional reasons, to mask his identity and keep his name from public identification. But this self-masking was more than a mere convention. By practising anonymity, he could write pieces that were alternative, anti-establishment, parodic, and satiric.

He was not only a journalist and an editor, but he was also "a bard" and "a minstrel." The writing of excellent poetry was his abiding preoccupation. At the same time, having been trained as a flautist in Dublin and Leitrim, he taught music to a number of students in Canada West and entertained audiences across the province with his deft and often flamboyant perform-ances. As a performer he had "few equals in America."[9] A devotee of Italian composers like Donizetti, he charmed listeners with beautiful melodies while his virtuosic flute solos drew frequent calls for encores from audiences and observers. Reviewers esteemed him a Mozart in the backwoods and a "modern Orpheus."

McCarroll was a man of many parts – too many, perhaps, for his own good. Certainly, they constitute a major challenge for his biographer. His scientific-literary image may remind the reader of a cheeky, latter-day Ben Franklin, with his finger in many pies and his refusal to be known as a specialist. In his Ben Franklin mode he was deeply interested in certain scientific questions and challenges. He read widely, even as he relied on his own observations and ability to hypothesize from personal experience. If he was wrongheaded in some of his conclusions and assertions, it did not bother him too much. He trusted himself and ventured outward according to his inclinations. Later in his life he patented and sought to manufacture inventions designed to prevent fires in elevators and to improve elevator safety.

This biography is the result of decades of digging and sleuthing in the numerous places that McCarroll called home in Canada and the United States. I have managed to gather much of what remains of the writing he was able to publish. Seen in one way, his life remains a fragmented but rich trove of early Canadian and, later, Irish-American cultural information. He was, in effect, a Humpty-Dumpty figure who fell precipitously from his Irish-Canadian wall in 1865–66, shattering both his oeuvre and reputation into shards of various sizes. My research has involved finding and gathering up as many of these as possible while at the same time identifying and interrogating the conspicuous gaps in the data. Each gap has led to disappointments. Seen more positively, however, the surviving fragments, when aligned and contextualized, provide their own coherence, insight, and narrative suggestiveness. At the same time, the missing material helps to explain, at least in part, why James McCarroll has remained for over a century Canada's lost poet, overlooked or forgotten by most early-Canadian literary and cultural historians.

Among my biographical challenges are the following. No McCarroll family papers have been found in any Canadian or American archive. Autograph letters from James McCarroll are few and difficult to locate.[10] Revealing looks into his personal life are, thus, rare indeed; so too are personal descriptions of him by others. In addition, several of the newspapers and periodicals he worked on, or in some cases developed himself, have not been preserved either in full or in part. The ephemerality of much mid-nineteenth-century journalism, a condition often bemoaned by scholars, has been a constant challenge as I have sought to track down his many journalistic connections. I estimate that only about 60 percent of what he wrote and published is retrievable today.

Each chapter of this biography provides a detailed look at a specific place in which James McCarroll lived and worked for a period of time. His Canadian experiences began positively in Peterborough (1832–47) and Cobourg (1847–51); then, as a provincial customs officer, he moved his family from Cobourg to Port Stamford (that new post at the Suspension Bridge put him in touch with St Catharines, Niagara Falls, and Buffalo from 1851 to 1853); then to Port Credit (with connections to Toronto) (1853–56); and, finally, to Toronto itself (1856–66) where he enjoyed his greatest prominence as a poet, comedic writer, and musician.

Then came the major sea change in his North American life – his plunge, following from desperate financial circumstances, into the Fenian movement in Buffalo. Tentatively at first, he relocated to Buffalo where he edited two Fenian newspapers for Patrick O'Dea and later wrote *Ridgeway*, a pro-Fenian historical romance (1868). Finally, drawing back from that movement as it faltered near the end of the decade, he completed his reinvention of himself as a seasoned journalist and man of letters in New York City (1869–92).

The particular details of his personal connections and the experiences that were dear to him in each place give body and shape to his curious, always forward-looking, ever-Irish odyssey. By following the sequence of his relocations, the reader is better able to measure his achievements and failures, his practical skills and his pugnacity, his humour and obsessiveness, as well as his ability to influence the lives and views of many who knew him. In terms of his social identity the reader is better positioned to consider the ways in which ordinary people – or, more accurately, not-so-ordinary individuals like McCarroll – lived and interacted with others during the nineteenth century. However, his tumble into the tangled web of Fenianism in 1866 caused numerous Canadians to mistrust his judgment and motives, although other observers saw his actions as reaffirming his essential beliefs and overall worth. Moreover, while he fell so precipitously from cultural prominence in Canada, his buoyant personality and literary abilities allowed him to recover and carry on with unsinkable verve.

James McCarroll was a much more substantial writer and poet than students of Canadian literary history have heretofore recognized or understand. In fact, his final two decades in the United States blur what had seemed – at least until 1864–65 when he was at the height of his literary productivity in Toronto – an instructive Irish-Canadian narrative, one that paralleled but also ran counter to the much better known story of Thomas D'Arcy McGee, with whom he, as Terry Finnegan, so joyfully and naughtily linked himself in a popular "correspondence." His various movements in Canada West as a customs officer provide one explanation for the much-fractured picture we have of his life. He was always on the move, ready to take up literary opportunities but, as a government official, needing to mask his identity. Everything came together for him in Toronto in the mid-1850s; a decade later, everything fell apart.

A number of early commentators have rightly observed that, despite his journalistic skills and musical performances, James McCarroll most deserves posterity's attention for his poetry. The Rev. Edward Hartley Dewart knew this: he considered him among the leading Canadian poets when, in 1864, he put together his path-breaking anthology *Selections from Canadian Poets*.[11] In fact, during McCarroll's decade in Toronto, the *Toronto Daily Leader*, one of the city's leading newspapers, published close to one hundred of his poems. This in itself was a remarkable output by a single media source in Canada West during that century.[12] More surprisingly, in 1885 a well-informed but anonymous critic wrote a series of profiles on the "Poets and Poetry of Canada" for the *Peterborough Examiner*. About McCarroll, the writer noted that, though he has been "long and favorably known to the reading public," "it is as a poet ... that his real powers are best seen, and upon this part of his work his fame will rest."[13] One must add here that this tribute to McCarroll's poetic skills was written twenty years after he had left Canada under a Fenian cloud. A few informed observers clearly remembered his "real powers." Accordingly, this biography offers a selection of his lyric and humorous poems; these poems deserve attention in themselves even as they provide insights into his formative experiences and his sensibility.

Poetry was but one area of achievement. Charles Lotin Hildreth, McCarroll's fellow editor at *Belford's Magazine*, observed in 1889 that McCarroll had "the honorable distinction of having edited or been connected with more newspapers, journals, and magazines than any other man in America."[14] This in itself is no small tribute to a writer during an era of heightened journalistic expression and expanding readership of many kinds. His various newspaper connections verify this extraordinary aspect of his literary career. Hildreth also suggests an important contextual aspect of the final third of McCarroll's literary life. He helps us to recognize "America" as a cultural entity that, for many people in the 1870s, included both the United States and Canada. Over his lifetime McCarroll moved from one world to the other with ease and poise. When pulled together, the descriptions and puffs that James McCarroll received as a musician and a writer provide a remarkable record of cultural recognition and achievement over nearly sixty years.

Prominent among his passions in the 1840s was his sustained and combative support of the Reform movement and the cause of "Responsible government" in the Canadas. A fervent anti-Tory all his life, he made many friends and enemies. Among his important allies were fellow Reform journalists Charles Lindsey and Francis Hincks, as well as the embattled lieutenant-governor of the period, Lord Elgin.[15] As a progressive thinker with a religious bent, he was drawn to the possibilities inherent in the spiritualism movement, which first caught his attention and that of many progressive-minded Canadians, including Susanna Moodie, in the early 1850s. He sought to balance that "enthusiasm" with an objectivity appropriate to the scientific side of his mind. Although nominally a Christian and a Protestant, he remained ever hopeful that a new direction might emerge out of the spiritualist movement, inspiring people to move beyond the tyrannies of religion, politics, and war that so evidently hampered the capacities for human progress in the world.[16]

It was in Toronto that McCarroll made several of his major contributions to the development of a then-nascent literary culture in English Canada. In addition to his poetry, two quite distinct enthusiasms merit attention. Both have either gone unnoticed or been ignored since that vibrant pre-Confederation decade of 1854 to 1865, in part because he carefully veiled many of his cultural ventures through the mask of anonymity. Over time, ironically, that then-conventional mask has assured not so much protection as loss and oblivion.

First, in 1854, while living in Port Credit and commuting to Toronto by ferry or train, he became the first serious critic of theatre in Toronto. His columns were part of an overall attempt by the *Daily Leader* to advance critical thinking in the arts beyond the polite system of puffery then in practice. This was the first such critical foray into quality theatre performance by a major Toronto newspaper and one that distinguished the *Leader* from its chief rival, the *Globe*. Its editor, Charles Lindsey, set McCarroll free as his critic to write a series of detailed reviews of local productions. The Royal Lyceum Company, under the direction of John Nickinson, was then resident in the city for part of the year and, not surprisingly, the company expected a continuation of that system of uncritical support for their efforts. In his unsigned reviews, McCarroll managed to anger and alienate both Nickinson and members of his company. The result was a dramatic kafuffle in Toronto that forced the *Daily Leader* to replace him as its chosen reviewer in order to defuse the uneasy situation.[17] In his place Lindsey employed the more genial and diplomatic Daniel Morrison who, later in 1854, also took on major editorial duties at the newspaper.[18] Lindsey refused to identify McCarroll who, thereafter, directed his critical attention to the music scene in the city, though, along with Morrison, he may also have written reviews of some of the productions by visiting theatre groups like the Italian Opera Company. In the Royal Lyceum incident the practice of anonymity generated a state of confusion that has lasted over 150 years.

Second, in the early 1860s McCarroll created a number of comedic voices while writing for small satiric newspapers like the *Grumbler*. The most popular of his voices was Terry Finnegan, a stage-Irish Paddy figure specifically designed for Catholic readers in Protestant Toronto. Terry proved to be a journalistic tour de force; his letters found immediate place in the homes of local Irish readers, be they Catholic or Protestant, as well as among many other readers of

British origin. The aim was to amuse, stimulate, and inform – and Terry did all that. Indeed, by positioning Terry on "Stanly Street" (today's Lombard Street) in one of the city's most notorious and unruly Irish ghettoes, McCarroll gave Toronto centrality in his "letters" and set a high-spirited, free-wheeling tone for his urban Irish humour.[19] Terry identified himself as the "lovin cousin" of Thomas D'Arcy McGee (of Montreal); he sent McGee a weekly letter filled with advice about how to respond in Parliament to political issues and opposition figures while providing commentary on various social events in the city.[20] Indeed, Terry's letters became something of a reference point for Irish readers trying to make sense of the shifting and uncertain politics of the day; at the same time "the inimitable Terry" offered "racy," amusing, sometimes outrageous looks at the major political players, among them John Sandfield Macdonald, John A. Macdonald, D'Arcy McGee, George Brown, Michael Foley, William McDougall, and George-Étienne Cartier. By late 1865 when he had ceased to write the letters, his name and Terry's had become synonymous in the minds of many city readers. The Toronto publication in 1864 of the "first series" of Terry's letters under McCarroll's name assured readers of the Finnegan-McCarroll connection.[21]

Relatedly, McCarroll was an influential player in what might be called Toronto's first subversive literary movement. Terry Finnegan's letters were the most noteworthy product of what was a collective effort to loosen the girdle of sobriety and restraint that held the Toronto media in its grip. This in-group was made up of a set of adventurous young writers and editors eager to snipe at the city's journalistic establishment, represented by George Brown and his influential *Globe*. They invented and financed a small-scale satiric press modelled on the success of *Punch* in London. It was a movement without a particular political agenda; rather its writers and editors sought to create various alternative points of view from which to mock and make light of the big political players and their policies. This spirited initiative led to a number of short-lived periodicals or satiric magazines, among them the *Grumbler*, the *Poker*, *Momus*, the *Latch-Key*, the *Growler*, and *Pick*. Thus far, there has been little attempt to study or make sense of this subversive literary activity. The fact that few of these small magazines were well enough financed to allow for runs of more than a few months certainly makes coherent study a challenge. So too does the practice of anonymity. In its three separate runs, the *Grumbler* was the most prominent of these magazines, but the fact that its runs were interrupted by lawsuits suggests that such satiric writing was a dangerous undertaking for editors and writers alike in 1860s Toronto.[22]

James McCarroll's role in this cultural blossoming was extensive. Not only did he contribute to *Momus* (1861) and the first coming of the *Grumbler* (1858–59), but he later made that magazine home for many of the "first series" of Terry Finnegan's letters. Then in 1863 and 1864 – years that proved very troubling for him personally and financially – he self-published his own little magazines, the *Latch-Key* (in 1863 and again in 1864), and the *Growler* (1864). All had short runs. He was also a regular contributor to William Halley's *Pick* (1865) where his final Terry Finnegan letters appeared.[23] Halley, Erastus Wiman, and John Ross Robertson were among the young Toronto journalist-entrepreneurs who fostered, edited, and published these satiric magazines.

Little scholarly work has been done on these "little magazines," though they represent the first eruption of counterculture journalistic energy in Toronto. A rare and misidentified James McCarroll letter provides valuable information about their modus operandi and interconnections. It is found in the William A. Foster collection, where it is misfiled under the name "Carroll."[24] Dated 5 September 1864, it reads as follows:

> My Dear Foster,
> The first number of a new series of the *Latch-Key* appears on Saturday next, positively. Give me some scraps and your name shall be held sacred if you desire it. The "posters" will be out tomorrow announcing the publication; and stating that it will contain exclusively Terry Finnegan's letters, as well as other articles from the pen of that genius. In addition, the bills will claim that all the principal writers on *Momus* and the first series of the *Grumbler* will also be contributors. Let me see you or hear from you. The *Latch-Key* will be published at Graham's – a door or two from you.
> Faithfully,
> J. McCarroll

The letter reveals McCarroll's active presence in this literary counterculture and the high place achieved there by Terry Finnegan and his vaunted "genius." It also suggests that most of the writers for these magazines knew each other and shared a desire to mock or criticize politicians and the life around them in Toronto, even as they required protection of their identity for practical reasons.

McCarroll's Terry Finnegan letters rose above the short-lived magazines in which Terry appeared. After the "First Series" of his letters was collected in book form in 1864, McCarroll began a "Second Series," many of which were published in *Pick* in 1865. A challenge for scholars today is to probe deeper into this culture of Toronto's satiric magazines, despite the constraint of lost runs and missing issues. So, too, McCarroll's own place in that milieu needs to be measured more fully.

In 1999 I approached the late Francess Halpenny, then general editor of the *Dictionary of Canadian Biography*, about the possibility of including James McCarroll in volume 12 (1891–1900). It was to be a very thick volume, she told me, and was scheduled for publication in 2000.[25] I realized then that I did not know enough about him to bring together the solid biographical information required to meet the deadline and the DCB guidelines; hence, Dr Halpenny decided not to pursue the matter further. With regret I had to agree with her; I recall, in fact, feeling some relief, given other demands on my time.

Since then I have brought McCarroll forward in a series of articles designed to call attention to his literary talents, his involvement with the Buffalo Fenians, and the extraordinary trajectory of his cultural life. I have required many years of intermittent sleuthing – three decades, in fact – with crucial help from several academic colleagues, fellow researchers, and research assistants, to gather up a sufficient number of the fragments from his life to present his story in the fullness it deserves.[26] In pursuing the details of his early Peterborough life, for example, I have consulted a variety of historical texts and newspapers for fragments of information. My search has unearthed a few previously unknown but important sources. These include two local court transcripts involving him. Nevertheless, his story is characterized by incompleteness. Early town records are thin at best and the passage of time has led to other losses. Moreover, the absence of family and personal papers assures that many details of their lives must remain absent.[27] Incomplete church and school records have hampered my gathering of details, as has the loss of nearly all the issues of the two Peterborough newspapers in which McCarroll was involved in the 1840s.

Indeed, since 2000 I have been delighted to unearth new information about James McCarroll. Fresh clues have led me to additional discoveries. Recently, for example, the Friends of Maple Grove Cemetery in Queens contacted me when they tracked down McCarroll's unmarked grave in New York City.[28] I have also discovered his employment as managing editor of and writer for *Watson's Art Journal* (1870–71) in New York City, a connection never mentioned in any of his obituaries.[29] I have no doubt that there is more important information to be found in archives and newspapers, both in Canada and the United States. However, I am now ready – with the steady encouragement of Jonathan Crago and McGill-Queen's University Press – to bring James McCarroll's Irish-Canadian story forward. I wish him well in his reintroduction to the world that has forgotten him.

Leitrim:
An Irish Education

THE IRISH LAD WHO WOULD BECOME ONE OF CANADA'S most neglected and misunderstood literary figures was born in the town of Lanesboro, County Longford, on 3 August 1814. That much is sure. So is the fact that more than two hundred years have passed since the birth of James McCarroll in that British garrison town near the banks of River Shannon. Much else remains uncertain.

Raised and educated in nearby County Leitrim, McCarroll's early life was closely connected to the Church of Ireland through his parents. Very few details about the family are available. But since he considered himself a Connaught man all his life, it is a near certainty that James spent his first sixteen years in the ancient province of Connaught, as the five western counties of Ireland had been known for centuries.[1] A few surviving details and descriptions provide glimpses into the conditions and influences that shaped his upbringing and education. His memories of those experiences don't begin to appear in his poems and stories in Canada until the late 1840s.

McCarroll's birth date coincides with the final months of the Napoleonic Wars and thus belongs to England's emergence as the most powerful nation in the Western world. England now proudly saw itself as the greatest empire, culturally strong at home and with colonial tentacles reaching around the globe. But in remote Leitrim, the least populated of the Connaught counties, the decade of the 1820s was still dominated by the long-standing traditions practised by rural Irish Catholics. Declan Kiberd has vividly described "the pre-Famine gaiety" that then characterized rural life in southern Ireland; he points particularly to "the old, joyful world of wakes and pattern-days, festivals and carnivals."[2] Raised as a Church of Ireland Protestant, McCarroll was nevertheless stimulated imaginatively by the rich communal life of the Catholic populace, even as he learned more about the political realities concerning English governance of Catholic Ireland. The advantages of empire and the social order assured by the English military presence in Ireland vied with the sheer energy and pursuit of pleasure evident in the daily life of the poor Catholic families in his observation.

McCarroll himself supplied a few pieces of information about his family to his (first) Canadian biographer, Henry Morgan, in the 1860s.[3] Documents in Canadian government land-grant files, news items in a contemporary Leitrim Protestant newspaper, and an advertisement placed by his father, Robert McCarroll, in the *Cobourg Star* in Upper Canada help to fill in the picture.[4]

James's father made his living in Leitrim as a military musician and a shoemaker. Music for him was a matter of personal passion, while a practical trade was essential to providing for his family. He held the position of bandmaster of the Leitrim Militia, whose home base was Carrick-on-Shannon, for twenty-one-and-a-half years.[5] The skills he passed on to his son proved invaluable to him in Upper Canada.

Although Robert McCarroll's military rank was that of a sergeant, and thus of relatively low status in the military hierarchy, his years of service made him eligible for a land grant of one hundred acres in Upper Canada. These were the early boom years of emigration and a large number of half-pay veterans of British militia units and regiments, many of whom had served in the Napoleonic Wars, found themselves pensioned off in Britain and in need of new opportunities. A number of them chose to make their way to Canada, lured by the assurance of free land and the promise of greater social freedom. The McCarrolls were part of a large contingent of Protestant emigrants leaving western Ireland from ports like Galway, Sligo, and Cork during the years 1829 to 1832.[6] In their reasons for emigration, the McCarrolls were not unlike the Anglo-Scottish families of John Moodie and Thomas Traill, though they left from Scotland and arrived in Upper Canada a year later. The land grant that Robert McCarroll received was in Emily Township, fifteen miles north of the town of Peterborough.[7]

Henry Morgan teased out only one story from James McCarroll about his father's life in Ireland. Robert had apparently enjoyed an early connection with the aristocratic Carden family of Templemore in Kilkenny. Morgan retold the story in *Sketches of Celebrated Canadians*: "His father's side of the house was, in some way or other, connected with the Cardens of Templemore, who evinced much interest in McCarroll's family; for, on his father running away to enlist,

Sir John Carden followed him with a view to providing for him more suitably, but, ere he had effected his generous purpose, the hand of the spoiler fell on the brave old knight, [and] he died" (757). Morgan's language romanticizes the value that Sir John Carden saw in Robert's potential, implying a high estimate of his musical talent. The anecdote also suggests the root of Robert's military career and perhaps implies an elopement, even as it raises more questions than it answers. Whatever the case, Robert McCarroll remains a mystery both in Ireland and North America.[8] Surviving information about him is very limited; I have learned only that his wife's family was named Kennedy.[9] A later account of James's life states that Robert died at Antietam in 1862 during the American Civil War.

James was a precocious and talented youth, blessed with literary inclinations and musical abilities, much like his father. Just as Sir John Carden saw a young man worth looking out for in Robert McCarroll, so many of his acculturated friends in Peterborough and Cobourg would soon see young James as a multi-talented individual. Curiously, after his death in 1892, one County Longford historical writer was so taken by the story of his success in Canada that he cited him "as an example of how successful the ordinary Irish Catholic emigrant, of some education, might become."[10] Successful James was in many ways, first in Canadian towns and then on the larger stage of Toronto in the immediate pre-Confederation era; little, however, did that Longford chronicler realize that the McCarrolls were in fact proud Church of Ireland Protestants from western Ireland, not "ordinary Catholic emigrant[s]."[11]

Robert McCarroll's connection to the Templemore estate clearly assumed a legendary status in McCarroll family lore, but their daily life in Leitrim was much more mundane. As militia bandmaster, Robert would have housed his family near the military headquarters in Carrick-on-Shannon, giving James many opportunities to wander farther afield to towns like Mohill, Rooskey, Toomen, and Boyle, and into the adjacent county of Roscommon. In Carrick-on-Shannon Robert practised his trade as a shoemaker while performing his military duties as required; he also sought to expand his own musical education and extended such opportunities to his son.

James spent his youth in Leitrim.[12] He told Henry Morgan that he "went early to school" and "studied earnestly and with success." There he "obtained a knowledge of the Classics" and studied music. Having begun his musical training under his father's guidance, he later took lessons from two prominent teachers then living in Ireland. As a result, music became the foremost aspect of his Irish education and a special bond with his father. A year after they moved to Upper Canada, Robert and his son placed an ambitious advertisement for a "Music School" in "Cobourg and its vicinity." They reported that they had "been for five years under the immediate instruction of two of the most eminent professors in Europe, Drs. [Domenico] Briscoli and [J.B.] Logier."[13]

It remains a mystery how the McCarrolls – father and son – managed, while living in Leitrim, to study for five years with two well-known music professors. From Carrick-on-Shannon to Dublin, where Logier and (likely) Briscoli were situated, was a journey of about one hundred miles by stagecoach. Nevertheless, for two individuals in the thrall of music, occasional trips may have been possible, while Logier and Briscoli may have given lessons outside Dublin.

Johann Bernhard Logier (1777–1846) and Domenico Briscoli were prominent musicians and composers in their day. Each had strong connections to military music and the preservation of Irish folk music. Of the two, Logier was the better known and the more closely connected to Dublin, though his fame was considerable in England. A German-born pianist, teacher, author, and composer, he had also been a military bandleader in England and Ireland early in his career and thus could offer Robert McCarroll the benefit of his experience and extensive martial repertoire.[14] In fact, Logier was in such demand around Europe that Charles Turner painted his portrait in London; his bust, by the Irish sculptor Peter Turnerelli, was exhibited in 1828 at the Royal Hibernian Academy.

Logier lived in Dublin for two periods of his teaching life. He kept a shop and studio on Lower Sackville Street from 1810 to 1817; then, after spending some time back in Germany, he returned to run a music shop and take on students on Upper Sackville Street in the late 1820s. The McCarrolls would have taken their lessons with him during these later years. Among his many musical publications were *Strains of Other Days, Being a Selection of Favorite Irish Airs, Arranged for Piano Forte and Dedicated to the Irish Harp Societies* (n.d.) and *Sacred Music, Adapted for Public and Private Devotion: The Melodies Selected from the Works of Handel, Haydn, Mozart, Hummel, Franc, Arnold, Webbe, Pleyel, Viotti and Beethoven*, which he co-edited in 1830.

Signore Domenico Briscoli was also a composer, teacher, and performer. In 1807 the *Monthly Magazine* in London identified him as "Composer and Director of Music to the Louth Regiment [Ireland] and Master of the Royal College of Pista de Torckini of Naples." Like Logier, he early on established a connection to regimental music in Ireland; he composed pieces for marching bands and provided instruction in various instruments, including the flute and harp. His well-known martial composition "The Battle of Egypt" (c. 1820) was a popular military piece available in Irish sheet music in the early decades

1.1 The statue honouring Turlough Carolan is located on the main street of Mohill, a town in Leitrim not far from McCarroll's boyhood home. Source: Wikimedia Commons, Sarah777, Creative Commons License.

of the century. Other compositions included the "Four Seasons" and "The Conversation of Five Nations."[15] Like Logier, he arranged compositions based on Irish (and early Welsh) popular airs. Most notable in this regard was his "Grand Duet for Pianoforte and Flute," which included "the favorite air of Paddy O'Rafferty" (1815). According to Francis O'Neil,[16] this sprightly air or jig, originally composed by Carolan, has continued to be part of the standard corpus of Celtic folk music for fiddle or flute to this day. Through the influence of Briscoli and Logier James McCarroll first came to understand the national importance of traditional folk airs, in particular the compositions of Turlough Carolan (1670–1738), the legendary blind harper of Leitrim, who is seen by numerous historical observers as Ireland's national composer.

Just as important was the development of James's poetic sensibility. It took early form in his attraction to the poems and songs of Thomas Moore (1779–1852). As a writer and performer, Moore was much celebrated in the first half of the nineteenth century as "the Shakespeare of Ireland" and Erin's master of melody.[17] By the 1820s he was approaching the height of his literary fame. Frequently compared to such acknowledged Scottish masters as Walter Scott and Robert Burns, and to his close friend, the notorious Lord Byron, Moore was often in the news, be it for his many writing projects or his personal

THOMAS MOORE.

1.2 Thomas Moore was McCarroll's chosen mentor and model as a poet. Source: Charles Dudley Warner, Hamilton Wright Mabie, and Lucia Isabella (Gilbert) Runkle, *Library of the World's Best Literature, Ancient and Modern*, vol. 18 (New York: J.A. Hill & Company, 1902), p. 10271, Wikimedia Commons.

adventures. Byron, who had been eulogized in a biography by Moore himself, died suddenly in 1824 and left his controversial memoirs in Moore's possession. This precipitous action led to many well-publicized twists and turns concerning the control and use of the manuscript. Through it all, Moore, the great poet, remained in the news.

Moore was also well known for his associations with eminent Irish noblemen like Lord Lansdowne, with whom he toured western Ireland in 1823.[18] That trip led to his first book of prose, *Memoirs of Captain Rock: The Celebrated Irish Chiefton, with Some Account of His Ancestors* (1824). A fictionalized and polemical autobiography, it was published widely in Britain and Europe and enjoyed steady popularity over the next decade.

McCarroll was ten years old when Moore's book on Captain Rock took Ireland by storm. By then, like many Irishmen, James would have known a number of Moore's *Irish Melodies* by heart; several volumes were then in circulation. His popular poems, often with musical accompaniment, were contributions to what Moore liked to call Ireland's "National Music." Often based on old Irish airs, they were his personal tributes to his country just as Burns had evoked and celebrated Scotland in his poems. Songs like "Tis the Last Rose of Summer," "The Minstrel Boy," "The Harp That Once through Tara's Halls," and "Oft in the Stilly Night" became the treasured music of the day for many Irish men and women, regardless of their religion. Lord Byron once claimed that he knew all Moore's songs by heart. Robert and James McCarroll would likely have made the same claim.

Moore's *Memoirs of Captain Rock* may have had almost as lasting an influence on James McCarroll as did his *Irish Melodies*. The book's evocation of familiar settings in western Ireland, its response to the burgeoning record of rural vigilante activities that so disturbed and terrified Protestants, and its creation of Rock as a semi-mythical Celtic hero appealed to many Irish-Catholic readers. Captain Rock became a Robin Hood figure, a crusader who attacked insensitive English landlords on behalf of the suppressed Catholic peasantry. A Catholic and a nationalist, Moore had been deeply upset by the poverty and social constrictions affecting the peasantry that he witnessed during his trip through Ireland with Lord Lansdowne. Combining outrage, parody, and myth making, he created a fictionalized version of the legendary Captain Rock, allowing him to tell his story in his own words. Moore presented a vivid account of rural vigilante activity designed to call attention to English mismanagement and misrule in rural Ireland, English injustice, and the desperate situations faced by many poor Irish Catholics.

It is not surprising that once his own literary career began to take shape, McCarroll dedicated a poem to his Irish mentor. "To Moore" was published in Peterborough, Canada West, in 1849 while Moore was still alive, though suffering from senility in Dublin.[19] The poem makes clear that McCarroll had read the entire corpus of Moore's writing. He was especially delighted by Moore's musical genius and lively word control, both of which he irreverently echoed in his tribute. The poem catches a duality and allusiveness in Moore's writing that McCarroll found fascinating and charming. Many years later he reported that he had written to Moore, likely in the late 1840s, and that he managed to have some correspondence with him before his death.[20] No doubt he sent him a copy of the poem.

With its bracing use of the brogue and its smooth integration of rough language, "To Moore" is one of McCarroll's best and most lively poems. It is surprising that he chose not to include it in his only collection of poetry, *Madeline and Other Poems* (1889), several decades later.[21]

Arrah, who would believe you're the boy who supposes
That love always lies on a *shake-down* of roses,
    Inhalin' its splindid perfume;
Whin you've seen him yourself – ay in all kinds of weather –
On a wad of ould sthraw, with a dozen together.
    And a different sint in the room!

Ah, thin lave off your jokes and your swindling *figaries*
That's sung from the poles to the bilin' Canaries
    Through the manes of *enchantment* I'm sure –
For you've ruined the Turks and the Frinch and all nashuns,
With your haythenish stories and thricks, and translachuns
    From that dhrunken, Greek son of a _____.[22]

From this kind of doins,' begorra I'm thinkin'
Your apt to "blaze blazes" at humbug and dhrinkin
    And "followin' out your own whim";
And by ____ what's more, mind "the divil is in it"
If half the young gossoons that know you this minnit
Shouldn't dash off their names with an "M"!

"But whare is the use?" – whin, to prove all I minshun,
We sarch your own books, you lade off our attinshun
    In a way that would puzzle an elf;
For just at the spot where we turn up our noses,
You schamer, you're ready to *Gul* thim with roses,
    Till we lose every thrace of yourself!

The poem celebrates Moore's ability to enchant his readers while exploring his "schamer"-like evasiveness, and one might imagine that in his early days McCarroll himself would have been one of those "young gossoons," so beguiled and gulled "with roses" as to want to be just like the dashing poet "followin' out [his] own whim."

In addition to the strong influences of music, poetry, and "the Classics," the natural beauty of the southern part of County Leitrim became rooted in McCarroll's sensibility. The novelist John McGahern has called Leitrim "the poor heart" of Ireland. The most northeasterly of the five counties making up Connaught, it remains largely unsettled and rural today, especially in its mountainous north. Indeed, in the 1820s its geography made extensive travel a daunting challenge, so much so that some observers casually dismissed the entire county as mostly "bogs, mountains and waste."

Such a bleak view overlooks the beauty and charms of Leitrim's geography. Although the county claims only a small piece of the western Ireland coastline and although much of its soil is thin, it is characterized by rivers, mountains, and green rolling hills. McGahern locates his attraction to Leitrim in its ordinariness. He writes, "There is nothing dramatic about its landscape, but it is never dull."[23] It is the home of several large rivers, the Erne and the Boyle in the north and the sinewy Shannon in the south, the tributaries of which, linked to adjacent lakes, run throughout large stretches of the county. The Shannon feeds Lough Allen, the largest of Leitrim's many attractive lakes. Drumlins rise above the lakes and valleys, and fringe the higher green hills and mountains.

Leitrim has been the home of at least two important artists – the harper Carolan and the novelist John McGahern (1934–2006), whose lyrical master-piece *For Those Who Face the Rising Sun* (2001)[24] paints a pastoral picture of southern Leitrim even as it probes many of the county's social problems. McGahern transforms the "bogs and waste" into sites of rural beauty of the sort that McCarroll knew well. But McCarroll also remembered that, partially hidden among the greenery near the Shannon, one could locate a few of the ruins dating from Ireland's legendary antiquity.

James McCarroll's memories of southern Leitrim's green landscape – its meadows, laneways, hedges, gorse, and lakes – resurfaced in romantic guise in his Canadian writing. Notable examples are his poem "O, Sainted Shannon," written for the *Irish Canadian* on 24 February 1863, and his serialized novel "The New Gauger; or, Jack Trainer's Story," which appeared in the *Anglo-American Magazine* (Toronto) in 1855. The Leitrim setting of "The New Gauger" affectionately describes the landscape and villages like Tooman, Roosky, and Drumsna; the author warmly recalls the quick-witted, high-spirited camaraderie of the Catholic menfolk who covertly made whiskey, one of the most prominent activities of Leitrim's underground economy.

"O, Sainted Shannon" evokes Ireland's distant but glorious past, emphasizing its beauty and the country's martyrdom over "seven hundred years." Written while his attraction to the Fenian movement was gaining ground, the poem draws on his boyhood memories. Here is the four-verse poem in full:

Oh! Sainted Shannon! – on thy banks I stray
From ancient moonlit, Ivied tower to tower
Whose mouldering stones, perfumed in their decay
By many a fragrant shrub or golden flower,
Oppress my spirit, at this lonely hour,
With dreams of glory long since passed away.

Ages have vanished since these crumbling walls
First echoed to the great O'Connor's tread –
Since fierce wassailers last swept those halls,
To harp and song, with flagons foaming red.
Say, shall one ray of sunshine e'er be shed
Through the sad, silent gloom that o'er them falls?

Or, on thy emerald waters, once again,
Thronging the warlike galley or gay boat,
Shall dark-eyed loveliness and haughty men
In all their wonted, regal splendour float
In pleasures leash, or to the brazen note
That called of yore, to mountain and glen?

Bright, from the flood of her baptismal tears,
With morning stars upon her pallid brow,
Shall not the martyr of seven hundred years
Break through the fetters that enchain her now?
Or shall she to that fortune ever bow,
That led her from her home among the spheres?

The banks and waters of the Shannon, still holding images of Ireland's past greatness, triggered in the poet a strong yearning for a return to the heroic times of Ireland's "splendour" and "glory." The Shannon was, after all, the river of his youth, flowing out of Lough Allen past Carrick-on-Shannon, Jamestown, Drumsna, and Rooskey, and deep in his imagination. But by the 1860s he had come to believe, with many frustrated Irishmen, that it was time for Ireland to break "The fetters that enchain her now." The poem argues that an uprising against English tyranny is the only valid response to Ireland's long martyrdom and misfortune. Although the poem mutes that aggressiveness, it reveals the distance that McCarroll had travelled from his freewheeling boyhood to his willingness now to affirm the Fenian vision of a free Ireland. Notably, the poem does not refer to the extraordinary promise made by American Fenians to free Canada by force from British control.

County Leitrim has had an under-celebrated history. T.M.O. Flynn's brief study, *History of Leitrim* (1937), concludes that "no native historian has arisen to give Leitrim its place of pre-eminence in the annals of Erin"; moreover, "No poet has tuned his harp to the glorious deeds of her sons."[25] Flynn knew of Carolan, the legendary harper of Mohill, but he had never heard of James McCarroll, who in 1831 had made his way from the banks of the Shannon to the banks of the Otonabee River in Upper Canada. Neither did Flynn live long enough to read John McGahern's evocative Leitrim novels.

Yet legends of Leitrim's heroic and rebellious past continued to live on in the memories of its people. During McCarroll's boyhood, the lively presence of the downtrodden, sometimes rebellious Catholic majority was impossible to ignore, though, as a young Protestant, McCarroll likely remained relatively unaffected by the political issues underlying their position. He remembered a people who were unwaveringly Catholic, mostly impoverished, characteristically buoyant, devoted to aspects of their flourishing underground economy, and always struggling to hold on to what little land they possessed or were allowed to farm as tenants for landowners. When potato famines began to strike Leitrim as early as 1828, the effects on the Catholic majority must have been striking. So too the restrictions and disciplinary treatment imposed on the peasantry by Protestant authorities were seen by many Catholics as reason to resort to vigilante violence.

As Protestants and members of the Church of Ireland, the McCarrolls were part of the privileged but uneasy minority of the county. Its major town, Carrick-on-Shannon, was Protestant by law. In the 1820s that meant, among other things, that Catholics had limited privileges and were not permitted to own property within the town's boundaries. On occasion, Protestant families like the McCarrolls may have found themselves in uncomfortable situations as they worried that Rockian violence might be directed at them. A growing sense of unease was likely a determining factor in Robert McCarroll's decision to emigrate in 1831. How much such dangers and the underlying politics affected young James is difficult to determine.

Flynn describes Leitrim in the 1820s as a threatening environment, especially from the point of view of the Protestant minority.

The history of Leitrim during the nineteenth century corresponds with the history of Ireland. Leitrim men were in the forefront of the fight for emancipation and the Repeal of the Union. The same monster meetings were held throughout the county that distinguished those movements elsewhere, but in Leitrim threads of a revolutionary nature ran through the fibre of the organization. The county was honeycombed with secret societies. The followers of "Captain Rock," "The Molly Maguires," [and] "the Stickmen" gave endless troubles to the authorities, but as they were more of an agrarian than a national character, they tended to divide rather than to unite the people on the big political questions.

No county in Ireland played a bigger part in the Land War than Leitrim, and it was in this struggle that those societies exercised their full powers. It must be admitted that they, more than the constitutional movement, played a big part in breaking the stranglehold of Landlordism on the unfortunate tenants. Many landlords, agents, and bailiffs met untimely deaths and the fear of consequences had a restraining effect on tyrannical actions. Hence it is only fair to say that the Land League owed much of its success to the driving force of those secret societies.[26]

"Threads of a revolutionary nature" bred by "secret societies" and their frightening night raids, ran deep in Leitrim in the 1820s. As Daniel O'Connell, the Great Liberator, fought steadily on behalf of Ireland's beleaguered Catholic majority, seeking to repeal the Acts of Union (which had been imposed in 1803) and gain emancipation for his people, Protestants worried that their once tranquil world and their personal safety were under increasing threat. Some kind of government action in England in favour of Catholic freedom was clearly needed, but local changes were slow to evolve during the decade; over the period corresponding to James's teenage years, covert vigilante activities by angry Catholics – loosely organized, periodic, and unpredictable – were seen as nightly threats by Protestant officials and their families living in the county's towns and countryside.

Such unrest was also widespread in adjacent counties like Longford, Roscommon, and Sligo, as secret societies or groups of "banditti" undertook occasional vigilante attacks. The feeling of fear grew. The power of rumour and the accounts of violence in weekly newspapers unsettled many Protestants, especially those who held positions of power, such as militia officers, agents, revenue collectors, bailiffs, and even clergymen.

The weekly issues of the only Protestant newspaper in the area, the *Roscommon and Leitrim Gazette*, published in the nearby Roscommon town of Boyle,[27] recorded the growing unrest and anger among its readership. Often under the heading "Alarming State of the Country," the ominous name of Captain Rock and, relatedly, "the Rockites" appeared in issue after issue from the paper's inception in 1822 into the following decade.[28]

The mere mention of Captain Rock's name sent a chill of fear through the paper's Protestant subscribers: reports regularly alluded to threatening letters, nighttime home invasions (in search of guns and money), personal injuries, and the insistence, under threat of death, that the victims swear an oath of support to Catholic interests, an oath that was, of course, obnoxious to Protestants. Reports of torn-down fences, house fires and barn burnings, violence done to farm animals and other property, the burning of stands of trees, and, most frightening, attacks on individuals in their own residences, heightened by the occasional mention of rape or murder, were weekly fare. These news items, often occurring in other counties, usually went uncorroborated; seldom, in fact, did individual reports lead to the verification of such information. Collectively, however, these reports fuelled the fear of midnight terrorism and heightened Protestant anxiety in the late 1820s. The *Roscommon and Leitrim Gazette* reported during 1829–30 that almost every night marauding "troops" were at large in the Leitrim countryside and other nearby counties. In October 1828, a news story reported on a night raid on the home of Captain Moreton of the Leitrim Militia. Several of his family members received "severe injury" during the attack, including Captain Moreton himself when he returned home suddenly to find the invasion in progress.

At the same time the newspaper paid close but dismissive attention to the doings and sayings of Daniel O'Connell. Because he was the major figure in Catholic politics at the time, the *Gazette's* editor regularly reported on his actions while routinely criticizing them and mocking his alleged stature. He was seen as the "Agitator-in-Chief" who issued periodic "Epistles" to the masses (16 October 1830); he was "the Lord of Misrule" (30 April 1831); his "Revolution" involved the unwanted and unnecessary "Repeal of the Union" (2 October 1830). But, as the *Gazette's* editor implicitly recognized, the movement for change that O'Connell sought to bring about was gaining momentum, even if it remained politically unfocused in Leitrim.

In this atmosphere of unease, vulnerability, and uncertainty Robert McCarroll began to rethink his future in Ireland. His employment in the Leitrim Militia must have involved him in occasional disciplinary actions against Catholics, either Leitrim residents or soldiers in his militia unit. Officers were obliged to arrest those suspected of illegal or violent activities. In general, Protestant militia officers, like others in prominent public positions, had some reason to fear retaliation in response to duties they had carried out or simply because of who they were. The nighttime attack on Captain Moreton's home and family stood as a stark reminder of their vulnerability.

The militia was composed of Protestant officers who oversaw Catholic foot soldiers. Its battalions could thus be tinderboxes of tension. Many local Catholics saw the militia as symbolic of British rule in the county, positioned to protect local Protestants from the increasing frequency of vigilante actions undertaken by disgruntled Catholics. Celebrating the militia as "one of the oldest constitutional establishments in the country" (7 March 1829), the *Roscommon and Leitrim Gazette* was duly alarmed by the recent news that the political powers in London had decided to reduce the size of local militias across the United Kingdom. This law was passed at the very time when, in southern Ireland, the increasing loss of respect for English law and order among the Catholic majority was a growing concern.

Parliamentary initiative in the first half of 1829 led, in fact, to a dramatic reduction in the overall size of county militias and the number of officers employed across the United Kingdom and specifically in Ireland. In January 1829, one such bill encouraged all current militia captains to retire on half pay. Retiring officers were also offered the opportunity to consider emigration to one of Britain's colonies where they could take up the offer of free land. Hence, while the local newspaper was continuing to call for "strenuous government intervention" to deal with the burgeoning night raids, the local militias were being severely cut back in a national cost-saving measure. Protestants living in places like Leitrim likely suffered from a double kind of anxiety – loss of position and income on the one hand and loss of protection on the other.

Robert McCarroll thus found himself facing mandatory retirement and the stark realization that his half-pay pension would be his only long-term security. Indeed, by the end of the 1820s, the Leitrim Militia was a shell of its former self. The bandmaster would have been among the first officers to be eliminated. Emigration became a practical alternative; it also promised a new start.

As he grew into his teenage years, James would have held to his family's Protestant position and outlook, even as he witnessed, with curiosity and some sympathy, aspects of the difficult situation facing local Irish Catholics. It is speculation to be sure, but he may have had some personal experience of Catholic friends and their families. Later writings make it clear that he remembered and admired the ability of older Catholic men to work subversively against the prevailing laws of Leitrim. As well, as he surely knew, there were regulations in place to curtail the freedom of ballad singers at country fairs and in public places. As a young musician and a student of Carolan, he likely delighted in their airs and stories, even as he noted in passing the litany of injustices and complaints that lay near the heart of such public music.[29] His later hatred of the English as insensitive and repressive imperialists who wilfully destroyed aspects of Celtic vitality and culture was rooted in the daily tensions he witnessed during his final years in Leitrim.

A Leitrim Story for Canadian Readers: "The New Gauger; or, Jack Trainer's Story"

James McCarroll's serialized novel "The New Gauger," written in Port Credit and Toronto in the mid-1850s, reveals his identification with and admiration for the buoyant Catholic folk of rural Leitrim and their successful underground economy.[30] The narrative, which is set in 1828 on "Wren Lough" (today Lough Rinn) near "the neat little town of Mohill" (113), vividly describes the landscape while dramatizing the high spirits of the men who operate their secret stills under the very noses of tax collectors and local gaugers. The making and distributing of poitin ("pottein") was a vital part of the subversive drinking culture embraced by Leitrim's menfolk. In dramatizing the outlook of these whiskey-makers and their zeal for camaraderie and storytelling, "The New

Gauger" presents a "Catholic" narrative by a Protestant author, one in which the good fellows of Leitrim cleverly get the better of officious outsiders, particularly Protestant-appointed revenue men or gaugers whose job it is to destroy their stills or tax their underground activities.

As its title suggests, the narrative involves a story within a story. The unnamed narrator is alone on a fishing expedition when a storm forces him to seek cover on an island in Lough Wren. Upon landing, he finds himself surrounded by ten to twelve "stalwart fellows" who are part of the secret team guarding "two large stills in full operation" (113). Recovering his equanimity, the narrator is amazed by what he sees when he is led to the ruined walls of an old castle linked historically to "the mighty O'Connors." There he encounters enormous stills in operation, "glowing, seething, and rumbling in all their illicit pride, and completing a scene which, I fancied, at the moment, the most picturesque that could be presented to the eye of mortal. The darkness, the storm, the men, and the fires reddening the huge rough angles that stood out like sentinels along the dim vaulted depths of the ruined pile [the castle], were in themselves the very essence of romance; and I then, for the first time in my existence, felt the full power of the antiquity of Ireland overshadow me" (114).

The narrator is so caught up in the vivid scene that his imagination, like McCarroll's, harkens back to centuries-old legends about the defence of the region "on the banks of the Shannon" (114) by fine Connaught soldiers. Although those heroic days are long gone, he realizes that they have their present-day counterpart in the underground activities of the high-spirited and daring men who operate the illegal stills near Mohill and Toomen, and ably fend off any lawful attempts to stop their work and destroy their kilns. In that same spirit of "pre-Famine gaiety" identified by Declan Kiberd, McCarroll celebrates the subversive nocturnal activities of these venturesome black-marketers.

McCarroll links the distillation of pottein in the castle ruins to the ancient warriors of old Ireland, and the outlaws of the present to old and lively traditions, be they wakes or marriages. Their florid use of the brogue matches their high spirits. Here is but one example of that language, voiced during a midnight story: "'Jack!' says he, as he landed beside me like a lump of wet spoddough, 'that's you ma bouchal! – give us your fist, your sowl you, give me your mitthogue,' says he, caperin' about me and givin' my right hand a squeeze that left it as dead as mutton for upwards of an hour, 'and I'm the boy that, at aither fair or Pattherm, will stick to your back, like broth to a soger, without inquirin' into the rights of it'" (327). As the men drink and carouse, a poetic spirit named "Terry" and a fiddler named "Paddy" are close at hand to raise the level of merriment and celebrate their doings.

The narrator is well treated by the company of bootleggers and their leader, Harry Thracy. He meets Jack Trainer, a "clark" from Toomen, who is urged by the group to tell afresh his story about Harry Thracy and his cleverness in dealing with Kelly, the "new gauger" who has come from away. Harry's highjinks dovetail neatly with his desire to marry his beloved Mary Corny, whose father is bent on scuttling the match, against his daughter's will. The two strands make up Jack Trainer's brogue-laced story, which comes neatly together in a colourful wedding ceremony where all things are put to right and Harry gets his girl Mary. The story takes up most of the stormy night on the island. After much drinking and some very belated sleep, the narrator is sent on his way back to Mohill by his amiable hosts.

McCarroll's Leitrim bootleggers are neither vigilantes nor criminals; rather they are "Irish rogues and rapperies."[31] The label serves as a poetic and alternative identity for the Irish peasantry in the 1850s (115). They do their secretive, survivalist work according to a strict code of behaviour that insists on avoiding unnecessary violence and ill will. To trap the suspicious gauger, for instance, they trick him in various ways before tying him up, thereby "disposing" of him without doing him "any sarious injury." Their code includes loyalty to family and friends (traitors are anathema to them), the enjoyment of plentiful drink and hearty laughs with their nocturnal colleagues, and great delight in finding creative ways to beat the system imposed on them by English law and Protestant authority. As a group they enjoy their "naggins" "amid jest and glee, with the utmost conviviality" (114).

"The New Gauger" owes much to the narrative tradition developed by such popular Irish writers of the early nineteenth century as Samuel Lover and William Carleton. It sparkles with McCarroll's command of the vernacular and his fine ear for the richness of the brogue. At the same time, while celebrating the creative ventures and high spirits of the outlaws, the narrative is soft on measuring the animosity and tension between the Catholics and the Protestants. It certainly underplays the increasing levels of vigilante violence that challenged law and order in Leitrim during that decade. There is no Captain Rock figure in "The New Gauger," only feckless gaugers and sergeants who represent the Protestant forces in control, but who are ineffective in their attempts to deal with and discipline the resilient and playful Catholic lads and their commitment to their successful underground activities.

In anchoring the adventures of "The New Gauger" in his boyhood days, McCarroll offers a measure of the loss he continued to feel for the vibrancy of the Ireland he had known before his departure to Upper Canada. By the mid-1850s, he had evolved into a writer who felt that it was his particular role to speak for and about Ireland as a whole; he wanted to bring together the world that included the dispossessed and struggling Irish Catholics of counties like Leitrim and the Irish Protestants of his family experience. As a writer and humorist he applied various strategies and created various styles as he attempted to broker a kind of literary rapprochement between the two sides. He wanted to speak out for the aching needs of his homeland, seeing Ireland as a distinct and complex entity rather than a broken island. In 1855 such an initiative was neither a practical nor a practicable undertaking; however, when framed and buoyed by humour, it could provide plenty of amusement and enjoyment for readers of many stripes. The politicized call of Fenianism in the early 1860s would soon imperil this delicate blending, even as McCarroll became more politically attached to the demands of the Catholic position.

Another persistent storyline in the pages of the *Roscommon and Leitrim Gazette* in the late 1820s were reports of boatloads of Protestant emigrants preparing each spring to leave from western ports like Cork, Sligo, Derry, and Galway for the United States or Canada. These reports increased year by year and became a seasonal staple late in the decade. The paper labelled the phenomenon "a rage" as increasing numbers of Protestants (who, it was reported, made up more than half the total number of emigrants) debarked for North America. Sligo alone reported that 3,000 emigrants sailed in 1831 (7 May 1831), while authorities in towns like Longford worried that "the Protestants of the Parish are disappearing fast" (19 February 1831). These emigrants were generally described as relatively well-to-do families. Among the reasons listed for their departure was the lack of legal protection available to them under current conditions, the fear of vigilante bloodshed, and the realities of famine that year by year further undermined southern Ireland's agrarian economy.

So it was that Robert McCarroll, Protestant in his religious affiliation and distressed, like many fellow Protestants, by the "savage ferocity" that had come increasingly to define daily life in Leitrim, joined the "mania" for emigration to Canada in 1831.[32] That desire to leave was augmented, of course, by the prospect of free land awaiting him as a pensioned British soldier in distant Upper Canada.

The McCarrolls arrived in Toronto in the summer of 1831 and bided their time for several months awaiting news of Robert's application for a land grant. Once he received the grant, the family looked into his new land in Emily Township in Upper Canada. Unprepared to turn themselves into farmers, however, Robert and James were quick to "prove up" and sell their land grant, seeking instead the "more genial atmosphere" offered by a settled community. Selling the Emily Township property at the first opportunity, they moved to nearby towns – Peterborough in James's case, while Robert chose to settle first in York (Toronto) with James initially in tow, then likely in Cobourg. Thereafter, he vanishes from the traceable record; indeed, the subsequent life of James McCarroll's parents in North America remains unknown.[33]

Starting Out: Peterborough, Upper Canada, 1830s and 1840s

JAMES MCCARROLL CAME TO PETERBOROUGH BY CHANCE. On 8 August 1831 his father had petitioned Sir John Colborne, the lieutenant-governor of Upper Canada, for a grant of land, available to him as a retired British soldier. The location of such grants was the luck of the draw, especially if one had no person of influence monitoring the process. Robert McCarroll received a grant of one hundred acres that he could turn to advantage for himself and his family.

The success of that petition brought the McCarrolls from York (Toronto) to the Peterborough area.[1] The family, according to Henry Morgan, "took up their abode" in "the wild forests of Upper Canada" on their half lot in Emily Township, and there they "encountered all the vicissitudes of a settler of that period." James likely provided the dramatic phrasing in response to Morgan's request for personal information for *Sketches of Celebrated Canadians*.[2]

Aware that there was plenty of "free" land still available, Robert McCarroll made a second petition to the government, this time in June 1833. He asked for an additional one hundred acres for his eighteen-year-old son. The document described James as his "son born in the army and ... now of age ... [but without] provision made for him." The request was rejected on the grounds that a retired soldier's son was ineligible. The pro forma reply might be seen as James's first setback in Canada. For the time being he was merely a young man "without provision" who would have to make his own way as best he could. And so he dug in. It would be two decades before Morgan would include him among his "celebrated" and worthy Canadians.[3]

In the Upper Canadian backwoods and towns of the early 1830s, those without capital had to work very hard and live by their wits. The physical demands were onerous and the margin of success narrow, especially for those who had to clear trees before they could begin to plant crops. A bush farm in that second tier of well-wooded, often rocky, townships north of Lake Ontario provided little immediate return beyond a rough home or shanty in which to live and whatever food the family could produce by gardening, planting, fishing, foraging, and hunting. McCarroll made it clear to Morgan that the "vicissitudes" of the farming life had little appeal to his father or himself.[4] By contrast, the possibilities of life in Peterborough called out to him.

In a matter of months he was comfortable there. In fact, his experiences in town provide a different perspective on how a talented and ambitious immigrant might make his way to recognition and success in Upper Canada. In 1832, Peterborough was a fledgling village of 500 in the Upper Canadian backwoods. Originally founded in 1819 as a mill site along the Otonabee River's western banks and formally named in 1825, Peterborough was beginning to emerge as a centre of trade for the back townships of the Newcastle District.[5] McCarroll soon made new friends, a number of whom had come from Ireland. The Otonabee River, with its vibrant greenness in spring, summer, and fall, reminded him of the Shannon. The river's fast-flowing waters drained a number of large, freshwater lakes to the north, flowing past the town, then through Rice Lake into Lake Ontario.[6]

The area was originally settled by a mix of British peoples, including a surprisingly high number of literate, middle-class immigrants who would serve as its first recorders. The earliest pioneers were Frances and Thomas Stewart, a well-connected Anglo-Irish couple who settled in South Douro in 1822–23 along with Robert Reid and his family.

Then came Samuel Strickland. In 1825 he arrived as a seventeen-year-old in Darlington from Suffolk, England before moving north to Peterborough. In 1831 he relocated to Herriott's Falls (now Lakefield) and built a log home there. Once settled, he encouraged his older sisters, Susanna (with her husband John Moodie) and Catharine Parr (with her husband Thomas Traill), to take up their military land grants near him. The Moodies and Traills arrived separately in the late summer of 1832.[7] Still later Anne Langton followed her brother John to the area in 1838. These pioneer chroniclers left their marks by means of narratives and letters. The mixture of English, Scottish, and Anglo-Irish families set a conservative social tone for the growing town. By contrast, the Catholic Irish families, of whom there were many, particularly because of the Peter Robinson emigration scheme of 1825,[8] were collectively far less impressive in their literary legacy. Most were hard-working labourers or struggling farmers; most had neither money nor old-world connections nor support; indeed, many were at best semi-literate.[9]

By 1835, McCarroll could feel that he was making progress. Blessed with musical talent and some classical education, he also had the advantage of being an Anglican.[10] But during his first decade in town he had to support himself as a shoemaker, a trade learned from his father, even as he began to give music lessons in the village. At the same time he became part of an informal group of young Irish-Protestant and Scottish men who were building their business lives and families there. Some of them, like William Cluxton, William McDonnell, and James Hall, would remain lifelong friends.

Music in the Backwoods: The Sacred and the Popular

Within a year of their arrival in Upper Canada, Robert and James McCarroll placed a grandiose advertisement in the area's only newspaper, the *Cobourg Star*. They announced their plan to establish a music academy to serve "the Inhabitants of Cobourg and its vicinity."[11] However, demographics, geography, and local transportation were not on their side. The ambitious scheme stood little chance of success.[12] Settlement in the area was thinly spread – there were less than 3,000 people living in the entire Cobourg-Peterborough corridor. Farming families were scattered widely and modes of transportation were limited and crude.[13] So, too, money for leisure pursuits such as music lessons was in short supply for most settlers.

Still, the McCarrolls were optimistic. There was a steady influx of British immigrants along that rugged corridor linking Peterborough with Cobourg and Port Hope. As Susanna Moodie later noted, "a Canada mania" was at play among "the middle ranks of British society."[14] Relatedly, improvements in transportation were underway; there were schemes for better roads, better stagecoach travel, and new steamboats to ply the region's lakes and rivers. Buoying local enthusiasm was the prospect of a government-funded canal system from Lake Ontario north to Peterborough and in due time to Georgian Bay. In the wake of the great success of the Erie Canal in New York State, Upper Canada had already undertaken the construction of the Welland Canal to the west and the Rideau Canal to the east.

The McCarrolls' advertisement offered an impressive suite of musical services and promised excellent instruction in "this the most delightful of all accomplishments." Music lessons would be provided for all the instruments requisite for "a complete band." There would be individual classes for ladies and gentlemen as

MUSIC SCHOOL.
Robert McCarrol and Son,

OF PETERBOROUGH, and late from the County of Leitrim, Ireland, (where the former for many years held the situation of Band Master in the Militia,) respectfully beg leave to announce to the Inhabitants of Cobourg and its vicinity, that they have made arrangements for the immediate establishment of an Academy in that place of the above description ; where one or both of them will be in constant attendance, to assist such Ladies and Gentlemen who may be desirous of acquiring a proficiency in this the most delightful of all accomplishments. In addition to the experience above noticed, R. McC. would observe, that both himself and son have been for five years under the immediate instruction of two of the most eminent professors in Europe, Drs. Briscoli and Logier, which perhaps may warrant them in a more confident assurance to their pupils, of a corresponding advantage on their part. Their favorite instrument is the Flute, but alike masters of the Flageolet, and every other requisite accompaniment to a complete band, they will at all times be happy to contribute their assistance at any select private assemblies, where the sublime studies of such spirits as Carolin, Weber, Mozart, Haydn, Handel, &c, may be considered a desirable introduction,

Attached to their instrumental instruction, they have it also in contemplation, to give lessons on sacred vocal music, the advantage of which will be apparent to all who have ever been familiar with this most essential part of divine worship.

TERMS—One Pound entrance, and an additional pound for every 12 lessons.

February 14, 1832. 5

2.1 Advertisement for Robert McCarroll and Son Music School, *Cobourg Star*, 14 February 1832. Microfilm, Cobourg History Information, Cobourg Public Library.

well as "assistance at any select private assemblies." Students could avail themselves of "sublime studies of such spirits as Carolin [*sic*], Weber, Mozart, Haydn, Handel, &c" and "lessons on sacred music, the advantage of which will be apparent to all who have ever been familiar with this most essential part of divine worship."[15]

This pipedream was grounded in the musical skills and experience that the McCarrolls brought with them from Ireland. The advertisement was not repeated. At best, it served to identify some local students for them. Robert, whose extensive experience was essential to the plan, may have begun to teach in the Cobourg area before returning to York (Toronto); some years later, he appears to have left the area entirely. James opted to settle in Peterborough. In a legal brief dated January 1842 he testified that he had been earning his living there over the past decade as both a cobbler and "a teacher of music."[16] Newspaper reviews in the 1840s confirm that he had already established a considerable reputation for himself as a flautist.

One of McCarroll's earliest pupils was William Cluxton (1819–1901). Five years his junior, Cluxton had come to Peterborough from County Louth, Ireland. Within a decade, he had developed a successful hardware business and general store on George Street and was on his way to becoming one of the town's most prominent and respected businessmen. In the early 1830s he began to study flute and voice with McCarroll. Reminiscing in 1897 about those early years and without mentioning McCarroll by name, Cluxton recalled his heavy work schedule as a general-store employee in the 1830s. "It was work, work! and plenty of it." But he also remembered "some pleasures [of] those early days. I often sat on the banks of the beautiful Otonabee River with musical companions on bright, balmy summer moon-light evenings playing duets, trios and airs on our flutes, when the world sat lightly on our shoulders."[17]

A shared affection for Ireland and the love of making music drew Cluxton and McCarroll together. McCarroll played his flute and lent his alto voice to glees. Others brought along their instruments and, if it could be arranged, there might be a piano, since, by then, a few Peterborough families had a pianoforte or harpsichord. The assembled would play songs by Carolan, or they might sing, individually or in glees, some of Thomas Moore's popular songs and melodies. Strains of Carolan's "Sheebeg and Sheemore," "Fanny Power," and "Bridget Cruise" might be heard along with Moore's "The Harp That Once through Tara's Halls," "The Meeting of the Waters," and "'Tis the Last Rose of Summer." In the late 1830s and early '40s music and nostalgia enlivened many a Peterborough boarding house as young men like Cluxton, the Rev. Robert J.C. Taylor, and William McDonnell joined McCarroll and his magical flute.[18]

2.2 This sketch by Henry Caddy captures the Court House and St John's Church on the hill above the fledgling town of Peterborough. McCarroll's *Peterboro Chronicle* print shop was across the road (later Water Street) at the base of Court House hill. Source: Trent Valley Archives.

Some of these young men became involved in the new choir being developed at St John's Anglican Church in Peterborough. Indeed, a fertile way to track McCarroll's life there is through the church and its first three ministers.[19] He served as St John's first choirmaster while Cluxton was a choir member.[20] In the early 1840s Cluxton would replace him as choirmaster.

The church began holding Sabbath services in the late 1820s under the Rev. Samuel Armour, but the construction of its impressive stone edifice, high on the hill overlooking the Otonabee River to the east and the town to the west, did not begin until 1837. In charge of the building was Armour's successor, the Rev. Richard H. D'Olier (1797–1839).

Hailing from County Longford in Ireland, D'Olier came to Peterborough in uncertain health.[21] A mild-mannered and gentlemanly individual, he was born in Dublin of "an aristocratic Huguenot family" and had served as vicar of Ballymore, County Kildare, before accepting an appointment to St George's Cathedral in Kingston, Upper Canada. Seeking a better climate for himself and an improved salary to support his large family, he came to St John's (1834–37) where, among his duties, he oversaw the purchasing of land and the construction of the church. As Frances Stewart reported in a letter to friends back in Ireland, D'Olier was "a pious good man," but he was "obliged to work like a labourer all the week" at farming in order to support his family.[22]

D'Olier hired McCarroll as the church's first choirmaster. The connection, likely forged in 1836 or 1837, was felicitous for both. As the decade wound down, St John's could claim to have the town's most impressive church building (its tower was erected in 1839), its most prestigious congregation, and the area's best choral music, though neither of the two church histories mentions the music. McCarroll's knowledge of sacred music found in D'Olier its first New-World supporter. As well, on 24 June 1837, D'Olier officiated at the marriage of his choirmaster "by licence" to Ann Davis. It was the one hundredth marriage he performed at St John's, and one of his last.

Ann was the English-born daughter of John and Susanna Davis of the White Cottage in Peterborough.[23] Two years younger than her husband, Ann was one of four popular Davis daughters. Her father, John (1791–1864), was a stonemason who had come to Peterborough in 1835 to work on the construction of St John's Church; he would continue his stone work on the town's impressive courthouse. McCarroll was likely a boarder at the White Cottage when he began his courtship of Ann. After their wedding they continued to reside with the Davises to minimize living expenses.[24]

A rather delicate complication for the newlyweds involved the birth of their first daughter, Emma, a mere three months later. On 19 September, Dr John Hutchison, the town's most prominent doctor, delivered the child.[25] If that birth produced a social reaction in the town, no record of it exists. Whatever scandal may have followed from the pregnancy and hasty wedding was soon put to rest. In 1839, a second daughter, Mary, was born, again overseen by Dr Hutchison. By then family stability and paternal responsibility had become important priorities for James.

D'Olier's consumptive condition finally forced him to take a leave of absence in the fall of 1837. Soon after, he returned to Ireland with his family where he died two years later.[26] His successor was another Irishman, Charles T. Wade. Born in County Meath and educated at Trinity College, Dublin, Wade came to Canada in 1836, serving first as a travelling missionary in the Newcastle District and then as D'Olier's temporary replacement. An eloquent preacher who beamed respectability and confidence, he won the admiration and esteem of such influential parishioners as Frances Stewart and John Langton, and of Bishop John Strachan of Toronto. Wade, who was forty-four when he took over as minister of St John's, was an accomplished writer who contributed to the Anglican newspaper, the *Church*. On a personal level he shared several characteristics with his choirmaster; they were creative and educated Irishmen who were sometimes visited by streaks of exuberance and indulgence. Both appreciated music, wrote poetry, and enjoyed a sociable drink. With Wade in the pulpit and McCarroll directing the choir, St John's underwent a "steady growth" during Wade's four-year tenure.

Within a couple of years, however, problems began to develop in Wade's incumbency. He became embroiled in disagreements with his lay leaders over land purchases, the control of church finances, and the "responsibility for the church debt." When the church clerk alleged that Wade had consorted publicly with a local woman of questionable character, Wade did not deny the charge, justifying his actions as innocent and well meaning, not "philandering." Meanwhile there was persistent gossip that he drank too much. But such rumours paled when a charge of "improper conduct" with a servant girl was brought against him. With pressure escalating in the summer of 1841, he was forced to resign his position. From Toronto, the Rev. A.N. Bethune spoke for other church leaders about their disappointment at this unseemly turn of events. "I never knew a man of whom I had once a better opinion," he wrote, "and it is not without a distressful struggle that I must surrender my sentiments of respect if I cannot those of anxious regard."[27] In disgrace, Charles Wade headed to Rochester, New York. Little further was heard of him.

Robert J.C. Taylor (1803–1852), Wade's successor, managed to calm the troubled waters left by Wade. Seven years earlier, in May 1832, Taylor, who had an undergraduate degree from Trinity College, Dublin, had taken over the "Peterboro' Government School" from Samuel Armour when the latter was forced to cut back on his missionary duties.[28] While teaching and also serving as a pastor in nearby Douro, Taylor realized that it would be best to advance his religious education. In 1837 he returned to Ireland to pursue a master's degree and prepare himself more fully for the ministry. Following additional pastoral experience in Dublin, Leeds (England), and Newmarket (Upper Canada), he returned to Peterborough. His return was somewhat delayed by cautious church officials who worried that he still "lacked that spirituality of temper, that forwardness of zeal or wariness of circumspectness of demeanor" required to fulfill his duties.[29] Nevertheless, so keen was he to return that he accepted a cut in the salary from his Newmarket post, despite the needs of his large family. He brought with him, if not the requisite "zeal," then a gift in money from Anglican supporters in England to help complete the building of St John's.

Church and newspaper records for these early years are thin, but it is evident that James McCarroll served the church under D'Olier, Wade, and Taylor. In the early 1840s he was able to redirect his energies toward teaching when Taylor offered him the position of assistant master of the local school.

His continuing friendship with Taylor is evident in a notice of their singing together at a St John's Church bazaar in 1850. In the *Centenary History of St John's Church, Peterborough: 1827–1927*, F.M. de la Fosse includes this single notice of James McCarroll's connection with the church; ironically, the event did not occur until a couple of years after McCarroll had relocated to Cobourg.[30] It does, however, provide a glimpse of how well he continued to be regarded in Peterborough. The January 1850 concert and bazaar was held to raise funds for the restoration of the already-weathered St John's roof. The *Peterborough Weekly Despatch* reported that a welcome participant in the event was "our old friend Mr McCarroll, whose reputation as a musician is now acknowledged throughout the continent. His alto, combined with Mr Taylor's bass, gave the choruses effect and power. Altogether," the report concluded, "we are safe in saying that no such concert was ever given in Peterborough."[31] Raising over one hundred pounds, the event was deemed an unqualified success.

Reform and Journalistic Opportunity: In the Wake of John Darcus

In early nineteenth-century Upper Canada, a man needed a reliable occupation in order to support himself and his family. There were no safety nets and few handouts. Fortunately, McCarroll was able to rely on shoemaking. Recognizing that sturdy shoes were more needful in the backwoods than musical instruction, he devoted his early working days to this practical trade. In the legal brief cited above, he described himself as "by trade a shoemaker," adding that "for some time prior to this time he had been working at his trade with Robert Bryson and for a former period by himself."[32] But to be simply "a mechanic" could not for long satisfy a man of his talents and aspirations.

He was determined to find opportunities for self-expression beyond leather soles. There was a musician, a poet, and a journalist waiting to break free, but, in the early 1840s, teaching offered him the best opportunity for advancement. However, school positions were few and, until 1837, there was no newspaper north of Cobourg. Yet there were many issues of the day – local and colonial, Irish and North American, Canadian and American – about which he had plenty to say once an opportunity presented itself.

The school-teaching opportunity came in 1841 when Taylor offered him the position of assistant master at the Peterborough Grammar School. Among his students were Catharine Parr and Thomas Traill's eldest son, James, a couple of Samuel Strickland's boys, including Henry,[33] and the younger sons of Thomas and Frances Stewart and of Robert and Maria Reid, the most prominent Anglo-Irish families of South Douro, who lived just north of the town and east of the Otonabee River.

But teaching paled before the appeal of journalism, especially in those heated days following the release of the Durham Report in Upper Canada. When fellow Irishman John Darcus began the *Peterborough Sentinel and Backwoodsman* in 1839, McCarroll must have been watching attentively. He likely volunteered to work for Darcus during his editorship. As a contributor he would have begun developing his Reform outlook even as he sought to have a few of his earliest poems printed there. In fact, as a poet he was already looking farther afield. His first poems in print appeared in the *Christian Guardian* on 17 November 1841. That paper was being published weekly in Cobourg.

The simmering grievances that led to the Rebellion of 1837 in Upper Canada engaged many of McCarroll's progressive-minded friends. They were eager to support the emerging Reform movement set in motion by Lord Durham's seminal report (1838). They were among the new leaders in the Peterborough business community, although Tory interests remained in control. They saw themselves as capable young men in the vanguard of growth and positive change; moreover, they were willing to face hostile, often nasty, criticism from influential conservatives who made unqualified loyalty to Britain and the Crown their central mantra and who clung to the political control they enjoyed.[34]

A strong class dimension informed this period of post-Rebellion tension. McCarroll's closest friends were men of modest background who had to rely on their resourcefulness and hard work rather than inherited wealth and old-world connections. They included Irishmen, Scots, and Englishmen, some of whom were Canadian-born. Anglican ministers like Wade and Taylor were quietly sympathetic to the Reform cause, even in the face of hostility from their leading Tory parishioners.

But beyond the tensions of the day, these young businessmen saw the potential for personal and material success in backing Reform. Chief among the vital changes needed in the united provinces of Canada was a more proactive and "responsible" kind of colonial government. Reformers rallied around the promises of change championed by Robert Baldwin and Louis-Hippolyte La Fontaine (in Canada East), and they were primed to initiate a new spirit of openness in colonial economics. As practical men of business, they also anticipated the advantages of patronage that would follow from a Reform victory at the hustings.

McCarroll committed himself to the emerging Reform agenda, thereby setting himself up for a heady roller coaster ride during the 1840s, a ride that took him from shoemaking to school teaching to a high point of local prominence and notoriety as a clever, outspoken newspaper editor.

The beginnings of his love affair with journalism were rooted in his connection with the Orange Order and fellow Orangeman John Darcus. An early supporter of Reform politics and a critic of Tory thinking, Darcus founded the *Peterborough Backwoodsman and Sentinel* in 1837. It was the first newspaper to be published in the town and it drew the ire of Tories in the area. But as Peterborough's only paper for that period (1837–41), it had a kind of free reign. Based on the available evidence, I postulate that McCarroll served a brief journalistic apprenticeship with Darcus, unpaid or paid, beginning about 1840.[35] His quick rise to journalistic prominence in town grew initially out of this connection and was further informed by Darcus's shift of political loyalty to the Tories in 1842.

After the *Backwoodsman* ceased publication, McCarroll waited only a year for an opportunity to set out on his own. His break came in December 1843 when a local bookseller named Thomas Messenger began a new Reform paper called the *Peterboro Chronicle*.[36] McCarroll was his choice as editor, likely based on his earlier work with Darcus. Local Reform leaders saw him as the right man to argue for their political interests and to challenge Tory hegemony.[37] McCarroll was glad to have his own weekly platform to speak out on larger issues and showcase his creative writing. Nothing else is known of Messenger, who left Peterborough within a year. Upon his departure, an ambitious James McCarroll raised the funds through loans and friendly support to buy the paper. For the next three-and-a-half years, he was the voice of Reform and cultural concern in Peterborough.

Military Errantry: Party Spirit after the Rebellion

The most useful facts about James McCarroll's Peterborough days come from the aforementioned court documents. Good reputation, of course, mattered increasingly to him. As choir leader and schoolmaster, he needed to convey a respectable public image. At the Peterborough Grammar School in the early 1840s he taught the offspring of some of the town's most prominent citizens, while at St John's he was charged with upholding the high standards of Anglican sacred music even as the church was being constructed.

But at heart he was a convivial and exuberant fellow; he enjoyed a collegial drink with friends and reflected a bonhomie and insouciance that

unsympathetic conservative observers found offensive. Nor was he the sort
of man to be pushed around by overzealous teetotalers – the Temperance
movement was slowly becoming a force in the 1840s – or by socially prominent
militia officers who dismissed him as pretentious and a mere shoemaker. The
Peterborough of the post-Rebellion years saw more than its share of swaggering
and self-serving misconduct by prominent young soldiers. It would have been
particularly galling for someone of McCarroll's Irish pride and high spirits to
be publicly mocked for his work as a mere "mechanic." His fighting spirit was
readily aroused.

In the wake of the Rebellion of 1837, Peterborough, like many Upper
Canadian towns, took on a lively military air. Among the 1,500 residents who
lived there in 1838–39, fears persisted about the continuing threat of American
invasion along the Great Lakes and the whereabouts and influence of the rebel
leader William Lyon Mackenzie. When Mackenzie took refuge in northern
New York in 1838, fears of future invasion grew. Better organized defences and
the creation of provisional militia regiments became top government priorities.
In the autumn of 1838 the Battle of the Windmill on Lake Ontario and other
related disturbances along the border quickened that concern.

In November 1838, in expectation of the creation of a local militia, a number
of volunteers began drilling in Peterborough under Captain Richard Birdsall.
However, it was not until Christmas Day that the official appointments to
the 7th Provincial Battalion of Northumberland were gazetted in newspapers,
touching off a wave of local excitement. It was announced as a "six-month"
battalion with a maximum of 300 men; its term of operation would be extended
if the government saw the need. Colonel Alexander MacDonnell would command the battalion. The first appointments under him were Richard Birdsall as
captain, William A. Shairp as lieutenant, and Thomas Fortune as ensign; this
list was likely based on the preliminary training exercises already taking place
in town. On 28 December a much longer list of appointments and promotions
was gazetted, which superseded those previously named. As a result the new
battalion went about filling its ranks and accelerating its training under Captain
James Gifford Cowell rather than Richard Birdsall.[38] Among the volunteers
who signed up, James McCarroll was appointed to the rank of corporal.[39]

In a matter of weeks the 7th Provisional, headed by the officers named
on 28 December, had established itself as a colourful presence in town; there
were regular drillings (on the site of the projected courthouse near St John's
Church), formal parades, and, unexpectedly, certain extracurricular antics
among the officers. In fact, it was not long before several members of the

battalion began to use their military rank and status as a means of launching personal and politically motivated attacks on those who had by that time identified themselves as Reformers. Public expressions of Catholic enthusiasm in Protestant Peterborough were also challenged.

In his *History of the County of Peterborough*, C. Pelham Mulvany put a saccharine spin on the brief – and ugly – saga of "The 7th Provincial Battalion of Peterborough": "It was comprised of volunteers from the militia of the county, who were called out *en masse* for drill and other service from January to May, 1839, their headquarters being in the Town of Peterborough. Their six months' service ended, they were inspected, received what appeared to be well-merited praise for their soldier-like appearance, and were dismissed. Colonel Alexander MacDonnell held the chief command, but the practical training of the battalion was carried on by Major Cowall [*sic*]."[40]

Mulvany's description omitted several less congenial activities involving the battalion's officers. Thomas Poole was closer to the truth in noting that "among those holding subordinate authority, were several whose zeal and officiousness outran their discretion."[41] In fact, the battalion suffered from organizational confusion and lack of discipline from the outset. Militia records indicate that officials in Toronto were so upset by the chaotic parades and disreputable conduct of its leaders that, in late January 1839, they "declined approving the pay lists of that Corps for the month of December."[42]

Then in March and early April, officers of the 7th were involved in several fracases in which the authority of two Peterborough magistrates was publicly mocked, leading to a state of near anarchy in the streets.[43] Old-world hostilities set the tone on St Patrick's Day, 1839. After the Catholics held their annual parade, there was a midnight response by the band of the 7th, abetted by several battalion officers and some unruly Protestants. It resulted in a stone-throwing attack on the barroom and boarding house of James Henthorn and the nearby house of Thomas Chambers, two Catholics associated with the parade and the Reform movement; several shots were fired and Henthorn was assaulted. A week later, when the Catholic church burned down, rumours quickly circulated. However, no arrests followed the fire because the magistrates deemed that its cause was an overheated stovepipe, not the actions of the Orange Order or the 7th Provincial. Still, the church fire further unnerved local citizens.

Led by John Darcus, the magistrates (or justices of the peace) sought to deal promptly with the St Patrick's Parade violence. The Tories viewed magistrates like Darcus as biased and therefore unqualified. Some militia officers led by

Lieutenant William A. Shairp (or Sharpe) took the situation into their own hands after a night of hard drinking. Shortly after the St Patrick's Day parade in 1839, effigies of Darcus and another justice of the peace, Dr George G. Bird, a medical doctor and apothecary, were carried through the streets of Peterborough. Shairp and his cronies delighted in publically mocking the *Backwoodsman* editor as "Dark Ass." For their part, Darcus and Bird dutifully took depositions from witnesses about the post-parade violence. It was their view that they might soon need outside military support because of the "strong party feeling" at play among some of the battalion's officers. Though they were assured of the full support of one of the most respected leaders of the regiment,[44] they still had reason to worry about "the peace of the town" as well as their own safety. When a hearing into the matter was convened, there were further acts of disdain and contempt; indeed, "some officers ... conducted themselves in a most unbecoming and improper manner." Outside the courtroom, one officer called for three cheers for the officers under investigation while Lieutenant Shairp followed by leading a chorus of "three groans" for the magistrates, targeting Darcus directly.[45]

In late March, rumours began to circulate about an upcoming duel between two officers of the battalion. Lieutenant Sam Strickland of Lakefield and Ensign George B. Hall were the principals in what was deemed a dispute of personal honour. A month earlier another duel – between former business partners Edward Duffy, an Irish justice of the peace, and none other than Captain James Gifford Cowell of the 7th – had only been prevented by the timely intervention of Duffy's wife.[46]

It was in the context of the impending duel between Strickland and George Hall that McCarroll's name appeared on the court record. On 28 March 1838, with a crowd gathering outside Darcus's printing office and the duel imminent, the magistrates tried to prevent the combatants from taking to the field. They did not realize that the duel might actually have been a hoax got up to embarrass them. Dressed in his uniform and evidently intoxicated, Lieutenant Shairp was prominent among the noisy crowd that stormed the printing office of the *Backwoodsman*. Darcus had ordered the town constable, Cottrell Lane, to bring in the four participants in the duel, Lieutenant Sam Strickland and Ensign George B. Hall, and their respective seconds, A.C. Dunlop, gentleman, and Lieutenant George Low(e). Bail was required of each of them. However, encouraged by the rowdy crowd, all four refused to pay. In fact, the defendants now laughingly stated that the duel was really a sham, designed to bait and embarrass Darcus and Bird.

Members of the crowd jammed into the outer office of the newspaper. As their jeering increased and the taunts grew more threatening, Constable Lane was assaulted as he attempted to arrest Shairp and to shield Darcus from the angry mob. When Shairp drew his sword and threatened Darcus across the counter, Darcus pulled out a pistol in self-defence – he would later claim it wasn't loaded. Though Lane succeeded in shielding Darcus from Shairp, he could do little else because of the size of the crowd. Hence, when Lane finally managed to clear the printing office, he was unable to make any arrests. The hostile mood continued later in the day in the form of another parade through town, this time featuring flaming effigies of magistrates Darcus and Bird. "Mr John Dark Ass" also received an anonymous letter threatening his safety.

"James McCarroll, Yeoman," was one of seven citizens who gave depositions to the magistrates two days later. He reported that he had been on the street near the *Backwoodsman* office at the time of the row. He clearly saw Shairp brandishing his sword and heard Caddy uttering threats against Constable Lane. Moreover, he reported that he had earlier received a visit from Mr Low of the 7th. As one of the seconds, Low wanted to borrow McCarroll's flute case to deliver the pistols to the site of the duel. In McCarroll's opinion, the principals were fully serious about the event; however, he did admit that he sensed that the seconds were less keen.

Matters soon calmed down. The duel was called off and Shairp, the catalyst of so much ill feeling, was at first cleared of wrongdoing. However, after further consideration of the evidence by the court, he was sent to the jail in New Amherst (Cobourg) for a time. Meanwhile in Toronto, wise heads prevailed, though not in the manner that Captain Cowell had hoped. The 7th Provisional Battalion suffered the ignominy of being terminated by the government a month before the completion of its six-month mandate. In May 1839 it was formally disbanded.

The public confrontations of March 1839 were, however, a sign of tensions to come. "Party feeling" – emotionally charged, highly personalized, and potentially violent – would characterize the politics of Peterborough, and much of Upper Canada, for the next decade. Colonel MacDonnell would blame the magistrates for the local disruptions. Darcus got up a petition designed to delay the creation of the new District of Colborne (replacing the old Newcastle District) on the grounds that it was not only an unpopular action but also one designed by "a few ambitious & greedy place hunters."[47] As the town's soon-to-be Reform editor, McCarroll would later play a role in the bitter episodes of partisan politics that on occasion made the streets of Peterborough dangerous.

Vandalism and torchlight parades were frequent. Once he became editor of the *Peterboro Chronicle*, he did what he could to raise the temperature of debate on behalf of Reform; he too would be burned in effigy on more than one occasion during his tenure by outraged Tory supporters.

One further note can be linked to the short-lived and undistinguished tenure of the 7th Provisional Battalion. In a letter to William Cluxton in March 1891, which he asked his old friend to pass on to the *Peterborough Examiner*, McCarroll reminded local readers that, in the wake of the Rebellion, he had voluntarily served the Crown as a member of the 7th. Nearing the end of his life in New York City, he wanted to remind the people of Peterborough that he had willingly supported the Queen and the British constitution during those highly charged times. Of course, he made no mention in this letter of his later engagement in Fenianism. At this late stage in his life he preferred to be remembered as a loyal British citizen rather than the hotheaded, sensitive, and combative Irishman that he had often appeared to be.

The second legal document involving McCarroll was drawn up two years later. It is the record of a lawsuit brought by him in response to his arrest in Peterborough in late January 1841. The legal action grew out of his support for his father-in-law, John Davis, in a complaint against William Lepar Scobell, an arrogant young military officer then living in town.

For several years, James and Ann McCarroll and their two daughters had been living in the White Cottage with Ann's parents. William Scobell was also a boarder there. He was a member of the 79th Regiment and a socially prominent officer from Kingston where his father, Joseph Scobell, was a highly regarded contractor. In fact, in 1835 Scobell senior won the contract to build St John's Church and in 1838 he had begun to oversee the construction the nearby courthouse and jail. Young Scobell had followed his father to Peterborough. John and Susanna Davis had two unmarried daughters still living at home. Scobell, it appears, had somehow convinced John Davis that he was properly married to one of them and was living respectably with her under her father's roof. In the lawsuit that daughter was unnamed.

Acting on information from McCarroll, John Davis became aware that his daughter and Scobell were not legally married. Outraged at the young man's brazen duplicity, Davis brought a charge of "Seduction" against him. Scobell, however, managed to forestall his own arrest by pressing charges against both Davis and McCarroll concerning debts that, he alleged, they owed him. Thus, to his personal embarrassment, James was arrested. He was held in jail for twelve hours before William Cluxton and William McDonnell paid his bail.[48]

Appalled by Scobell's high-handed actions and acutely sensitive to the threat that imprisonment posed for his reputation, McCarroll brought a countersuit against Scobell in July 1841 on the charge of "Malicious Arrest." In court McCarroll's lawyer, James Gardiner Armour, argued that Scobell was a "wild, dissipated and unprincipled" individual who showed no regard for matters of public decency and who had no reasonable grounds for the charge he had brought against his client. Judge B.Y. McKeyes heard the evidence and ruled in McCarroll's favour. He issued a court order requiring Scobell to pay McCarroll damages, including lawyer and sheriff fees, amounting to 14.5.3 pounds.

This second deposition, like the first, identifies James McCarroll as an engaged citizen who was quick to stand up for himself and to bear witness; he did not hesitate to speak out against unscrupulous behaviour when he experienced it. In both instances, he responded to challenges presented by socially prominent, English-born Tories who flaunted their military positions and social status. He held his own as best he could, sometimes with the help of friends. However such misadventures may have wounded him personally, they did little to undermine his sense of Peterborough as an amiable, progressive town alive with opportunities for advancement. He had chosen it as his home and, by December 1842, he was ready to take up the new challenge of being a newspaper editor on his own, poised to speak out on political and social matters affecting local and provincial levels of government.

The Patchwork of Backwoods Journalism

Only four issues of Darcus's *Backwoodsman and Sentinel* and two of McCarroll's *Peterboro Chronicle* (December 1843–July 1846) have survived. Many more issues of the first Tory newspaper, the *Peterborough Gazette* (1845–48), are available, but even its run is broken in places.[49] One finds occasional mention of McCarroll as journalist and poet in the *Cobourg Star* and other provincial papers of the period. Before 1850, the *Star* was the most prominent of the region's newspapers and the voice of Tory politics. To date, no investigation of consequence has been undertaken into the evolution and nature of Peterborough's newspapers during the 1840s.

The combined force of Reform and Irish-Protestant interests had found its first sympathetic voice in John Darcus's *Backwoodsman*, a paper he set up as the northern counter to R.D. Chatterton's *Cobourg Star*. An Orangeman from Londonderry, Darcus arrived in the Peterborough area about 1832. After five years spent trapping and farming on his property in Emily Township, he moved into Peterborough in 1837 and began his newspaper. In 1838, he was appointed a justice of the peace, but soon thereafter broke his ties with local Tory leaders and shifted his support to Reform. Then, in 1841, after terminating the *Backwoodsman*, he broke off his Reform connection; his Tory "reward" was his appointment as clerk of the District Council for the Colborne District, a much sought after position paying 300 pounds annually. The move angered local Reformers – among them McCarroll – as it appeared to be a self-serving about-face in political allegiance.

A few years earlier McCarroll would have readily approved of Darcus's dual commitment to the Orange Order and Reform. In the "new Prospectus" for the *Backwoodsman*, dated February 1840, Darcus articulated his passion for celebrating the Irish: "The town of Peterborough is the centre of the Newcastle District," he wrote, "a district where Irish loyalty and Irish industry have so prominently displayed themselves." As well, McCarroll would have applauded him for locking editorial horns with Chatterton, the most influential voice of Tory and Family-Compact interests east of Toronto. A ready fighter from his editorial chair, Darcus contended with Chatterton over such crucial matters as the appointment of a new lieutenant-governor and the bullying behaviour of Tories in the Oshawa area.

McCarroll learned much from observing Darcus in action.[50] When, for instance, Darcus challenged George Elliott, a powerful Tory in Durham Township who sought to rally Orangemen along the Front against the Durham Report, McCarroll would initially have concurred. Like Darcus, he supported Reform and felt that the Orange Order in Canada should keep itself at a distance from the Tory party, especially since Tory insiders were determined to make loyalty to Britain the major issue among their supporters.[51]

How "Radical" was Darcus? The surviving issues of the *Backwoodsman*, all from 1840, provide little evidence of his politics or style. However, the *Cobourg Star* readily attached such labels as "Radical" and "Reformer" to him and his paper. In the wake of the Durham Report, Canada West was witnessing, in community after community, the hardening of two sharply opposed political positions and the emergence of party-like affiliations in support of each view. By 1841 the political die was cast. One had to be either a Tory or a Reformer. There was little room for conscientious independence.

For an Irish Protestant and Orangeman like Darcus, a consistent and coherent political position was often elusive. In supporting the new Canadian goal of limited responsible government, he found himself at odds with many fellow members of the Orange Order. He could declare himself and his newspaper committed to the British Constitution, and opposed to "Republican forms" and ideas, but could he be, as a Reformer, as conspicuously loyal to Britain as Orange Order members required? Caught in this conundrum, he aligned himself with another Irish-Canadian editor of note, the flamboyant and outspoken Ogle Gowan of Brockville, himself a past Grand Master of the Orange Order in British America. Both men sought to establish a middle ground wherein matters of local government could be placed in the hands of elected Canadian representatives without compromising their loyalty to Britain and without allowing the intrusion of American ideas into colonial life.

In 1868 Toronto editor James Moylan charged that McCarroll had once served as secretary of the Orange Order in Peterborough. This accusation should be seen in the light of Darcus's contradictory position twenty years earlier.[52] As a young journalist and Irish Protestant making his living in Peterborough, McCarroll would have welcomed the opportunity to be a part of the local Orange Order. He was an Anglican by habit and faith, and most of his close friends were Protestants. Moreover, like many members of the Orange Order at that time, he would have preferred to be seen in a non-political light; their organization was devoted to celebrating Ireland's Protestant past, not engaging in current political debate about loyalty. In the wake of the Rebellion and the rise of the Reform movement in Upper Canada, Tory leaders like George Elliott sought to enlist Orange Order support in both their attacks upon the Reform opposition and their hostility to Irish-Catholic demonstrations.

Such thinking was designed to categorize Reformers as disloyal – hence disreputable and little better than traitors to their heritage. Thus, the role of the Orange Order was one of the major issues facing Reform leaders and their supporters in the early 1840s. They had to appear to be fully loyal to Britain even as they campaigned for an increased control of government by elected, Canadian representatives.

Within this hotbed of loyalty, certain Peterborough leaders sought to articulate and celebrate the new voice of Reform. A weekly newspaper was crucial to that support. In December 1842, after the demise of the *Backwoodsman* and the fact of Darcus's conspicuous betrayal of Reform, Thomas Messenger launched a successor to Darcus's newspaper. Calling it the *Peterboro Chronicle*, he named himself publisher and hired James McCarroll as his editor, likely on the basis of his previous involvement with the *Backwoodsman*.

At last, then, McCarroll had the journalistic opportunity to which he aspired: he had his own editorial pulpit and the opportunity to promote both Reform ideas and his cultural interests. Ownership befell him soon thereafter. Initially he proceeded with caution and calm. The *Cobourg Star* took note of the *Chronicle*'s beginnings by welcoming a journal that promised "to steer clear of politics altogether." Such a promise was a fiction; it was merely for the record, as Chatterton knew well.[53]

Though the only Peterborough newspaper from December 1843 to 1845, the *Chronicle* was a small operation. From its print shop on Brock Street (near Water Street) it kept Reformers in town and the surrounding townships, especially those of Irish background, engaged and informed. Its circulation was likely between 500 and 600, given that its potential reading audience would have been more or less split between Reform and Tory supporters. Its balance sheet also depended on printing contracts with local government and businesses. How Catholics, and particularly Irish Catholics, responded to the voice of the *Chronicle* is not clear, but many of the latter supported Reform principles. In later years it was a matter of pride for McCarroll that, in his capacity as a journalist and writer, he had made it his personal goal to speak for all Irish interests in Upper Canada, regardless of religious affiliation. Imaginatively, he balanced his boyhood interest in Irish Catholics with his Anglican identity.

While McCarroll and Darcus shared Reform sympathies prior to 1842, it is an irony of local events that he was appointed to serve as Darcus's interim replacement as district clerk two years later. In *A Sketch of the Early Settlement and Subsequent Progress of the Town of Peterborough*, Thomas Poole rightly implied a connection between Darcus's appointment as district clerk in 1842 and his retirement from the *Backwoodsman*.[54] Awaiting him was a patronage plum from the Tories. Realigning himself with that "party" paid off handsomely for him, but Peterborough Reformers saw the appointment as a base betrayal.

They were outraged when, at a meeting in the Market Square (31 January 1844), the Peterborough Tories gathered to "to express their confidence" in Governor General Charles Metcalfe's decision to accept the resignation of his elected cabinet (all Reformers) and set up an advisory cabinet of his own choice.[55] Metcalfe's initiative was shocking in itself and a blow to Reform interests, though it was certainly within the range of his executive powers. While Metcalfe's move overrode the legitimate concerns of the duly elected Reform parliament, the Tories cheered it as a signal victory for their side.

Front and centre among the speakers was the apostate John Darcus, now rubbing shoulders with local Tories like Samuel Strickland, Thomas Traill, Dr John Hutchison, John R. Benson, G.B. Hall, J.G. Armour, and Captain A.S. Fraser. Darcus had been strategically selected by the Tories to move the first resolution of the rally, applauding Metcalfe's autocratic initiative. He spoke at length in support of conservative interests, noting "he ever had and ever would advocate a *Constitutional* Responsibility, and trusted that neither himself nor his children after him would ever advocate the Responsibility of the Baldwin and Hincks' Cabinet."

Later that same year Darcus, still the district clerk, found himself in court. Charged with fraud, he was tried and found guilty. His crime seems modest today – he reportedly claimed the money ($6 per head) for seventeen wolf kills in his jurisdiction, few of which could be verified as his. The court found that he had forged the certificates of documentation submitted by several local individuals who subsequently denied having any knowledge of the kills. Whether Darcus had been set up for his fall by irate Reformers or was simply the victim of his own petty fraud is lost in time; he was forced to resign his position and was replaced temporarily by none other than "James McCarroll, Esq." who, while currently editing the *Chronicle*, was appointed to serve as "acting" county clerk "for a few weeks."[56] A couple of months later, after an embarrassed Darcus had left the area, the clerkship was bestowed on another local Tory, Walter Sheridan, by Governor General Charles Metcalfe. Metcalfe bypassed the acting county clerk, who in any case would have found it difficult to produce the sureties required for the job. For McCarroll, it was but another instance of government patronage conspicuously favouring Tory supporters.[57] What he made of Darcus's actions is nowhere evident in the surviving issues of the *Chronicle*. What is clear, however, is that, as editor he had Sir Charles Metcalfe squarely in his journalistic sights.

The Editor's Chair at the *Peterboro Chronicle*

Occasional comments about the *Chronicle* in other provincial newspapers and the copies of its two extant issues –Tuesday, 27 May 1845 (vol. 3, no. 12) and Tuesday, 3 February 1846 (vol. 3, no. 46) – suggest that James McCarroll was not long in making a name for himself as an outspoken Reform or "Radical" editor in Upper Canada. Self-described as "A weekly journal devoted to Agriculture, Commerce, Science, Public Improvement, the Diffusion of Morality, useful Knowledge, and General Intelligence," the *Chronicle*'s masthead carried the motto "We Have Nothing to Fear from Prerogative but Everything from Undue Influence." McCarroll prefaced the paper's editorial section with words from the Durham Report: "The Responsibility in the United Legislature of all officers of the Government, except the Governor and his Secretary, should be secured by every means known to the British Constitution. The Governor as the Representative of the Crown, should be instructed that he must carry on his government by Heads of Department in whom the United Legislature should repose confidence, and that he must look for no support from home in any contest with the Legislature except on points involving strictly Imperial interests." This statement took direct aim at the autocratic mode of governance in Canada West as practised by Metcalfe, the fiery incumbent of the day.

McCarroll strongly supported Robert Baldwin, Louis-Hippolyte La Fontaine, and especially their emerging journalistic contemporary Francis Hincks. Hincks, a fellow Irishman, had successfully published two newspapers designed to advocate the implementation and development of responsible government – first the *Toronto Examiner* (1838–42) and later the *Montreal Pilot* (1844–48). Like Hincks, McCarroll "thoroughly enjoyed the vituperative journalism of the day."[58] He was a quick study as editor of the *Chronicle*. He knew that success in Canada West had much to do with one's political affiliation and that patronage appointments could be earned by effective party support.

For decades patronage had been a deep-rooted aspect of Upper Canadian life; it confirmed one's affiliation and connections. Members of the Family Compact in Toronto and elsewhere had made it their business to control the ear of London's representatives to the colony by catering to their interests. Having enjoyed the support of the lieutenant-governors and exercised a monopoly over most aspects of colonial life, Tory supporters had come to see themselves as part of a New-World, Anglo-aristocratic ascendency. Their control of patronage and business opportunities over several decades did much to spur the outrage of William Lyon Mackenzie and his cohorts, leading to the Rebellion in Canada West.

By the early 1840s, the politics of Reform had gained an impressive level of public support across the province. Increasing numbers of citizens chose to align themselves with the promises of responsible government as envisioned in the Durham Report and brought forward by Baldwin, La Fontaine, and Hincks. There were growing hopes for a more representative and effective legislative assembly and a wider range of economic opportunities within the colony. Young businessmen welcomed the freer exercise of business promised by Reform policies.

As editor of the *Chronicle* McCarroll made it his business to meet the rhetoric of the Tories head on. In his editorials and columns he exercised a more powerful voice than he could muster by means of a poem or story. "There is a certain prestige in Editorship, which contributes not a little to its ascendancy," wrote the editor of the rival *Peterborough Gazette* on 15 August 1845.[59] Young McCarroll had eagerly embraced that prestige. He was poised to critique and tease the Tory establishment of Peterborough while exercising his new role as a "gentleman of the press" and cheerleader for the town.

McCarroll set up his printing operation in a frame building below the impressive hill topped by St John's Church and the new courthouse. The office was not far from the house on Water Street that he would soon purchase for his family. His friend and printer George Haslehurst had charge of the *Chronicle*'s Washington Press. Born in Nova Scotia, young Haslehurst (1825–1861) was related to McCarroll's mother-in-law, Susanna Davis (Haslehurst). The Haslehursts lived close to the Davis's White Cottage.

McCarroll operated the paper for three-and-a-half years (the *Chronicle* began its third volume in March 1846).[60] It was a weekly production of four pages. Neatly laid out and printed, it offered its audience the standard journalistic fare of the day – potted European and American news, items of Canadian interest, local observations, and Reform-oriented editorials, all leavened by his poetry, cultural musings, and humorous gambits. Peterborough would not see so creative an editor for another hundred years – that is, until Robertson Davies took over the reins of the *Chronicle*'s successor, the *Peterborough Examiner*, in 1942.

Once settled into his editorial saddle, a confident and buoyant McCarroll took on his political enemies while lending support to his colleagues and friends. Often he did so in a wry or satiric manner, occasionally introducing comic voices. Such *jeux d'esprit* (sparkling with calculated misspellings and grammatical errors) were condemned as illiterate, flippant, or lacking in seriousness by local Tories, especially T.H. Dunsford, the Methodist editor of the *Peterborough Gazette*, who, in 1845, began to respond dismissively to McCarroll's offensive sallies. Publicly, McCarroll committed himself to four goals: first, to promote responsible government in the Canadas while attacking Tory interests; second, to champion the character and accomplishments of the Irish people, be they Protestant or Catholic, patrician or pauper; third, to celebrate Peterborough as a vibrant and pleasant community in which to live; and fourth, to express his faith in his community by, for example, challenging joyless attacks on social drinking and entertainments such as theatre performances, country fairs, and circuses that were regarded by many as morally dangerous and ungodly. He enjoyed writing pseudonymous essays and letters "to the editor," the better to amplify his arguments and mock his enemies. In the 1840s such tactics were characteristic of the politicized journalism in towns across Canada West.

Targeting Sir Charles Metcalfe: Earning Provincial Attention

One of McCarroll's attacks on his Tory enemies appeared in the spring of 1845. In seeking a dramatic way to call attention to the autocratic leadership of Governor General Charles Metcalfe, he linked the cancerous growths on Metcalfe's face to his slavish reliance on Tory advice. Metcalfe's cancer, which had been treated in England prior to his arrival in Canada in 1843, had recurred in Toronto; in fact, his condition was steadily worsening. Hesitant at first to enter the political situation he found in the Canadas, Metcalfe soon adopted a position of firm support for the Tories. He set himself against the wishes of the Reformers, despite the fact that they constituted the majority of members elected to the Legislative Assembly. McCarroll honed in especially on Metcalfe's refusal to pay heed to his duly elected Canadian representatives.

By 1845, Metcalfe had thoroughly alienated most Canadian Reformers. He forsook the more conciliatory strategies of his predecessors Sir Charles Bagot and Poulett Thomson (Lord Sydenham), who had followed the direction and spirit of the Durham Report. (Sydenham's term was ended by a fatal accident.) Metcalfe came to power operating under more conservative orders from London and urged on by his own desire to re-entrench British autonomy. He deliberately set aside the recommendations of the Durham Report. He regularly used his power to block or dismiss the legislative initiatives of the elected assembly; he made all the political appointments within the Canadas himself, refusing to listen to the advice of his elected officials; he chose to ignore current legislative initiatives in the assembly such as a law to ban secret societies. By the end of Metcalfe's term, "politics" had been "made a business," and a matter for party affiliation. In an editorial entitled "The Canadian Press" on 16 February 1844, the conservative *Toronto Patriot* argued that the press bore much of the blame for the growing party hostility and for "embitter[ing] the public mind."

In November 1843 all but one of the Reform members of cabinet, led by Baldwin and La Fontaine, resigned their positions after a lengthy and heated parliamentary debate. The resignations of the council members plunged the colony into a state of heightened anxiety. Cool and reserved in manner and making no concessions to popular feeling, Metcalfe simply accepted the resignations and chose to operate under the banner of "royal prerogative," a strategy that he had used in previous colonial appointments. Needing a practical way to carry on with his government, he appointed an unrepresentative Tory triumvirate to govern the colony in the interim.

In effect, Metcalfe "practically suspended" constitutional government during much of his two-and-a-half years in power, thereby raising the tempers of Reformers to the boiling point. In response, a "monster Reform Association was established in Toronto, with branches all over the Province," and, as Dent added, "party ferocity reached an [unprecedented] pitch in Canada."[61] Violence was a common occurrence at both Reform and Tory meetings while there were pitched battles at the hustings among voters and party watchdogs during local elections.

Peterborough was no exception. The *Chronicle* showered a steady stream of criticism on Lord Metcalfe. He was now viewed as a despot, an "obstructionist," and an "opponent of the popular will."[62] Reform journalists applied nicknames like "Charles the Simple" and "Old Squaretoes" to him. McCarroll's cancer motif, mean-spirited as it was, may well have been adopted by other editors.

In the provinces, the newspapers were "almost entirely engrossed by the struggle."[63] McCarroll, whose editorship coincided with Metcalfe's term in office, waded into the controversy at every available instance, prompting angry responses from various conservative newspapers, which served to bolster his sallies. An issue of the *Kingston News* delighted in describing a triumphant Tory rally in Peterborough in December 1843, the very month that McCarroll took over the *Chronicle*. Under the title, "Great Rejoicings in Peterborough," it reported that, on the occasion of the mass resignation of the Reform leaders from Metcalfe's cabinet, there was an illumination and bonfire at the Market Square attended by many prominent conservatives. Baldwin and Hincks were hoisted on poles and burned in effigy "with the star-spangled banner floating over their heads and holding each a *Peterborough Chronicle*." As the effigies were consumed in the flames, "Cheers were given for the Queen and the Governor General, and groans for the late Ministry."[64]

In 1845 McCarroll's attacks on Metcalfe's facial cancer drew the fire of the *British Colonist* in Toronto. He was chastised for his "brutish spirit" and "violent Radical[ism]." The venerable and long-suffering Metcalfe, the paper wrote, deserved fairer treatment and more respect, even from his political enemies. On 27 May 1845 McCarroll offered a somewhat apologetic reply to the *British Colonist*, allowing that the governor general was "a kind man in private however misguided in public affairs"; he even conceded that "we regret his sufferings as much as the *Colonist*." True to his pugnacious editorial guise, however, he tempered his apology by calling attention to Metcalfe's "renowned political pliancy" and questioning the objectivity of the *Colonist* itself. He mocked its slavish propensity to fawn over "our noble Governor, etc., etc." at the expense of any recognition of the political matters at stake.

Local Hospitality in an "Amiable Community"

As a Peterborough resident for nearly fifteen years, McCarroll carefully read "the passions of the hour" and kept a close eye on the local Tories, many of whom were influential citizens and acquaintances. They had to be treated with some care, despite the sometimes blatant abuses of civic order they occasionally encouraged. While such questionable actions needed to be challenged, an editor who had his own financial challenges and was aware of the tenuous nature of his social identity in his class-conscious community had to tread carefully when it came to hurling brickbats. The better strategy was to square off against opposing journalists as fair game while attacking fallible government figures like Metcalfe. Choosing his targets with care, McCarroll mixed eloquence with spleen, wit with satire, according to the occasion. By such strategies he flourished in the editorial crossfire that characterized Peterborough journalism during the *Chronicle*'s final year of operation.

Active journalistic sniping became a local reality when a group of Tory leaders finally agreed to set up a rival newspaper. The *Peterborough Gazette* came into being on 15 August 1845, financed by "a Company of Proprietors" one of whose aims was to put the uppity James McCarroll firmly in his place. Its editor was an elderly Methodist minister, T. Hartley Dunsford, a man of some means who held to strict standards of written English, enjoyed quoting Latin, and supported the Temperance movement. However, Dunsford's health was so infirm that within six months he had to turn over the *Gazette*'s editorial reins to a much younger man, the flamboyant James Northey.

In a two-column editorial in the tenth issue of the *Gazette* (17 October 1845) Dunsford launched a prolonged attack on McCarroll for "his insolence towards the leader of the Government" and "the use of the vulgar tongue." Dunsford argued that McCarroll's "talents" for vulgarity were "unquestionable" and "flow[ed] much more readily from his pen, than any other style of language."[65] Then he charged him with a litany of sins – "surpassing ignorance" of history and matters of taste, "so small a quantity of knowledge," general offensiveness, mendacity and "scurrility," abusiveness, "trashy and braggadocio remarks," all outfitted by weak arguments and faulty grammar. Dismissively, he concluded, "We certainly did not expect this from one, who has heretofore filled the respectable and useful situation of Instructor of Youth."

McCarroll relished the name-calling and met it forcefully. He courted trouble and welcomed the dance of insults. Though respectful of Dunsford's age and profession,[66] he was not about to diminish his stylistic experiments in letter writing and voice – the sort of writing that the stuffy Dunsford so vigorously dismissed. As a forward-thinking editor, he particularly enjoyed tweaking the noses of arrogant Tories and local Temperance advocates. He mocked their moralistic zeal and offered by contrast a far more positive picture of Peterborough's drinking and social culture than his teetotalling adversaries deemed allowable. He was personally delighted to be recognized as one who enjoyed a convivial drink. His editorial of 25 June 1846 (under the title "Temperance in Peterboro") drew a righteous response from the *Gazette*.

McCarroll had written quite frankly that he was "proud … to bear testimony to the fact, that a more amiable community [than Peterborough] has never blessed any portion of the habitable globe." Amiability included the opportunity to share a glass of "Irish tay" with friends during or after a busy workday. However, the *Gazette* saw his happy sense of community and its daily social interactions as a gratuitous slap to the Temperance cheek. Dunsford responded by publishing two anonymous letters to the editor, each attacking McCarroll's stance and calling into question his personal behaviour and moral outlook. "A Lover of Truth" and G (*Gazette*, 4 July 1846) complained that while there was but one struggling Temperance Society in Peterborough, the town's 2,000 inhabitants had access to twenty places to drink, as well as three distilleries, a brewery, and plenty of "Whiskey and Liquors" imported from Cobourg and readily available in the basement of William Cluxton's store. Dunsford targeted the camaraderie that McCarroll and Cluxton shared with their drinking friends. Fearing that Peterborough's reputation as a disreputable, hard-drinking town was growing apace, and worrying about the future of its struggling Temperance society, "A Lover of Truth" accused the *Chronicle* of "a *low standard* of moral rectitude" and suggested that McCarroll must have consumed an extra gin cocktail before "he penned the disgusting article under consideration."[67] It was by then pro forma for the *Gazette* to debunk the young editor – he was, to Dunsford and his rival newspaper, a so-called "great man," an upstart, and an indulgent "weather-cock."

A week later another letter in the *Gazette*, again from G, deplored "the onward strides of baccanalian activities in Peterborough," chastising McCarroll for his breezy and thoughtless advocacy of so serious a problem. In the *Chronicle* McCarroll had apparently prefaced his acerbic reply by inviting the *Gazette*'s Mr G to "step down into Cluxton's wine-cellar" where, over a bottle of champagne purchased at his personal expense, he would happily contest G's views about the nature of "moral rectitude." G sealed his moralistic outrage with a melodramatic image: "But, let not the *Chronicle* invite me to be an accessory to his 'atrocious crime' – let his blood be upon his own head – the widow's frowns shall not fasten upon me. I beg to apologise for applying the epithet *weather-cock*, to your contemporary, at which he appears to have taken umbrage, and I candidly acknowledge that, although his career has been one of almost incessant changes, he has hitherto maintained a certain degree of consistency – he has steadily adhered to the example of the Vicar of Bray." That same label – "the Vicar of Bray" – had been pinned on Francis Hincks by the Tory press of Toronto because of what they deemed his donkeyish editorials.

On 18 July 1846, G was back in the *Gazette*, renewing his attack. Again deploring McCarroll's cavalier attitude to Temperance, he was clearly mortified to learn that the *Chronicle* editor claimed to have no idea of who he – Mr G – was. Adopting a musical motif the better to mock McCarroll, G wrote, this time altering his signature to "G. Flat or F. Sharp":

> But it seems that I am also a "Flat," for noticing the "great man's" flippant *Editorial* on the subject of "Temperance in Peterboro." Now, Sir, the editor's musical genius might teach him that a flat on the left side of a note is a sharp on the right side of another, and on the right side I will always endeavour to be found. In doing so, I trust I shall be, at least, as sharp as the editor of the *Chronicle*.
>
> The slovenly attempt at satire in his last, in which every fourth or fifth word is misspelt, concludes with pronouncing me to be a consummate _____. It is easy enough to guess the intention of the writer, as to filling up the blank, but whether or not the suppressed word be applicable to him rather than to me, I am willing to leave to be determined by those who do not frequent wine-cellars. At all events, we have high authority for saying, that only "Fools *make a mock of sin*."

McCarroll had indulged his penchant for the comic vernacular in mocking the sober self-righteousness of G, aka G Flat. We cannot, however, know precisely what he wrote, given the loss of the issues cited.[68]

As the 1840s unfolded, McCarroll's sense of Peterborough as an up and coming place continued to develop. Jean Cole has accurately described the period: "The mood in the mid-1840s was one of hope and optimism."[69] Signs of growth were everywhere, from the numerous mills and foundries along the river to the range of stores and businesses along George and Charlotte streets.[70] A new lock had been built below the town, a new bridge was being proposed across the Otonabee, and James Hall was promoting the construction of a railroad from Port Hope to Peterborough.[71]

Moreover, as McCarroll happily noted in his editorials, the town's social life was rich and enjoyable. Here one could share good times with friends and here, as he knew, a man could rise from humble beginnings to public prominence, even if his critics persisted in mocking his mutability and ambitiousness. Friends like Cluxton and William McDonnell, James Hall and the Rev. R.J.C. Taylor, Charles Perry, John Albro, and George Haslehurst were nearby, ready to lend a hand should he find himself in need. One new friend in Peterborough was Sandford Fleming, a young Scot who lived with a relative, Dr John Hutchison, in 1845–46 during his first two years in Canada. Fleming was an aspiring surveyor and engineer. In June 1846 he offered his map of the town of Peterborough for sale to interested townsfolk. McCarroll signed up for a copy only a month before the fire that destroyed his print shop. No doubt he bought his copy with the *Chronicle* in mind, but he also knew that Fleming was a friend not only of Hutchison, his own doctor, but also of James Hall. Fleming would marry Jean Hall, James's daughter, in January 1855.

Here as well his creative juices were flowing productively. His ability to write evocative poems was now well established even as he continued to seek further outlets for his work.

The growing town on the Otonabee would continue to exert an imaginative hold on him long after he left Peterborough.[72] When in the spring of 1859 he returned on a visit, now an established writer and notable citizen in Toronto, he was overtaken by memories of "these scenes of my youth" and disturbed by the many changes that had taken place since his arrival. His nostalgic tribute to the place where "my old shaded haunts … once moved to song and soft whispers alone" appeared in the *Toronto Daily Leader* (1859) under the title "Lines, Written at Peterborough, Canada, April, 1859."

The Poet Testing His Several Voices

In his 1862 profile Henry Morgan wrote that, once settled in Peterborough, "McCarroll began to contribute scraps both of prose and verse to some of the provincial journals"; moreover, "the manner in which they were received, was so gratifying, that it may be said to have determined his after literary career."[73] McCarrroll's poems were indeed well received and sometimes highly praised. The accolades of provincial editors encouraged him. Initially, however, his progress was modest, given the paucity of available outlets and his commitment as an editor. How many of his poems he published in the lost issues of the *Chronicle* must remain unknown.

Opportunities to receive payment for creative work in the Cobourg and Peterborough area were scarce in the late 1830s and early 1840s. So too in Toronto. In *Roughing It in the Bush* (1852) Susanna Moodie painted a dismal picture of the few paying outlets available to her during her time in the bush. As a modestly well-established English writer seeking to make a name for herself in Upper Canada, she found no publications willing to pay her for her writing until John Lovell sought her out in 1838 to contribute to his new

Montreal magazine, the *Literary Garland*.[74] Nevertheless, during that decade Moodie sent her poems to local newspapers and short-lived Toronto magazines, grateful for the opportunity to place her poems before some readers in Upper Canada. The *Cobourg Star* was initially the only local publication available to Moodie, who lived in Hamilton Township from 1832 to 1834 and then north of Lakefield for the rest of the decade.[75]

By contrast, James McCarroll was a younger and unknown entity. He could not trade on a family literary name as Moodie could, and did.[76] His first known appearance as a poet was in 1841, although it is possible he had previously contributed a poem or two to Darcus's *Backwoodsman*.

Two McCarroll poems appeared in the *Christian Guardian* for 17 November 1841. Both were sent from Peterborough. Begun under the editorship of Egerton Ryerson in Cobourg, the *Christian Guardian* had been in weekly production for some twelve years and occasionally included poems of a religious or uplifting nature. McCarroll's efforts were likely inspired by observing his two daughters who, in 1841, were two and four years of age. Entitled "To a Beautiful Child" and "The Father to His Sleeping Child," the poems celebrate a father's love for a daughter, the vulnerability of women as child-bearers, and Time's tyranny over fragile human lives. In an accompanying note, the editor described McCarroll as "a correspondent who has not till lately favoured us with an effusion from his pen."

The latter poem, which McCarroll included in *Madeline*, focuses on a deceased woman whose beautiful features survive in her sleeping daughter. It recalls the beauty of the mother through the smile, eyes, and hair of the "Dear miniature of her who's sainted now." It explores the emotional gap between the remembered beauty of the mother and the living presence of the slumbering child. The poem offers a poignant reflection on the vulnerability of Victorian women in pregnancy and childbirth, as well as the poet's love for both his lost love and his sleeping child. It reads as follows:

How like thy mother – every circling hour
As thus I gaze, more fully I trace
The beauteous semblance of that faded flow'r
    In thy sweet face.

Dear miniature of her who's sainted now,
Her wonted smile seems sweetly lingering there;
And that dark tress which shades thy shining brow,
    Is her own hair.

Oh, let this fervent kiss thy slumbers mar,
That I may gaze upon her speaking eye,
Which seem'd a fragment of the vesper star,
      And deep blue sky.

Sleep on, sleep on, thou lonely lovely thing;
Owe the unruffled calmness of thy breast
To thy own angel mother's golden wing
      That guards thy rest.[77]

Surprisingly, this poem had first appeared in the *Literary Garland* for November 1841. It is the only known McCarroll poem to have been accepted by that popular magazine.[78]

The other poem, "To a Beautiful Child," invokes a grimness keyed to the inescapable shadow of "the silent tomb" in life.

Heir to the silent tomb, how sad thy lot!
Sport of conflicting passions, child of gloom,
Why weep'st thou not,
      Heir to the silent tomb!

Like meteor flying thro' yon midnight sphere
In evanescent glory's wild illume,
You journey here,
      Heir to the silent tomb.

Burst thro' the morn of life like laughing brow
Through sapphire blaze, and wreath of rich perfume;
And where art thou,
      Heir to the silent tomb?

Thy trembling spirit yields its latent breath,
While joys becalm, or shipwrecked hopes consume
Thou art in death,
      Heir to the silent tomb.

Although simple in structure and thought, the two poems are impressive in their verse building, dramatic sense, imagery, and word choice. Twenty years later, the Rev. E.H. Dewart chose seven of McCarroll's poems in his anthology of Canadian poetry, *Selections from Canadian Poets* (Montreal, 1864). While Dewart included more poems by Charles Sangster and Alexander McLachlan, McCarroll was more fully represented than well-known poets like Susanna Moodie and Thomas D'Arcy McGee. Dewart considered him a special kind of poetic talent – graceful, lyrically fluid, light of spirit, at times deftly humorous, capable of celebrating elements of enduring beauty while acutely aware of the fleeting present.[79] It would appear that, in 1864, Dewart did not know McCarroll personally; rather he selected his poems from contemporary newspapers and magazines, especially the *Toronto Daily Leader*. Critics and scholars have often overlooked his perceptive tribute to McCarroll as an early Canadian poet.

In November 1843, the *Christian Guardian* published a third McCarroll poem entitled "Time"; its text was taken from the pages of the *Peterboro Chronicle*.[80]

> Could mortals be lash'd to the lightning's red *steed*,
> To be hurried away to the tomb,
> They'd shudder at once, through his terrible speed,
> Being ingulf'd in its mystical gloom.
>
> On their courser of flame they would tremblingly ride,
> And believe every plunge was his last;
> As the thunders told forth of that measureless stride,
> In whose swiftness the future seems past.
>
> Yet onward! and onward! they carelessly dash,
> Nor conceive that they rapidly fly;
> Tho' compared with the speed of their course, the wild dash
> Seems at rest on the face of the sky.
>
> A charger unseen, while they're trifling around
> Sweeps along with that echoless tread,
> Which bears them away with a mightier bound!
> To the desert-like waste of the dead.

The wild journey deathward on a shaft of lightning reveals a young poet capable of vividly ominous imaginings. The sense here of time as lived and time as eternal is effectively dramatized and suggests a vision adept at evoking images of recklessness and inevitable death.

But McCarroll was a poet of many moods. The issue of the *Chronicle* for 27 May 1845 includes a poem in a lighter vein. Its two verses celebrate the light and warmth of human "gladness" that, passing from one individual to another, helps the latter to deal with loss and overcome sorrow. Perhaps it should also be read as a testimony to his own powers of balance and recovery. He would need to draw on those powers within the year. The poem appeared without a title.

Here's a smile for the past with its sunshine and shade,
For no tear can restore us one joy that's decayed;
E'en an urn, when sunlight is over it thrown,
No more seems the record of sorrow alone;
For the brightness that Heav'n has lovingly shed,
Seems to tell us how calm is the sleep of the dead.

A smile, still a smile, tho the flowers which appear
On our pathway of life may yet cradle a tear:
Still the light of your gladness each drop will illume,
And the warmth change our grief to the spirit's perfume:
Then why should we sorrow, when gladness can shed
A light o'er the living, a calm o'er the dead.

But while he was writing poems in the *Chronicle*, he was also on occasion publicly ruminating about culture and literature. As a Canadian journalist, for instance, he was well ahead of his time in writing an essay (again on 27 May 1845) about the nature of poetry. Here he called attention to two powerful couplets from Edward Young's poem *The Last Day* (1713):

The world alarm'd, both earth and heaven, o'erthrown
And gasping Nature's last tremendous groan;
Death's ancient scepter broke, the teeming Tomb,
The righteous Judge, and man's eternal doom.

These lines from Young (1688–1735)[81] awakened his poetic instincts and stimulated his vision of eternity: "how condensed, yet luminous! how enumerative, yet brief! how metaphorical, yet true! [Young] rises into the inexhaustible style, it seems without an effort." Deeply moved, he responded as a reader to Young's visionary effects: "'Both earth and heav'n overthrown.' What conception! The whole system deranged, signals of distress meet the eye from every quarter. The abode of man about to disappear, and to disappear under circumstances which the past allows the imagination to form. – The world dissolving, monarchies and kingdoms breaking up, thrones trembling, crowns and sceptres lying as useless things." Though disturbed by Young's picture of "general ruin" and "the infinite of woe," he also welcomed the "light of revelation" and the hope of "new heavens and new earth" introduced by the poet. A pure vision was necessary to allow humanity access to the "heights of felicity" in the future. A work-a-day journalist McCarroll might be, but he was much more as well – a poet, a visionary, and a secular minister. The *Chronicle* allowed him opportunities to bring forward many of his enthusiasms and concerns.

Personal Tragedy, Fire, and Bankruptcy

The year 1846 was James McCarroll's *annus horriblis*. There were two devastating losses. Late in April his first-born son, William, died at the age of three weeks. His death was hard on both parents in many ways.

A few months later came the second loss. On a July evening a sudden fire destroyed the frame building on Brock Street that housed the *Peterboro Chronicle*. The town's volunteer fire fighters, ill-equipped and not well organized, valiantly sought to control the blaze but with little success. However, while the building and the newspaper's records were lost, the firemen managed to save some of the office equipment, including the Washington Printing Press and much of the typeface.

For a few heart-rending hours, James McCarroll watched the bottom fall out of his world. His high spirits and optimism were horribly dashed. Suddenly, he seemed to have no future. While his grief at the loss of William was private, the losses he suffered from the fire were public. Indeed, within weeks he would be gazetted as "a Bankrupt." Already encumbered with a large debt for the *Chronicle*, he now found himself the image of conspicuous failure, facing a bleak future and unable to pay his creditors. Ahead lay the possibility of imprisonment.[82]

In the Peterborough of 1846 log and frame dwellings were the order of the day. Brick houses were still a rarity, though the sale of bricks was growing.[83] Minimal fire-fighting resources were available and insurance costs were too high for most residents. A business that depended for its income on a limited number of (sometimes reluctant) subscribers and access to job-printing contracts was vulnerable. At the best of times James McCarroll had little extra capital; in fact, though he now owned his own house, he likely had sometimes to rely on support from Ann's family and his friends. Still, until the fire, his fortunes had been following an impressive upward arc. "Weather-cock" he may have seemed to his adversaries, but, by small, deliberate steps, he had raised himself up; he had become the owner and editor of his own newspaper even as his reputation as a poet and musician was beginning to grow.

In existing reports there is no intimation of arson with regard to the fire. Certainly, some local Tories would have liked nothing better than to see an end to the *Chronicle* and McCarroll's editorial voice. But whatever the cause, the result was inescapable. McCarroll's losses were "heavy," both financially and emotionally. On 30 July his debt to a man named Nathan Lyman was docketed and certified.[84] Despite the moral and financial support of McCarroll's friends, it was impossible to forestall the inevitable. On 12 September 1846 the *Peterborough Gazette*, which for a few weeks had been the only newspaper in town, announced that "James McCarroll, Printer and Publisher" had appeared in "the Insolvent Court for the Colborne District" before Justice B.Y. McKeyes. The notice added that the court had appointed William Cluxton and James Hall as "Assignees of the Estate." However, in part because Judge McKeyes was suffering from a serious illness, the certificate of indebtedness was not issued until 27 October. No further report on McCarroll's bankruptcy appeared in surviving issues of the *Gazette*.

A Phoenix of Reform Rises from the Ashes of the *Chronicle*

Despite this crushing setback, James McCarroll could or would not remain silent for long. Some of his "office" was put up for auction as part of his bankruptcy settlement. That sale was scheduled for Peterborough's most prominent hotel, the Albert House, on 12 March 1847. The printing equipment would be sold at a (minimum) cost of 350 pounds under the close watch of "Mess'rs Cluxton and Hall."

By then, however, the *Chronicle*'s printing press was already back in operation. In November 1846, perhaps to no one's surprise, it was leased for three years by the *Chronicle*'s successor, the *Peterborough Weekly Despatch*, at a rate of 40 pounds per annum. The lease effectively assured the continuation of the voice of Reform in the region while allowing McCarroll to continue with his job-printing contracts. The arrangement also positioned him to provide

editorial support and advice to George Haslehurst, his former printer, who
was announced as the *Despatch*'s editor. Politically and personally, it was the
best possible interim solution.[85]

The *Weekly Despatch* began its run on 19 November 1846. So close in purpose were the two papers that the *Despatch* used the *Chronicle*'s motto on its
masthead: "We Have Nothing to Fear from Prerogative, but Everything from
Undue Influence." Surviving issues reveal that after a few months McCarroll
began contributing to its pages, but now under a playful pseudonym. Though
less creative and ebullient than his former boss, Haslehurst was not long in
renewing hostilities with the editor of the *Peterborough Gazette*, the Rev. J.H.
Dunsford, and his young protege, James Northey, who, having returned from
a European excursion, would soon be announced as the *Gazette*'s acting editor
in place of the ailing Dunsford.

Where McCarroll had been and what he had been doing since the
announcement of his bankruptcy is not clear. The actual terms of the court
case are not known, although, as a debtor under the law, he could certainly
have faced time in prison. Judge McKeyes, the veteran Tory who heard the
case, was in fact dying. His ill health likely led to delays in the action against
McCarroll; whatever the case, no record has been found indicating the kind
of punishment imposed on him by the court.

If he did go to jail, it was not for long. More likely, he remained quietly in
Peterborough, struggling with a personal depression brought on by his double
tragedy. During his recovery he likely withdrew into an emotional "desert
place" such as he imagined in his poem "Lines" (How oft, while wandering in
some desert place).[86] In fact, brief bouts of depression seem to have afflicted
him on later occasions, however upbeat he sought to be. He was, in George
Haslehurst's apt phrase, "now out of harness" (*Despatch*, 25 March 1847). He
needed time to recover his bearings, regain his fighting spirit, and develop
new plans for the future.

One major task he faced was to find a new way to provide a living for Ann
and their three daughters, Emma, Mary, and Kate.[87] This meant looking to
employment opportunities beyond Peterborough, for he knew that he could
not continue to rely on the generosity of his friends there. Hence, he turned
to Cobourg where he had some friendly connections and where he knew there
was a market for his skills as a music teacher and an editor. In fact, Cobourg
would soon provide him with a fresh journalistic opportunity: he was invited
to edit a new Reform newspaper on the Front. Printer Joseph Leonard set
up the *Newcastle Courier* in the fall of 1847 and invited him to promote the

campaigns of Reform candidates in both Cobourg and Peterborough during the run up to the important election of January 1848. Two of his good friends were involved. James Hall had been named as the Peterborough candidate and William Weller of Cobourg made a late entry into the Northumberland campaign. McCarroll was eager to support them. In addition, he was able to back the Toronto campaign of Francis Hincks, who was also being touted as a prospective attorney general should the Reformers once again muster a majority.

For about six months he had been uncharacteristically silent. Until the spring of 1847 there is no clear sign of his presence in the pages of the *Weekly Despatch* where, as usual, articles were unsigned. But recover he soon did! He re-entered the journalistic fray, disguising himself in the *Weekly Despatch* with pseudonyms readily apparent to those in the know.[88] In Peterborough his jaunty, aggressive style was recognized by most readers, be they Reformers, Tories, or independents. Even though he had moved to Cobourg that year, he was often on the move, remaining in close contact with Haslehurst, providing editorial advice, and rekindling his quarrels with the *Gazette*. In particular, he took strong exception to James Northey's high-toned and artistic airs; here was yet another pretentious Tory whose arrogance and insensitivity needed schooling. As well in 1849 he would contribute a number of important poems to the *Weekly Despatch*, at times using pseudonyms and at times his own name. In fact, in that year, at least eleven new McCarroll poems appeared in the *Despatch's* pages.

From St Patrick's Day (17 March 1847) until 9 April 1847, he adopted the voice of CRUX in a sequence of letters to the *Weekly Despatch*. Still smarting from earlier wounds inflicted by the *Gazette*, he chose the Irish Catholic holiday to launch a fresh attack on Dunsford and Northey.[89] His particular purpose in the first instance was a defence of the "members of the late Peterborough Fire Company – whose services are still remembered with gratitude by many individuals here." Though the company had since been disbanded, he appreciated their efforts; nevertheless, with tongue firmly in cheek, he admitted that the volunteer firemen had been forced to work with a fire engine that was "no better than a common watering pot." Still, he took offence at the *Gazette's* unfeeling attack on the company, arguing that it was a "gross insult" to the brave men involved. It was offensive in its intention, unfair in its allegations, and wrong-headed in its judgment; indeed, it was worthy of a public "tanning." Why the fire company had been disbanded is not clear from surviving columns, though inadequacy of equipment and the lack of capable volunteers would likely have been reasons. For his part, McCarroll could not forget his "gratitude" for the company's effort and the risks they faced in rescuing his valuable printing equipment from the *Chronicle*'s conflagration. His letter called for more "caution" and "respect" in the treatment of future firefighters.

A week later CRUX was back, responding to counterattacks in the *Gazette* and addressing the surprising news that "the reverend gentleman" [Mr Dunsford] had, for reasons of health, vacated his editorial chair. Dunsford, the *Gazette* implied, was responsible neither for the article about the disbanded fire company nor the pretentious attempt at "light literature" published in a recent issue.

McCarroll, however, was having none of it. A knowledgable editor, he argued, could not so easily distance himself from what appeared in his paper nor could he conveniently retire "behind his man Friday." Playing on the theme of Dunsford's "studied misrepresentation" of the facts, CRUX directed his spleen at the "host of barbarous scribblers" whose "vulgar" personal attacks often appeared in the *Gazette*. These writers of letters to the editor appeared above such initials as A.B. and X.Y.Z. With the kind of verbal flourish he reserved for his attack mode, he concluded that, at the very least, "I may be entitled to some consideration for having stirred up the stagnant pool by which the *Gazette* is surrounded, and brought to the surface, animalcula so extraordinary as A.B. – X.Y.Z. and VINDEX, inasmuch as I am confident that the public have been amused, in no ordinary degree, at the cleverness that could suggest an idea so admirable as that of coming forward, in such alphabetical array, to annihilate a gentleman for having written under an assumed name" (*Weekly Despatch*, 25 March 1847).[90]

Admitting to being CRUX, McCarroll responded to subsequent "animalcula" in letters in the 31 March and 7 April issues. In the first, CRUX observed that the *Gazette*'s editor seemed unable to detect the "legitimate humour" that had characterized his previous letters, calling it "vulgar falsehood." In the second, he took exception to the fact that VINDEX (presumably Northey) had demeaned his previous vocation as a "mechanic" – or shoemaker. CRUX mocked VINDEX's pretentiousness and his tasteless violation of "the spirit [of equality] that characterizes the day" in Canada. Such undemocratic "prejudices" were the expression of an "unreflecting, and ill-read simpleton," the sort of man who "affects to view every mechanic with supreme contempt."

He then launched into a vigorous ad hominem attack under the rhetorical guise of not wanting to "indulg[e] in gross and unwarrantable personalities" such as "*Master Vindex*" does. He knew his man and felt that Northey's insults required an equally mean-spirited response. Here, then, is the pseudonymous McCarroll in full vindictive rant:

However stupid or uneducated this friend of the *Gazette*, he will, doubtless, wince under the observations that have already been made; although I am satisfied that such persons are always able to find sufficient balm for their wounds, in the pleasure which they derive from being noticed publicly, in any way whatever – the only solace of scribblers; still, sir, though severe, I trust that, throughout the course of my remarks, I have not betrayed a spirit, similar to that which imbues the tissue of purile [*sic*] falsehood that has created so much unqualified disgust here, or stooped to supply the place of common sense by indulging in gross, and unwarrantable personalities. True, sir, [if] I could so far forget myself, it would be quite easy for me to assert, that this same *Master Vindex*, who affects to sneer at honest trades-people, is but a miserable young pettifogger, who, in the meagerness of his mental acquirements, and profound ignorance of his profession, is, absolutely, obliged to hang upon the misplaced friendship and liberality of a certain individual of this place, for the purpose of sustaining, amongst other things, a tolerably decent exterior! – And, Sir, might I not add, that there resides, at this moment, in a neighbouring town, an undoubted gentleman who insulted him in the public street, and would have followed up the matter, in the usual manner, had not master V sneaked off, quietly, for the purpose of avoiding the prompt and merited treatment he was about to receive? And further, Sir, could I not but state that, from his mischief-making propensities, and *penchant* towards low gossip, he is, jetty locks, macassar and all, but barely tolerable in ladies' society, and treated with the most marked indifference by many of the principal families amongst us! – while, to crown all, were I mad enough, I might publish to the world, that, in connexion with being denied unlimited intercourse with all respectable and good men, he is known throughout the length and breadth of the District as a person unworthy [of] private confidence, and far from occupying an enviable position in town![91]

Often mocked because of his cultural pretensions and his former occupation as a cobbler, McCarroll was acutely sensitive to attempts to demean his talents, abilities, and hard-won social stature. He valued the position he had attained in Peterborough and was scornful of those he judged to be pretenders to rank and respect in local society. Hence, he unloaded the range of his scorn on the likes of Master (VINDEX) Northey.

George Haslehurst stood firmly by his friend in his letter-writing ripostes. In supporting CRUX's second letter on 25 March, the editor lamented the criticisms put forward by the *Gazette* writers, especially in their continuing campaign to demean "the tone and character of the late *Peterboro' Chronicle*." Rather, he argued that CRUX's letter of 17 March had been "principally a *jeu de mots*, which, strange to say, has been completely lost on the lucid individuals who have taken up the matter with such gentlemanlike warmth." Furthermore, he warned that, given such criticism, McCarroll might be "goaded, once more, into the indulgence of those propensities, which have left, at least one individual, a standing jest throughout the length and breadth of this province."[92] CRUX's letter of 7 April was just such a response.

James Northey tried to put an end to the war of letters by publishing an "apology" which he alleged was written by CRUX himself. On 1 May 1847 he had CRUX offer a "sudden retraction of everything which may be deemed offensive to the retired editor of your paper." CRUX contritely admitted to his "present self-abasement," begged forgiveness for his sins, and offered a promise of "good behaviour" henceforth. The letter was, of course, merely an escalation in Northey's personal attack. He deemed McCarroll's pseudonymous letters "an abomination to respectable citizens" that revealed his "low" reputation for "veracity and honesty." Northey also has CRUX admit to being caned in public, deservedly, and also punched in the nose. Finally he makes him confess that he used pseudonyms for the simple reason that "if I used my own name, no one would care a straw for the contents, or believe a single word I might say."

McCarroll's answer to Northey's mischief is missing, but it is clear that such persistent and nasty ad hominem attacks could not continue for much longer, even though Northey found other ways to irritate McCarroll, especially in writing an insensitive and dismissive attack on famine-ravaged Ireland.[93] Finally, on 25 April, a *Gazette* editorial proposed a truce for the mutual benefit of the rival newspapers. An end to the name calling between the parties would allow, it argued, better business opportunities for both. However, in the absence of any reasonable ground for agreement and in the wake of such a long series of insults, an uneasy truce was the best that could be hoped for.

Haslehurst's reply to the offer was a firm no. Reviewing old insults directed at his illiteracy and his editorial clumsiness as the "new head-organ … grinding [out of tune] for the radicals in this district," he had no desire to take the "whining" peace proposal seriously. Rather, he cast doubt on the *Gazette's* ability to survive as a business, mocking the "idiocy," pretentiousness, long-windedness, and "*blatherim boo*" of its "*paste-board* sub [editor]." Further, he scorned the idea that he might seek the advice of a former editor to help in the reconciliation. "Better to turn to a writer who, though advocating political principles different from our own, we could answer without being ashamed of our antagonist. If the *Despatch* would consult its own interest, it would try to secure the co-operation of that *gentleman*, and save itself from its present *friend*."[94]

Haslehurst rather relished the reversal or "contrast" in attitudes implied in the *Gazette*'s second proposal. The idea of a truce may have appeared generous, but it was, to his mind, the hypocritical suggestion of an "impracticable dunce." Rejecting the peace offering, he would, within the year, have the satisfaction of seeing his prediction fulfilled. The *Gazette* was forced out of business in 1848.

In his short and understated reply of 1 May 1847, Northey could not resist a further jab at Haslehurst. "We have read, without surprise, the column of delicate notice, bestowed upon us by the last *Despatch*," he wrote. "Fully recognizing the style of the old *Peterboro Chronicle*, we decline the *honour* of further contest. We might hope for victory in argument but pretend not to an equal talent for abuse." The persistence of hostility confirms that, at least for the first half of 1847, a revitalized and bristling James McCarroll remained close by Haslehurst at the *Despatch*. A seasoned veteran of the cut-and-thrust party politics in a two-newspaper provincial town, he emerged from his losses in fighting form. By late 1847 he was again ready to savour the challenge of meeting abuse with abuse. More importantly, he was busy gaining a toehold in nearby Cobourg, confident that a brighter day lay ahead for him.

One final journalistic note adds a surprising instance of generosity to McCarroll's final months in Peterborough. He personally donated 1.5 pounds to aid in the relief of the Highland Scots and the Irish in the spring of 1847.[95] While the victims of the Irish potato famine and the Scottish expulsion were issues close to home for him, the fact that he gave generously at such a stressful time is noteworthy. It suggests as well that, constrained as things must have been for him after the fire, he was not utterly bereft. Like many immigrants to Canada, he empathized deeply with his fellow Celts, particularly the impoverished Catholics of southern Ireland. Perhaps it would be more accurate to say that in 1847 his personal finances were temporarily limited. His close friends in Peterborough – among them Cluxton, Hall, and Haslehurst – did what they could to tide him over and help him recover. He was able to draw some income by means of job-printing contracts through the office of the *Weekly Despatch*, but he was determined not to let down struggling Irish families far "across the herring pond" in their time of great need.[96]

Sounding the "Magical Flute": Cobourg, 1847–51

The "Professor of Music" at the Globe Hotel

IN 1847 A REVITALIZED JAMES MCCARROLL began to seek out opportunities in Cobourg, a larger town on the shore of Lake Ontario. He planned a fresh start professionally with both music teaching and journalism in mind. At thirty-three, he was sufficiently resilient to reset his priorities, despite the death of his son, the fire, and subsequent *Chronicle* bankruptcy. Once again he would be a small fish in a larger pond, but he had few doubts about his ability to meet his new challenge.

Cobourg, a town forty-five kilometres south of Peterborough and 150 east of Toronto, had begun in the 1770s as a small village and harbour. Its early struggles led to such nicknames as "Hardscrabble" and "Port Misery."[1] By 1847, however, it had grown into a substantial town; boasting close to 4,000 inhabitants, it was more than twice the size of Peterborough. Moreover, it was once again promoting great expectations for its future.[2] Its harbour serviced many ships plying Lake Ontario while the town continued to be the landing place for many British immigrants arriving via Quebec and Montreal. With "the black years of emigration" affecting famine-plagued Ireland in particular, Irish newcomers flooded into Cobourg in the late 1840s where they were temporarily housed in hastily constructed "sheds." Businesses in town provided a wide range of supplies and services to "back-township" centres like Peterborough and Lindsay. The town was now known for its well-stocked stores, advances in transportation, and up-to-date hotels. In the 1840s Cobourg continued to vie with Kingston, Belleville, and Port Hope as a major centre for services and transportation in the eastern part of Canada West. The town had long since relinquished its claim to be a rival to Toronto as the province's primary port, but Cobourg could brag, for instance, that, in fledgling Victoria College, it had its own fledgling university. Headed by Egerton Ryerson, the college was opened in 1838 by the Wesleyan Methodists. As well, thanks to William Weller, the town had become an important transportation hub along the Front and was developing plans for a splendid town hall to be named for Queen Victoria.

The first indication of McCarroll's relocation to Cobourg was an advertisement in the *Cobourg Star* on 1 August 1847. Recurring weekly thereafter, it announced that he had "decided on residing permanently in Cobourg" and that as "Professor of the FLUTE," he would offer music lessons to residents "in his rooms" at the Globe Hotel or "in private." The Globe Hotel fit his needs perfectly. The commodious building on King Street, the town's main thoroughfare, had been rebuilt in 1846 after a fire. It advertised not only a new standard in "comfort and convenience" for travellers, but also the largest ballroom in the colony. Supplementing that "great room" were a comfortable reading room and a smoking den. In fact, it had established itself as the centre for large social and cultural events in the Cobourg area.[3] In an 1850 article, McCarroll wrote effusively about its "whist parties, *frigidum sine*,[4] and [the] jolly good fellows" who frequented the Globe. He was delighted to find a congenial, mostly male milieu in which to live, since circumstances had forced him to leave his family in Peterborough. For meals and relaxation he could frequent Robert Sinclair's popular saloon on nearby Division Street.

The previous month, on 8 July 1847, he had made his concert debut in the Globe's ballroom. A review, reprinted from the *Cobourg Star* in the *Peterborough Weekly Despatch* (15 July), offered a "well-merited testimony to the talents of our respected fellow-townsman, Mr JAMES M'CARROLL, on his first appearance in public as a flautist." Likely written by H.J. Ruttan, the *Star*'s new editor, the report began by noting that, although McCarroll was "evidently a little deficient in nerve," he performed like "a perfect master of his instrument." Both his playing and the quality of his alto voice earned high praise. Along with several local gentlemen he sang songs like "Life's a Bumper" and "Fill the Bowl,"[5] but it was his work as a flautist that transfixed the *Star* reviewer. His observations are noteworthy and detailed:

> Never have we met a flautist (and our experience is by no means limited) who could produce such variations of effect with such truth of tone. The Flute in his hands appeared instinct with life, and promptly obeying

3.1 Rebuilt in 1846, the Globe Hotel was Cobourg's finest hostelry until it was destroyed by fire in 1856. This colourized print of *View of Cobourg*, c. 1852, attributed to Owen Staples, shows the Globe Hotel, numbered 2. Platinum print, coloured with watercolour and with mat opening indicated in pencil, of wood engraving, 1916. Toronto Reference Library, JRR 3506 Cab.

the slightest mandate of his will – now braying forth in trumpet tones some war inspiring strain, and anon gliding into the softest and most silvery cadence – now hastening on with lightning speed over the most elaborate and difficult passages, and again pausing to dwell and luxuriate amid the touching beauties of some simple melody.

Some of the highly ornate pieces which he gave were of surprising brilliance, and what is of rare occurrence with rapid players, there was no sacrifice of tone to execution; all the notes were not only clear and distinct, but level – the few melodies he played were beautiful. "Auld Robin Gray," "Molly Asthore," and "Kenlock of Kenlock," were given in a style not to be surpassed.

We said that this gentleman is a perfect master of his instrument; in further proof of which we need only to say that he stopped with corks the upper holes of the flute, and with ONE HAND played the beautiful song of "Oh Nancy, wilt thou gang wi' me," with elaborate variations and embellishments! On a previous occasion, in private, he astonished us with a duet, the double notes being as perfect and the harmony as correct as though two instruments were employed.[6]

The review also noted that McCarroll had announced his intention to "visit and give concerts in most of the cities and towns of Western Canada this season."[7] Despite his reputation as a Peterborough Reformer who had often locked journalistic horns with R.D. Chatterton, the *Star*'s founding editor, McCarroll must have been delighted to find that he had knowledgable admirers in Cobourg. For young Henry Ruttan, music, poetry, and personal relations trumped politics, at least in quiet seasons. Their evolving friendship helps to explain why McCarroll's poems began to appear in the *Star*'s pages, starting with "To the Spirit of Light" on 22 September 1847 and continuing into the 1850s.

McCarroll did not undertake the concert tour, although one obituary suggests that he did. Rather, for the time being teaching music in Cobourg was his main source of income. The tour would have involved detailed planning, advanced advertising, and financial backing, all of which were wanting. Realistically, he knew that he was too inexperienced to become a travelling performer. Such, however, would not be the case two decades later when, in 1865, he developed a one-man variety show to tour Canada West. In the meantime a relocation of his family to Cobourg was too costly and inconvenient. Instead, he maintained his home in Peterborough where Ann and their three daughters remained near her family and friends. It was not until November 1847 that Francis Connin placed an advertisement in the *Weekly Despatch* announcing that the McCarroll house was for sale.[8] Ann and the girls continued to live there until the sale was completed, then moved back into the White Cottage with her parents. On 27 May 1848 Ann gave birth to their fourth daughter, Charlotte. A coterie of loyal friends helped to support Ann during her pregnancy and her husband's extended absences.

McCarroll travelled back and forth to Peterborough, drumming up new students, building social connections, and writing for George Haslehurst at the *Weekly Despatch*. His main goal in Cobourg was to land a patronage position through the new Reform government. Here he was closer to the centre of political activity in Canada West. Here too he could avail himself of the hospitality of a new set of influential friends. Most prominent among them was affable William Weller (1798–1863), a Vermont-born lawyer who had achieved prominence and considerable wealth as a leading entrepreneur in the transportation business in Canada West. Other companions included Henry Ruttan, merchant Thomas Eyre, local publisher Joseph H. Leonard, saloon owner Robert Sinclair, and Terence Duignan, the Irish-born proprietor of the Globe Hotel, his home away from home.

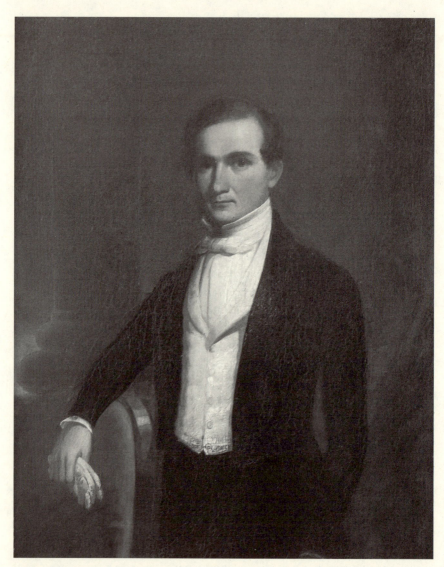

3.2 Paul Kane painted this 1834 portrait of William Weller, "the stage coach king," in Cobourg. Oil on wood, 34.5 cm x 27.4 cm. Art Gallery of Northumberland.

Cobourg historian Percy Climo had ample grounds for dubbing William Weller "the stage coach king."[9] Beginning in the early 1830s, he began to operate not only a tri-weekly stage and ferry service between Cobourg and Peterborough, but, much more importantly, the main east-west stagecoach line linking Hamilton and Montreal through Toronto, Prescott, and Cobourg.

While he undertook the government contract to deliver the Royal Mail along the Front and to settlements to the north, he promised travellers comfortable passage and a reliable schedule. He was also involved in developing the telegraph business in Cobourg, operating lakeside warehouses for shipping, and establishing a local carriage-making firm and hostelry. One of Cobourg's most energetic, sociable, and civic-minded citizens, Weller was also a keen sportsman whose passion for horse racing and steeplechases was on display during local fair days and exhibitions. As Weller's friend, McCarroll enjoyed his hospitality and was witness to many of his successes.

Politically, Weller was a Reformer. Despite his immense popularity, he was not part of Cobourg's inner circle of "aristocratic" families. In the election of January 1848 he belatedly put forward his name as a candidate for a seat in the provincial assembly. His slogan was catchy: "Wheat at a dollar a bushel and good roads close to your door."[10] He had filled a variety of municipal positions, all the better to promote his commercial interests and encourage local development. He was elected mayor in both 1850 and 1851; his years in office thus coincided with McCarroll's rise in public stature in the town.[11]

Weller's large estate, The Hill or Weller's Hill, was the birth-place of many of his twenty-two children (he had eleven by each of his two wives)[12] and it was there, overlooking Lake Ontario, that McCarroll spent many a congenial Cobourg evening. Locally renowned for his hospitality, Weller drew comparisons to Dickens's jovial Sam Weller. At The Hill he kept an "open house" for friends and visitors. McCarroll gave music lessons to some of Weller's children, including his youngest daughter, the light-hearted and attractive Emily Melissa. In tribute, he dedicated a poem to her, "To E.M.W. on her eighteenth birthday," which appeared in the *Cobourg Star* on 11 March 1850. Likely he attended her wedding later that year, on 26 November, at St Peter's Church, Cobourg, to George McKenzie Clark, a barrister at law from nearby Newcastle.[13]

In the mid-1840s the advance of railway lines was much in the news in the Canadas. Begun in England, the railway boom spread quickly through the northern United States, raising local expectations to a fever pitch. Nevertheless, the daunting costs of laying track and purchasing heavy equipment meant that such plans were more slowly realized in Canada West. The entrepreneurial William Weller kept a close watch on these new possibilities; however, he pragmatically applied most of his energies and money to developing better roads for stage travel. Accordingly, he involved himself in the organization of the Cobourg and Rice Lake Plank Road and Ferry Company, which he initiated in 1846. When it opened for business in September 1847, a passenger could board

Weller's steamboat, the *Forrester*, piloted by McCarroll's Peterborough friend John Albro,[14] at the Little Lake dock in Peterborough and, after transferring to a stagecoach at the Plank Road below Rice Lake, be in Cobourg in half a day. Such were the miracles of travel in the 1840s. Weller deemed railroad travel a thing of the future; for a time he was right.

For a few months in the fall of 1847 McCarroll was involved with Weller's new company. In the *Cobourg Star* (25 September), the Plank Road and Ferry Company reported that Weller had been elected company president. He had been nominated by two influential company directors of Tory persuasion, D'Arcy E. Boulton, a local lawyer, and James Smith, while his young associate, "Mr James McCarroll, Esq.," was appointed secretary, pending his ability "to furnish security to the satisfaction of the Directors in the sum of 500 pounds upon entering upon his duties." Given his recent setbacks, the requirement was not in his favour. A few months later, the *Star* announced that Mr James Beatty, Jr had been named the company's secretary to replace him. Not surprisingly, McCarroll could not muster such a large surety. Nevertheless, he would be a frequent passenger on Weller's improving ferry and stage service, travelling north to visit his family or perform in Peterborough musical events. Indeed, for a time he appeared to be a townsman of both places; certainly, he was a figure of gossip and interest in both. He was welcomed and admired by many, but mistrusted and even despised by others, especially because of his reputation as a radical Reformer.

Among his detractors was the writer of two letters to the editor in the *Cobourg Star* (11 and 25 April 1849), attacking him for his support in the *Peterborough Weekly Despatch* of James Hall and the controversial Rebellion Losses Bill (for Canada East).[15] His record as the pugnacious editor of the *Peterboro Chronicle* remained fresh in many Tory minds. In this instance, "I" or J.I. of Emily Township took several shots at him as the (anonymous) author of a pro-Reform column in the *Despatch*. "I" deemed any Reform support of the bill to be part of the "French faction," and he mocked the "pigmy *Despatch*" for its continuing inadequacies as a newspaper. "I" alleged that McCarroll had to be the author of the column because it smacked so clearly of the "fertile imagination and perverted talents" of the late *Peterboro Chronicle*. In both letters "I" characterized him as a relentless and failed "office-seeker" eagerly pursuing every municipal or provincial position in and around Peterborough.

True to form, McCarroll soon had his fingers in as many Cobourg pies as possible. As "I" concluded, he was an opportunistic place-seeker, hopeful that his long-standing support of the Reform cause would lead to a patronage appointment. In the late fall of 1847 he had sought to further this goal by accepting Joseph Leonard's invitation to edit a new Cobourg newspaper, the *Newcastle Courier*. From here he could support William Weller's election bid in South Northumberland and James Hall's bid for re-election in Peterborough, while vigorously attacking Tories and their policies.[16] Moreover, since this was the period of the worst potato famines in Ireland, he called special attention to the plight of the long-suffering Irish Catholics, some of whom were now immigrants struggling to make their lives anew in Canada.

The Magical Flute: A Hunger for Music

McCarroll edited the *Newcastle Courier* for five months – from December 1847 until April 1848 – even as he engaged in several musical performances in both Cobourg and Peterborough. Newspaper reports indicate that his reputation as a musician was growing rapidly. In February 1848, for instance, he took the musical lead in a special evening held to celebrate the opening and dedication of Peterborough's first Odd Fellows Hall.[17]

At the request of William Cluxton and other close friends involved in the mushrooming Odd Fellows movement in Canada West, he was the featured performer at a concert that drew an audience of three hundred. The *Weekly Despatch* carried a notice of the event in its issue of 17 February 1848 along with a review signed "No Odd-Fellow." Oddly, the piece was copied from McCarroll's former rival, the *Peterborough Gazette*.

No Odd-Fellow praised contributors like vocalist Mr Green and "Mr Kelk and his Lads," and effusively deemed the concert an event unsurpassed by any set of "Amateur Singers and players in the Province." McCarroll came in for special praise: "What shall we say of McCarroll? Simply this: – He possesses a power in the use of the flute, seldom equalled, a voice for its tones and capacity of modulation seldom surpassed, and a disposition to please the most cheerful – may he continue to gain as well-merited laurels as he did in Peterborough on the evening of the Concert."

The records of two other musical events in Peterborough also survive. The first, previously mentioned, took place at St John's Church on Wednesday, 30 January 1850. On this occasion "our old friend, Mr McCarroll" played the flute and sang a duet with his friend, Robert Taylor. In March of 1851 he was again in Peterborough, this time to participate in a fundraiser to retire the debt on the Wesleyan parsonage-house. The *Weekly Despatch* reported that "Our old friend J. McCarroll, Esq. of Cobourg, the magical flute, was there, and the accompaniments on the piano were characterized by taste and execution of the highest order."

No review of the St John's church bazaar during the winter of 1849 has been found, but McCarroll was likely involved, if only on the business end. A report on this fundraising event appeared in the *Weekly Despatch* on 26 July 1849. Among the itemized expenses was the payment of 3 pounds each to Mr Dunsford (of the *Gazette*) and Mr McCarroll for "Printing costs."[18] Brief as it is, it indicates that, by agreement with George Haslehurst, McCarroll still did job printing on his old printing press.

In Cobourg he appeared to great advantage in three special "entertainments" at the Globe Hotel. The star of the evenings was Mr Arthurson, a "talented and highly finished vocalist" who, according to the *Cobourg Star* (20 March 1850), had toured Canada and the United States to much acclaim. No report was printed about the third concert at the Globe in April,[19] but the first event, "a Soiree Musicale," held on 29 January 1850, drew "a highly fashionable audience." After describing Arthurson's "thrillingly beautiful" renditions of "some of the most charming songs and ballads that ever [have] been sung on this side of the Atlantic," the *Star*'s reviewer – again likely Henry Ruttan – noted that Mr McCarroll "assisted" in the program by performing three solos – "Il soave e bel contento" and "Allegretto" by Giovanni Pacini and "The Swiss Hunter" with "elaborate variations by Lee, &c."[20] Ruttan added, "We cannot praise Mr McCarroll's performance on the flute too highly. He is equally capable of pleasing those who are fond of hearing a simple melody as he is of astonishing where execution is looked for. The secret, however, is – Mr McCarroll is a thorough musician by *nature* and *art*." A longer review on 12 March praised Arthurson's second concert, this time of sacred music.[21] He was joined by a quartet comprising two women – Miss Leonard (the daughter of publisher Joseph Leonard and a McCarroll student) and Mrs Cameron – and two men, Mr Macdonald and McCarroll himself. Together they performed "I Waited Patiently" and "I Would not Live Away." Authurson sang evocatively from the works of Handel, Haydn, and Mendelsshon, while McCarroll provided a flute solo: "Mr McCarroll's performance on the flute elicited much admiration and his execution of Handel's beautiful piece, 'Ah, Perdonna,' was rapturously encored. Although we think this gentleman's execution of difficult and brilliant passages can scarcely be surpassed, yet, we would much prefer listening to his soft flowing melodious strains as exhibited on this occasion – the effect of these two instruments, the flute and the piano, was touchingly beautiful."

During his four years in Cobourg Mac became a familiar figure at Duignan's Globe Hotel. These were the days when Kivas Tully's stately Victoria Hall was in the planning stages, slated to be built further down King Street. Until the Globe was destroyed in 1864, again by fire, its ballroom was the acknowledged centre for public performances in town. It also contained Weller's ticket office for his stagecoaches.[22] The affable Duignan did his utmost to make the hotel a vibrant venue, attractive to townsfolk, travellers, and itinerant performers alike. Professional singers like Mr F. Gardner and Mr Arthurson, performers like the Phieffer Brothers and "the celebrated T.P.B." (Mr Thomas Pope Besnard of the Royal Lyceum Theatre in Toronto),[23] and the young gentlemen of the Cobourg Lyceum who put on amateur theatricals and saucy melodramas like "Black Paddy Morgan's Ghost"[24] rented the ballroom and entertained the growing number of residents who were eager to take in live theatre and music.

The Stage-Irish Voice:
Humour and the Power of Expression

The comic possibilities of the Irish voice must have percolated in McCarroll's imagination as he listened to "An Hour in Ould Ireland," T.P. Besnard's charming blend of monologue and songs, and as he attended "Paddy" plays performed by the Cobourg Lyceum troupe. Besnard brought his popular one-man show to the Globe Hotel from Toronto, supplementing his signature lecture with performances such as "The Sprig of Shillelagh" and "The Shamrock." His tour included Cobourg, Port Hope, and Peterborough. To those who responded too literally to the excesses of Besnard's comedic blarney, the *Cobourg Star* politely recommended an adjustment of perspective. The paper detected nothing but an entirely good-natured purpose behind Besnard's presentation. Neither mockery nor nastiness was intended, however excessive the brogue and over-rich the verbal exaggerations might seem. Rather, "as an Irishman himself, and a most enthusiastic one too," Besnard simply portrayed the eccentricities of the Irish and dramatized to "perfection" various comic examples of "their so perabundant wit."[25] Feeling an increasingly strong attraction to that comic approach, McCarroll began to tap its potential in his own vernacular poems.

He would also have been delighted by Ruttan's frequent inclusions of the comic letters of "Terry O'Driscoll" (or "Terry Driscoll") in the *Cobourg Star*.[26] While Besnard offered the dramatic flourishes and verbal delights of stage-Irish patter, Terry O'Driscoll's letters put the brogue vividly on the page, mixing chatty vernacular prose with snippets of poetry and amusing doggerel. Written from Stoneybatter in Ireland to Mr Taddy O'Donohue of St Giles, London, Terry's letters, appearing under the headline "Ireland and the Irish," enjoyed a steady popularity during the late 1840s both in Ireland and in several Canada West newspapers.

Published weekly in the *Dublin Warder*, Terry Driscoll's letters were the work of John Jackson (d. 1857), a career journalist from Kilrush, County Clare, on the banks of McCarroll's beloved River Shannon. Drawn to their wit and liveliness, Canadian editors like H.J. Ruttan and William Kirby of the *Niagara Mail* reprinted them a month or two after their Dublin appearance. While they provided free "old-sod" copy for Canadian editors, they gave Canadian audiences, especially those of Irish descent, welcome moments of pleasure and amusement. An obituary of John Jackson, reprinted in the *Cobourg Star* on 8 April 1857, verifies the high regard in which his vernacular humour was held in Canada West: "No Irish writer, Carleton not exempted, exceeded 'Terry O'Driscoll' in his peculiar style – his spontaneous humour, sly sarcasm, graphic portraiture of character, vivid pictures of life and manners, and his succint [*sic*] and pointed allusions to the political and local incidents of the day. His pen and ink sketches [had] much of the artistic ability of Cruickshank, the wit or earnest and useful purpose of Hood, [and] no writer was more thoroughly Irish in his phrases and style."[27]

McCarroll's own Terry Finnegan, whose comic letters first appeared in print in Toronto in 1861, owes much to the Driscoll legacy and to other journalistic examples of vernacular humour in letter form. Columns by Artemis Ward, "Yankee Doodle," and Thomas Haliburton's Sam Slick appeared frequently in Canadian newspapers in the 1830s and 1840s. A devoted newspaperman by the mid-1840s, McCarroll read as many weeklies as he could and recognized the comic potential in such forms of expression. Like John Jackson and Artemis Ward, he was a humorist by inclination. A vernacular Irish letter in the *Cobourg Star* in 1851 is the first known example of his experimentation with the stage-Irish voice in prose. That September he wrote to H.J. Ruttan from Port Stamford, where he was settling into his new custom's position.[28] He enclosed a comedic letter signed by "Denis Finnegan." Four years later he wrote a serialized novel, "The New Gauger" (1855), that bubbled over with the same high-spirited and exuberant love of the stage-Irish vernacular. The use of that voice is also evident in his poetry from the late 1840s.

Another Reform Newspaper — Another Platform

While he kept a hand in job printing and writing antagonistic columns for Haslehurst's *Weekly Despatch*, McCarroll could not resist the invitation to edit a new Reform newspaper in Cobourg, one designed to counter the Tory rhetoric of the *Cobourg Star* during a crucial election in the Canadas. In publishing the first volume of his "cheap" monthly magazine, the *Canadian Gem and Family Visitor*, Joseph Leonard had included McCarroll among its contributors. Now he began a Reform newspaper. Given the opportunity to promote the local campaign of William Weller and that of James Hall in Peterborough, McCarroll accepted Leonard's offer. He knew all too well that, whatever salary he might earn, it would not be commensurate with the work involved or the energy required of him. He saw it as a temporary but important opportunity.

Aware that Cobourg and area had been a Tory stronghold for years, McCarroll announced the beginning of the *Newcastle Courier* with a pro forma "Prospectus," dated 9 November 1847. Publication began on 2 December. As with the *Peterboro Chronicle*, he declared his commitment to responsible government in Canada: "the Advisors of His Excellency," he averred, must "be responsible to the Majority of the Representatives of the People of Canada." At the same time he promised a paper which would operate under the motto *Fiat justitia ruat ca[e]lum* (Let justice be done, even if the heavens fall), "from a sound conviction that such a sentiment [spoke to] the Genius of British Freedom whose benign influence is now felt to the most remote corners of the earth." He also declared his commitment to the "temperate discussion of all useful subjects," though he knew well that the intense political rhetoric of the moment did away with high principles. Platitudinous prospectuses were expected.

Welcoming his new journalistic rival, H.J. Ruttan wrote in the *Cobourg Star*, "As liberal men we are confident we shall agree in good manners, however we may differ in our views of the occurrences of the day" (17 November 1847). The fact was that Ruttan and McCarroll were already friends. H.J. was a well-established Cobourg citizen; he was the son of one of the town's best-known citizens, Henry Ruttan, who had served as a member of parliament and was the sheriff of the Newcastle District until 1847. Henry Ruttan Sr had once been the partner of the *Star*'s founder and editor, R.D. Chatterton, and had schooled his son in conservative politics. Nevertheless, in terms of culture and the arts, Henry Jr was more liberal and open-minded than Chatterton or his father. As a lover of cultural expression he admired McCarroll's talent and conviviality. Together they glided easily over the political divide that separated them and relished spending leisure time together.

By 1847 the two were fast friends. The old antagonism between McCarroll's Tory-slagging *Peterboro Chronicle* and Chatterton's *Cobourg Star* faded once McCarroll took up residence in the Globe Hotel and began to align himself with some of Cobourg's leading citizens. His editorship of the rival *Courier* did not pose a worry or threat to Ruttan. Likely he saw the operation as a one-shot deal on Leonard's part, aimed mainly at promoting Reform interests for the election of 1848.

From Belleville, Susanna and John Moodie, Reformers themselves, warmly encouraged McCarroll in their *Victoria Magazine*. However, they suggested that he would be wise to eliminate conspicuous violations of decorum in his future editorial work. Commenting on the second number of the *Newcastle Courier*, the Moodies wrote,

> The *Courier*, from its outward appearance, and the well known talents of its Editor, promises to take its stand among the first periodicals of the same class in the Colony. Mr McCarroll's views are liberal; he has the well-being of the country, and of mankind in general, at heart. A man of an enlightened and elegant mind is not at all likely to stain his pages by low and vulgar abuse, a practice too commonly resorted to by the editors of papers, who enjoy a certain popularity, by fostering malignant feelings of others. We hope as the Colony advances in literature and refinement, to see this disgraceful abuse of the glorious privilege of the freedom of the press, gradually disappear before the force of reason and the light of truth; and we know no person more able to lead the van in the march of improvement, than the accomplished editor of the *Courier*. From our heart we wish him and his paper success.[29]

McCarroll was well known for his editorial pugnacity. In earlier days he had allowed his penchant for invective and ad hominem abuse in the name of Reform to blur his liberal views and misdirect the energies of his "enlightened and elegant mind." As an editor in Cobourg he continued to direct his attacks at Tory politics, but aimed his arrows more at the *Peterborough Gazette* than the *Star*.

Regrettably, as is too often the case with early Canadian newspapers, and especially those that did not complete a full year of publication, few issues of the *Newcastle Courier* have survived.[30] More lamentable, the two that are extant belong to the period after McCarroll resigned as editor. Overall, the *Newcastle Courier* lasted about six months, even though, early in 1848, Joseph Leonard successfully outbid Cobourg's other two newspapers, the *Star* and the *Provincial*, for the town's yearly printing contract. Cobourg was not able to provide sufficient subscriber and advertising support for three newspapers; thus, the *Courier* and the *Provincial* ceased publication in less than a year. The demise of the *Newcastle Courier* itself probably had more to do with Joseph Leonard's changing plans. His absence from the Cobourg section of the *Canadian Directory* of 1850 and the coincident appearance of the *Canadian Gem* in Toronto in that same year suggest that he opted to leave Cobourg for a bigger market.

For his part McCarroll saw no long-term future with the *Courier*. He was there to have an effect on the January 1848 election and deal with its aftermath. Though the odds were against William Weller, he fought hard for him. Predictably, Weller did lose the Northumberland district seat, but McCarroll had immense satisfaction in seeing James Hall win in Peterborough. In April 1848 he resigned his editorial position. The *Cobourg Star* gave cheerful notice of his resignation, congratulating him on becoming a "free man" once again.[31] Freedom meant the opportunity to travel more readily to Peterborough, to undertake more public performances, to devote more time to his poetry, and to pursue connections in his quest for a patronage appointment. Being "in [editorial] harness" had less appeal for him in Cobourg than it had once had in his beloved Peterborough, especially since his musical and literary efforts were now being more widely appreciated. As well, with the overall success of the Reform party in the 1848 election, he now had more reason to lobby for that patronage position.

Examples of McCarroll's editorship can only be found in occasional columns reprinted in the *Peterborough Weekly Despatch*. These indicate that he persisted in his combativeness, especially when he felt personally challenged. For example, with the Irish Potato Famine of 1847 squarely in the public eye, he vigorously attacked the disparaging, anti-Irish comments made by James Northey in the *Peterborough Gazette*. George Haslehurst included one of his *Newcastle Courier* columns in his issue of 11 May 1848. It was entitled "Ireland." Northey had categorically dismissed Ireland as "The curse of herself, of England, and the world!" Haslehurst reported, perhaps a little smugly, that the *Newcastle Courier* was a newspaper "with which we dare say [the editor of the *Gazette*] is well acquainted," as "he has already received some severe castigations from its Editor."

In his defence of Ireland, McCarroll began by questioning whether the ailing editor of the *Gazette*, Dunsford, could possibly have written such an insensitive piece. Surely, some "contemptible interloper" must have usurped the editorial chair, even as he admitted to being well aware that Northey had assumed that position. The "villainously illiberal tone" of Northey's article was not that of a competent and judicious thinker, but of a "malicious," "addled," "vicious," and "irreclaimable dunce." It "affect[ed] to sneer" at "our unfortunate country," mocking its reputation for beauty and glibly dismissing the wide range of Ireland's military, naval, and cultural contributions to Britain and the world. By way of measuring Northey's ignorance, McCarroll drew on a book published in 1842 (he does not give its title), citing a variety of authorities on Ireland's historical importance, among them Henry Grattan, Wolfe Tone, Lord Collingwood, and Sir J.C. Hippisley.[32]

Calling attention to some of the most notable achievements of the Irish, McCarroll asked rhetorically, "Was Ireland a curse to England, at the famous battle of Waterloo, where, it is asserted, upon the best authority, that *two thirds* of the British forces were Irish?" Similarly, "In 1796 two Thirds of the Whole British Navy were composed of Irishmen ... Was Ireland a curse to England then?" To these points, he added, "'It is thoroughly understood by those at all conversant with Irish history,' says a modern author, 'that Ireland under the reign of her own Kings was famed for her learning; and that the surrounding nations benefitted much from the light which adorned her; and further, it is now confidently asserted that there are but few seminaries on the face of the Globe in which a distinguished Irishman may not be found.' Is this anything like being a curse to the world?"

His strong defence of his homeland presages the views of many later interpreters, not least Thomas Cahill in his best-selling book of 1995, *How the Irish Saved Civilization*. As persuasively as he could, McCarroll made the case for the accomplishments of the Irish that had been overlooked, particularly in England and by the English. He hoped that the future would see not only the breakdown of the barriers between England and Ireland but also the unification of Britain as "one impenetrable phalanx." He presented himself as an aspiring Irish nationalist, even as he remained strongly tied to the idea and ideal of a united Britain. Above all, he was a vigilant defender of Ireland in the face of uninformed and thoughtless aspersions. He realized that a marked increase in attacks on Ireland in the press was abetting the economic and social troubles at home. He also called attention to continuing evidence of English tyranny in Ireland and England's delayed and inhumane response to

Ireland's current problems. Such concerns would emerge more forcibly in his writings of the 1860s.

It was likely during this period – 1847 to 1850 – that McCarroll also contributed to the *Morning Chronicle* (Quebec) as a columnist. While I have found no direct evidence of this, he reported the connection to Henry Morgan. He may well have sent columns about Ireland and reform issues.

Poet at Large: Tribute to Tom Moore and Lord Elgin

With his recovery, McCarroll's inclination to write poems increased noticeably. By 1847 this fresh burst of creative energy was in full flower. His poems had begun to appear in the *Christian Guardian* in 1841 and were often included weekly in the *Peterboro Chronicle* during his editorship. But after 1847, it was as if, in escaping the daily grind of editorial work, he was able to devote more time and energy to his creative efforts.[33] Moreover, he was encouraged to do so by editors and receptive readers; on a few occasions one of his published poems elicited a published tribute from a sympathetic reader. One such reader, George M. Noland, was so taken by McCarroll's poem "The Dreamer" (*Cobourg Star*, 29 November 1848) that he sent his own poetic response to the newspaper. Noland's "Lines Suggested on Reading 'The Dreamer' of J. McCarroll, Esq." appeared in the *Star* on 7 February 1849.[34]

"The Dreamer" creates a picture of a private, dream-like space that serves as a necessary refuge in a world of change and loss. It asserts an existential need for a place where memory can flourish despite "the waste of the past." It was republished several times.

I've a world of my own! I've a world of my own,
That is brighter by far, and more happy than this;
A creation so pure that the spirit alone
Is permitted to taste of its fountains of bliss;
Where the mystical drops, though they glance but in dreams,
May be quaff'd with an exquisite thrill to the last,
For the depths where they sparkle are fed by those streams
That still sprinkle with verdure the waste of the past.

I've a world of my own! I've a world of my own,
With its morning – of blushes that waken no more;
With its noontide – of smiles that once brilliantly shone;

And its starlight – of eyes whose last beamings are o'er.
And thither from earth I oft wing my lone flight,
To revisit the scenes that to me were so dear,
And to listen again to that phantom of light
That was once all that heaven could grant to me here.

I've a world of my own! I've a world of my own;
A bright spot in this desert-like bosom of mine;
Where I meet with the spirit of joys that are flown,
In an oasis blooming 'round memory's shrine.
With the shadows I cherish, there, there, let me dwell –
Would the hand not be cold that would tear us apart?
Gaze in silence and sadness, but break not the spell –
Wake me not! wake me not, from – that dream of my heart.

Henry J. Ruttan published a number of McCarroll's poems in the *Cobourg Star* from 1847 to 1852. Of a strong literary bent himself, Ruttan was eager to encourage local writers to write for the *Star*. In addition to McCarroll's poems, he welcomed pieces from writers like Rhoda Ann Page and George Coventry.[35] There were two McCarroll poems in the fall of 1847 ("The Spirit of Light" and "From the French of Rousseau"), two in 1848 after he had left the *Courier* ("Impromptu – A True Friend" and "The Dreamer"), one in January 1849 ("Ocean"), four in 1850 (the aforementioned "For Miss E.M.W. on her Eighteenth Birthday," "Mick O'Grady," "Hindia's Song," and "Lines [Addressed to an Old Friend]," one in 1851 ("Lines" [How oft, while wandering through some desert place]), and two in 1852 ("Morn" and the then-untitled vernacular poem "Ah! Thin, take down that image that hangs near the althar"[36]). Most were written "expressly for" Ruttan's paper. A missing year of the *Cobourg Star* from August 1849 to August 1850 prevents a fuller inventory of his output during this period.[37] Both 1852 poems appeared under the pseudonym SOPRANO and were written from Port Stamford near Niagara Falls.

McCarroll also found opportunities in new magazines. The Moodies included two of his poems ("Otto's Soliloquy in the Storm" and "A Fragment" [All heaven's lost in silence! – and the cry]) in their short-lived *Victoria Magazine* (1847–48) in Belleville. In 1849 he placed three more ("Lines" [I hate the world – I hate its empty show], "Tyre," and "The Storm Fiend") in Joseph Leonard's *Canadian Gem and Family Visitor*, the first volume of which was published in Cobourg while he was working there.

Despite his fertile Cobourg connections, McCarroll published his largest number of poems during this period in George Haslehurst's *Peterborough Weekly Despatch*. In 1849, ten appeared in its pages. A final poem, "Lines" (How oft, while wandering through some desert place) was printed in the *Despatch* (6 February 1851), having appeared four days earlier in the *Cobourg Star*. "Lines" connects a meek and sensitive image – "the poor, pale thirsty little flower" – with those humans "who feel affliction's chastening rod" in "this fair land of ours." For the flower, there is, at least belatedly, a refuge provided by God. But "how few" among human beings, he asks, are ready for the solace of His "deep'ning cup"? The poem reads as follows:

How oft, while wandering through some desert place,
I've met a poor, pale, thirsty little flower
Looking towards heaven, with its patient face,
In dying expectation of a shower.

And when the sweet compassion of the skies
Fell like a charm upon its sickly bloom.
O, what a grateful stream gushed from its eyes
Towards Him who cared to snatch it from the tomb.

And O, when all its leaves seemed folding up
Into the tender bud of other days,
What clouds of incense, from the deep'ning cup,
Rolled upwards with the burden of its praise.

And then I thought, in this fair land of ours
How few who feel affliction's chastening rod,
Are like the poor, pale, thirsty flowers,
With their meek faces turned toward their God –

How few, when angry clouds and storms depart,
And all the light of heaven reappears,
Are found with incense rising in a heart
Dissolved before his Throne in grateful tears.

These *Despatch* poems, occasionally written under pseudonyms, provide a glimpse of McCarroll's thematic range and the careful structuring of his verse.

"Aurora Borealis: An Extravaganza" and "Impromptu: To a Butterfly" celebrate the natural world while "Creation" and "One Hope" contemplate the mystery and power of God's presence in the world. In "Gold" he offers an almost stereotypical lament about the march of materialism and in "Lines" (When early passion's deadly, flaming sword) he considers the dangers of excessive emotion in amorous relations. "Stories for Sucking Statesmen: The Beauties of W, or the French and the Fly-flap" mocks politicians and their airs while "The Hero of a Hundred Fights" considers the nature of heroic action.

Two of these poems stand out as particularly important, though, surprisingly, he included neither in his retrospective volume of poetry, *Madeline and Other Poems.*[38] "The Bruce," which appeared on 16 August 1849, celebrated the enlightened leadership of Canada's new governor general, Lord Elgin (Sir James Bruce). The poem links Lord Elgin's inspiring leadership and conduct in Canada during the stressful months in 1848–49 to the long-celebrated nobility and military history of his famous family.[39] Elgin had assumed the office of governor general of Canada early in 1847, replacing Lord Cathcart. During his tenure Elgin proved to be the most important Reformist counter to Sir Charles Metcalfe (1843–46), the controversial governor general who had been the bane of Reformers and liberals in both provinces during his three years in office. McCarroll had been one of Metcalfe's most acidic critics.

Not long into his appointment, Elgin encountered significant opposition. Despite his caution and preparation, he found himself under attack by disaffected Tories who saw him as blindly favouring the Reform agenda. When he opened the Canadian parliament in February 1848 he chose his executive council from the newly elected majority party headed by Robert Baldwin, Francis Hincks, and Louis-Hippolyte La Fontaine. In so doing, he opened the door to responsible government for the first time in Canada's history.

Tory leaders like Sir Allan MacNab were outraged by what they saw as a capitulation to the forces of change and conspicuous disloyalty to the Crown.[40] They labelled Elgin a puppet of Francis Hincks and the servant of the most dangerous kind of radicalism. Encouraging a strident Tory press that welcomed hostility within the Orange Order and as usual catered to Anglican support, MacNab and others threatened violence against Elgin and his government. At the same time, in Lower Canada, Joseph Papineau was using the fragile political situation to stir up national feelings among French Canadians. Reflecting the general state of economic depression in North America and the news of dangerous rebellions underway in both France and Ireland, the mood in the Canadas was for the time unsettled and grim.

Tensions came to a head in the spring of 1849 when the Baldwin-La Fontaine government passed the Rebellion Losses Bill, providing financial relief for those who suffered losses in Lower Canada (Canada East) during the Rebellion. Weighing the issues carefully, Elgin, who was personally conflicted and hesitant to support the bill, did not feel he could undermine the legislation as set out by the elected members of the House of Assembly.

The result in Montreal, then the seat of government, was chaos and near insurrection. On 25 April when Elgin signed the Rebellion Losses bill into law, Tory rioters attacked Elgin's carriage with stones and rotten eggs as he left parliament and that night an angry mob burned the parliament buildings to the ground. For months thereafter Montreal remained in a state of civil unrest, although marked more by a war of words and threats than actual deeds. Virtually imprisoned in his Monklands estate near the city, Elgin cautiously rode out the tensions with as much calm and restraint as possible; on one occasion he faced up to an angry mob while putting his personal safety at risk. A state of martial law seemed imminent.

It was in response to these heated and difficult days that McCarroll wrote his poem about Lord Elgin. From Monklands where he welcomed a newborn son (the new Lord Bruce), Elgin was quietly planning to move the seat of government to Toronto and was preparing, despite persistent threats from the "ruffian horde" and public burnings of his effigy, to undertake a tour of Canada West. McCarroll knew all this; his poem celebrates Elgin's courage under pressure and, above all, his refusal to overreact to Tory hostility. Elgin saw the long-term advantages of a more responsible kind of Canadian government – hence, "his gen'rous sword" and the "grateful thousands [in Canada who] fondly turn / To bless thy proud descendant's sway." Forgotten today, the poem deserves to be recognized as a contemporary tribute to Lord Elgin and the important role he played in peacefully supporting Canada's emerging political system. Overall, it traces the Bruce family legacy from Robert Bruce's famous victory for Scotland over King Edward II at the Battle of Bannockburn in 1314 to the enlightened leadership of the current Sir James Bruce in Canada.

Shades of the Bruce of Bannockburn,
The glory has not passed away;
The dust within thy sacred Urn,
Must own its wonted fires to-day,
While grateful thousands fondly turn
To bless thy proud descendant's sway.

'Though ages – like a mighty flood –
Between us roll their voiceless tide,
We still possess thy noble blood –
Thy name – thy honour and thy pride –
As true a man as ever stood
At Bannockburn by his side.

What, though their country's dregs and shame
On his forbearance dared to prey,
England's best George once felt the same,
And, too, in mercy turn'd away
To quench his anger's struggling flame,
Else, such foul locusts, where were they?

Then boast we that his gen'rous sword
Drinks not the blood of dogs, in fight,
But deigns to spare the ruffian horde,
Till time shall frown them into flight: –
When Justice owns herself restored
And exiled Peace returns to light.

Thus, when his glorious sands are run –
When Heaven shall grant his cares a truce –
The sense that he has nobly done
Shall those frail bands serenely loose,
While he bequeathes us in his son,
The hand – the heart – the pride of Bruce!

Especially important in the light of McCarroll's writing career is his vernacular tribute – cheeky, witty, and suggestive – "To Moore."[41] In 1849 Thomas
Moore was the most celebrated and famous of all Irish poets. As poet, prose
writer, humorist, and musician, he was a model artist and an inspiration for
aspiring Irishmen like McCarroll. The poem is a lyrical, four-stanza romp,
praising Moore's romantic images and enchanting language, while criticizing
his over-reliance on "whims" and "swindlin figaries." It suggests that, while
Moore could lead the reader to forget the realities of human experience (that
"old sthraw" and that "different sint" which are often involved in love-making),
he remained a master of romantic effect. He had a wonderful ability to "gul[l]"

his readers "with roses" and "lade off [their] attinshun" with flights of fancy. At the same time, McCarroll implies a desire to see the master reaffirm his commitment to the celebration of Ireland rather than turning to other places and cultures. Though Moore had vividly adapted the voice of Anacreon ("that dhrunken Greek son of a ___") to modern sensual concerns, he revelled too much in the orientalism of "Lalla Rookh" and the lures of Paris (the Fudge family). Nevertheless, his tribute makes it clear that in 1849 he wanted Moore to remain for readers the consummate Irish poet, a voice celebrating the Irish imagination, be it in Ireland or Canada.

Journalistic observers and rivals sometimes criticized McCarroll for his perverse misspellings and conspicuous grammatical errors. Typically a stickler for good literary form within the English tradition, he also knew that he could create certain literary effects by drawing on the stage-Irish tradition that was then very popular in Irish fiction. He wanted to draw on the dramatic possibilities of the lower-class, rural Irish voice. He loved the blarney of "Paddy" or "Teague," and sought to amuse his readers with the comic doings and vivid language of his own Irish lads. Drawing on the evolving tradition of the "stage Irishman," which he knew well through the work of writers like William Carleton and Samuel Lover, and popular journalists like John Jackson,[42] McCarroll sought to develop a cultural connectedness between rural Ireland and colonial Canada. In poems that belonged to his "Irish Anthology,"[43] he loosened his traces, de-romanticized typical poetic conceits, and offered charming insights and verbal perspectives that would have been impossible in a straightforward "English" poem.

"Mick O'Grady" and "Ah! Thin Take Down That Image"[44] are, like "To Moore," early experiments in the use of Irish vernacular. "Mick O'Grady" is an expansive vernacular love song. It appeared in the *Cobourg Star* on 5 June 1850 along with "Hindia's Song." Unlike "To Moore," he included this poem in *Madeline*. His delight in the Paddy idiom is fully evident in its five rolling stanzas. It moves from the high-blown romantic hyperbole of the lover wandering among the stars to the more earthy pursuit of "something solider," as Mick makes melodic and extravagant love to his "own darling Molly Mallowney":

If I could, throth I'd hop into one iv thim cars,
    And be off, like a shot, up yon glittherin height,
Just to bring you down lashins and lavins ov stars
    To encircle that neck and that forehead this night.

Don't you see where a river iv light seems to sthray,
    Where the beautiful azure appears to be riven?
Och! I'd dash into it, and take bagfuls away,
    For they say that's a mine iv those jewels of Heaven.[45]

Arrah, maybe you think I'd prove false on the road,
    If I step'd into Vesta or Juno or Ceres;
And that I'd be apt to soon scatther my load
    Amongst their could phantoms iv Judies and Marys.

Is it me? Blur an ounthers! It's you that well know
    That I've no earthly raison to live in the skies,
Whin I've got purer blue and more light here below
    In my own darling Molly Mallowney's two eyes.

And, thin do you b'lieve I'm a ghost iv a man
    That would spind all his life with a vaporish lady?
Throth I'll have something solider, dear, if I can;
    Cock thim up, to be sure, with the likes iv Mick Grady!

Encouraging the Arts and Culture in Canada West

Henry Ruttan and James McCarroll shared a passion for poetry and music. In these years Cobourg had a modest share of visiting singers and performers, but the community had little say in what came its way or about acceptable standards for performance. McCarroll kept his eye on such events and offered to contribute a few humorous commentaries to Ruttan. Two of these personal pieces appeared in 1850 under his new penname SOPRANO. The first, entitled "Excrescences," was printed in the issue of 20 February and the second, "Belshazzar's Court," on 6 March. There may have been more such pieces between August 1850 and August 1851, but those issues have not been preserved. However, the two pieces showed McCarroll's awareness of the limited critical ability among Canadian journalists. He himself was a critic in the making.

These two pieces were followed on 13 March by Ruttan's editorial calling for the establishment of a "Cobourg Athenaeum," or, at the very least, a renewed effort to create a Mechanics Institute, designed to provide education to young working men in the community. His editorial closed with a pointed reference to "SOPRANO's Musical Festivals," the subject of one of McCarroll's columns in which he decried pretentious and disappointing "festivals" that symbolized the humbug passed off for culture in small towns like Cobourg. Ruttan's editorial was progressive and business-like in spirit. By contrast, McCarroll's style was exuberant and playful, the better to make his points while amusing his readers.

A committee considering the creation of a new Mechanics Institute and Library Association held its first meeting in Cobourg in February 1852; the meeting, however, came a year after McCarroll had moved to Port Stamford. Thus, while Mac contributed his mite to this cultural initiative, Ruttan would continue to promote the idea of an institute in the *Star* even as he grew increasingly impatient with delays in arranging meetings and failures to raise the funds required.

"Excrescences" is McCarroll's attack on the third-rate musical performers who too often preyed on the innocent audiences of North American towns. He also critiqued those members of the press who failed to call attention to their lack of quality or to warn readers about the vulgar deceptions being practised. He asserted his own commitment to both high standards of musicianship and a more informed criticism of musical performance than was the colonial norm. He began by asking whether "the mysterious influences of Climate" or "the more occult necromancy of the Editorial Sanctum" can account for the sad state of musical criticism in Canadian newspapers. Citing those promoters who sweep down upon "some country town" with their "flaming programmes," announcing a "Musical Festival" and highlighting their not so "modest assertions" about their European musical connections and the pedigree of the company, he turned his attention to the members of the Fourth Estate who failed to see through such puffery and false promises. He urged journalists to be more vigilant in identifying pretenders and less impressed by their purported connections to the likes of "Herr Splutterkroots" and "Signore Ditantipalpiti." Otherwise, Canada, he warned, will be forced to witness again and again "the extraordinary process by which a tap-room bawler from the old world is suddenly metamorphosed into a 'finished artiste' of the new!" Such was the naive level of criticism in the Canadian colony.

"Belshazzar's Court" is a personal anecdote that exposes the kind of shoddy performance too often foisted on Cobourg audiences. Recalling an evening when he went arm in arm with a friend (likely Ruttan) to the Globe Hotel for an evening billed as "An Exhibition," McCarroll exposed the crude and mismanaged "magic'" of an illuminated diorama, presented by a travelling American huckster.

Entering "the great hall" of the Globe after the performance had begun, he found himself separated from his companion in a darkened apartment only partially illuminated by "a feeble ray of light" projected through a large dark curtain. The audience was patiently awaiting the promised vision of Belshazzar's Court, complete with exotic religious symbols. But as the image slowly became clear, what appeared, in the words of a spectator standing next to him, was less like a regal court than a "Babylonian brick yard." Despite the slangy language of the wand-waving master of ceremonies, who talked of "astonishin' picturs" and "divine genus" as he explained to the audience what they were seeing, the poor quality of the projected images and the weakness of the lighting drew a barrage of complaints. The scene is vintage Mark Twain, years before Sam Clemens took up journalism.

Moreover, McCarroll found himself so positioned in the dark room that, alone among the audience, he was privy to the angry comments directed by the "learned interlocutor" to his hapless young assistant who stood behind another curtain. The boy in question was an awkward, inexperienced Irish lad named Bill. When Bill missed his cue to bring up the image of Daniel's famous writing on the wall, the master of ceremonies muttered a venomous, yet flamboyant condemnation, "Bill, you critter of hell, that's Dannel apointin at nothin! – Why don't you make the writin flare up, you vital thing you! – Guess I'll flatten you out when this bizness is over, you cussed distressor of human natur, you."

This outburst, McCarroll reports, was "more than ['human natur'] could bear." "[O]ne convulsive burst of laughter directed every eye present to where I was standing; restoring to me, at the same time, my lost friend who kindly stepped over to make some polite enquiries as to my saneness, neither he nor any other person in the room having the slightest idea of the true cause of my sudden mirth." Soon enough the image of Daniel's writing was illuminated, thus directing attention away from McCarroll's outburst. Still, the problems with the lighting recurred twice more. In the end, having gruffly dismissed the disappointed audience, the master of ceremonies rushed past McCarroll "muttering an imprecation of undoubted originality ending in 'I'll boot him by ____.'" Poor Bill is then cuffed about backstage in a scuffle that embarrassingly brings down the "huge black curtain" separating the departing audience from the operatives behind it. McCarroll's final line resists an obvious moral. "I was soon in the street with a hold of my friend's arm, relating the particulars of the scene with Bill, and regretting that I had not witnessed the whole exhibition."

Patronage at Last

Following the election of a Reform government early in 1848, James McCarroll continued to lobby the new leadership with his claim to a patronage appointment. Observant Tories no doubt regarded his efforts as further evidence of the corruption now rife among self-serving Reformers. Still, it must have been a welcome surprise to read Henry Ruttan's sympathetic editorial on behalf of his lobbying efforts. For Ruttan, patronage was a given: an elected government that did not duly reward a loyal and supportive party journalist was a cause for shame. Under the title "Ingratitude of Ministers," he put forward the case for McCarroll even as he tarred the new Reform "Ministers" with a thick Tory paste. His admiration for McCarroll lay behind his editorial (5 December 1849).

> Put not your trust in princes is an old saying which contains good advice, but the admonition might be materially strengthened and brought home to the feelings of the partizans of the present Cabinet, if the word *Ministers* had been substituted for *Princes*. –
>
> Our attention has been called to this subject of ingratitude, by a friend remarking that Mr McCarroll, who for many years, rendered such important services to the present Cabinet, by writing and publishing in Peterboro' at great pecuniary loss, a paper devoted in its interests, is still unprovided for, while men of yesterday, such as Messrs. Black and Co., have an unlimited command of the spoils. Mr McCarroll is, undoubtedly, a gentleman of talent, and the ingratitude of those whom he has assisted in placing in power, is deserving of the severest reproach. Every Editor in Canada should make Mr McCarroll's case his own, for there is no telling how soon in the ups and downs of parties he may be placed in a similar position.

Ruttan was no doubt echoing McCarroll's own impatience, shared on numerous occasions, man to man, friend to friend, editor to editor, across his desk at the *Star* or over a dram in Robert Sinclair's saloon. Hope was certainly not lost at this point, but McCarroll's patience was being tried. His waiting game, however, would soon be over.

There was always keen local competition for patronage positions when they became available. With rumours abounding that the position of landing waiter at the Port of Cobourg would soon be reassigned by the office of the inspector general, a Cobourg businessman named William Butler applied directly to Francis Hincks, identifying himself as a Reformer with connections to the harbour; his list of references included James Hall of Peterborough.[46] However, despite his Cobourg address and connections, his case was not compelling enough. That same month, Lord Elgin formally announced that "Mr James McCarroll, of Peterboro" was appointed "to be a Landing Waiter and Searcher in Her Majesty's Customs."[47] Though the announcement did not specify where he would be working, McCarroll was soon on the job at the Port of Cobourg where he had previously undertaken short-term positions as they became available. The appointment came on the recommendation of Inspector General Francis Hincks.

Beyond party loyalty and support, Hincks had to be concerned that there was an ongoing probe, begun in 1849, into the work of the current collector at the port. In its issue of 21 November, Ruttan voiced some distress in the *Cobourg Star* when he announced that an "investigation" was underway into William H. Kittson by Mr Whitehead (collector at Darlington) on the charge of "neglect of duty." The new cabinet in Montreal had identified the Cobourg office as a problem site; in fact, customs headquarters viewed the Cobourg office as unstable and problematical.

Ruttan was not at all sympathetic with the investigation, even though he reported that Mr Kittson had offered to resign rather than have the inquiry proceed to its inevitable conclusion. In the same editorial, he added, "The witnesses called by the prosecutor, without exception, spoke of Mr Kitson [*sic*] in the very highest terms. It is really too bad that a gentleman so amiable and kind hearted, and withal so attentive to his important duties, as Mr Kitson, should be subject to such continued annoyance from the department to which he belongs. We hope this is the last we shall hear of such proceedings; if it be not, we shall expose the parties implicated, and show them up in their true colors."

The review of Kittson, Ruttan implied, was yet another instance of witch-hunting by insensitive, power-hungry Reformers and office seekers. He suggested that the long-standing collector and the former secretary of the Cobourg Harbour Company had been the subject of continual harassment. There was no legitimacy in bringing charges against so fine a man. Ruttan saw Francis Hincks's actions to improve and regulate all aspects of the customs service in the interest of bureaucratic precision and revenue collection not so much as a necessary government responsibility but as yet another instance of Reform tampering.

But why did McCarroll get the position so keenly pursued by William Butler? The answer likely lay in McCarroll's record as a Reform journalist. Like Hincks, he had cut his teeth in defending Reform ideas and policies; then, in the recent election, he had returned to continue the good fight along the Lake Ontario front. Who better to reward for work done well? Who better, as a relative outsider, to be placed in this strained situation to face the ongoing problems in the customs office? After all, he was already living in Cobourg and had been doing occasional work at the harbour itself.

In December 1849, McCarroll was appointed landing waiter at Cobourg. His annual salary was 50 pounds. What he found at the customs office bore out Hincks's concerns. The office records were in shambles. In fact, he found that there was no one there on a daily basis to direct him in his new duties and advise him on recent events in the office. Collector Kittson was too much preoccupied by his own problems to come to the port with any frequency. As well, the two landing waiters who immediately preceded McCarroll were nowhere to be seen. The waiter whom he replaced, Herbert Lennon, had already been reassigned to the Port of Newcastle. The other landing waiter, an unstable fellow named Henry McCarty, who came from a prominent Cobourg family, was personally involved in the Kittson inquiry, having brought the charges against his boss under cover of anonymity (19 October 1849). But McCarty was so mentally unwell that he claimed to be unable to attend to his daily duties. Thus, shortly after receiving his appointment, James McCarroll found himself in charge of the messy and moribund Cobourg customs office. Opportunistic and resilient as ever, he did not let his inexperience hinder his approach to his duties.

A second ongoing problem he faced was the drama of the harbour itself. Various parts of the waterfront needed major improvements. The problems had begun in the early 1830s when a few Cobourg businessmen formed a joint stock company, the Cobourg Harbour Company (CHC), to improve the capacities of the harbour and increase its revenue. The build-up of silt in the inner harbour, caused by the prevailing easterly winds, was a yearly challenge. The company first built a 16-foot wide, 300-foot long pier on the harbour's east side. However, a plan to construct a second (or western) pier was delayed because of lack of funds. When it was finally constructed, it was much shorter than the eastern pier and remained incomplete. Dredging continued on a yearly basis, but thereafter little was done by way of necessary improvements, though the CHC produced a steady profit for its stockholders.

By the early 1840s, while the harbour continued to provide dividends, it had earned a reputation for inadequate repairs to its docks and was increasingly regarded as a dangerous stopping place for larger ships, especially in windy weather. The longer eastern wharf, which was fast deteriorating, could not provide adequate protection for ships entering harbour's waters. At the same time, the continual silting made access to the harbour more dangerous year after year. In 1842, the CHC finally negotiated a deal with the province's Department of Public Improvement. Its aims were threefold: to oversee necessary changes to the east pier, to build a new west crib and pier, and to dredge the accumulated silt on the western side of the harbour.

A government-appointed engineer named Russell undertook the work at a cost in excess of 10,000 pounds. Both his appointment and the results of his work, however, dismayed the Tories in town. The *Cobourg Star* soon began complaining about Russell's inadequate progress and his lack of skill. The paper also accused him of double billing, in effect, of doing 5,000 pounds of improvements for twice the money. In the meantime, facing increased competition from ports like Port Hope and with the CHC hobbled by a large mortgage from the government for the (inadequate) improvements, concerns were mounting about the future of the harbour as a viable port and the town itself as a progressive business community. By the time that McCarroll began teaching music in Cobourg, Ruttan was warning his readers that the harbour was "rapidly filling up with sand and unless dredged early in the spring will be totally useless" (22 November 1848). Again on 30 January 1850 – a month after McCarroll's customs appointment – Ruttan groused that "if something is not immediately done to improve the harbour, it would soon pay nothing," either to the CHC or the government.

It was in this quagmire of silt, wind, debt, and political opposition that James McCarroll launched his new career as a public servant. His courteous but neglectful superior, Kittson, was too distracted by the ongoing government inquiry to offer much advice. At headquarters, J.W. Dunscombe, the provincial surveyor of customs, had identified the Cobourg office as producing too little revenue and showing little evidence of improvement. Meanwhile, McCarroll was well aware of the immediate threat of competition from Port Hope, just eight miles to the west. He also knew that there were individuals in Cobourg like the aforementioned William Butler (the current harbour master and a Reformer), who coveted his customs position and resented his appointment as an outsider. But, above all, he wanted to serve his government's bidding as effectively as he could and to make a name for himself in terms of accountability, good management, and wise counsel. Francis Hincks was a heroic figure to him and he meant to prove himself a loyal and grateful employee.

Over the course of his first six months at the port, circumstances changed significantly.[48] In early May 1850 Kittson resigned as the collector of tolls, ending months of speculation about his future. On his own and with little experience, McCarroll did his best to clean up Kittson's mess and put into practice the new laws announced in An Act to Amend the Laws Relative to Duties of Customs, by an Order in Council on 1 December 1849. As well, during that winter and spring, he watched closely as contentious negotiations undertaken by Mr Thomas Scott[49] and Ebenezer Perry led to the purchase of the harbour by the town of Cobourg from the directors of the CHC and from the harbour's major investor, the Canadian government. On 1 July 1850, the Town Council of Cobourg – the council of the newly incorporated town, headed by its newly elected mayor, William Weller – formalized its agreement to commit 10,500 pounds to purchase the harbour outright and to dedicate another 6,000 pounds for immediate improvements to the cribs, piers, and wharves as well as to provide for necessary dredging of the harbour basin. Weller and other businessmen like D.E. Boulton, Thomas Scott, and Ebenezer Perry (the Tory father of McCarroll's Peterborough friend Charles Perry and the brother of Peter Perry, an independent-minded and controversial politician) took the lead in negotiating what was a very large financial commitment by the town, one upon which, in the eyes of many citizens, its commercial future depended.[50]

Ruttan's *Cobourg Star* proudly crowed that Cobourg now had its "Harbour of Refuge," a worthy symbol of "the future prosperity of our good Town" (3 July 1850). In a subsequent editorial,[51] he compared Cobourg's rapid growth from 1810 to the present day to the awakening that Rip Van Winkle experienced in revisiting the Catskills after his long sleep. So much had changed over those four decades, and very much for the better. But nothing compared to the town's brilliant coup in finally taking ownership of its most crucial asset and in stepping forward aggressively to implement necessary improvements to the harbour. Sadly, however, while the optimism of 1850 continued for a few years, it began to flounder within a decade. By 1859 the ongoing debts from the purchase and the yearly costs of maintaining the harbour threatened to bankrupt the struggling town.

A close look at the Custom's House Papers at the National Archives of Canada reveals that McCarroll was from the outset no shrinking violet, despite his lack of experience. He proved a quick study and he persistently wrote letters and reports to his superiors.[52] He relied on his pen to present himself as a reliable and trustworthy official who was willing to do all that he could for his government and who undertook his now-expanded duties as professionally as possible. At the same time he occasionally reminded his superiors that he was working under particularly stressful conditions.

Indeed, his letters reveal that self-interest was never far from his mind. He assumed that this concern was a given that his superiors understood. As well, despite his inexperience, he saw himself as a spy in camp watching out for ongoing Reform interests. His job was in part to analyze past Tory practices and make pragmatic suggestions for improvements in present operations. Knowing that his benefactor, Inspector General Francis Hincks, was only a letter away, he always had pen and paper close at hand.

His first three letters to headquarters dealt with ways to augment his salary of 50 pounds. Writing to J.W. Dunscombe on 19 March 1850, he sought advice about whether it was permissible for him to hire an individual of his own choice to serve as "Custom House broker" for the upcoming shipping season. The chosen broker would pay McCarroll "a certain sum on the amounts received for Entries." He wanted Dunscombe's assurance that "my acceptance of such a sum … would [not] be repugnant to your wishes, or not in accordance with the spirit of my appointment."[53] On receipt of Dunscombe's positive response, he hired Thomas Eyre in place of the previous broker, George Coventry, who, it was reported, was leaving town.[54] Coventry was both a notable Tory journalist and a poet of local renown. In the late 1840s, one was just as likely to find a Coventry poem in the *Cobourg Star* as one by McCarroll.

On 22 March he wrote directly to Francis Hincks urging that if, as he had heard, a new collector of tolls was to be appointed to replace Kittson, he might be considered for the position, given his "present position in the Customs" and his "intimate knowledge of the books and affairs of the Harbour Company, gathered during the present investigation, at which I have occasionally assisted in a subordinate capacity." Though he had only been on the job for four months, he assured Hincks that he was "peculiarly adapted to discharge the duties of the office." At the same time he used the letter to thank Hincks again for "the instance of your goodness I now enjoy."

McCarroll made it clear to Hincks that he was virtually running the office himself. However, were he to be appointed as collector he would need two local "sureties" and this, he knew, would be a significant task to meet within a short time frame. He had no property and little personal capital; moreover, he was a relative newcomer to the town. Nevertheless, his creditable work in the customs office counted heavily in his favour. Hence, on 11 May 1850 he was appointed "Acting" collector of tolls. While the new appointment began immediately, he knew that to become the full-time collector would require that he bring forward his two sureties as soon as possible. They proved to be Thomas Eyre and William Weller.

Before being promoted, however, he had increased his salary by another strategy. On 4 April he reported to Dunscombe that the daily servicing of the Cobourg lighthouse, built on a small island in the harbour, had declined because of a change in the lamplighter's situation. He offered to oversee that job himself, assuring that the lamp was lit every evening and that an adequate supply of oil was on hand. "My constant attendance on the wharf would enable me to see that the person to whom I might entrust the lighting of it, did not neglect his duty," he assured Dunscombe. Subsequent payment of office accounts indicate that he did indeed receive that extra salary (25 pounds) in 1850 under the expanded title "Acting Collector of Tolls and Keeper of the Lighthouse."

Later letters reveal his increasing engagement with business challenges affecting customs work at the port. He explained various decisions he had made and recommended a number of changes, especially to the harbour facilities. In a letter to Dunscombe of 11 May 1850, he presented an overview of the competitive situation of the port. Cobourg, he noted, was still in a favourable position because, in contrast to Darlington and Port Hope, which he had looked into, the town charged less than the allowable limit in terms of current toll rates. The physical state of the harbour, however, was a different matter. Discretionary money was required to make immediate repairs to the surface of the east wharf and to undertake improvements to the much shorter west wharf. The latter, he reported, "is not used at all from the want of a proper entrance." If such work were not undertaken during the coming summer, he argued, "the eastern pier will be literally torn to pieces with Teams [of horses] and choked up to the total obstruction of anything like business." The head office sent him twenty-nine additional pounds for work he had overseen during the year.

In the same letter he reported that he was investigating the precise amount owed to customs for toll monies collected by a former Cobourg surveyor, Mr Bertram, who was now serving as collector at the Port of Presqu'ile. He also reported that he had served notice upon Mr Ebenezer Perry for a bill of 450 pounds, which remained on the Harbour Company's books. It was a bill that was sure to displease Perry. In general, however, McCarroll emphasized his ongoing frustration with the incomplete records that he found in the customs ledgers. Though he was now "thoroughly acquainted with [the] books," he found the tracing of certain transactions "almost next to an impossibility, as the outstanding debts are scattered amongst bankrupt estates, broken down Merchants and persons residing at the extreme end of this, and the adjoining District." Still, he was confident that, "in a few days," he would be in a position to pass on "a respectable portion of the amount, and give you that description of

<u>satisfaction</u>, which, I trust, will insure a marked good opinion of my treatment of the matter."

Two months later (31 July), he had still not supplied Dunscombe with either the reclaimed funds or a detailed explanation of his progress. Rather, he now argued that he needed to consult "Mr Kittson," who, "from his other duties [has] been totally unable to afford me the necessary assistance." Again, as was typical of his business letters, McCarroll worried out loud that he not be seen as neglectful of his duties.

Regarding Ebenezer Perry's outstanding bill, McCarroll was not long in realizing that he was up against a formidable foe, one whose grasp of the historical and business issues at the harbour he could scarcely match. Neither could he match Perry's personal stature and formidable tenacity of purpose. Perry was an importer and exporter who ran a grist mill and a large dry goods, hardware, and grocery business at the foot of the harbour, specializing in exporting flour, lumber, and produce to the United States. For years he had worked in collaboration with numerous merchants on both sides of Lake Ontario. Faced with McCarroll's bill, he refused to pay. Instead, he cited "high legal authority," arguing that, since the government had taken over the harbour company (1842–43), it had not lived up to its commitment to make the necessary improvements to the harbour; hence, as a disappointed former stockholder and an ongoing client, he had no obligation to provide payment for services not provided. It did not take long for McCarroll to sidestep what would have been an impossible confrontation. He advised Dunscombe to refer the matter to the "law officers of the Crown," for he worried that Perry's strategy of citing the expiration of the company charter might "find its way into the heads of others, and interfere with my settlement of the affairs of the Company."[55]

His final letter from his Cobourg office attempted to answer "the implied charge of a wilful neglect of duty" recently launched against him and sent to the inspector general's office. The complainant was the disgruntled William Butler. As harbour master, Butler cited two alleged misdemeanours to Hincks – first, the manner in which McCarroll collected "Harbour Dues" and, second, the preferential treatment he offered to clients regarding the use of storage warehouses on the piers.

McCarroll's explanations, while plausibly rendered, carried a clear note of political favouritism. It was implicit in his sense of duty that, where possible, businessmen who were Reform supporters should be advantaged by his decisions and that old political allies from Peterborough should receive better treatment from the Cobourg office than had hitherto been offered. Butler specifically complained to the inspector general that the actual customs warehouse lay "empty – or nearly so" while the private warehouses of William Weller were much in use. McCarroll defended his assignment of goods to Weller's buildings on the grounds of the inconvenient location and poor condition of the customs warehouse. Not surprisingly, Butler himself owned that customs warehouse, which he occasionally advertised for storage purposes in the *Cobourg Star*.

In regard to the immediate collection of duty on imported goods passing through the port, McCarroll argued that he did not feel he could enforce the payment of tolls "upon any of the exports and imports of Peterborough before they left the storehouse here." If he had done so, "the whole of trade of that town would have been transferred to Port Hope instantly." He asserted that his take-it-now-and-pay-me-later strategy actually allowed him to collect more tolls from regular customers than the office had managed to do in the past. He further argued that the amount he returned for the quarterly reporting period was, for the present, larger than had been produced "by any of my Predecessors, even under the prosperous circumstances, altho' the rate of Toll was reduced to nearly one half at an early period of my servitude." Still, when one notes that merchants and businessmen like William Cluxton, Robert Nicholls, John Albro, and Charles Perry were among those allowed a grace period by the acting collector, one can identify a well-connected scheme of favouritism in play.

When the inspector general's office complained to the acting collector about the amount of money it was owed by Cobourg customs (20 July 1850), McCarroll reminded his superiors that the collection and return had been complicated by the government's own order on 29 June "to deliver up to the Corporation of Cobourg, all the property belonging to the Harbour Company." In complying with that order, he had paid to the president of the company "all the monies then in my hands, as well as the Books, &c." There had been no slacking in his collection of tolls, he argued; rather, the results reflected his prompt response to the particular pressure created by the government's ongoing debt to the company and his dutiful efforts to implement the orders he received.

While the situation facing him as acting collector of tolls remained fraught with unresolved issues through 1850, matters of contention seemed to lessen in 1851. The collector's office was adjusting to the new laws and conditions, and McCarroll was doing his best to straighten up the customs books and to make the Cobourg office run as efficiently as he could. Such was his success – or, perhaps better, such was the success of his explanations – that in the late spring of 1851 Hincks surprised him with a promotion. McCarroll would now have the rank of collector, but he would serve in that capacity at Port Stamford, the port of entry at the Canadian end of the newly completed suspension bridge over the Niagara River. The bridge was located three miles below Niagara Falls and close by the famous whirlpool in the river. Ironically, he had been assured by this time that his Cobourg friends William Weller and Thomas Eyre were ready to serve as his local sureties.

When one reads the correspondence to and from the Cobourg customs office to government in 1850 and 1851, James McCarroll – poet, musician, storywriter, and journalist – vanishes from sight. Yet, from sources already documented, we know that he was far from being creatively fallow during the sixteen months in which he served his first customs appointment. He persisted on all fronts as time allowed, penning poems for Haslehurst in Peterborough, for Ruttan and Leonard in Cobourg, writing articles on the arts for Ruttan, and performing in concerts in both Cobourg and Peterborough. Now, however, as an experienced government employee, he had before him a new opportunity, one that would allow him to reunite with his family and receive a much-improved salary.

A bankrupt five years before, he had recovered his financial equilibrium and landed squarely on his feet, thanks in large part to Francis Hincks and the Reform Party. He could now count on a better annual salary than he had ever previously earned and he could bank on receiving it with regularity. Moreover, he had been appointed to the prestigious rank of collector, though at a new and small port of entry. Most importantly, he would at last be able to live together again with his wife and four daughters, moving them with him across the province to the scenic, world-famous area of Niagara Falls. There, they would have opportunities to explore an exciting environment and to make a new set of connections in the St Catharines-Niagara Falls region, perhaps even across the border in New York. A gregarious individual with a penchant for making friends wherever he went, he was eager to test these fresh waters. Here too he could seek out new opportunities to develop his reputation as a writer and musician.

For his part Henry Ruttan had no doubts about McCarroll's talents. While publicizing McCarroll's promotion to collector position at Port Stamford, he described his friend as a musician he could not praise too highly and a "witty, funny, and altogether agreeable" wordsmith.[56] In the same editorial, Ruttan introduced a comic letter he had just received from Port Stamford, adding that McCarroll was "one of the best writers we have ever had the pleasure of putting in print."

4

The Suspension Bridge:
Port Stamford, 1851–53

IN MAY 1851, THE INSPECTOR GENERAL OF CANADA, Francis Hincks, promoted James McCarroll to the position of collector of tolls and customs at Port
Stamford, Canada West. It was another patronage appointment, Irishman to
Irishman, Reformer to Reformer; however, Hincks's concern about how the
new port on the Niagara River would operate may have led him to engage
McCarroll in a testy experiment. In that sense he could be seen as a gladiator
sent to meet the American lions on the bridge (and alternatively the Tories of
the Clifton area) or a rising star among Canadian customs officers who had
earned a challenging position.

With his two Cobourg sureties in hand,[1] McCarroll became the first
Canadian customs officer formally appointed to the Suspension Bridge post.
That bridge spectacularly spanned the Niagara River gorge just above the
famous whirlpool, some 4 kilometres (2.5 miles) below the Horseshoe Falls at
Drummondville (Niagara Falls, Canada West). Awaiting him at Port Stamford
was a new set of opportunities that initially covered over ongoing border issues
and less obviously political challenges in Canada West. As collector he enjoyed
a position of authority and an improved annual salary. As well, new friends
and fresh musical opportunities awaited him in the St Catharines-Niagara
Falls region. Inevitably, local Tories, led by Samuel Zimmerman (1815–1857)
and Gilbert McMicken (1813–1891), kept a close watch on his every move.[2]
McMicken had been the influential and wealthy Zimmerman's choice for the
position, but Hincks had other ideas.

The small village of Port Stamford, then also known as "Suspension Bridge,"
was located in the Township of Stamford, Canada West. Two years later the

4.1 This photograph shows the famous Suspension Bridge linking Canada West to northern New York State. In McCarroll's time, it was used by wagons, stages, and pedestrian traffic. Clifton House, on the Canadian side, is visible in the background to the left. Date and photographer unknown. Niagara Falls Heritage Foundation Collection, record ID 97544, Niagara Falls Public Library.

village would be renamed Elgin in honour of James Bruce, the current governor general of Canada, whom McCarroll greatly admired. Lord Elgin was at that time completing his turbulent tenure. Little wonder that the numerous name changes of the village at the bridge have led to confusion among later observers. Port Stamford, Suspension Bridge, and Elgin are all forgotten names today. Elgin was first absorbed by the larger town of Clifton in 1856 and subsequently by the city of Niagara Falls.

Envisioned by St Catharines businessman and politician William Hamilton Merritt, the Suspension Bridge was designed to expand commerce and traffic between Canada and the United States at the closest local point of contact.[3]

So phenomenal and awe-inspiring was the bridge as an engineering project that it was immediately regarded as a major attraction in itself, ranking just below the famous Canadian falls. Located fourteen miles west of St Catharines and twenty miles east of Buffalo, New York, the Suspension Bridge spanned the 251 metres (825 feet) across the deep Niagara River gorge. Between the bridge and the Canadian Falls was the Clifton House, a first-rate hotel popular with sightseers and vacationers seeking a close view of one of the world's Seven Wonders.[4] Canadian government officials, after several extensive delays, opened a customs office at Port Stamford in 1851 in order to collect tariffs and duties. Well aware that border vigilance had been slack on the Canadian side for years, officials hoped to mount a more effective means of controlling both legitimate trade and the smuggling that was then flourishing across the Niagara River.

When construction of the Suspension Bridge began in 1848, a still larger vision was at play. Beyond pedestrian and carriage traffic, the plan was to build an upper-level bridge capable of carrying trains across the gorge. Railroad companies were fast advancing toward the river's edge from both sides. Nevertheless, plenty of skeptics were concerned about the bridge's long-term viability and durability. Who would finance its construction and who would control the right to collect usage fees? How long would its structure last? And would the bridge actually be able to support both a railroad track and pedestrian traffic as envisioned by its engineers?[5] Since 1818 three ferry depots along the river had served local business interests.[6] The village of Chippewa and the town of Drummondville[7] would continue to serve as the Canadian ports of entry for boat traffic even after the bridge opened. Thus, McCarroll arrived at a propitious yet difficult time.

Overall, progressive engineering generated a climate of optimism. The pedestrian bridge at Queenston, six miles to the east, was the only other bridge crossing the Niagara River at the time. When the Suspension Bridge was first opened in August 1848, a steady stream of pedestrians, stagecoaches, peddlers, and carters crossed from Manchester (now Niagara Falls, New York) into Canada. Accompanying the two-way business traffic was a flood of American tourists eager to view the wonders of Niagara Falls from the Canadian side and enjoy the hospitality of the Clifton House. One American carrier alone made fourteen trips in a single day across the bridge, his stagecoach crammed with sightseers. The Suspension Bridge now made the trip to the Canadian falls an affordable and pleasant excursion for middle-class American tourists. The monied classes, be they American, European, or Canadian, had long since agreed that Niagara Falls, viewed from the Canadian side, was a very special North American destination.

However, for three years legal issues and lawsuits kept the Suspension Bridge from being used regularly. Finally, on 11 March 1851, by an Order in Council from the Canadian government, the customs office at Port Stamford began regular operations.[8] Initially, a local man named Hemphill served as acting collector.[9] Two months later when James McCarroll arrived at the bridge, he was shocked by the inadequacies of his new post. Confidence had never been his problem, but the absence of facilities certainly was. There was neither an actual customs office at the bridge nor suitable accommodation for his family. Nor was there a warehouse to hold goods and shipments for valuation or transfer. There was no copy of the Provincial Statutes or "Instructions to Collectors," nor were there the office supplies essential to conduct transactions and keep records. Immediately, he began making urgent written requests for supplies like blank entry forms and "writ[s] of assistance" to support his efforts in making seizures.[10]

Port Stamford was barely a hamlet in 1851, with only four or five buildings near the bridge although plans were afoot to develop the adjacent lands.[11] Rents were unusually high and there was no ready space for an office or living quarters. The nearest "post town" was Drummondville and the closest bank was in St Catharines, fourteen miles away. The small and serviceable Elgin Hotel, located near the bridge, had little space to rent. Nevertheless, McCarroll soon became friendly with its proprietor, Theodore Griffin, who allowed him to conduct some of his official business with peddlers, importers, and travellers at the hotel itself.

Leaving Peterborough, the McCarrolls travelled as a party of seven by steamer from Cobourg to Port Dalhousie at a cost of 7 pounds, 10 shillings. Appointed at short notice, McCarroll had to borrow the money for the trip; then upon their arrival he was faced with finding accommodation for his wife and himself, their four daughters, and Ann's brother John Davis. Temporarily, he rented office space in the wing of a small grocery store, and furnished it with a desk and chairs borrowed from Mr Sears, the genial manager of the Clifton House.[12] Meanwhile the family moved into a "rickety old wooden building that appears to have stood from time immemorial." It featured "a miserable small sitting room and two infinitely more small and miserable bed rooms." For this he would have to pay thirty-nine pounds a year – more than half his annual salary.[13]

A month later he was still searching for affordable accommodations. He could not imagine his wife and daughters living in that "miserable" building during a Canadian winter. At the same time he had to abandon his office in the small backroom of the grocery store whenever the landlord required the space to accommodate beer-drinking patrons or weary travellers. However, with R.S.M. Bouchette's encouragement at headquarters, McCarroll submitted a proposal that called for the building of a house for the collector and his family. It would have two wings, one for bedrooms and living space, and the other for the customs office. He estimated the total cost for the land and construction (including fences and sheds) would be no more than 200 pounds. Bouchette visited Port Stamford in July to verify McCarroll's needs and then began to move the recommendation through government channels.

Still, McCarroll was alert to other possibilities. While awaiting the promised "parliamentary action," he lost the use of his grocery store "office" and made a new arrangement to share some of the space occupied by the directors of the Suspension Bridge Company. Then in early October, with winter approaching, he took the initiative to rent a house that suddenly became available at 6.5 pounds a quarter; that structure would serve temporarily as both an office and a home for his family. In a letter he begged Bouchette's "approbation" for his action, providing a compelling justification for a lesser expense than the government seemed ready to approve. In fact, nothing came of his construction proposal during his two-year tenure at Port Stamford. It was not until the completion of the Zimmerman Bank in 1853 that the custom's office found a suitable location next to the new Port Stamford Post Office.[14]

Meanwhile McCarroll was introducing himself to local people and building his reputation as a courteous government employee. In his letters to head-quarters, he argued for the growing importance of the customs service at the Suspension Bridge and suggested improvements in its operations. He was quick to report on impressive gains in revenue collection and to argue that further savings could be implemented by bringing the Niagara Falls ferry service under the control of the Port Stamford collector rather than maintaining it at Chippewa. Above all, he sought to impress Bouchette with his efficiency as an employee and his continuing loyalty to the Reform government.

Meeting the Press and Making a Splash

Always able to make friends quickly, McCarroll nevertheless often found himself an outsider in Port Stamford. To some local folk he was an interloper and an unwanted political appointee. The way he conducted himself and his office was closely watched. To local Tories, he was yet another insult foisted on them by the "vile" Reform government.[15]

By contrast, he soon discovered a friend and champion in James Lamb of St Catharines. Lamb proved an ideal observer of the talented and congenial McCarroll. A fellow Irishman, Lamb was the editor of the *St Catharines Evening Journal*, but he was also a prominent Reformer and a lover of music. Like McCarroll, he had recently received a patronage appointment as landing waiter at the port of St Catharines. The daughters of James and Catharine Lamb, Nora and Anna, soon became good friends with the four McCarroll girls.[16]

Writing in the *St Catharines Evening Journal* on 14 August 1851, Lamb made a grand to-do about an impromptu visit to the new collector at Port Stanford. They had met on business at some earlier point, but in August their acquaintance flowered into friendship. Frustrated at having missed the stagecoach from the Suspension Bridge back to St Catharines, Lamb called on McCarroll at his home. Comparing the residence to a backwoods shanty, Lamb was delighted to receive a kind Irish welcome – "a Caed Mille Faithe" – and was introduced to several of the interests and talents of his genial host. Without naming McCarroll, he sang his praises in grandiose terms: "That shanty, reader, contained a man holding correspondence with some of the most popular *literatti* of the day, as also a writer of articles for the most widely circulated periodicals of the world; and well may those repositories of thought rejoice in such a correspondent, as in prose or verse, this denizen of the bush may take his position beside all that is elegant, refined, imaginative and pure."

Lamb made his new friend's list of literary correspondents (which would eventually include Dickens, Longfellow, and Oliver W. Holmes) seem extraordinary though he offered no particulars.[17] Nor did he provide specific examples of the "widely circulated" periodicals he wrote for.[18] Little matter! The new collector could "shine in any galaxy, however bright and glorious." As evening approached, his host produced his own telescope and took Lamb outside to study "Mr Jupiter and his moons." Here was a newcomer well versed not only in the arts but the sciences.

But there was also music. "Some time having been spent in literary conversation, music was introduced, when we found our rusticating friend equal to a good song, and quite indifferent to the source of the music, whether the most exquisite to be found in the German and Italian operas, or the simple but melodious compositions of his own country – Ireland. We found our friend quite an adept in his execution on the flute, making the instrument disconse passages of the most difficult kind, and anon stealing in[to] the soft and melting mood."

Because the celebrated Swedish soprano Jenny Lind was then much in the American and Canadian news while residing at the Clifton House, Lamb did not hesitate to mention her popular male partner, Giovanni Belletti, in his description:

> We found our friend with a marked Connaught accent, as though he had come last week, fresh and fasting, from the bogs of Leitrim. No affectation of classical attainments – no literary puppyism – nothing of the blue stocking *coterie*, to indicate this diamond contained in a rough-looking casket enough. Our friend will pardon us when we say this, but we will add that Belletti, with all his polish, could not induce us to forego the pleasure of hearing "Widow McCue," or "She sat in the low-backed car," for all the Italian buffo-dramatic songs [that Belletti] sings so well.

Lamb completed his portrait affectionately: "We must contrive to be late for the stage, the next time we pass that way."

Lamb's enthusiastic description of McCarroll was not long in drawing a snappy journalistic response. A week later the *St Catharines Constitutional's* editor, John Richardson, who knew McCarroll from Cobourg, answered Lamb with a mocking column entitled "The Literary Galaxy" (20 August 1851). It was an unsparing attack on Lamb's "absurd, inflated, pompous and preposterous editorial," mocking his pretentious attempt to play Homer to Achilles or Boswell to Samuel Johnson. He held up Lamb's spelling ("literatti") and his sloppy use of Latin phrases as obvious signs of failed writing, and he made fun of his having designated Port Stamford as a backwoods refuge. He also called into question the validity of "such fulsome eulogy," even though, like Lamb, he chose not to reveal the identity of the Samuel Johnson figure in question.

The dispute soon escalated as old grudges were renewed. Richardson was clearly not amused by Lamb's star treatment. For his part, McCarroll was angered by Richardson's attack. Adopting the penname CRUCIBLE, he launched into his old attack mode in a letter to the *Evening Journal*.[19] Dismissing Richardson as "not worth an arrow from a schoolboy's bow," he labelled him a Tory hack, "a mischievous idiot" of "inordinate vanity" whose editorial work was "utterly degrad[ing]" and whose writing was little less than "illiterate vulgarity." More pointedly, he challenged Richardson's editorial credentials, identifying him as "only the alternate printer and traveling agent of the *Newcastle Advertiser*, or the [*Cobourg*] *Star*," not the experienced editor he claimed to be.

Richardson shot back, threatening to call up old complaints about McCarroll, a man he claimed to have known for fourteen years.[20] CRUCIBLE's letter was, he reported, typical of his usual nastiness, "abound[ing] in personal abuse" while maintaining anonymity. Richardson, however, continued with the policy of not naming his adversary. As was typically the case in such ricocheting abuse, the invective soon tailed off; Richardson contented himself by returning to his attacks on Lamb's journalistic ineptness and stylistic infelicities; he also questioned, as a Tory had to do, the patronage job and extravagant salary Lamb had recently received.[21]

The effect of Richardson's attacks was to throw Lamb and McCarroll closer together. They were Irishmen, fellow Reformers, customs officers, and family men. Lamb often called attention in his newspaper to McCarroll's cordial and efficient work at the Suspension Bridge as well as his musical talents. He viewed him as "the best amateur flautist on this continent" and a performer with "a critical knowledge of the laws of harmony inferior to few artists" (14 October 1852). Informally, Lamb became McCarroll's local publicist as he began to perform in a new environment.

The Divas at Niagara Falls

Local historians have paid scant attention to the fact that 1851 and 1852 were extraordinary years for music lovers on the Niagara frontier. With good reason, John Richardson of the *Constitutional* described St Catharines as "music mad" during this period. Typically, St Catharines' residents bemoaned the fact that travelling companies and visiting musicians too often bypassed their town because it lacked a performance space large enough to yield a good house. Early in 1851, however, things changed. The well-known English soprano Anna Bishop sang in nearby Buffalo as part of what has been called the first international tour by a leading European singer. Her tour included Toronto. On a lesser scale, an Italian-trained singer named Madame Theresina Rank performed two concerts at the St Catharines town hall in July 1851. "The celebrated flute player" James McCarroll was the headliner among local "distinguished artistes" included in Madame Rank's program. While this was likely his first appearance in the Niagara area, the billing indicated that he was now being recognized as a distinguished musician.

Another reason for the local music madness lay in the newsworthy movements of Jenny Lind (1820–1887) in and around Niagara Falls that summer. She had generated tremendous international excitement when, after breaking off her controversial contract with P.T. Barnum, she chose to sequester herself for several months at the Clifton House. Her goal was to rest her voice and reformulate her North American commitments. Sharing an enthusiasm for her voice and her person, both Richardson and Lamb kept local residents informed about her doings.

Affectionately known as the "Swedish Nightingale,'" Jenny Lind had emerged as the world's most famous soprano, in part because of her excellent European reputation but more persuasively because she had been lured to America by Barnum and his grand promise of Yankee dollars. In 1851 she was in the midst of his lengthy tour and had taken North American audiences by storm. As her tour manager, Barnum had laid out a gruelling series of 150 concerts at $1,000 per night, all of which were publicized and promoted by some twenty paid agents and a "caravan" of reporters. The scale of the promotional hype was unprecedented and the release of information was carefully controlled. The American public was duly enthralled. Capitalizing on her voice, her warm presence, and her well-known generosity, Barnum took a huge financial gamble on the tour even as he successfully ushered in the dawn of newspaper-generated celebrification in North America.

One of Barnum's reporters hailed Lind as the singer who "changed all men's ideas of music as much as Bacon's inductive system revolutionized philosophy." Odes were written about her. Jenny Lind dolls, hats, and chocolates were sold as souvenirs. Schools, boats, and vehicles were named for her, including a fire engine in St Catharines. There had never before been such a well-promoted phenomenon as Jenny Lind as she toured North American cities under Barnum's watch.

Despite the pervasiveness of "Lind-mania," Lind had reached a personal breaking point by the summer of 1851. Having completed all her concerts to date and the exhausting travel involved, she knew that she needed a rest; moreover, she knew that she would be better off financially if she broke with Barnum now that she had met the major requirement of her contract – the performance of ninety concerts. Hence, only two months after James McCarroll moved to Port Stamford, Lind announced that she had ended her agreement with Barnum and would strike out on her own, vowing to make good on the entire tour schedule.

In early July she took refuge in a suite of rooms at the Clifton House and began assembling a new team of musicians and confirming the remaining dates of her tour. Of particular note, she had to replace her able musical director, Julius Benedict, who had opted to return to Europe. Her durable and handsome singing partner, baritone Giovanni Belletti, had agreed to continue on with her. The general public had long favoured a love match between Belletti and Lind. She, however, had her own plan in mind. She called on her old friend Otto Goldschmidt to take Benedict's place as her pianist and musical director. Goldschmidt arrived at the Clifton House that month to take up his new duties.

A devotee of serious music who closely followed news of Jenny Lind's doings, James McCarroll observed some of her local activities and attended to the rumours buzzing about her personal life. Living only a mile from the Clifton House, he was well positioned to follow her movements, especially when she crossed the Suspension Bridge on afternoon outings to New York State; she did so, for instance, on 22 July 1851. In a "letter" that he sent back to the *Cobourg Star* as its "Niagara Correspondent,"[22] he adopted for the first time in prose a stage-Irish voice that allowed him to play fast and loose with Jenny's situation and her wonderfully pristine reputation.

In the voice of "Denis Finnegan," he reported that Jenny had sung by request at the Clifton House for a political function and had chosen several "profane" songs for the occasion. This, as most readers realized, was not something Jenny would ever have done, but it made for provocative gossip and the sort of stage-Irish excess that McCarroll was testing. From personal observation, he was also able to speculate about her romantic life, indicating – correctly as it turned out – that she was now lavishing her attention on Otto Goldschmidt, who accompanied her on her outings. Thus, she was forsaking the dashing Belletti, who so many observers of the early concerts had hoped would win her heart: "If I was Belletti, I'd brake the bones of the little jarmin that's always riding about wid Jenny, meandherin wid her attords the whirlpool, and payin her toll at the bridge. Nabocklish, [my boy], the splindid Italian'll never get her; for although the little fella was hish'd for his peeanna playin in the Shtates, begorra, he may be more shkillful among the sthrings of a lady's heart. – Besides, she appears to have a wondherful lanin attords matrimony lately, beein continually handling the landlord's little boy." In that same comic letter McCarroll let loose his Irish pride and bias regarding the qualities that make for a great soprano:

> But I'm thinking that, wid all her liberality, she's a very shrewd kind of a woman; for well I know, she'd have gone home [to Sweden] this Fall, if Catherine Hayes wasn't expected in this country. Rely on it, she'll shtart, from this place, about the beginning of the month, for the purpus of crassin the thrack of the new-comer, and contindin wid her in the great cities of

4.2 Jenny Lind, 1850 (*left*). Photographer unattributed, retouched version of daguerreotype, original plate in Library of Congress. Source: Wikimedia Commons. Catherine Hayes (*right*). Source: Music Division, New York Public Library, item ID 1231874, http://digitalcollections. nypl.org/items/510d47df-8d6f-a3d9-e040-e00a18064a99. The two European sopranos were all the rage in the Niagara area in 1851. McCarroll saw both perform and favoured Kate Hayes, his countrywoman, in his comments.

the Union. She fears the dazzling fame that follows her rival from Italy, as well she may, for it is now generally admitted by the best judges upon airth, that God has tshuned the throat of the Irish Thrush, to more than mortial melody – [my boy], b'lieve me, the paper grows dim afore me, whin I think of the way her bussum will heeve undher "The Harp that Wansht."

Less smitten by Jenny Lind than many observers, Denis Finnegan neverthe-less applauded her extraordinary vocal range, her fine enunciation, and her abil-ity to "operate" on an audience "like a peeled inninan." For his part McCarroll himself arranged to attend her performance in Buffalo (15 October 1851) and was likely in attendance at one of her Toronto concerts (21 and 23 October).[23]

Catherine Hayes (1818?–1861) provided another exciting musical drama for the people of St Catharines. Popularly known as the "Swan of Erin," the "Irish Thrush," "the Hibernian Prima Donna," and the "Queen of Song," she had arrived in North America on a tour with the Royal Italian Opera Company but had broken her contract in order to undertake her own tour of the United States and Canada in the wake of Jenny Lind's extraordinary success. News of Catherine Hayes's concerts spread rapidly. Like many people in the Niagara region, especially those of Irish descent, McCarroll and James Lamb were as wild as schoolboys to hear her in person. Writing in the *Evening Journal*, Lamb favourably compared Kate Hayes and Anna Bishop with Jenny Lind, noting their respective abilities to sing so beautifully the ballads of England, Scotland, and Ireland.[24] At the same time he lamented the news that the latter part of Jenny Lind's tour, the part she organized herself, was being plagued by "a pack of sharks." In a column dated 7 August 1851 Lamb wrote that "Barnum was a prince compared to these commissionaires."

The news of Kate Hayes's concerts in Boston, Montreal, and Toronto was reported in both St Catharines newspapers. John Richardson attended her Toronto concert on 24 May 1852, rapturously describing her as an "enchantress whose Fame as a singer had been wafted on the breeze to every part of the world, and who had proved so great a gem to the Emerald Isle of the Ocean." "There was," he added, "a majestic appearance about her, as well as a most plaintive and beseeching look – an expression that penetrated the inmost soul and fixed [the audience's] every thought and commiseration upon her who was about to give vent to the plaintive character of the Irish nation." She was quite as good as Jenny Lind, he reported, and far better liked by audiences.[25] Kate appeared on stage in a white muslin dress, with embroidered shamrocks rimming the neckline.

A young soprano of impeccable moral reputation, Kate Hayes had risen above the poverty of her childhood through the patronage of the bishop of Limerick.[26] After training in France and Italy, she debuted with the Italian Opera in 1845; she also played extensively at Covent Garden, had links to Franz Liszt and Giuseppe Verdi, and sang for Queen Victoria, encoring that performance with a stirring rendition of the popular Irish ballad "Kathleen Mavourneen." That royal encore helped to define her career as much as her earlier operatic triumph in the title role in Donizetti's *Lucia di Lammermoor*.

Bird imagery prevailed in the *Evening Journal* as Lamb compared Kate to a nightingale rather than a swan (a more musical bird!) and published a poem dedicated to her entitled "Happy Birdling of the Forest." Moreover, during the late spring of 1852, Kate Hayes stayed at the Clifton House. She rented the suite Jenny Lind had occupied and made her presence felt locally.[27] She gave a sold-out concert in Buffalo on 6 May, drawing forth Lamb's effusive praise. "Never was triumph more complete," he wrote, asserting that "Jenny Lind cannot sing a ballad like Kate Hayes."

Lamb provided a fuller account of her second Buffalo concert, which he deemed "a brilliant triumph." Performing before a full house that included many leading musicians, she sang such favourites as "I Know That My Redeemer Liveth," "The Harp That Once through Tara's Halls," and "Kathleen Mavourneen" with grace, modesty, and pathos, ably supported by Mr LeVanu on pianoforte, Mr Kyle on flute, and Mr Graybiel (Griebel) on violin, along with baritone Herr Mengis. Furthermore, Lamb reported that Hayes was contemplating a Canadian tour. St Catharines, however, could not be included because its town hall would not draw the necessary $700 in audience revenue as a guarantee.[28]

That same issue of the *Evening Journal* contained another instance of Lamb's praise for McCarroll's efficient work as a collector. On this occasion Lamb had travelled to the Suspension Bridge by the horse-drawn Erie and Ontario railroad, crossed over the Niagara River at Port Stamford and continued on to Buffalo by train to attend Kate Hayes's concert. McCarroll joined him at Port Stamford: they attended the concert and stayed in Buffalo at the moderately priced, 200-bed American Hotel.

Kate Hayes's final local concert was a more intimate performance at the Clifton House on 21 July. It might have been better had she opted to take a loss and sing at the St Catharines town hall. Her performance in the hotel's large dining room disappointed both Richardson and Lamb. Lamb felt that she sang too many difficult pieces, leaving insufficient time for the ballads he enjoyed so much.[29] Richardson offered another explanation. The "overflow" crowd and "the never-ceasing fall of the great cataract" nearby forced her to struggle to be heard. "We are heartily sorry Miss Hayes attempted a concert here," he wrote, "as strangers who were present could not rightly appreciate her vocal powers."[30] Thus ended the battle of the sopranos and the Niagara area's brief immersion in musical greatness.

McCarroll himself was not long in becoming more involved in the St Catharines music scene. He took part in several local fundraising concerts and performed, as previously mentioned, with Madame Theresina Rank in two concerts at the town hall in July 1851. Three months later he was a special guest at a "grand concert" (October 1852) in Chippewa, performing with Herr Frederick Griebel and Dr Thomas C. Macklem of that town.[31] This was likely the first time he shared the stage with Griebel, the acclaimed violinist who had originally come to Canada with Kate Hayes. He also joined James Lamb's daughter Nora as a featured guest at a fundraising concert for St George's Anglican Church Bazaar in St Catharines on 29 October 1852.

It is noteworthy that John Richardson in the *Constitutional* set aside his political biases and the memory of CRUCIBLE's insults in waxing eloquent about McCarroll's contributions to that concert. Clearly, music could trump politics in Richardson's outlook. Describing McCarroll's flute solo, "O Dolce Concento," he wrote,

> [it] far surpassed anything we have ever heard: – it was indeed "the soul of music," and every judge must at once confess that it could not be surpassed this side of the Atlantic, or probably in the Old World itself. We have known Mr McCarroll as a flautist for many years, and could only wish he had favored the audience with his favorite piece "Molly Asthore" as we have heard him on many occasions, – for in it he throws all the pathos and feeling which make the Irish melodies excel all other music: – but should another opportunity offer we shall expect Mr McCarroll to entertain the audience with this beautiful piece as we have seen him perform it with one hand. (3 November 1852)

Despite receiving acclaim for his performances in St Catharines and Chippewa, McCarroll had one unhappy concert experience that winter. It was a gala holiday event planned for 29 December 1852 in support of Miss Graydon, a local music teacher and soprano. The invitation called forth the elite of St Catharines, including William Hamilton Merritt, who was a member of the committee of management for the event. McCarroll was chosen to manage the concert and to perform. Hopes were high that it would fill the town hall. Herr Frederick Griebel was billed to appear with Miss Graydon, McCarroll, and Dr Thomas C. Macklem. However, for reasons that remain unclear, Griebel did not show up for the concert.

Frederick Griebel (1819–1858) was no minor figure in the musical world of the day. A German-trained violinist of immense skill and impeccable reputation, he had come to Canada on tour in 1848 and decided to stay.[32] Kallmann has described him as "the first fully professional violinist to have settled in Canada."[33] Having come to the St Catharines area while touring with the Musick-Gesellschaft Germania, he broke with that troupe and, after brief appearances with both Jenny Lind and Kate Hayes, he decided, for reasons of health and family responsibility, to leave off the demands of touring and settle in the Niagara Falls area as a teacher and performer. His close connection with his friend and student Dr Macklem of Chippewa played a large part in his decision. Like James Lamb, McCarroll had developed a personal friendship with Dr Macklem based on their mutual love of music.

Three things are certain about the infamous concert. The night of 29 December was stormy, the concert went off as scheduled, and Griebel was a no-show, though he had reportedly journeyed to St Catharines from Niagara Falls that very evening. James Lamb, who had helped to promote the concert in the *Evening Journal*, promised that "the very well known musical talent of the principal performers" [Griebel and McCarroll] would be "a host in themselves." He gave Dr Macklem special credit for helping to engage Griebel's participation.

Why then did Griebel stay away? Was it indisposition? Exhaustion? A misunderstanding about dates? Artistic pique? Forgetfulness? Weather? An inadequate fee? Whatever the case, his absence became a gentlemanly *cause celebre* in the St Catharines newspapers. For several weeks the *Constitutional* and the *Evening Journal* kept the issue alive.

Lamb triggered the controversy in reviewing "Our Concert" on 6 January 1853. After praising McCarroll for his admirable "management" of the evening and "the delicious tones" that characterized his flute solos and accompaniments, Lamb recalled that, in his own presence, he had heard "Mr Griebel" volunteer his services and "promise to attend and play at the Concert, without any stipulation as to time or other arrangements – leaving all such things in the hands of his friend Mr McCarroll." Clearly, Lamb wanted to vindicate McCarroll and the committee (of which he was a member) in light of Griebel's unexplained absence.

In a letter to the *St Catharines Constitutional* dated 18 January, Dr Macklem (using the penname "An Admirer of Merit") defended Griebel from "a most undeserved censure" in the *Evening Journal*. Such an article might, he argued, damage Griebel's professional reputation just as he was setting up in Drummondville (Niagara Falls) as a "teacher of Piano Forte, Violin, etc." Identifying McCarroll only as "a Gentleman residing in this vicinity," he asserted that Griebel had never agreed to perform in the concert and that, in his own presence, he had turned down an informal invitation. Macklem added that on a later occasion when he was approached by Lamb to see if Griebel might still be convinced to take part, Macklem cited "certain conditions" necessary for Griebel's agreement. As a committee member, Lamb could not agree to them.

What were Griebel's "conditions?" Was he concerned with remuneration, or top billing, or the absence of a formal invitation? Perhaps he was uninterested in performing with local amateurs like Miss Nora Lamb and Miss Atkinson? Macklem did not name those "conditions" in his letter, but he did suggest that the concert promoters had unwarrantedly used Herr Griebel's name in its advertisements. Rather, he blamed James Lamb and his newspaper for creating the confusion, even as he admitted that he and Lamb were usually on "friendly terms."

McCarroll sent his own reply to James Lamb. Addressing his letter from the "Suspension Bridge, 1st February 1853," he deferred to Dr Macklem, who had recently agreed to serve as his custom's surety and whom he knew to be a gentleman and a doctor of high standing. He argued that there had been a misunderstanding that involved two separate concerts:

> The concert at which Mr Griebel refused to play, was that in connexion with the Bazaar. Mr Griebel, although he may have forgotten the engagement, volunteered cheerfully and kindly, at his own house, in both [James Lamb's] presence and mine, to assist at Miss Graydon's concert whenever it took place, and, subsequently, at my own residence, consulted me as to what pieces he should perform. These few lines are penned with a view of meeting an allusion made to me in the communication now before me, as well as in justice to the Committee of Management, who made the announcement in question in good faith.

One final letter followed on 19 February 1853. Macklem wrote to Lamb at the *Evening Journal*, this time under his own name. Regretting that he had "to appear in this matter" and having "no ambition to be a newspaper correspondent," he nevertheless felt obliged to defend both Griebel and himself. Again not identifying McCarroll by name, he registered his criticism of the use of anonymous letters and the assertive tone so evident in the newspapers of the day, a complaint that certainly fit McCarroll's reputation. "Mr Griebel," he wrote, "still denies having so promised or at least having any recollection whatever of having so promised, and I can positively assert, (and if requisite prove) that whenever addressed on the subject in my presence Mr Griebel uniformly declared his intention not to appear on the occasion alluded to." In closing, Dr Macklem suggested an end to the controversy. Better that "such of your readers as it may interest (numerous no doubt)" be left to judge "assertion against assertion." He concluded, "There has evidently been a misunderstanding somewhere but I trust no *intentional* departure from truth on the part of any one."

Relations between Macklem and McCarroll may have continued to be strained during the last few months of McCarroll's time at Port Stamford. Such, however, was not the case with his relationship with Griebel. They performed together at concerts in Oakville and Hamilton later that same year (1853) and stayed in close contact during Griebel's time in Hamilton and Toronto, performing together, for instance, on August 1855.[34] In 1858 McCarroll would help to raise funds for the violinist and his family during Griebel's final illness; indeed, he generously made a place for Griebel in his own family plot with St James's Cathedral in Toronto.

"The Adventures of a Night"

After McCarroll moved to his new customs post at Port Credit in 1853, he returned to St Catharines on occasion to visit James Lamb's family and he sent him numerous poems for the *Evening Journal*. But he also drew on his memories of life at the Suspension Bridge in crafting one of his best stories: "The Adventures of a Night" was published in the *Anglo-American Magazine* in Toronto in its December 1854 issue.[35] It was based on the Niagara River's reputation as "one of the most notorious smuggling points on the whole frontier." His narrator – a veiled version of himself – lives with his family at the Suspension Bridge on the Canadian side of the Niagara River and claims to "kn[o]w the river thoroughly." Indeed, he tells us that the local residents had access to a hidden key should they need to cross the gated bridge after it had closed for the night.

The story is a dark-and-stormy-night narrative that draws together two plot lines – the pursuit of smugglers along the Canadian side of the river and the harrowing escape of a newly married black couple being hunted down by bounty hunters on the American side under the authority of the dreaded Fugitive Slave Law.

One evening, while spending time with his family, the narrator reads an American newspaper account of the desperate flight of the young black couple. Then, in the course of his efforts to break up a band of smugglers on the river, the two plots converge. While pursuing the smugglers on the American side, he meets and rescues two hooded figures who turn out to be the newlyweds. Then at midnight, during a furious rain and lightning storm, he leads them across the Suspension Bridge to safety. In so doing the narrator calls into question "the boasted freedom of the neighbouring Republic" even as he entertains his readers with his dangerous adventures and descriptions of the landscape: we see the Niagara River in all its fury; we see the rapids below Chippewa, the towering walls of the Clifton House, and even the *Maid of the Mist*, moored on the river's dark shore

The *Toronto Daily Leader* praised the story's originality, "local relation, exciting plot, and the racy style in which it is written." James Lamb was as usual very positive in his *Evening Journal*. He described the narrative as "the stuff ...

to contribute to our home literature": "The localities – the plot – the style of this [story] give evidence that James McCarroll could not confer a greater benefit on this country than to supplant the miserable trash imported from the neighbouring republic, by something substantial and, interesting and impressing. If imagination, poetry and language be absolute essentials to composition, Mr McCarroll can scarcely fail to amuse and instruct the reading public" (14 December 1854).

Border Blues: What's a Displaced Collector to Do?

James McCarroll's two-year term as the collector at Port Stanford provides a good deal of information about his daily life and preoccupations. (The customs service had begun in Canada in 1841, having heretofore been a British operation.) The records of the Customs Department (now the Canada Revenue Agency) offer important glimpses into his work habits and misadventures on the job. These files include numerous letters to his superiors, other correspondence, and occasional petitions sent by individuals to government criticizing his service and behaviour. By examining his own letters – particularly to the commissioner of customs, R.S.M. Bouchette, and, more personally, to the inspector general of Canada West, Francis Hincks – one learns a good deal about the state of the customs service at newly opened Port Stamford, the kind of work that McCarroll had to undertake, his modus operandi, and the pride he took in being a Canadian official. His letters make fascinating reading both for what they say and what they don't say.

McCarroll found himself working in a place where his Reform credentials were often in question. Behind the scenes was the powerful Samuel Zimmerman, one of Canada West's wealthiest men, who was not willing to forgive Francis Hincks for parachuting his man into the place he – Zimmerman – so valued.

McCarroll made a point of regularly assuring Bouchette about his courtesy and dutifulness: "it shall be my constant aim," he wrote on 25 July 1851, "to facilitate the intercourse peculiar to the Port, between the two Frontiers, and endeavour to, amicably, [address] the little omissions which must, often necessarily arise from forgetfulness on the part of Travellers who, wrapt up in the attractive novelties of this locality, omit to report themselves to this office." Such was his view of how he sensitively and ably conducted himself.

On a more public level his friend James Lamb regularly placed a kind word in the *St Catharines Evening Journal* about McCarroll's cordiality and proficiency as collector at the bridge. His editorial squibs paint an attractive picture of high-quality service and throw some light on McCarroll's success in collecting tolls and duties. On 12 February 1852, for instance, Lamb reported that the receipts from Port Stamford were remarkably high.[36] Moreover, he added, "We find that all hours of the night, the collector at Stamford, James McCarroll, Esq., gives his attendance when called upon, so that parties meet with all possible attention, and are never delayed by the absence of that officer, or his unwillingness to oblige those pressed for time, in requiring to pass at unseasonable hours." On 13 May, Lamb praised the amount of duty collected at Port Stamford.

> We recollect that when Stamford was made a point of entry, some of our grumblers found fault with the arrangements, as involving an unnecessary expense. But the results very clearly prove that the Customs Department exhibited a thorough knowledge of the advantages which would arise from the arrangement.
>
> The Collector at the Port of Stamford has not only promoted the interests of the revenue, by giving every facility to importers, but also by suppressing smuggling to a very great extent. Every facility that can be given to the Suspension Bridge Company is extended by this accommodating officer.

At the same time, letters and petitions in the custom's files reveal that, in the eyes of some business people – mostly Americans – McCarroll was far from a perfect government collector. When faced with difficulties, he could always offer an excuse to his superiors. Not least among them was the fact that, in a matter of months, the Suspension Bridge had become "the most difficult point [of entry] in the province."[37]

As collector, McCarroll had a number of responsibilities. The most susceptible to criticism was his power to seize goods that he judged to have been illegally brought into the province. In the vicinity of the Suspension Bridge, smugglers often risked the dangerous waters of the Niagara River to cross with saleable goods under cover of darkness. Once the bridge was in place, peddlers or small businessmen frequently tried to bring their wares into Canada without making a declaration. If caught, they could claim that they were unaware of the law or that they didn't realize that they had crossed an international border. Or they could pay up. For his part, having managed to seize undeclared goods, the collector had to hold them for a designated period of time in a warehouse, before putting them up for auction, thereby claiming a percentage of the proceeds as his fee. Seizures were a significant source of income for collectors across the province.[38]

McCarroll inherited the paperwork of a few seizures made by his predecessor, but during his two years as collector at the bridge he made several of his own. Horses, jewellery, oysters, and photography equipment were among the items seized. Most seizures, like the daguerreotype equipment taken from Francis Parsons, a St Catharines businessman, were resolved with limited fuss.[39] The Customs Department ruled that the seizure of Parson's goods be disallowed since it was contrary to a section of the act. However, by early 1853 two particular McCarroll seizures had become fractious enough to involve not only the two border communities but also leading Canadian government figures. Taken together, the two had a major effect on his immediate future.

One involved Milton H. Wheaton, a "[licensed] American peddler of jewellery" who brought from New York a supply of "common jewelry," hoping to sell his goods to the scores of well-heeled visitors to the Canadian falls. An agreeable, well-educated chap with a family to support, Wheaton had his trunk seized by McCarroll in July 1852; his unclaimed goods were subsequently sold at auction for 160 pounds.

Wheaton's response was to enlist a number of prominent American colleagues who appealed on his behalf to the Canadian government for reparation on the grounds of McCarroll's "duplicity" in misleading him about his options. McCarroll reported to Bouchette that Wheaton "told me an untruth about the contents of his box"; moreover, he registered surprise that Wheaton, whom he had invited to dinner at the bridge, would turn against him in what had been a normal border procedure.[40] McCarroll felt fully vindicated, having previously received a "voluntary official communication" from headquarters to the effect that there were "no grounds for interfering in any degree whatever with the case at issue."

Still, the department was more sympathetic with Wheaton than McCarroll had anticipated. In a letter to Hincks, Wheaton had claimed that the seizure "leaves me not worth a penny." As a result much of the proceeds of the auction – that is, the Crown's share – was returned to him as a cash payment "after deducting all expenses."[41]

While the Wheaton appeal was proceeding, a second seizure by McCarroll became a matter of special concern in Bouchette's office in January 1853. There were in fact two matters that turned some heads against the collector.

McCarroll himself was responsible for the first problem. In January 1853 he had submitted a flawed quarterly and year-end report to headquarters.

After Bouchette criticized him for his mathematical carelessness, McCarroll admitted to his accounting blunder, blaming it on his own "anxiety" and hurry to meet the department deadline and the flawed assistance of an unidentified associate whom he had assigned to do the additions for him. On 4 February he hurriedly submitted "a correct account of Annual Imports," bathing his re-submission in profuse apology.[42]

But a much larger border problem had begun in July 1851 and, by the autumn of 1852, had gained increasing notoriety. It involved three seizures of horses and equipment owned by George E. Hamlin and Company, Stage Proprietors and Livery Stable Keepers, of Manchester, New York. The Hamlins were the prominent livery outfit in the area, running as many as thirty "pleasure carriages" a day over the bridge to the Canadian falls as well as three regular delivery routes to St Catharines and related locations.

Free trade and precise border regulations were the issue. It would appear that George Hamlin and his brother Samuel were not inclined to treat Canadian revenue regulations with due seriousness, especially as they were relatively new and had been slowly implemented. Their drivers either disregarded Collector McCarroll or treated him with disdain. Part of the problem was that Canadian laws encouraged American carriage traffic north of the border while Canadian carriers were prohibited from advertising their services or picking up passengers after they crossed the Niagara River. Strong advocates of American enterprise, the Hamlins were inclined to treat Canada simply as an extension of their working territory; they paid only token attention to the niceties of international laws that now pertained at the Suspension Bridge.

Their drivers would cross the bridge, pay the required toll, and then carry on as if the collector were invisible. Although McCarroll insisted that all such vehicles must check in with him so that the contents of the carriage could be duly examined, the Hamlin drivers ignored that standing order. In frustration McCarroll reported to Bouchette that he had "threatened and remonstrated" with Samuel Hamlin on numerous occasions and sent after his drivers at least "fifty times."[43]

As the collector saw it, the Hamlins operated in an "impudent and swaggering manner" that irritated him and angered many Port Stamford bystanders. Indeed, hostility toward the Hamlins and their highhanded ways seems to have run high on the Canadian side. Karen Dubinsky's study of the records and reminiscences of travellers to Niagara Falls provides a useful context for the difficult situation facing McCarroll. She has documented a litany of complaints made by travellers in Canada about the crude and hostile behaviour of hack drivers in the Niagara area during this period.[44] Given the unsettled mood at Port Stamford, McCarroll must have felt that he could count on the support of local citizens as he sought to make the Hamlin drivers pay heed to Canadian law once they were on Canadian soil.

A seizure was inevitable. On the morning of 21 July 1851, McCarroll stopped a Hamlin driver who, according to his report, refused to check in when he crossed the bridge. Ordered to report to the customs office, the driver, who was a Spaniard, first claimed that he did not know where the office was. While this was a plausible enough response given the limited customs facilities, he then declared his American colours: "This is a Yankee horse and buggy," he said, making it clear that he had no intention of reporting to "that damned Customs Officer." Instead, he carried on with his passengers to the falls.[45] On his return, however, McCarroll invoked his vested power and seized the horses and the buggy.

Reporting immediately to Bouchette about his action, he made it clear that the Spaniard spoke fluent English and should not be allowed to use the excuse of language to justify his actions.[46] He also reiterated that he had given the Hamlins numerous warnings that their drivers had to abide by Canadian regulations once they crossed the bridge.

Five days later George Hamlin paid the 50 pounds required to reclaim his horses and carriage from customs. Still worried about perceptions of his professional conduct, McCarroll offered to gather signed affidavits in support of his seizure. Bouchette quickly set his mind at ease; in fact, he commended him for his intervention.

But George Hamlin was not a man to forgive or forget. Before a year had passed, he would deliberately force the collector to take action against his firm for a second and then a third time. Clearly, a border vendetta was percolating. It led to a showdown; neither George Hamlin nor James McCarroll was willing to back down, even as matters became more complicated and vexatious.

Seeking to address the inadequacy of stagecoach service from Buffalo to St Catharines and the Canadian falls or simply to confound McCarroll's authority, the Hamlins bought "a large amount of stage property" from Robert Fields of St Catharines on 6 December 1851. The purchase included twelve horses and three post-stages. Two days later they began their operations in Canada as an extension of the Canada West Stage Company. By this means, George Hamlin cleverly set the scene for his next confrontation with McCarroll.

On 11 December two Hamlin stages proceeding in opposite directions met at the Elgin House hotel. The stage from St Catharines had four American horses pulling a Canadian coach while the stage from New York was an American coach with four Canadian horses. With McCarroll's permission, the passengers were allowed to transfer from one stage to the other while their baggage was being checked. However, with that process underway and with the collector otherwise distracted, the drivers managed to change the horses from one stage to the other, thus avoiding the duties applicable to the use of American horses in Canadian territory. McCarroll learned of the switch only after the stages had departed for their respective destinations.

The result was confrontational, if not downright ugly. Canadian observers at the bridge, many of whom were fed up with the manoeuvrings and arrogance of Hamlin's Yankee drivers, insisted that McCarroll act immediately against the Hamlins, given their flagrant violation of the law. They told him that if nothing were done, they would take their complaint to the Queenston customs office and personally initiate an action against him. These "noisy individuals," as George Hamlin dismissively labelled them, effectively forced the now wary collector to undertake a new action against the Hamlin Company.[47]

The next day – 12 December – McCarroll called in a Hamlin representative and informed him that, given their conspicuous violation of Canadian revenue law, he had to seize the stage then returning to Port Stamford from St Catharines. His action led the Hamlins to post a bond of $1,600 (400 pounds) and to show cause to the Canadian government why their property should be returned without cost. A month later, after the bond had expired, McCarroll notified the Hamlins that, by his estimate, they still had to pay $800 in order to reclaim the horses, coach, and harness that had been seized.

While the specific seizure was a matter of current revenue laws and government procedures, the larger issue had to do with a system of rules that favoured American business enterprise on Canadian soil and penalized any Canadian initiative. As a Canadian customs officer, McCarroll had to be sensitive to the noisy local lobby at Port Stamford. But he also had to undertake his duties in as civil a manner as he could manage. He was well aware that the Hamlins were deliberately prodding him and undermining their Canadian competition. But he also realized that the Suspension Bridge was their gateway to ever-increasing profits. Their business was booming, though they were paying very little for their business opportunities on the Canadian side since passengers were required to pay their own tolls.

The dispute lingered into autumn even as the stagecoaches continued to roll across the bridge. The Hamlins maintained that McCarroll had promised that they would suffer no loss from the seizure; they specifically alleged that he promised that the coach and team would be returned, the bond rescinded, and the $800 returned in full. In February Hamlin sent a "memorial" to the Canadian government, requesting a full refund of the $800 bond.[48] In that document and its accompanying letters of support, McCarroll was described as an accommodating man who had the Hamlins' interests at heart and wished above all not to be seen as "a fool." One of Hamlin's witnesses, George Swain, the collector on the American side, even swore that McCarroll had said in his presence that Samuel Hamlin was "as innocent as a babe."

McCarroll, however, remained resolute concerning Hamlin's offences and the validity of the seizures he had made. Reporting to Bouchette on 7 May, he alleged that Samuel Hamlin was indulging in "deliberate falsehood[s]." He included his own set of affidavits from five "ear and eye witnesses" and sought to clarify how and why he had acted as he did. Above all, he refuted the assertion that he had "deliberately led an ignorant person into a breach of the laws of the land." He assured Bouchette that Hamlin was fully aware of what he was doing in his operations.

Canadian government officials found the situation problematic. "The case," they noted, "has elicited a vol. of evidence on both sides containing the most conflicting statements." They could see that the Hamlins had been playing tricks on McCarroll, but the bigger issue from the government's point of view had to do with what McCarroll had agreed to allow as collector. The report defined the conflict thus: "The seizure seems to have excited a good deal of interest in Stamford & the neighbourhood, the proprietors of Coach property in Canada being anxious that the seizure should he upheld whilst the American feeling is of course that this long an investigation of the case on the spot would be the safer course to come to a decision."[49] Further delays ensued and temperatures continued to rise.

A month later, upon hearing rumours that the Canadian government had decided not to support his actions, McCarroll launched another of his characteristic self-defences. In letters to headquarters (7 May, 8 June, 21 June 1852) he continued to describe the challenging conditions along the Niagara River border and to justify his own civil conduct. He was tired, he stated, of "the impertinent interference and curiosity of the minions of Mr Hamlin" and dismissed as outright lies Samuel Hamlin's charges that he had used inappropriate language in the matter and at one point had explicitly promised the Hamlins the full return of the $800 bond.

With the matter of the $800 still hanging in the balance, McCarroll made his third seizure of Hamlin property. On 13 September he reported that he had seized a Hamlin carriage, driven by a man named Alexander McKenny, on the grounds that McKenny was guilty of soliciting paying customers while travelling in Canada. The American answer was to deem such illegal payments a "present" to the driver rather than a fee for services. Such pick-ups of Canadian passengers by American stagecoaches were not uncommon, especially if the driver had carriage space available while on Canadian soil. There was, however, a specific law against such actions, designed to protect Canadian livery operators who were prohibited by American law from picking up American passengers while they were travelling in New York State.

The third seizure led the Hamlins to increase their pressure on government authorities. As managing partner of the firm, George Hamlin sent a second petition to Lord Elgin, dated 11 October 1852.[50] It called for the replacement of James McCarroll by a more competent, less vindictive collector. Among his allegations Hamlin reported that McCarroll had lied to him and misled his firm, harrassed his drivers, and acted improperly on many occasions, thereby "bringing discredit to Your Excellency's Government." More damningly, Hamlin closed with an ad hominem attack, characterizing McCarroll as "notoriously a person of very dissipated and intemperate habits" who was often "much intoxicated" on the job.[51] Elgin duly passed the petition on to the Customs Department and the inspector general.

Faced with increasing pressure and this new set of charges, Hincks wrote to McCarroll on 7 March, delicately expressing his concern about matters of "public service" at the bridge. By way of consolation and in response to the difficulties he knew McCarroll was facing, he was prepared to offer him an escape from the prickly situation. He could choose between two positions – the collector at Napanee or the collector at Port Credit; both ports would be much less difficult than Port Stamford. McCarroll's immediate response was to turn down the offer and request "an impartial investigation of the charges preferred against me."[52] But, even as he sent the letter off to the inspector general, he was reconsidering the advisability of continuing to fight the charges against him.

It took only a day for him to change his mind. Now feeling the need to "escape from a locality where I can no longer be courteous to every man I meet" as well as the need to provide some relief for his family, he accepted the position at Port Credit "as a post more eligible for me." Send me there, he affirmed; that way I will be "without the curse of Swift."[53] It was a curse that both he and Hincks recognized.

So ended James McCarroll's two-year stay at Port Stamford. They were busy years on many fronts and they were his baptism by fire as a collector for customs in a new territory. In his own mind, he had fought the good fight and happily escaped from a stressful and disagreeable position. Likely Hincks now regretted having parachuted him into a difficult situation that proved even more challenging than he had anticipated: at Port Stamford McCarroll faced new challenges that even the government had difficulty in sorting out and he found that he had few powerful allies there to help him. As a Reformer and an Irishman in a new place he was more vulnerable than he realized. James Lamb could do only so much for him, though he persistently tried to build a case for his good work on the job, as well as for his courtesy and efficiency.

To some extent McCarroll may have been the victim of his own open and cheerful nature; initially, he tried to be as accommodating as possible to all those around him, be they Americans or Canadians, and he sought to do a duly professional job in protecting the Canadian border from lawbreakers and smugglers. But when threatened, he could be pugnacious and he was not inclined to back down. If, as he claimed, he was on duty daily from 6am to 10pm, he was likely open to the charge that at times, like Leacock's teacher in Mariposa, he drank a little in the line of duty. Certainly, he was no tea-totaller. By nature a bon vivant, he enjoyed entertaining travellers and friends over a drink at the Elgin House Hotel or at dinner in his own home.

Whatever the case, it was his time to go. And "go" he did, whisked away on Francis Hincks's magic carpet. However, he left Port Stamford to take up the collector's position at Port Credit with reluctance. Only when it became clear to him that his continuing vendetta with the Hamlins was likely to work out against him did he take up the offer of a less stressful posting. It is less clear how much he realized that Samuel Zimmerman was delighted to see him go.

In a matter of weeks after his departure, much changed at Port Stamford. In short order Zimmerman, the local financier and wealthy Tory, announced the construction of a new bank and office building at the village, one that would include ample space for the customs collector. Responding to Zimmerman's pressure, Hincks appointed Gerald McMicken to the collector's position in McCarroll's stead. McMicken was a Niagara Falls man with strong Tory connections. Moreover, he was Zimmerman's man, and Zimmerman served as one of his sureties.

What conclusions can be drawn from McCarroll's busy but tempestuous stay in the Niagara region? The challenges facing a customs collector at a busy pedestrian border crossing make for interesting reading, especially when that officer was a literate, self-promoting, and engaging individual. Then as now, the fact of American incursions into Canadian territory and the attitude of

Americans to Canada and Canadians could be irritating, challenging, and controversial. Then as now political stakes often underlay events on the surface.

McCarroll's Niagara experiences demonstrate a high level of cultural engagement. He had a protean energy for the arts and a strong commitment to writing, music, and performance that is too often missing from the record of – indeed our general sense of – life in nineteenth-century Ontario. Along with James Lamb and John Richardson, he did much to feed the musical appetites of "music-mad" St Catharines in the early 1850s. The three shared a desire, with a fond backward gaze to Ireland and the old world, to encourage both the local musical culture and what Lamb called the creation of a "home literature." Lamb saw his friend McCarroll as one of those rare creative forces to be promoted and valued. Little wonder then that he began to publish a number of his poems in the *Evening Journal* soon after McCarroll left for Port Credit.

Evading the "Curse of Swift":
Port Credit, 1853–56

AS FRANCIS HINCKS HAD PROMISED, there was less activity and certainly less controversy for a customs collector at Port Credit. Located eleven miles east of Hamilton and eighteen miles west of Toronto on the shore of Lake Ontario, the port at the Credit River provided McCarroll with one stellar advantage; it offered daily steamer service to Toronto and Hamilton. He held the post from April 1853 to May 1856, and during this time he was drawn magnetically to the literary, musical, and theatrical opportunities available in Toronto. He spent at least a day each week in the city, staying overnight at a hotel near the waterfront. Toronto became his new cultural home, the site of his most notable achievements and literary experiments, and a place where he could hobnob with some of the musical greats of the age.

In 1853, Port Credit was a small, sleepy village on Lake Ontario. Its harbour was in poor condition, not having been deeply dredged for years, and it had a notoriously unhealthy climate. The 1851 census reported a population of only 250 for the village, though work on the Great Western Railroad line was moving west from Toronto and had given rise to "Corktown," an Irish shanty settlement on Port Credit's eastern outskirts. The Cottons, a local Tory family who had emigrated from County Roscommon in western Ireland, not only controlled several of the village's public facilities but also owned the Port Credit Harbour Company. James Cotton (1812–1888) was the postmaster and owner of a number of wharves and storehouses while Robert (1809–1885), a justice of the peace, ran a store and the shipyard. A third Cotton, Thomas, would become the collector of customs after McCarroll was transferred to Toronto.[1] But being farmers and shopkeepers at heart, James and Robert Cotton were unwilling to undertake the improvements needed for the harbour. No doubt, they were also wary of the economic changes that would follow the completion of the Great Western Railroad.[2] Thus, by the time McCarroll arrived, Port Credit's harbour was in need of a large capital infusion to improve its operations; in the meantime, only small-scale dredging was being undertaken on a yearly basis.

By contrast to the bustle of salesmen and tourists around Port Stamford's international bridge, customs traffic at Port Credit was modest at best and predictable by season. It was by no means a plum appointment in the customs service; nevertheless, as collector, McCarroll would earn a comfortable salary of 125 pounds per annum while enjoying relief from the pressures he had faced at the border.[3] Lumber and wheat were Port Credit's leading exports, the former in the spring and the latter in the fall, spurred by the needs of British and allied troops then engaged in the Crimean War. The dates of that war – 1853–56 – coincided exactly with McCarroll's appointment at the Credit.

The port at the Credit had earned an unpleasant reputation not only because of its inadequate docks and yearly silting but also because of the low-lying, swampy conditions of the harbour. Writing from nearby Streetsville in 1858, the Rev. R.J. MacGeorge called Port Credit "that Goshen of ague" in his Laird's column for the *Toronto Daily Leader*.[4] McCarroll's predecessor as collector, James Royce Yedding, had begged his superiors for a transfer because of the unrelenting ill health of his entire family. He complained to Commissioner Bouchette about "the unhealthiness of Port Credit" and the debilitating effect of the ague. In August 1852 he reported that the recurrent malarial disease, always at its worst in the summer months, was "killing us." He further claimed that the illness was so bad that it was affecting both his mind and his body.[5]

These complaints finally led Bouchette to recommend a change in the collectorship for Port Credit, facilitating McCarroll's exit from Port Stamford. Given a choice of ports,[6] McCarroll had opted for the Credit, thereby avoiding what he called "the curse of Swift" – the bane of active, intelligent Irishmen everywhere – while positioning himself closer to Toronto's more active cultural life.[7] Nevertheless, while hoping to restore his solid record as a customs officer, he inadvertently exposed his family to the mosquito-plagued environs of the Credit harbour. Inadequacies in the collector's house and office may also have been factors in Yedding's complaint, but there is no record of McCarroll's complaining about that aspect of his Port Credit appointment.

The malarial harbour was not long in affecting the McCarroll family. Within three months McCarroll wrote to Bouchette requesting a leave because one of his daughters had taken so ill that their doctor had recommended an immediate ·change of scene for her (25 July 1853). He asked specifically for permission to "accompany her to my late Post, or some other point, for a short period," leaving his brother-in-law, John Davis, in charge of the office. The business in late summer, he reported, "is … scarcely worth referring to" and young John had already gained valuable experience in helping him with his Port Stamford duties.[8]

A brief holiday was, however, no relief from the unhealthy conditions affecting the family. During his three-year tenure McCarroll persisted in such complaints. In a letter dated 4 February 1854, he described the climate at the port as "malarial" and "devastat[ing]." A year later, on 20 April 1855, he reported that his family had "never enjoyed a single week's health" since their arrival and that "three of them, at this moment, are afflicted with sickness."[9]

James Lamb and his family in St Catharines were very much on McCarroll's mind during the spring and summer of 1853; his family missed the Lambs' supportive congeniality and shared musical evenings. While the leave he requested – a rare "indulgence" as he called it – allowed them to visit the Lambs, previously scheduled concerts likely spurred the visit. Two months before McCarroll requested his leave, he had travelled to Oakville, another village on Lake Ontario, just west of Port Credit, to perform in a church bazaar concert with two of his former St Catharines' musical partners, pianist and singer Miss Graydon and her pupil, Norah Lamb. Joining the trio was the popular Toronto tenor James Dodsley Humphreys. In puffing the concert, the *Streetsville Review* spoke highly of Humphreys as a singer while assuring its readers that "Mr C. has not his equal as a flutist in Western Canada."[10]

As well, Lamb had begun to publish McCarroll's poems in the *St Catharines Evening Journal*: "Lines" (How oft' while wandering thru some desert place) (12 May 1853) was followed by "Ocean" (2 June), "Gold" (16 June), "Hindia's Song" (30 June), and "Lines" (What gorgeous streaks the horizon now unfolds) (3 September). The "beautiful lines" of McCarroll's "Gold" even elicited a poetic response from one "Samuel Sawbones," a pseudonymous contributor to that newspaper.[11] As he had done after leaving both Peterborough and Cobourg, McCarroll sought to keep his memory fresh by sending back poems to his St Catharines readers. Such poems were not, however, new. Four had been published either in the *Cobourg Star* or the *Peterborough Weekly Despatch*.

Port Credit in the 1850s: The Backwater Blues

During their three dull and uncomfortable years at Port Credit, the McCarrolls witnessed two notable events. The first, in 1855, was the long-awaited completion of the Great Western Railroad. It passed through Port Credit, linking Toronto to Hamilton and points west, including St Catharines and Port Stamford. The train gave Mac quicker access to Toronto and Hamilton than the two Lake Ontario steamers, the *Eclipse* and the *Queen*, could provide. Thus, his travelling propensities were given freer rein. By rail he could journey to Toronto for 37½ cents each way and to Hamilton for 75 cents one way. Nevertheless, railway construction brought its own problems and in Port Credit there was a notable riot in August 1855 involving the Irish and Dutch labourers who inhabited the Corktown shanties some two miles from the village. As acting magistrate, Robert Cotton had the job of restoring the peace and later apologizing to the local public because it took police from Toronto over eight hours to arrive at the scene.[12]

In April of that same year there was a severe fire at the harbour, originating in James Cotton's warehouse near Nelson's Tavern. It roared through many of the wooden buildings serving the port. While most of the boats and ships were saved, the fire left the docks on the west bank "a blackened ruin."[13] This was the busier and more accessible of the two wharves. The fire also destroyed seven adjacent buildings and warehouses, several of which were owned by one or other of the Cotton brothers. Losses were reported at $30,000 and harbour operations were partially curtailed for a time.[14] Since newspaper reports do not mention it and McCarroll did not file a report among his infrequent letters to headquarters, it is likely that the collector's house and office were unaffected.

In his letters to customs headquarters McCarroll had little to say about the town of Port Credit and the people he interacted with there. His letters are distinctive only in the regularity of his complaints about the ague and its "wretched" effects on his family. In one missive he even implied that it might be a solid business decision for the department to close down the port, given its several drawbacks.[15] In fact, business was so slow that, to some observers, it hardly seemed worth it for the department to pay the collector a yearly salary. Not surprisingly, Commissioner Bouchette noted on one of McCarroll's letters that the collection of fees at the port for one quarter was a mere 150 pounds, only marginally more than the collector's annual earnings. The implementation of the Reciprocity Treaty with the United States in 1854, encouraging free trade between the countries, seems to have had little effect on the income generated at the Credit, at least during McCarroll's time.

Like Yedding, McCarroll could not resist badgering his superiors about a more congenial appointment. Indeed, he was not long in making himself familiar with customs personnel in Toronto. A few days after the 1855 fire at Port Credit harbour, he wrote to Bouchette requesting a Toronto appointment but making no mention of the losses experienced at the harbour. It would appear that Bouchette had earlier promised him a new posting, "after a certain period, say 3 years." However, having learned from Collector Meudell at the Port of Toronto that there was increased need there for someone to fill "certain arduous and indispensable duties hitherto discharged inefficiently,"[16] McCarroll quickly put his name forward. Were he to receive such a "kindness" from government – "a kindness of no ordinary kind," as he put it – he asked only that he be allowed to "retain my present rank" and that "if any notice of my appointment appear officially, that it shall be so worded as to place me correctly before the public."

A positive official announcement was as important to him as an improvement in his current salary. While he needed the income, he knew that his real capital lay in his public reputation. Since some observers might see his writings as contrary to official government positions and as evidence that he was misusing his time, he frequently used pseudonyms, especially in Toronto, to disguise his various literary forays.

The Lure of Toronto

The attractions of Toronto quickly took hold of James McCarroll's imagination. A move there, he knew, would be better for his entire family. Having suffered considerably from the ague at Port Credit, his four daughters would benefit from better health and greater opportunities for friendships and music training. Ann and her brother John would be able to see more of their mother, who had moved to the city from Peterborough. There too he would enjoy the challenge of a more demanding customs position, the opportunity to mix with a wide circle of literary and musical people, and the cultural life available in the city. Thus, despite his Port Credit duties, he and Ann travelled to Toronto as often as once a week. On such occasions he left his brother-in-law in charge of his customs duties.

A look at the register of guests at prominent Toronto hotels (published daily, but somewhat irregularly in the *Daily Leader*) reveals the frequency of his visits. Usually, he stayed at Russell Ingles's Wellington Hotel, located on Wellington

Street near the harbour. He was there with Ann on 19 July 1853, for example,[17] and there he sometimes met old friends like William Cluxton and Charles Perry of Peterborough, William Weller from Cobourg, William McDonnell from Lindsay, and Frederick Griebel, who came in from Hamilton to perform.

During his visit of 21 November 1853, he attended a memorable concert at St Lawrence Hall, the city's new music venue. Located on King Street, near Yonge, it had been built in 1850 precisely for big cultural occasions. The headliner that evening was the *petit* Ole Bull, the "marvelous and famed violinist" from Norway who was appearing in what he called his "farewell North American tour."[18] Ole Bull performed on the following two evenings as well. Accompanying him were tenor Salvatore Patti and his much publicized daughter and protégé, nine-year-old Signorina Adelina Patti (in later years recognized as "the foremost singer of the nineteenth century"), and the "swashbuckling" conductor-impresario Maurice Strakosch, a well-travelled Czech pianist who had married Adelina's older sister Amalia.[19] Ole Bull also played two concerts in Hamilton. Twice that same year (31 August and 17 October) the celebrated English soprano Madame Anna Bishop, who would prove to be the most durable of the travelling divas of the mid-nineteenth century, gave bravura performances at St Lawrence Hall, accompanied by her partner and harpist, Nicolas-Charles Bochsa. They too chose to stay at the Wellington Hotel during their visits.[20]

Such events were pure joy for McCarroll, fulfilling his desire to hear and meet some of the greatest European musicians of the day. Well-known performers were increasingly drawn to North America in the 1850s by the prospect of big-money concert tours. P.T. Barnum had raised the threshold with his highly publicized Jenny Lind tour of 1851. Though Ole Bull (1843) and Anna Bishop (1851) had toured North America prior to 1853, there was a new level of awareness among ambitious impresarios and musicians of the profits to be made from music-hungry audiences in America, Canada, Mexico, and Cuba. Notably, Bull's 1853 visit to America was described as "one of the most popular and lucrative tours" of his long career. For his part, McCarroll had delighted in hearing both Jenny Lind and Catherine Hayes in 1851 (see chapter 4) and had closely followed Anna Bishop's numerous visits to Canada. A decade later Terry Finnegan would wax poetic about Bishop's Toronto concerts. The Italian Opera came to the city for the first time in 1853, performing the first full-length opera, *Norma*, ever heard in the city.[21] Basking in the excitement of these occasions, McCarroll planned his visits accordingly. Moreover, he was eager to write about such events and to help raise the level of audience appreciation of talented visiting musicians.

"A Modern Orpheus" in Hamilton and Toronto

McCarroll continued to perform in public concerts either by invitation or when opportunities arose. From 1852 to 1855 he took part in concerts in Oakville, Hamilton, St Catharines, and Peterborough, all while living in Port Credit. In 1856, after moving to Toronto, he began to appear in a number of charity concerts in the city. His performances there numbered close to twenty over the next decade.

Aside from the Oakville concert with J.D. Humphreys in 1853, he was invited to perform in the first of three Grand Concerts beginning on 4 October of that year in conjunction with the annual Provincial Agricultural Exhibition and the Building Fund for Christ Church, Hamilton. R.G. Paige of the Toronto music company Small and Paige, and the organist at St James Cathedral, organized the event and brought together McCarroll, soprano Mrs John Beverly Robinson (nee Mary Jane Hagerman), Jules Hecht, J.D. Humphreys, organist W. Ambrose, and himself on piano.[22] McCarroll was billed in advertisements as "a Flutist of great reputation in the Musical World, though an Amateur."[23] Reviewing the concert, the *Hamilton Gazette* made special mention of "that delightful flutist, Mr J. McCarroll of Port Credit – a modern Orpheus – whose sweet melodies imparted a kind of enchantment and charmed the whole soul and body" (10 October 1853). He played Forde's "Fantasie" with Paige on pianoforte and then joined Paige, Hecht, and Humphreys in the glee that served as the concert's finale.

McCarroll performed with J.D. Humphreys and Frederick Griebel in a concert on behalf of the Odd Fellows of the town of Dundas on 2 August 1853. An evening musicale in St Catharines, billed as a fundraiser for Stephenson House, followed on 23 August 1855. Likely there were more such events, small or large. Information depends on newspaper advertisements and reviews and the preservation of the relevant newspaper issues in local archives.[24]

Making Literary Inroads:
The *Toronto Daily Leader* as Home Base

The *Toronto Leader* began its operations at a fortuitous time for James McCarroll. James Beaty, a shoemaker from Ireland who had become a very successful businessman in Toronto, started the paper in February 1852. He chose as his editor Charles Lindsey, the son-in-law of William Lyon Mackenzie and the former assistant editor of the *Toronto Examiner*, the Reform newspaper begun by Francis Hincks.²⁵ Like Beaty, the English-born Lindsey favoured the Reform cause and championed Hincks's political career and ideas. By 1851, after Robert Baldwin's surprising retirement from active politics, Hincks had evolved from Baldwin's heir apparent in Canada West to the leader of the Reform Party.²⁶

By July 1853 when the *Leader* became a daily, it began billing itself as "the first liberal daily journal ever published in Canada."²⁷ Moreover, it had begun an aggressive campaign to challenge George Brown's *Globe* as the widest circulating and most important daily in Canada West's largest city.²⁸ Liberal-conservative politics, Hincks's economic plans, the doings of Lord Elgin, homeopathy, spiritualism, railroad ventures, city development, "bloomerism" (dress reform), and anti-slavery issues vied for attention in its columns.²⁹

McCarroll found a friend and kindred spirit in Charles Lindsey. They shared a liberal-conservative, Reformist political vision, but they also agreed that they could make a mark by encouraging an improved level of cultural awareness and activity in the city and in the Canadas as well. A shrewd appraiser of journalistic talent, Lindsey recognized in McCarroll a useful and versatile colleague who, by talent and experience, could speak to and promote the arts far more authoritatively than he could. He also saw much to admire in the prolific and urbane Tory Robert Jackson MacGeorge, a Scottish-born Anglican minister then living in Streetsville and editing that town's newspaper. Later in 1854, Lindsey brought to the *Daily Leader* Daniel Morrison, an experienced journalist and theatre critic, and a few years later he engaged the eldest of James Beaty's three young relatives, the Belford brothers, who had arrived in Toronto fresh from Ireland. Charles Belford would later become the *Daily Leader*'s editor while the youngest, Robert, would remain a close friend of McCarroll in New York.

Though living in Port Credit, McCarroll offered four kinds of literary input to Lindsey. He eagerly contributed "original" poems for publication, thus bolstering an aspect of the *Leader* not seen in its early issues. Second, he wanted to become a music and theatre critic when his customs schedule allowed him the time to attend performances. Third, he was a dedicated Irishman who could speak enthusiastically for Irish interests in Canada, a subject that was certainly dear to James Beaty's heart; in this way he could offer a friendly Celtic counterpoint to MacGeorge's cheerful Scottish excesses. Finally, by means of pseudonyms, he was prepared to write editorial pieces that would address aspects of the paper's political opinion, be supportive of Hincks's political manoeuvrings, and add an "objective" voice to the discussion of such controversial topics as spiritualism.

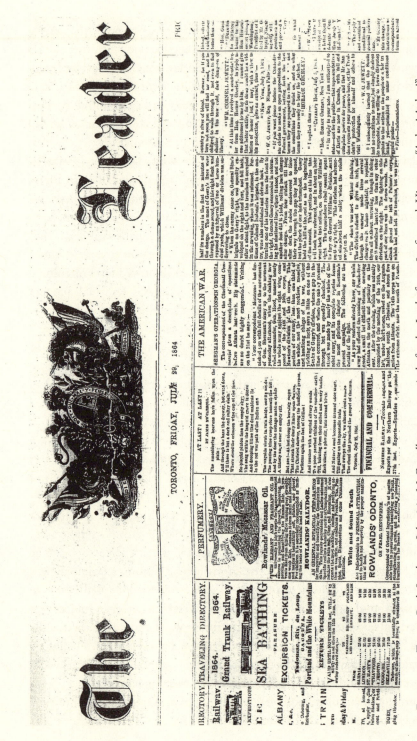

5.1 Front page, *Toronto Daily Leader*, 29 July 1864. McCarroll wrote extensively for the *Leader* from 1863 forward. His poem "At last! At last!" appears on the centre of the page just below the date on the centre of the page. Bata Library Microfilm Collection, Trent University.

Charles Lindsey, like MacGeorge, was no spiritualist. Still, because the movement was arousing a great deal of public curiosity, he was willing to indulge McCarroll's personal enthusiasm. If Lindsey was a straight and somewhat sober shirt as an editor, McCarroll readily served as his loose-fitting sweater: he was more wide-ranging, more inclined to humorous takes, more prone to be outspoken, and more open to articulating everyday human experience, though always attentive to prevailing social standards.[30]

McCarroll's first appearance in the *Leader*, other than in the lists from hotel registers, was his poem "The Woods," which appeared on 23 October 1853. "Written for the Leader" from Port Credit, it is a mood piece about the approach of winter. Notable for its facility with image and its somber restraint, it predates by several decades Archibald Lampman's evocative Ontario poems like "In November." "The Woods" vividly captures the sense of loss that accompanies the chill onset of winter and the sudden "blast" of a snowstorm in the Canadian woods:

The mourning woods now bare their aching breast,
    And wildly toss their naked arms on high
O'er the last shreds of their autumnal vest
    That float in eddies through the cold, bleak sky.

The sear earth wraps its sackcloth round their feet,
    And snows like ashes fall upon their head,
While many a bitter tear of cutting sleet
    Is darkly o'er the leafless ruin shed.

And the chill fingers of the wintery blast
    O'er their wild harp-strings are in sadness swept,
Till one might feel the beauties of the past
    Lay not unsung, unhonored, and unwept.

"The Woods" ushered in what would be a virtual showcase of McCarroll's poetic range and themes in the *Daily Leader*. Recognizing him as a significant poet, Lindsey gave him privileged space in his paper. From October 1853 until 1865, close to ninety McCarroll poems appeared in the *Leader*, occasionally under pseudonyms but most often under his own name. Notably, the poems were usually found on page three in the editorial material, rather than in the upper-left box on page one that typically served as the "Poet's Corner." This positioning privileged him. Few nineteenth-century Canadian poets could claim such a special place for their work. It is not surprising that his poems caught the attention of Edward Hartley Dewart as he searched for the leading "Canadian" poets to include in his path-breaking anthology. Dewart was an attentive reader who responded positively to the quality of his poems in the *Daily Leader*.[31]

By the end of 1855, seventeen of McCarroll's poems, most of them new and original, had appeared in the *Daily Leader*. The output was the result of the free time and surge of creative energy McCarroll experienced while living so quietly in Port Credit. Notable among these poems are "To Bacchus," "Tennyson," "Impromptu" (What, now? – Signor Tenore, what's the matter?), and "Lines" (There's a pool of Bethesda in each of our hearts).

"To Bacchus" appeared in the *Daily Leader* on 8 February 1854 and in James Lamb's *St Catharines Evening Journal* the following day under the pseudonym YOD. It was a penname that McCarroll used often from 1853 to 1855 as a convenient means of disguising his columns for the *Daily Leader*. It is a provocative poem by a man who enjoyed a congenial drink or three. Adopting the melodramatic schematization of the Temperance movement (an ongoing and growing campaign strongly backed by both the newspapers), the poem nevertheless envisions a powerful psychological reality that McCarroll knew well – the "dark deceit" and attractive "spell" that can seize control of "the votary of the bowl," thus encouraging creativity on the one hand but rendering the votary a breaker of hearts and the agent of his own destruction on the other. Outwardly, the poem applies the language of Temperance, but on a deeper level, and especially in the second stanza, it recognizes the extent of human attraction to the welcoming bowl and to Bacchus's "sunny wreath." In recognizing the role that wine has played in "a thousand glories of the past" and in the pursuit of "Fame," the poem subtly affirms McCarroll's personal agenda as a poet, even as it acknowledges aspects of the creative spirit with which he had to wrestle in his private life. The poem also represents the kind of dour moral commentary at work in the society of the day, a commentary very much at odds with his glowing tribute to the magic of still-brewed whiskey in his rollicking novel "The New Gauger," which he wrote two years later:

As did the Olympian Thunderer's last embrace,
In ashes lay thy Boeotian mother's charms,
So now, from age to age, the human race
Lies crushed to dust within thy iron arms.

O'er every clime and tongue thy spell is cast;
And Fame, herself, while blushing for our sires,
Owns that a thousand glories of the past,
Catch half their lustre from thy wanton fires.

Tear from thy brow that sunny wreath – false god,
To thee belongs no leaf of vernal bloom;
Thy vintage from the broken heart is trod,
And thou should'st wear the emblem of the tomb.

Unmask, and let the votary of the bowl
Feel, for a moment, all thy dark deceit; –
Fear not – he'll clasp thee closer to his soul,
And live and die a leper at thy feet.

With the Crimean War dominating international news, he wrote three related poems. The first, "The Six Hundred" (20 February 1855), commemorated Tennyson's freshly famous poem about the charge of the light brigade. From that crushing loss of men, it gleans "a Thermopylae" won, "glorious to [England]." Then on 18 May, again from Port Credit, he honoured Tennyson himself in an exclamatory mode. Tennyson's "sublime" and weighty poetry was music to his ears, a symphony to be chanted "in booming chorusses" above the storm. Tennyson was, for him, a poet for the ages, a maker of music capable of outlasting Parnassus. Writing as a fellow poet from one of "the pilgrim nations," he gave voice to the great admiration shared by many in Canada for Tennyson's achievements. "Tennyson!" reads as follows:

Lord of the thunder-toned, colossal lyre
Whose huge, harmonious cables swing, sublime,
O'er the foundations of thy monument
Those ponderous masses of immortal rhyme –
Vast, glowing blocks of adamantine fire
That bid defiance to all change and time,
From proud Parnassus by the lightning rent,
Until, at last, its total bulk shall lie
Beneath thy feet, and thou shalt upwards climb
Into the great, broad, startled firmament.
There thou shalt blaze, half hid from mortal eye,

Above the glorious sea of the last cloud,
Where never shadow quarreled with the sun,
Or tempest raged, unbitted, to and fro.
There, thou shalt mark the pilgrim nations come
To chant thy deep-toned symphonies below,
And, when the booming chorusses are done,
Behold them wave ten thousand hands on high,
Towards thy fierce-flaming head that cleaves the sky.
And shout, "Hail Tennyson! – Immortal Tennyson!"[32]

Such high and solemn praise stands alone, but, as was often the case, the humorist in McCarroll found outlets in current events. In "Impromptu" (12 May 1854), he brought together his love of accomplished professional singing and the ongoing public concern about the Crimean War. The celebrated Italian tenor Mario (Giovanni Matteo), who was then performing in New York, had publicly announced his intention to enlist and fight under the banner of Victor Emmanuel, the King of Sardinia.[33] Always attuned to news about music from Europe, McCarroll made light of Mario's apparently high-minded ambition. He placed music and the pleasure it delivers to audiences far above the call of war and what he saw as a case of knight errantry. Such talent must not be wasted, whatever one's loyalties; "damn it," he wrote firmly, "it's some new piece we want and not your fighting."

Rich in musical and military reference, the poem cleverly blends the comedic and the colloquial in identifying a decision that could lead to a terrible waste of talent. Gleefully punning to the finish (excessive punning was much favoured by many poets of the day, including McCarroll), he urged Mario "To stay where the tenor of your way is blest":

What, now? Signor Tenore, what's the matter?
You, whom we used to fete and feed and flatter,
Now going to rob us of our purest pleasures;
You, who have been so long our ears delighting
    With your Andante and Allegro measures,
And gambols through the much astonished gamut,
Come, tell us, have you lost your senses – damn it!
    It's some new piece we want and not your fighting.

In spite of France, Victoria or Emmanuel,
Or all the rest, the Russ, may chance to tan you well.
A rolling fire is not your proper role:
Your troupe, Signor, should never be at war,
    Nor be a troop of horse; and, 'pon my soul,
Our Cantatrices shan't be Cantinieres,
Or if in love with military airs,
    They shall not take them from "Etoile du Nord,"

And, then, suppose, for instance, that a bullet
Should ever graze your thorax or your gullet,
You might, forever afterwards, be wheezy;
And when Sardinia was to peace restored
    And you unto the arms of Giulia Grisi,
I can assure you, you'd look very droll,
With all your honors at your button hole,
    To find "*come gentil*" was not encored.

Or when you met the "Rounds" at night, I'll wager
If "who goes there?" was sung out, in G major,
You'd lose yourself, and quite forget the word;
And if there followed, "stranger, quickly tell,"
    You'd answer, in a fine sonorous third,
With such a glorious run and mellow roar
As fine, old Braham gave in days of yore,
    "Above, be-e-e-low, good-night, all's well."

Although her faith to you may never waver,
This crotchet must make Donna Giulia quaver –
To see you madly rushing into Russia,
Where all the armies of the mighty Czar –
    Or some of them, at least, – are sure to crush you:
And just because, you who have shone so long
In one bright sphere, the Lucifer of song,
Should fancy to become a shooting star.

Stay where the tenor of your way is blest;
The Opera suits your operations best,
What do you care for a small country King?
You who have robbed the critics of their spleen;
　　You who have made the pit and boxes ring;
The Crimea you would find in such a state,
That you'd cry *mea culpa*, when too late,
Like that old, titled noodle, Aberdeen.[34]

"Lines" (There's a pool of Bethesda) is a short and hopeful lyric that appeared on 26 September 1855. It speaks to McCarroll's increasing familiarity with Toronto and his sober recognition of the impoverished and down-trodden condition of so many of his fellow beings, even as it celebrates "that spirit of Mercy" and "compassion" that dwells deep in human nature. The poem, dated "Toronto, 23 September," is the first of many in which he pictured the overworked and the misunderstood poor of the city, especially the Irish immigrants who had recently flooded into Toronto in the wake of the potato famines. The poem calls for a pure and humane response to the "strangers" and sufferers among us:

There's a pool of Bethesda in each of our hearts,
　　Where an angel descends at some hour of the day,
To stir up its depths till the shining foam starts,
　　In the hope that we'll sprinkle mankind with the spray.

Every drop in a shower of compassion should fall,
　　On the poor weary ones that are strangers to rest,
Till a rainbow of hope hanging over them all,
　　Blazes full of love-light that pours from our breast.

Then, let not that spirit of Mercy, in vain,
　　Dip his plumes in this innermost fount of the soul,
Nor those waters subside into coldness again,
　　Till some leper that weeps on their verge is made whole.[35]

Pseudonyms and Masks

In deciphering authorship in mid-nineteenth-century Canadian newspapers, a reader is bound to falter. It is almost impossible to identify a writer of individual pieces, be they editorials, reviews, or letters to the editor, unless one comes with a particular clue in hand. Writers were rarely identified by name. However, one often finds catchy pseudonyms on editorial pages or in columns, a few of which can be traced to specific authors. Some contemporary readers would, no doubt, have been curious to know the identity of contributors named CATO, FAIR PLAY, CLEOPS, CIS, VIATOR, MARCO POLO, LAIT-IN-THE-DAIE, or CRUX, while others would simply have accepted the convention for what it was. By contrast, insiders would have known who was who, for newspaper offices were meeting places for the politically like-minded in the towns and cities of Canada West.

Thus, those who examine surviving newspapers from the 1840s and 1850s in search of specific authors beyond the editor usually draw a blank. Even the authorship of editorials can be a mystery: there is no guarantee that the paper's current editor wrote all the editorial material, especially in a busy city environment.

To this challenge, James McCarroll proves a partial exception. To find him one has to follow his movements closely. Some of his alternative names can be verified by checking poems published with pseudonyms against the poems he published under his own name in *Madeline and Other Poems* (1889).[36] For example, "To Bacchus" (see *Madeline*, 179) appeared in two newspapers over the name of YOD.[37] In *Madeline* under the title "An Easy Lesson in Humor and Versification" (287–9), one also finds YOD's comic poem "A Yarn" ("In the style of [Thomas] Hood"), which appeared in the *Daily Leader* on 23 March 1854. He used that same pseudonym for some of his columns in both the *Toronto Daily Leader* and the *St Catharines Evening Journal*. YOD, and relatedly TEMA, became two of his editorial signatures in the early 1850s.

McCarroll used pseudonyms from the beginning of his journalistic career. His pre-Toronto writing reveals at least four jaunty masks, notably CRUX in the *Peterborough Weekly Despatch*, SOPRANO in the *Cobourg Star* and the *St Catharines Evening Journal*, CRUCIBLE in the *St Catharines Evening Journal*, and, on at least one occasion, DENIS FINNEGAN in the *Cobourg Star*. Such disguises allowed him to play fast and loose with events or to attack rival editors while protecting his own identity, especially after he became a public official. They gave him the freedom to speak out about current social and political matters; they provided a platform for attacking particular individuals; and, on occasion, they provided the opportunity to experiment with comical vernacular voices. His most significant later pseudonyms, TERRY FINNEGAN (following from the experiment with "Denis Finnegan") and SCIAN DUBH (Celtic for "black knife"), would appear in the 1860s.[38] Certainly, TERRY FINNEGAN became the most popular and durable of his ventriloquisms; it was the name most closely associated with his literary reputation in pre-Confederation Toronto.

Writing Reviews for the *Daily Leader*

During the mid-1850s, while still living in Port Credit, McCarroll became a reviewer of musical and theatrical performances in Toronto for the *Daily Leader*. It remains unclear, however, when and for how long he wrote such reviews. Reviews were usually unsigned and there is no extant information concerning which writers Charles Lindsey chose for specific reviewing assignments. Furthermore, city newspapers produced several editions on a daily basis in the 1850s; thus, a search for specific columns is further stymied by the absence of other published editions.[39]

In 1853 McCarroll convinced Lindsey to let him review musical and theatrical performances. He later wrote reviews of music for the *Colonist* as well. It was an assignment he coveted. He told biographers like Henry Morgan that he wrote reviews in the *Leader* and the *Colonist* – as if to say, don't forget what I did. Indeed, he saw himself as a pioneer in arts reviewing.[40] As Charles Hildreth later phrased it, his "long and useful career" took place "in the very marketplace of life, among the busiest toilers of the world."[41]

Lindsey was convinced by friends like McCarroll to make the *Daily Leader* Toronto's first large-circulation paper to adopt a critical approach to the arts. On 15 February 1854 Lindsey published a feisty letter from a correspondent named TEMA under the title "Musical Criticism." TEMA, whose sharp views and range of references suggest McCarroll, deplored the mediocre state of criticism, "musical or otherwise," in Canada:[42] "With talismanic rapidity, every fiddler, squaller and hurdy-gurdy player is transformed into a Vieuxtemps, a Sontag, or a Liszt; and gentlemen of the burnt cork, banjo and horse bones, wonder at finding themselves locked in the same patronizing embrace, which, but a few hours previously, had clasped, with enthusiastic fervor, the unrivalled Kate Hay[e]s, Alfred Jael or Ole Bull!"[43] TEMA urged "members of the Fourth Estate" to take the lead in raising critical standards as opposed to undermining them through misrepresentation, flattery, and puffery.

On 1 May, in an unsigned editorial – perhaps written jointly by Lindsey and McCarroll – the *Daily Leader* reiterated the view that "Criticism, musical, literary, theatrical has not yet become a necessary part of journalism in Canada." Instead, a "system of ignorant or servile puffery" prevails. As a corrective the editorial announced that the *Daily Leader* would take special aim at "current musical productions." Rather proudly, the editorial further noted that the paper had already printed several reviews of plays at the Royal Lyceum; these reviews, by their surprising forthrightness, had created quite a buzz in the city. "The result has been to create no little commotion among the gossips of the city and some slight trepidation among the actors." McCarroll was the cat in that particular henhouse.

His hand was evident in "Music and Composers" (31 May 1854) where, in seeking "simply, to arouse a spirit of inquiry," he lamented that the achievements of the great European composers were being overlooked in Canada because of the excessive attention paid to American musical fads. He particularly deplored the deluge of "Polkas innumerable" and what were termed "Nigger-songs." With this flood of American popular music, he feared not only a vitiation of taste but also the emergence of "a rattle-trap style" among the young. The only counter to this "musical idiocy" lay "in the hands of professional men" who could speak out in informed ways against the tyranny of pap.

Furthermore, the problem in Canada lay not only in the lack of informed criticism but also in the limited ability of Canadian composers. In that spirit he launched an attack on Toronto musicians who set themselves up as "Mus. Bacs," based on either spurious credentials or less than mediocre abilities. He took direct aim at one "James P. Clark, Mus. Bac." whose songs were then appearing in monthly issues of the *Anglo-American Magazine*. Finding no quarrel with Clark's actual credentials, he itemized the numerous faults in his compositions. They lacked a musical backbone and were "devoid of life, of beauty, of expression." While the article ended somewhat apologetically, it left no doubt that, as "a writer of songs," Mr Clark was very weak.

It is likely that McCarroll also began to write reviews of significant musical performances in the city, beginning with Anna Bishop's concert (17–18 October 1853) and Ole Bull's "Farewell" concert in November.[44] After moving from Hamilton to Toronto earlier in 1854, Griebel announced that he would perform a series of concerts in the city. As an insider and a musical authority, McCarroll was eager to provide positive coverage for his friend. He had no doubt that Griebel was "the most accomplished artist we have ever had among us."

Griebel's January concert included J.D. Humphreys, Mr Hecht, Mr and Mrs Hayter, Mr Haycraft, Mrs J.B. Robinson, and members of the Toronto

Philharmonic Society. McCarroll praised both "the superior tones of the grand piano" and Griebel's performance; moreover, because of his close relationship with the violinist, he was able to report that Griebel's next event would be "a promenade concert" with "everything even better arranged." As a rule, McCarroll was sympathetic with the Toronto musicians and singers who helped to make these concerts successful, and on occasion, he performed with them.

Frederick Griebel also participated in Mr Haycraft's memorial concert (6 October 1855) at St Lawrence Hall in which Mrs J.B. Robinson excelled in her singing of "The Soldier's Funeral." McCarroll noted, however, that, as an Englishwoman, she was less successful in singing Thomas Moore's famous ballad "The Harp That Once through Tara's Halls" as her encore. Similarly, he highlighted Griebel's participation in concerts in November and December 1855. He used his review of the 9 November concert to dress down an over-eager audience for its insistent call for encores, the effect of which was to prolong the concert; "when in twelve pieces, five are encored, there is an absence of [audience] discrimination, as well of all proper feeling." As usual, he praised Griebel, "the magician of the bow"; this time he included allusions to Dean Swift and Samuel Johnson, noting that Griebel's playing would alter Johnson's "reservations about violin playing." He also criticized the flute playing of a local rival, Mr Eccles. Again on 20 December at Mr Haycraft's concert, he praised Griebel's two solos as "masterly exhibitions of the skill of this eminent violinist." In another review in 1855 McCarroll reported on the first-ever Toronto performance of Handel's *Messiah*. Griebel was one of the musicians involved.[45]

Whether McCarroll fouled his own nest by critiquing Toronto musicians like Eccles is difficult to ascertain. It would appear that he was inclined to engage in personal vendettas with some of the city's more influential musicians – for example, James Clark and Henry Carter – thereby undermining his own prospects as both a performer and a critic.

But that would be in later years. Shortly after moving from Port Credit to Toronto, he joined Herr Griebel in at least two concerts. The first, on 17 April 1856, was a Promenade Concert for charitable purposes and the second was a Grand Concert on 16 June 1856. Both took place at the St Lawrence Hall and involved the usual set of Toronto musicians. In each case he contributed a flute solo.

McCarroll's theatre criticism remains shrouded in mystery today. All his reviews were unsigned and he chose not to use a pseudonym for his theatre columns. In fact, Canadian theatre historians have long puzzled over the identity of the *Daily Leader*'s first theatre reviewer. Patrick B. O'Neill, the scholar most closely engaged in this research, was forced to conclude that the person in question had to be Scottish-born Daniel Morrison (1826–1870), largely because it was known that, at some point in 1854, he joined the newspaper as Charles Lindsey's assistant editor and theatre reviewer. But what O'Neill could not have known was that James McCarroll had an earlier connection with Lindsey and was writing in different capacities for the *Leader* by the fall of 1853. Nor could O'Neill be precise about the date on which Morrison began to write his *Leader* columns. What O'Neill did note was "a dramatic change of tone" and the diminishing of a "noticeably cruel streak" in the reviews after 1854. In considering the reviews of 1855–56, he wrote, "It is difficult to recognize the same [fearless] critic" who so upset John Nickinson and his troupe of actors at the Royal Lyceum Theatre during the summer of 1854.[46]

Several factors converge in pointing to McCarroll as the *Leader's* first theatre reviewer. In biographical notes, he made it clear that he wrote music and theatre reviews for both the *Leader* and the (Toronto) *Colonist.*[47] He had a strong personal interest in drama and in later years wrote several plays, one of which was published in New York.[48] Clearly, he welcomed the anonymity that protected his workaday identity as a government employee, leaving him free to be frank and even outspoken in his assessments of play selection and the performances of actors, and to proceed as learnedly as possible, at least until the anger and complaints of Nickinson and his Royal Lyceum Company became a problem for Lindsey.

In this revised scenario Daniel Morrison entered the fray at Lindsey's request to mend fences and establish a milder, less antagonistic line of criticism. Certainly, McCarroll's inclination to write forceful criticism is evident in these early reviews. Morrison's approach was equally well informed but less "ferocious" and more sympathetic to the company's struggles and efforts. No doubt his more positive reviews helped to repair the relationship between the *Daily Leader* and the company; as well, they played a part in his courtship of the company's leading lady, Charlotte Nickinson, whom he married in 1858.[49]

Given the opportunity granted by Lindsey, McCarroll dispensed with the complacent puffery and non-critical adulation that was the norm among Toronto "reviewers" at the time. Beginning late in 1853 he sharply criticized the Royal Lyceum's uninspired productions of Shakespeare's plays, arguing that the company lacked sufficient depth and ability to meet the challenges of staging *Hamlet* and *Othello*. His 1854 reviews included *The Corsican Brothers* (24 March), Sheridan Knowles's *The Wife – A Tale of Mantua* (24 April), Harrison Ainsworth's *Jack Shepherd* (4 May) and *The Soldier's Daughter* (17 May), Bulwer-Lytton's

Money (10 August), and Buckstone's *Green Bushes* (21 September). In each instance the reviewer appeared to be detached and well informed, but the cumulative effect cast a negative light on the quality of the company and the abilities of its more prominent members. In fact, the columns show a greater range of theatre knowledge and practical awareness than might have been expected from a man with as little stage experience as McCarroll. What he knew was based less on his own limited attendance at plays than on his careful reading of New York newspapers and magazines like the *Edinburgh Review.*

In 1853 John Nickinson's Royal Lyceum Theatre Company (RLTC) was undertaking its second season in Toronto. T.P. Besnard had encouraged the company to come to Toronto, and their commitment made Toronto the first Canadian city to support its own resident company, though only for parts of the year. The thirty-four-member troupe, first organized in Utica, New York, played nightly in Toronto to good houses, presenting a variety of plays in repertoire from March to September. Then the RLTC would move on to Hamilton and other Canada West cities. Featuring travelling stars like C.W. Couldock and G.K. Dickinson, the company adjusted its selection of plays to fit the skills and favourite roles of particular visiting stars.

McCarroll's reviews were typically long and thoughtful; they involved an extensive plot summary and insights into recent theatre history.[50] Having noted the current popularity of Dion Boucicault's *The Corsican Brothers* in New York, London, and Paris, he deemed the Nickinson production but tolerably successful. The play lacked backstage arrangements (false doors, quick set changes, and convincing scenery) effective enough to dramatize its spectacular illusions. Arguing that the play would have been better if certain scenes had been cut, he concluded that while Nickinson had done well with the script, he could have done better. A month later, after seeing *The Wife – A Tale of Mantua*, he confirmed Sheridan Knowles's strong reputation as a playwright but critiqued certain casting choices and the onstage mannerisms and weak enunciation of a number of the company's lead actors. He particularly deplored the choice of Eliza Nickinson as Count Florio, "a character totally unsuited for her sex"; the effect undermined the play's attempt to create "the feeling of reality."[51]

A more severe note accompanied the review of *Jack Shepherd.* For McCarroll it was a low and "filthy" piece of theatre, "calculated to gain sympathy and favor from the mob." As such, he deplored its inclusion in the season, even though it was well attended. Plays, he argued, had to have "some higher object [and beauties] in view." The crude representation of low-life vice and reckless living was not itself worthy of dramatic presentation.

We should regret being the means of depriving Mr Nickinson of the receipt of one shilling at the box-office; but he cannot expect us, even though he be unused to criticism, to suppress our views, merely because he thought proper to produce it at his theatre. We believe, too, Mr Nickinson was unwittingly in error when he produced a play so obnoxious where its character is well known; for we believe that gentleman would not willingly bring before the public a play really offensive to refined female taste, and that he has some higher motives besides merely crowding his benches.

In the mode of a high-minded gentleman of the theatre, McCarroll queried Nickinson's play selection. Both moral standards and the abilities of his cast had to be considered when choosing plays for performance. With a coolness that must have sent a chill through the entire company, he added,

'Tis true the staff of the Lyceum are not competent to do full justice to the Shakespearean tragedies and others of scarcely less note they have attempted, and it would be well to make a more judicious selection consistent with the abilities of the company. We have never applied any criticism to the pieces produced in the Lyceum as contrasted with theatres dependent on wider resources, and more opportune appliances; but making every allowance for difficulties in the way of a theatre "so far west," and without intruding beyond our duty to the drama loving public, we should not think it any great enterprise on the part of Mr Nickinson were he to import actors of recognized ability, and at least confine his staff to those who do not "murder" the Queen's English most unmercifully.

Little wonder that Nickinson and his actors found themselves increasingly angry under such sharp scrutiny. Soon therafter, Nickinson pulled his daily advertisements from the *Leader*.

Subsequent reviews sustained the attack. The reviewer continued to critique Nickinson's play selection and the second-rate acting of the company. *The Soldier's Daughter* was a "comedy itself in no particular way deserving of note" and the acting of both G.S. Lee and Nickinson himself was faulted for "want of adherence to the text." By contrast, McCarroll viewed Bulwer-Lytton's *Money* as well chosen in terms of the company's abilities; he praised Lee here for his comedic rather than his dramatic skills. However, his praise seemed faint in light of his other critical judgments. He concluded the review by putting his own efforts into a sympathetic perspective:

we make every allowance in our theatrical notices for the difficulties incurred by Mr Nickinson, in procuring and maintaining in this city, a clever dramatic company and … in reviewing the performances we take no high criterion for our standard. In stating so much we merely do so in order to inform the worthy disciples of the "sock and buskin" that we have no designs upon their reputation, although we have not indulged in anything like the eulogies of contemporaries who sought to persuade every scene shifter in the Lyceum that he was a Macready or a Charles Matthews in his way, and fiercely attacked us for venturing anything to the contrary.

Furthermore, he chided individual Lyceum actors for holding on to such a "primitive notion of criticism" in this more "enlightened" age.

McCarroll's final review – of Buckstone's *Green Bushes* – brought matters to a head. A furious Nickinson had already pulled his Lyceum advertisements from the *Daily Leader*, but he and his company continued to be upset. Even before the *Green Bushes* review, other Toronto newspapers had begun to question and rebuke the severity of the *Daily Leader*'s theatre reviews. The *Patriot*, for instance, took up the case of the wounded egos of actors like Sir William Don and cast blame on Lindsey himself as editor. Lindsey, however, hit back by defending "the exercise of the critic's office"; he added that "the character of some of the performances at the Theatre [were] indefensible, – impure beyond the ordinary license of the drama at the present day."[52] However, he chose not to identify "the gentleman who has usually written on the subject of the drama in our columns."

It is an interesting commentary on early Toronto that neither Lindsey nor his rival editors chose to identify the by-now infamous reviewer in question. In his *Green Bushes* review, McCarroll could not contain his strong Irish pride or his need to answer aggressively those who publicly challenged his opinions. He began by taking issue with a play that depended on national stereotypes long since out of date. The play's overdone Irish character, he wrote, was a fiction perpetuated by English plays: "The leading or Irish character in these productions was made to perpetuate the most stupid blunders conceivable, although with singular inconsistency, he was allowed to exhibit extreme cunning and sagacity. The coarsest farcical humor intended for the supposed national wit, was the chief trait of his conversation, while his disposition was assumed to be of such an extremely volatile nature that he was alternately pugnacious and loving to every person that unluckily crossed his path." After critiquing this unattractive stereotype of "the eternal Paddy," he examined the play itself, deeming it "a drama totally deficient in every desirable feature, except a fair share of novel incident."[53] "A Donnybrook, a dancing-drinking scene, and a 'who'll tread upon the tail of my coat' scene were all jumbled together without the smallest connection to the thread of the play."

Turning to the actors, he gave Madame Duret credit as the "Amazonian" female lead but chastised others in the cast for their elocution and failed attempts at an Irish accent. He ended by offering a riposte to Sir William Don, the popular actor who had criticized the *Daily Leader* reviews in the pages of the *Patriot*. He acknowledged Don's capacity to draw laughs for his comedic portrayal of Master Grinnidge, but severely undercut him with his final critical salvo: "he will be laughed at so long as he remains in his present capacity of 'low comedian' to a fourth class theatre."[54]

At times astute and at times cruelly personal, McCarroll clearly went too far in labelling the Royal Lyceum "a fourth class theatre." It was an unconscionable insult that required either a huge apology or a quiet retreat from the field. John Nickinson's public response forced the *Daily Leader* to offer a defence of its "gentleman" reviewer, but it left the newspaper little choice but to replace him in that capacity. Thus, Lindsey repositioned McCarroll to music criticism and brought Daniel Morrison to the rescue. McCarroll was allowed to retreat – identity still masked and dignity intact – to continue with his poems, musical reviews, political columns, and accounts of spiritualism for the newspaper. The fact that he was still living in Port Credit must have played some part in allowing him to maintain his anonymity.

Some informed people kept the controversy alive in a way that praised the unidentified McCarroll. O'Neill reports that the *London Prototype* criticized Morrison for being too gentle while regretting the loss of the earlier critic who had become "a martyr to public opinion."[55] Thus, McCarroll's venture into theatre reviewing had a more powerful effect than much of his music criticism.

Practising Spiritualism in Muddy York

In his early columns for the *Daily Leader*, McCarroll's preferred pseudonym was YOD. YOD is the tenth or smallest letter in the Hebrew alphabet, hence an iota or a very small entity. He perhaps meant it to signify a brief poem or a short opinion piece sent out to the larger world; he might too have meant to indicate the then modest nature of his literary presence. He used YOD as a cover when he identified and challenged failings of the Canadian press and disputed certain public pronouncements made by leading church officials. He first used YOD in a letter to James Lamb at the *St Catharines Evening Journal*, published on 17 December 1853.

The subject was spiritualism or "table-turning," an increasingly popular but highly controversial movement to which he and his family, like the Moodies in Belleville, were attracted during the early 1850s. McCarroll was responding to an editorial in the *Hamilton Canadian*, which Lamb had reprinted in the *Evening Journal*. Thomas McQueen had dismissed the current mania about spiritualism as "twiddle twaddle" and "bunkum."[56] In his reply McCarroll was deferential, showing due respect for McQueen as a fellow Reformer and poet. Nevertheless, he held that people needed to be more open-minded about the possibilities of enlightenment through the study of supernatural agency. One had to think beyond the New Testament and church protocol, in the full light of nineteenth-century scientific knowledge; then one could proceed to personal inquiry "within the fireside circle of every individual." Our assumptions about Providence, he argued, need to be queried and adjusted. Miracles are not as unlikely as we may be inclined to think and "Hell" is a concept that required enlightened inquiry.

As YOD, McCarroll fired off a second volley in his defence of spiritualist activities, this time addressing "The Editor of the *Leader*," on 27 December 1853. Noting the hostile and unconvincing responses in the press to "this startling agency," he urged greater openness as the most effective means of accessing the truth. "Families of respectability in Toronto" were "almost hourly" experimenting with such possibilities. Then, tongue-in-cheek, he wondered, "Is there not, then, amongst the corps editorial, some scientific-anti-eternal-progressional gentleman willing to step forward and expose this reputed fraud, increase his subscription list, and above all, rescue his darling hell from the utter annihilation threatening it by the doctrines embodied in the new revelations?" The challenge was directed at the likes of Thomas McQueen and his colleagues Charles Lindsey and Robert Jackson MacGeorge, all of whom were firmly opposed to spiritualist "nonsense." Eliminating the concept of our "darling hell" from the rhetoric of institutional religions appealed strongly to McCarroll, as it did to many leading spiritualists. The idea of fire and brimstone was a daunting barrier to progressive thinking.

On 17 January 1854, McQueen replied to YOD's letter in the *St Catharines Evening Journal* under the heading "Modern Spiritualism." In an even-handed manner, he allowed that, while certain events boasted by the spiritualists might involve "wonderful facts," they offered nothing new with regard to the traditional Christian view of immortality. "'Yod' and his fellow spiritualists," he cautioned, needed much more than the mysterious opening of a rusty old lock to make their case.[57] McCarroll answered back on 31 January querying McQueen on his lack of understanding of the factors underlying the enthusiastic support for spiritualism. He found his authorities among the prevailing "experts" of the movement – Dr Dexter, Governor Talmadge, Edward Fowler, and Judge Edmonds – and he noted spiritualism's larger, Christian objectives.[58]

McCarroll's approach to spiritualism was cautious, integrative, and positive; his thinking, he insisted, was not at odds with Christianity:

> Although I am not a convert to spiritualism, I have given the subject some consideration; and can assert, without fear of contradiction, that the professed object of this alleged superhuman intercourse is to alleviate "physical suffering," to dispel "ignorance," to diminish "immorality and gross wickedness," and to promote "love, peace and purity." Upon this, as upon almost every subject, the isolated scraps and garbled extracts that reach us, through the public prints, are an unsafe foundation for the superstructure of our opinions or belief. We must lay our prejudices, or preconceived ideas, aside, and approach the whole mass of evidence, for and against, in the garb of stern philosophy. We, then, as Christian metaphysicians, might, possibly, arrive at the conclusion, that spirit, whether disembodied or in connexion with "this mortal coil," is identical and under the direct control of the Creator.

On 4 February, he responded testily to a "pastoral on table-turning" sent out by the Archbishop of Quebec, Pierre-Flavien Turgeon, which Lindsey had republished in the *Daily Leader*.[59] The archbishop emphasized the pagan and superstitious aspects of the craze and warned Catholics that they were playing loosely with the sin of "divination" in attempting to speak to spirits, be they "blessed" or "damned." Lindsey had praised Turgeon's clear reasoning and eloquence. McCarroll, however, would have none of it and, in the voice of YOD, he conveyed his displeasure to his editor friend.

He chastised Turgeon for his "clerical interference" and for hiding behind "the ban of the church." What the archbishop could not concede was the repudiation of eternal punishment as advocated by well-meaning spiritualists. Such narrow views were inappropriate for "this enlightened age of the world," he asserted, echoing the charge he had made against McQueen. He confidently believed that the world was changing for the better and that some of the old tyrannies of the church would soon have to be viewed from a new perspective.

Drawing on an old Irish joke, he concluded, "I have watched, as narrowly as [the archbishop], the progress of that influence, and confess myself totally unable to arrive at the conclusion he adopts so readily on this head. Nor can I comprehend, clearly, the novel idea that induces him to urge us to abstain from table-turning until we can explain the phenomena on scientific principles, as, it appears to me, to place our thirst for knowledge in a position similar to that occupied by the boy on the bridge in Limerick, when he exclaimed, 'If I had a boat I'd gaff a salmon, only I have no gaff.'"

When Lindsey published a second letter warning against spiritualism – this time by a Rev. Dr Taylor in the Montreal *Gazette* – YOD became more personal. Taylor had declared that rapping mediums "were generally infidels, and [that] their pretensions [were] … as absurd as they were wicked." McCarroll responded by offering a convivial picture of spiritualist experiments conducted in his own Port Credit home. For several nights in January, he reported, four members of his family had sought by means of a spiritual assembly to make "a small work table" move. One night they succeeded because of the presence among them of his nine-year-old daughter Kate who proved "a powerful medium." Given her age and "long established innocent sincerity," there could be no question of infidelism or guilt on her part. Casting himself in the role of detached observer, he described what happened next: "The little walnut gentleman became suddenly animated, until, at last, after waltzing about the room in superb style, [he] commenced answering the interrogations that were showered upon him, by raising two of his feet and stomping three times for 'yes' and once for 'no' – this being the mode agreed upon, as orthodox, by all present."

McCarroll then outlined a series of tests he conducted on Kate as medium, aimed particularly at defining her physical and emotional relation to the dancing table. In these tests he was deliberately scientific. First, he substituted a heavier table, using a fine oil to detect the pressure of her fingers on the surface; then he tested the answers she drew from the spirits by asking Kate to pose questions to them far beyond her own years and experience. His conclusions were muted and mild. Where one might have expected enthusiastic reportage, he admitted that Kate's powers, such as they were, were "unconnected, totally, to any supernatural agency." They arose, he concluded, from her "mental identification" with the events and her personal level of emotional excitement. Still, though he was frustrated by these experiments, he was not, like Taylor, ready to be dismissive. "I never questioned the creed nor the sincerity of thousands of respectable citizens who placed implicit confidence in the spirituality."[60]

Perhaps, he conjectured, we might learn something more relevant to this powerful issue if we looked to the religions of the East for guidance.

Over the next year YOD appears to have been silent on spiritualism. The *Hamilton Canadian* went out of business. The religious disclaimers of Turgeon and Taylor were soon old news; but McCarroll persisted in his fascination. YOD's last word came in a letter – from "our correspondent" – to the *Toronto Daily Leader* on 8 October 1855. Offering no specific reasons, he confessed to his deeper engagement in the spiritualist movement. Since his earlier letters, he had had "opportunities of testing it to the fullest extent; and now I rest," he reported, "in the settled conviction of its being a palpable truth." Drawing authority from "some of the ablest and most astute minds in the community" (that is, thinkers from "the upper stratum of society") and from the evidence of his own "investigations," he had thrown caution aside and gone over to what Susanna Moodie in Belleville rather grandly called a "glorious madness."[61]

Imaginative and curious beings like McCarroll and Susanna Moodie were susceptible to the spiritualist call, but, once they became converts, it appears that their enthusiasm could not endure for long. Some kind of deflating insight, some new disappointment, disrupted their enthusiastic commitment and led them to retire very quietly from the field of spiritualist inquiry. No self-proclaimed spiritualist wished to admit publicly that he or she had been wrong-headed, misdirected, or deceived. There was no further word on the subject from YOD in the *Daily Leader* or the *St Catharines Evening Journal*, though in later years McCarroll would return to spiritualism with renewed enthusiasm.

YOD also proved a useful veil for McCarroll when he wished to address the fast-changing political situation in Canada. A devoted supporter of Francis Hincks from his Peterborough days, he wrote a strongly worded vote of confidence in the premier of Canada West for the *Daily Leader* on 23 March 1854. These were troubling times for Hincks, who had kept the various interests of Reform Party supporters under control longer than anyone thought possible. While his strong support of agrarian and commercial interests was paying dividends for Canada West and while the progress of the Grand Trunk Railroad (and the Great Western) was helping to boost provincial business and optimism, Hincks himself was under public scrutiny for allegedly having reaped personal profits from the negotiations and transactions related to railroad development. In fact, in March he was but a few months away from having to resign his office in the face of mounting opposition pressure. Dismissing as trivial the persistent carping of Tory politicians and journalists, McCarroll voiced his strong support for "the magic touch of this distinguished individual."

Hincks was, for him, one of the "great men of our times." A man of "rare abilities," he was a superior statesman and an enlightened leader "who was ever on the lookout for Canada's 'peculiar interests.'" More than any other Canadian since 1837, he had overseen and helped to encourage the development of the country's "magnificent future." In negotiating a railroad deal with British partners instead of American capitalists, he "has done more to make this a thoroughly British Colony, and to strengthen the bonds that unite us to the mother country, than had ever been accomplished in the history of Canadian legislation." Furthermore, in helping to set up the reciprocity agreement with the United States, "[he] recently reduced the taxes on our imports and still kept the revenue of the country at high tide; while, through the inflexible and enlightened character of his policy, he has kept the neighboring republic within its proper, relative, commercial bounds – a line which it seems ever ready to transgress." If he had "enriched himself" while in office, YOD allowed, he did so "without realiz[ing] one shilling of his reputed fortune at the expense of the interests of Canada." A firm believer in pragmatic politics, McCarroll was ready to justify self-serving means if they achieved important political ends.

Later in 1854 YOD praised Sir Allan MacNab for his pragmatic rescue of Hincks's political interests by helping to form a Reform-minded coalition government in the wake of Hincks's resignation.[62] Hincks, McCarroll maintained, was "scarcely divested of any strength" in stepping down from the premiership. That strength was evident in his recruiting of MacNab to the liberal cause. An influential Tory, MacNab had long been an anathema to Reformers, especially when, in 1849, he persistently attempted to undermine Lord Elgin's credibility as governor general. Since that time, however, he and Hincks had been on friendly terms. They agreed that the economic advantages for Canada West were rooted in Hincks's economic and legislative plans. YOD viewed MacNab's role in the new coalition government as a case of well-considered pragmatism and an indication of the "progressive character of our mental constitution." The politics of the future would call for more enlightened compromise among politicians and less "narrow" adherence to old, outmoded views. In adapting his conservative stand on the long-standing and divisive Clergy Reserves question, MacNab demonstrated real "progressiveness" and leadership. McCarroll ended the column with a tribute to the (now deposed) Hincks and expressed the hope that "Forgetful of the past, he may, if but indirectly, generously throw his great experience and weight into the scale on our behalf, until identified more ostensibly with whatever future projects may affect, in our day, the interests of this fine province."

The *Anglo-American Magazine* (1852–55)

Beyond the pages of the *Daily Leader*, McCarroll's biggest literary opportunity in these years was Thomas Maclear's *Anglo-American Magazine*. Begun in Toronto in July 1852, it set out to be a national showcase of Canadian literary talent and a counter to the flood of American material into the English-Canadian market. Effectively, it replaced Montreal's *Literary Garland* with a Toronto-centred magazine. Its editors were a pair of Scots, the aforementioned R.J. MacGeorge and Gilbert Auchinleck.[63] The magazine lasted nearly four years before succumbing to a lack of paying subscribers and the depressed economy of Canada of 1855. However, it provided substantial opportunities for British-born writers like Catharine Parr Traill, Alexander McLachlan (1817–1896), MacGeorge, and belatedly James McCarroll. He became a contributor once he had settled in Port Credit.

Trained in the Scottish Episcopal Church, MacGeorge immigrated to Canada in 1841 and was ordained by Bishop John Strachan as the Anglican incumbent at Streetsville, a village on the Credit River north of Port Credit.[64] A man of strong literary interests and some journalistic experience in Britain, MacGeorge started the *Streetsville Weekly Review* in 1846 and made it one of the liveliest newspapers in the Toronto area. He also contributed literary articles to the *Globe* and the *Daily Leader*, and edited the *Church* for a time. By 1852 he had developed such a strong reputation as a writer, critic, and humorist that he was for Maclear an obvious choice as editor. However, his literary work and participation in the Orange Order of Canada put a notable strain on his pastoral work and must have caused some concern for Bishop Strachan. In fact, in 1858 MacGeorge would lose his Streetsville parish and return to Scotland.[65] But when McCarroll moved to Port Credit in 1853, he found in "neighbour" MacGeorge a kindred Celtic spirit, though of a pronounced Caledonian stamp.

There is an interesting parallel in their literary careers following from their respective beginnings in Canada. The two writers connected through Lindsey's *Daily Leader*. They had mutual interests in classical or old-world music and they liked to explore the possibilities of vernacular humour in their native idioms. In 1854, MacGeorge was clearly the more prominent of the two. Through his newspaper and the *Anglo-American Magazine*, he had achieved considerable literary stature in the Toronto area; by contrast, fresh from his previous customs appointments in Cobourg and Port Stamford, McCarroll was eager to find a larger audience for his imaginative offspring. MacGeorge became an influential supporter. They shared a passion for their Celtic heritage, though, as a Scot, MacGeorge reserved his warmest praise for a young Scottish poet named Alexander McLachlan who lived on a farm near the village of Erin. In the dandified "Scots" language that MacGeorge used in his "Editor's Shanty," young Alex was a "lovite" and a poet to be lauded. By contrast, McCarroll had little good to say about the dour and turgid McLachlan; a decade later he would use his Terry Finnegan voice to dismiss him as a Lazarus at the gates of poetry, especially after D'Arcy McGee presented McLachlan with an award in Toronto.[66]

Their connection began when MacGeorge, impressed by a McCarroll poem in the *Daily Leader*, republished it on 8 April 1854 in the *Streetsville Weekly Review*. "Lines" (When Winter, that crusty old rogue, brushing by) offers a warm and humorous perspective on winter's cold and gloom that appealed to him.[67] Seldom had geese been put so vividly to poetic purpose.

> When Winter, that crusty old rogue, brushing by,
> Plucks our woods just as if they were geese,
> Oft I notice a smile in his merry, gray eye,
> As he sends their brown tatters adrift through the sky
> To play shadows among its white fleece.
>
> 'Tis because that his lot is not hard after all
> For, while traveling onward, he knows,
> When he shakes a sweet shrub or a forest tree tall,
> That the seeds of wild roses, and acorns fall
> In the print of his frosty old toes.
>
> And this hint with a lesson I'm sure should be rife
> To those wretched old croakers of ours,
> Whose teeth and short nails are forever at strife,
> And who never could see that the blasts throughout life
> Always scatter the seeds of some flowers.[68]

Despite MacGeorge's recognition, it took more than a year in Port Credit for McCarroll to break into the columns of the *Anglo-American Magazine*. Once he did so, in volume 5, no. 5 (November 1854) with his poem "Lines" (How oft, while wandering through some desert place),[69] he was not long in becoming a major contributor of stories, poems, and articles. However, sadly for him (as was too often the case in Canada), the magazine did not last long.

Its final year was 1856. The aforementioned "Lines" speaks to the poet's ability to provide an uplifting perspective in worldly but Christian terms for people struggling "in this dry land of ours." The full text is given in chapter 3.

McCarroll broke through as a poet and writer in 1855. Because his Port Credit duties demanded less of his time and presence on site, he was able to spend more time at his writing desk and to visit Toronto with regularity. Still engaged in his spiritualist experiments but removed from his theatre reviewing for the *Daily Leader*, he continued his musical reviewing and, from Port Credit, he wrote pieces for two major Toronto publications. He contributed eight poems to the *Daily Leader* in 1855,[70] but more impressively he wrote two pieces of fiction for the *Anglo-American Magazine* – one a long story and one a serialized novel – along with an article entitled "The Origin of Printing" and several new poems.[71]

The two narratives drew plenty of positive journalistic response. "The Adventures of a Night," a story belonging to his Port Stamford experiences is treated in chapter 4. "The New Gauger; or, Jack Trainer's Story" appeared in seven installments in the *Anglo-American Magazine* from February to August 1855. At approximately 55,000 words, it is the longest narrative that he completed in his lifetime.

Set in County Leitrim, it is an adventurous tale that takes the reader deep into the good-hearted, "boys-will-be-boys'" world of the Irish-Catholic countryside in 1828. The plot of the novel is described in chapter 1, but here it is worthwhile to consider the effects of McCarroll's vivid use of the "Irish" language he so ably called upon in connecting his Toronto readers with "the full power of the antiquity of Ireland" and "the very essence of romance" inherent in the story.[72] Serving both as a test run for Terry Finnegan's linguistic romps and as a nostalgic return to the world of rural Connaught, "The New Gauger" is a story in love with "Irish talk." It is a comic romp designed to amuse and entertain readers who continued to cherish memories of their Irish antecedents.[73] Still a quintessential Irishman after twenty-five years in Canada, McCarroll threw himself into the narrative, his nationalistic identity in full flower.

"The New Gauger" is peppered with stage-Irish tags, vernacular jokes, and poetical effusions. The text abounds in words and phrases like "ma bouchal," "cugger," "blur and agers," "begorra," "mavourneen," and "goosson." The rural Irish penchant for mispronouncing names is wittily tapped: Jack tells us that Father Conlin attended the "Sorra bun" in Paris as a student, while places like "Bottomy Bay" and "Gibberalther" pop up in conversation. Colourfully colloquial and sometimes surprisingly modern phrases enliven the linguistic flow – "yalla as a kite's claw," "in a pig's whisper," "Go tache your mother to milk ducks," "dead as a duck," "The man in the moon," and "the heavens be about you" are examples.

The story celebrates the hardy drinking culture of male friendship and rural life that helped to sustain Catholic Ireland in the early decades of the nineteenth century. Jokes shared by the boys, "a little sport … in rale style," reflect their rough and ready approach to life, their love of sports like hurling, and their respect for the wisdom of the local priest. Father Conlin's word is law but his vision is deeply sympathetic to their interests; he shares with them an essential joyfulness in life and spirit of fun; merriment, they know, is a worthy counter to "a melancholy sthrain [that] pervades the music of poor ould Ireland, it bein' neither more nor less than her vocal history."[74]

Part of the merriment is the brogue itself and the freedom of expression it allows. All the characters speak in the brogue; even Kelly, the government-employed gauger, who turns out to be an old friend of Father Conlin and a better man than any gauger ought to be, speaks it. Kelly himself offers a nationalistic tribute to the "scalthieen" produced in Harry Tracy's celebrated still:

I think that the devil a witty thing was ever said in Ireland, or fine song composed in the same place, but owes its characther to a dhrop of the same sort. Punch, of course, has conthributed to the fame and litherature of the country; but the startlin' points that make the Frinch or English stare, are all traceable to this necther of necthers itself. Punch, I admit, at the ninth or tinth tumbler, is powerful in unlockin' the threasures of the sowl and mind, and givin' a middlin' dacent scope to the tongue; but look at scalthieen. What is it? Nothin' but the pure crayture, itself, and a thrifle of thrimmin's – an eggshell of carraways, a quarther of butther, and a half pound of sugar, to a half gallon was our way in Roscommon; but I give up to this – A more direct appale to the head and heart I have never met with. Look at scalthieen … Let your eye rest on it, and see how it glitthers like glosserlane in a bog hole. Put your nose over it, and tell me, if that heavenly scint didn't prompt Tom Moore to say that you might smash a flower pot into smithereens, but that the pieces would still smell afther all … Now did you ever hear of a man sayin' a dacent thing on beer? It's this sedate sort of stuff that makes the English so cool and calculatin – that makes them walk so slow, and look so fat and dhrowsy like; although if you were to believe books and writins' you'd think they

all play aethers and tumblers, and almost aquel to the Frinch ... Be this
as it may, the dhrink of a nation is an index of the caracther of the people.
Light wines for the Frinch – frishky beer for England – heavy Pottieen
for Scotland and Ireland – Hurra! Whack[,] mavournieen, if they only
stuck together.[75]

In this narrative James McCarroll breathed fresh life into still-vivid memories of his Leitrim boyhood and made effective use of the poetics of the
stage-Irish brogue he delighted in. "The New Gauger" was his opportunity to
revive those memories and give them a shape designed to amuse and cheer Irish
readers in Canada. Gregarious Jack Trainer is his voice of the Irish people in
the story. He's "the boy that can do it," whatever "it"' might entail.[76] Jack has
a poetic streak that enriches his descriptions; he can bandy Latin phrases with
Father Conlin; but he is very much one of the boys and their acknowledged
leader. He is typically a step or two ahead of them imaginatively and in practical
matters, but he never lords his leadership over them.

For MacGeorge, the story merited a strong puff: "we can testify that it is a
production of no ordinary merit, and abounds with humor of the most sterling
order. *The New Gauger* is an Irishman to the backbone, and will doubtless create
a sensation."[77] It attracted positive response elsewhere but nowhere more keenly
than from James Lamb in his *St Catharines Evening Journal*. While the *Toronto
Daily Leader* praised the story's originality and "laughter-provoking" qualities,
Lamb praised each part of the serial as it appeared.[78] He lauded McCarroll as
"one of our best writers" in the line of "light literature" in the country; he is
a literary figure who hides "more talent under these light productions than
yet appears." Lamb compared McCarroll's approach to Dickens's realism and
pronounced his sense of "Irish character" impeccable.[79]

In his final notice Lamb waxed particularly euphoric. Noting that the
installment "contains the best description of an Irish wedding we have ever
met with," he added, "The subjects, the language, the *prupria persona*, are all
so good, so racy, so true to nature, that if Mr McCarroll had never written
anything else, this alone must place him on a highest pinnacle of Irish manners.
The Priest, Father Phelim, as a type, is worth any money."[80] Finally Lamb voiced
the hope that "The New Gauger" would soon be published as a book. It would
be a sure thing for booksellers and a pleasure for readers, be they Irish or not.[81]

What followed was disappointing, if not predictable, given Canadian
markets at the time. Despite garnering so much praise, "The New Gauger"
could not save the *Anglo-American Magazine* from its "untimely grave." Nor

was McCarroll able to find a book publisher.[82] In its 3 March issue, which incidentally featured twinned McCarroll poems, "Noon and Midnight," the *Daily Leader* expressed concern that "the magazine was too large for the money, considering that it must labour under the disadvantages incident to any similar publication in a new country, with a population not greater than ours."[83] So it was that, after completion of its seventh half-year volume, the *Anglo-American Magazine* succumbed, a victim of American competition, too few paying subscribers in Canada, the increased cost of paper, and rising taxes. Canada's only literary magazine of the decade thus died a quiet death.

Neither was a publisher found for "The New Gauger." McCarroll certainly tried, but he met roadblocks wherever he turned. He was still trying in 1862 when he wrote to Charles Dickens in England looking for publishing help.[84] He could not afford to self-finance a publication and he knew that most commercial publishers in Canada West were unwilling to enter into that kind of venture unless the writer could muster a large subscription list. This might have been possible in Toronto, but as yet he had limited connections there; moreover, such work would have been exhausting and time-consuming. But in 1856, as he prepared to leave Port Credit for Toronto, he had hopes that he would soon connect with new literary ventures in the province's largest city.

"The New Gauger" has languished in its original form for over 150 years. Arguably, it should be included among the best of Irish writing of the 1850s, as it compares well with the popular stories of Lover, Carleton, Banim, and Lever. It sets its vision well beyond and above the stereotypical Paddy that a year earlier McCarroll had dismissed with disgust in his review of *Green Bushes*. On its own, it constitutes an important example of his Irish-Canadian writing. It is a fit companion for Terry Finnegan's letters to D'Arcy McGee and the comic poems belonging to what McCarroll called his "Irish Anthology."

Making It and Losing It in Toronto, 1856–66

Making It, 1856–63

THE TEN YEARS THAT JAMES MCCARROLL SPENT IN TORONTO brought him new levels of literary acclaim, public recognition, and political involvement. Independent-minded and talented, he was engaged in several aspects of the city's developing cultural marketplace. He attached his own name to many of his poems but also used a variety of pseudonyms to expand his cultural reach while protecting his professional identity. Then in September 1863, with the sudden elimination of his customs position, he began what he called a "slow probation," perhaps more accurately described as a painful descent from the recognition he had achieved among people in the know in Toronto.

During that descent he began to align himself more closely with the Fenian promises that were much in the air at the time. Ultimately, that allegiance was both wrong-headed and badly informed. It was a choice for which he suffered grievously in the long run.

Questions abound about why McCarroll chose to align himself with militant Fenianism. Why did he allow himself to go over so precipitously to what was at best a dubious possibility? Were there special influences working on him or extenuating circumstances in his private life that unsettled him? Was he the convenient scapegoat of an angry Premier John Sandfield Macdonald or had he, by September 1863, become an aggressive nuisance who deserved to lose his customs position?

Furthermore, did he realize that he was risking his literary reputation in Canada West by taking up the Fenian banner? Was he misguided in putting so much faith in John A. Macdonald's repeated promise to help him when the moment was right? Was he, in the end, simply an impulsive Irishman forced by a situation of his own making to turn traitor against his adopted country and seek a new home for his talents? Had he become another frustrated Canadian place-seeker, forced to find a refuge in the United States?

In May 1856 no such concerns were at play. James McCarroll moved to Toronto eager to take up his new position as assistant outdoors surveyor for the Customs Department. He planned to extend his musical, literary, theatrical, journalistic, and political connections even as he threw himself into his new duties. Given what he had accomplished from Port Credit, much seemed possible.

In the late 1850s Mr James McCarroll cut a buoyant, confident figure in the fast-growing city. Always well dressed and well groomed, he was short in height but tall in spirits, a broad-chested, bantam-rooster of a man with a thick Connaught accent and a congenial manner. He was a popular figure in downtown life where his literary and musical reputation preceded him. By times he was a hard-hitting journalist, a music and theatre critic, an acclaimed amateur musician, a lyrical poet, a popular humorist, and a talented storywriter. There were few such versatile figures on the Toronto arts scene in those years. Newspaper reports indicate that he attended numerous public banquets and events; he hobnobbed in private homes, at hotels, at such King Street establishments as McConkey & Carlyle's Terrapin Restaurant, and at city drinking establishments like Joe Gregor's. At evening parties (typically for men only) he was a witty conversationalist, an amusing storyteller, and a popular musician, his flute usually close at hand.

In his early Toronto years, McCarroll devoted much of his time to his work at the port; he was determined to build his reputation as a reliable, competent civil servant, thereby confirming Francis Hincks's confidence in him. Evidence suggests that his reputation as a customs officer in Canada West gained considerable traction during this period.

With several new railways passing through Toronto and the increasing traffic in the port itself, the customs office was a busy place by the time that McCarroll became assistant outdoors surveyor. But as progressive as the city sought to be in business terms, it remained visibly tethered to its agrarian past. Pigs and cows wandered the back streets, building construction was often shabby, fires were frequent, roads were often muddy and impassable, and intersections were dangerous even for wary pedestrians. The city's boundaries were tightly defined by proximity to the Lake Ontario waterfront. Weston was a village off to the west and Yorkville lay to the north, although it was far south of the village of York Mills. The McCarrolls rented homes in various parts of the downtown – first on Shuter Street (east of Yonge in 1856), then 159 Church Street (1857–58), Parliament Street (1858), and finally 54 Bay Street, just north of Front (from about 1861 until 1865).[1] He always located his family near the port and railway stations as well as the theatres, music halls, newspaper offices, and the city's business centre.

McCarroll was quick to adapt to his new workplace. As assistant surveyor, his responsibilities required him to be on the move around the city. He delighted in the mobility. If he had an office, it was likely a desk in a corner of the department's "Long Room." He was at the port or at each of the city's three railway terminals several times each week.[2] His duties included "charge of the Lockers, Landing Waiters, Wharves, Warehouses [and] Railway Stations," surveying "all vessels and check[ing], at stated periods, goods in Bonded Warehouses, and arrang[ing] all out-door matters connected with the Port; that is, not of sufficient importance to be brought under the notice of the Collector."[3] As he settled into his ambulatory routine, he sent a letter to his superiors emphasizing "the arduous nature of my duties" and the many demands on his time each working day. He reported that he was often on the job before 6am and regularly put in long hours. By his own evaluation he was an energetic, responsible official who was prompt in meeting shippers' and warehouse needs. As well, he could be confident that his colleagues admired his business instincts and his ability to detect signs of smuggling in what appeared to be standard shipments.

Within months of taking up his duties, an antagonism between McCarroll and Muedell began to fester. The collector was sometimes neglectful, then overly fastidious and autocratic. McCarroll found he had many allies among his co-workers: Meudell was a cranky and aloof boss. Initially, the collector objected to McCarroll's constant movements and ordered him to remain at the Don Station until further notice.[4] Realizing the folly of that command, he rescinded it. By the spring and summer of 1857, a mischievous McCarroll found other ways to challenge Meudell's officiousness.

In setting up the public sale of one of his seizures, he made a conspicuous end-run around the collector. After seizing a large shipment of nails (110 kegs) and observing the month-long waiting period, he put the kegs up for public auction. However, according to customs procedures, a sale of this size required the collector's approval. When Meudell discovered what had transpired, he immediately objected to McCarroll's high-handedness. He called off the sale even though it had been duly advertised. That in itself constituted a breach of public faith and reasonable expectation. Letters flew back and forth from Meudell to Commissioner Bouchette's office. In the end little seems to have come of his complaint about McCarroll, except to make it more evident to headquarters that simmering dissatisfactions about Meudell were coming to a boil. In a private letter to Commissioner Bouchette that he sent requesting a brief leave (15 November 1857), McCarroll wrote with curt frankness about his boss: "the antipathy to the latter individual is so general that no person likes to have any communication with him."

Earlier that same year McCarroll had been involved in a situation concerning his nephew Alexander Munro. A landing waiter who had been moved into the Longhouse as the acting manifest book clerk, Munro had lamented to his superiors that, despite his increased responsibilities, his salary remained unchanged. Facing a domestic situation "a little short of absolute want" – he was struggling to provide for his "widowed mother and seven children" – he wrote to Inspector General William Cawley asking for help and mentioning the support he enjoyed from his uncle.[5] A sympathetic Cawley sent the request on to Commissioner Bouchette and within a week Munro's salary was raised to $200 per annum. However, at an earlier stage, McCarroll had advised his nephew to alter his own salary and rank on the quarterly pay list before he submitted it to the collector. Not noticing the changes, Meudell signed off on the list. When he discovered his error, he had to overturn his own approval; moreover, his immediate reaction was to fire Munro on the charge of "tampering." But when he discovered that the young man had made the alterations on the advice of his uncle, Meudell reinstated Munro and sought some way to reprimand McCarroll.

Nothing formal came of this episode. However, an elderly customs colleague, Edward Curzon, sent a letter to the department on 24 March 1858, defending young Munro as the unwitting victim of his uncle's manipulations. In his letter he argued that behind McCarroll's backroom actions lay an ugly family feud between him and his widowed sister. Using words like "malice" and "a perverted influence," he drew attention to what he regarded as McCarroll's mean-spiritedness toward both Munro and his family.[6]

After Alex Munro was reinstated and received his raise in salary, Meudell was demoted from Toronto to the Port of Belleville.[7] When the Honorable Robert Spence succeeded Meudell as collector, most customs employees greeted the change with enthusiasm. Meanwhile, McCarroll forged ahead, apparently pleased by the results of his own behaviour. He continued to build his reputation. In the next few years he blew the whistle on a number of inadequate employees and recommended several improvements to procedures in the workplace.[8] In such matters he worked harmoniously with the new roving inspector of ports and stations, Thomas Worthington. Little wonder, then, that in 1858 McCarroll was promoted to surveyor. The customs fonds for 1857 include a number of individual testimonials to his work habits by his outdoor colleagues. It would appear that he had carefully sought such tributes in the light of Meudell's ongoing hostility to him.

These testimonials underlay the tribute that he received from his fellow workers in early May 1858.[9] A delegation of his "out-door" colleagues, led by Mr James Stitt, one of the port's "Lockers," arrived at McCarroll's Parliament Street home to present him with "a valuable piece of plate" in recognition of his work habits and good judgment. The notice of the presentation (*Daily Leader* [11 May])[10] was placed by either his colleagues or himself.

On behalf of the out-door officers of this port, I have, Sir, great pleasure in presenting you with this trifling token of their appreciation of the eminent qualities, personal and official, which have distinguished you since your first appearance amongst them. Although prompt, energetic, and conscientious in the discharge of your important duties, you have ever been kind, considerate, and obliging; and in so far as you have come into contact with the mercantile community here, your popularity in that direction is but another corroboration of the justice of what I now assert. Hoping, then, that you may long live to enjoy your present connexion with us, and be spared, for years to come, to your amiable wife and interesting family, I beg your acceptance of this slight mark of esteem at our hands.

In response McCarroll thanked the delegation for "the elegant and substantial token of your regard," especially "at a time when financial embarrassments are so widely felt."[11] Praising "a staff so intelligent and efficient," he hoped that "under the able guidance of our upright and efficient chief [Robert Spence] to whom we all now look up with such confidence," we will be "bound together more closely in our endeavors to assist each other in the performance of our respective duties."

Arrayed in platitudes, the presentation buoyed his sense of importance as an officer at the port. He had been an assistant outdoors surveyor for only two years and was working with a large staff for the first time in his eight-year customs career. But in that short time he had made a positive impact on both his colleagues and members of the Toronto "mercantile community." Despite his ongoing disputes with Collector Meudell, he had achieved a high level of departmental success, and functioned as a leader under trying circumstances.

Two painful personal losses occurred in 1858. On 8 February, the *Daily Leader* carried the announcement that James Macdonald McCarroll, the two-year-old son of James and Ann McCarroll, had died. No other notice followed that stark announcement. Whether the boy had been sick from birth (he was likely born in Port Credit during the family's last year there) or had been struck down by an illness is not known. Whatever the case, the loss was difficult for both parents. He was their second son and the second to die at a very young age. Young James's death may have further disturbed Ann's health, which by this time was a concern for the entire household. She had come to rely on her four daughters to carry out many of the household duties. Additionally, given Ann's age and increasing ill health, James was their last chance for a male heir.

Less than two weeks later, McCarroll's good friend Frederick Griebel suddenly fell ill. He died on 19 February 1858. In the words of music historian Helmut Kallmann, Griebel had within a few years established himself as "the first fully professional violinist to have settled in Canada"; some twenty years later he was still regarded as "the greatest violinist ever resident in [Toronto]."[12] Griebel's passing was a great loss not only for his young family but also for serious music lovers in Toronto. Only thirty-eight years old, he left behind a wife and two children who had relied on him for their livelihood.

Despite his grief at the loss of his son, McCarroll was quick to respond to Griebel's dangerous illness. First, he arranged to take him into his own home during what proved to be the final days of his life, and then he did what he could to help Frau Griebel and her children after his death.[13] The year 1858 would see a number of fundraising concerts set up by the "Griebel Relief Committee"; McCarroll was on hand either to help with the organization and publicity or to perform.[14] He even provided a burial site for his friend in the plot that he had bought for his own family through St James Cathedral.[15]

But Ann's health continued to weigh on McCarroll during that dark spring. In July, he sought and was granted a ten-day leave from his custom's work on her behalf; "since the death of her only son [she] has not been well and requires change of air," he reported in a letter to his superior, the Honorable Robert Spence.[16]

Anglo–Irish Confidence and the Edges of Darkness .

During his first seven years in Toronto, McCarroll's literary stock rose steadily. In addition to his special connection with the *Daily Leader*, he developed supportive relationships with other city editors of Irish birth, notably Ogle Gowan, the outspoken and controversial Orangeman who had recently moved to Toronto from Brockville and who, after 1854, owned and edited the *Toronto Patriot* for several years; James Moylan, the editor of the *Canadian Freeman*, which functioned as the voice of support for Thomas D'Arcy McGee and Catholicism in Toronto and Canada West; and Patrick Boyle, the editor of the *Irish Canadian*, the city's Hibernian, or pro-Fenian, newspaper which began its weekly publication on 7 January 1863. Boyle and Michael Murphy, leading voices in the Hibernian Benevolent Society, became McCarroll's friends early on; in fact, they agreed to be sureties for his customs position.[17]

McCarroll's range of creative interests found supportive, if often short-lived, outlets. His ambitions were evident in the arc of his poetic output even as he carried on with his customs duties. Year after year a number of his poems appeared in the *Daily Leader*, mostly under his own name, and a few were reprinted in provincial newspapers. In all, the *Daily Leader* published more than seventy McCarroll poems between 1856 and 1865 along with a number of his anonymous columns. He continued to review musical performances for the *Daily Leader* and on occasion for the *Daily Colonist*,[18] paying special attention to the concerts of such international stars as Anna Bishop, Maurice Strakosch, and Henri Vieuxtemps.[19] In the years just before Confederation, Toronto had emerged as a reliable stop on the celebrity concert circuit both for individual performers and for companies like the Italian Opera. In his enthusiasm for serious, professionally performed music, McCarroll was eager to pay close attention to visiting stars; in fact, over time many became his friends.

There was, by contrast, a notable void in literary periodicals in Canada West following the termination of the *Anglo-American Magazine*. McCarroll remained alert to fresh opportunities and was quick to place poems in two subsequent Toronto magazines, the *Home Journal* (1861) and the *British American Magazine* (1863–64). William Halley's *Home Journal* makes an interesting case in point. It lasted only twelve issues although it was a bargain at four cents per issue ($1.50 per annum).[20] McCarroll was a contributor from its inception. In addition to stories, a poem, and an article entitled "Fragment on Ancient Music and Musical Instruments,"[21] he began his second serialized novel there. Entitled "Black Hawk. A Tale of 'The Plains,'" it was set on the grassy plateau rising

The Irish

VOL. I.—No. 1.   TORONTO, C.W., WEDNESDAY,

For the Irish Canadian.

RESURGAM.

BY JAMES M'CARROLL.

Come! let us form a solid square,
No matter what our creed or clan,
And plant our drooping standard, there,
Beside some wounded Dalgais' man.

Till all its emerald folds unfurled
O'er yonder sea of kindred sheen,
Shall mid-way meet, before the world,
Its brighter half of living green.

Then shall a rainbow span the skies—
A pledge of countless, glorious years—
The light of a young nation's eyes
That flashes through her joyous tears:

While in his ancient glory decked,
Beneath its arch of dazzling rays,
The haughty Celt shall stand erect,
As he was wont in other days.

Toronto, Jan. 1, 1863.

* The favourite troops of Brien Borombe, some of whom wished their Monarch would cause them to be lashed to stakes stuck in the ground by the side of a wound man, so as that they might still do battle.

THE LATE BISHOP POWER.

It is a source of much gratification to us that we are enabled in our first number to present our readers with a portrait of the late lamented Right Rev. Dr. Power, R. C. Bishop of this Diocese.

We have selected his name as a subject, believing that none other can be more appropriate for a Journal like THE IRISH CANADIAN. The fact of his having been a Bishop of the Catholic Church alone, we are aware, would be sufficient to make our effort acceptable to a large number of our persons. Ours is not a religious journal, but the motive that has impelled us in selecting this ecclesiastic as a subject for our first illustration, must be obvious. The good Bishop was esteemed and respected by all classes of the community, and religious differences did not prevent him from enjoying the good will of his Protestant fellow-countrymen.

Though strictly speaking he was not an Irishman, or an Irish Canadian, yet his associations were much nearer at once to identify him with both Irishmen and Canadians, and all were proud to acknowledge him as of themselves. If there is

tion on the 18th May, 1842, as Bishop of the Diocese of Toronto, which ceremony, gratifying to his flock and the members of the church generally, and reflecting like credit on the deceased's exertions in the ministerial office, took place in St. John's Church, a large stone edifice erected by himself, at Laprairie. He formally entered into possession of his See in the Church of St. Paul, Toronto, on the 26th of June, the same year.

In the summer of 1843 he made the first visitation of his diocese, accompanied by the Rev. Mr. Hay; he had, however, previously, in 1843, visited Penetanguishene and the Manitoulin Islands, accompanied by the Rev. Mr. Proulx, who alone of his many clerical associates now resides in our midst.

From the day of his arrival to that of his death his energies were taxed in every way to advance the interests of his sacred calling and improve both spiritually and temporally the condition of his flock, to whom he spoke became dearly beloved.

The erection of a suitable edifice for the purpose of a Cathedral, soon engaged his attention, and with such energy did he pursue this object that the corner stone of the imposing structure of St. Michael's was laid on the 8th of May, 1845, and on the 29th September, 1848. it was consecrated to the worship of God by his Lordship Bishop Bourget of Montreal, and during the administration of the Rev. Mr. Carroll.

To the accomplishment of this great work Bishop Power devoted his private means, having himself purchased the ground upon which the Cathedral is built as well as that occupied by the episcopal residence, which was commenced at the same time.

In January 1847 the Bishop visited Europe,

but threw his whole energies into the labour of rendering spiritual consolation to the many immigrants congregated within the walls of the fever hospital and sheds. The Rev. Mr. O'then at Niagara, learning the situation in his Bishop was placed, came over to Toronto, joined him in his labors. About the 20th of tember, however, the good man, himself contracted the disease which in a few days over forever from his beloved flock, and removed from the midst of a community that was generous but which had learned to respect the Bishop on account of the amiability of his man. His demise took place in the morning of that day, the first of October, 1847, more than fifty years after his decease of the See of Toronto, and in the following year he can in no time exhibit the features of sorrow with which the tidings of his death were received more than half of the population can now tread in his footsteps, in the newspaper city (the British loyalist) at the time. The article was frequently contact with him, and whose death since been lamented as a useful member of the community (the late Hugh Scobie), who with many eyes and sorrowful heart penned the following quote:—

"It is not for us to pronounce his eulogy. The sorrow of his flock, the regrets of the community, the members of which have learned to appreciate his exertions to promote peace and brotherhood among us, the tears that moisten the eyes of so many persons not within the pale of his church, to whom we have spoken of his untimely death, are the best evidences of the loss sustained. May it be our lot to see a successor pointed to the episcopate whom all may love as well."

above the western shore of Rice Lake, south of Peterborough. The eponymous hero was the brilliant and athletic son of a Huron chief and a genteel white woman. Having received a European education, Black Hawk wore his native attire only when he came home to the Canadian forests. Ambitiously, the novel promised to "correct ideas regarding early Pioneer life in Canada, as well as of Indian habits and character."[22] It began with the magazine's fifth issue and was suspended with its twelfth and final issue. In the midst of his struggles to keep the magazine in circulation, Halley, who placed high hopes on McCarroll's serial, sent out "An Appeal," seeking new supporters for "the only literary publication in Canada." Alas, his call for support could not forestall its demise.[23]

William Halley became a prominent literary figure in Toronto during the 1860s, but his various efforts as a publisher have been largely overlooked today. He first came to prominence in helping John O'Donohoe to set up James Moylan's newspaper the *Canadian Freeman*. He backed other Catholic projects geared to encouraging support for Thomas D'Arcy McGee in Protestant Toronto. Then in 1865 he became the publisher of *Pick*, the last of Toronto's pre-Confederation humour magazines. *Pick* lasted less than a year but it served as the final home for McCarroll's Terry Finnegan letters. Regrettably, no copies of this "little magazine" have survived nor have those final Finnegan letters. Neither is there much available information about the Halley-McCarroll connection.

After the failure of the *Home Journal* in mid-August 1861, McCarroll sought a new home for "Black Hawk." Andrew D. McAllister had begun a new newspaper, the *Cobourg Sentinel*, and welcomed the opportunity to publish it; in fact, McAllister made its forthcoming appearance the centre of a special subscription campaign for 1862. Billing it as a "great Canadian story" from "the brilliant pen of James McCarroll," the paper deemed it "one of the most interesting ever published."[24] Its serialization began with the first issue of the new year (4 January 1862) and lasted until the issue of 1 March. In all, nine chapters appeared, the same chapters that had appeared in the *Home Journal*. When the serial suddenly broke off, the newspaper announced that the author was ill. Although the break was described as "temporary," "Black Hawk" was not resumed and no further explanation was offered.

"Black Hawk" bears similarities to John Richardson's *Wacousta* (1832) and other early Canadian novels involving indigenous characters.[25] It is unusual in the McCarroll canon. Black Hawk is the son of Grey Eagle, a wealthy Huron chief, and a white mother who dies young and whose origins remain mysterious. He spends his early days (the summer of 1825) among "the gigantic pines" near Peterborough and Rice Lake, just after the Peter Robinson Emigration. Following his own marriage (a case of true love, of course) and the death of his young wife in Europe, his story focuses more on his privileged white friends and their Anglo-Irish connections than the indigenous characters associated with his Upper Canadian life. While grieving as a widower, Black Hawk visits Ireland and meets a gentleman named Stanhope Kavanagh near the village of Roscrea.[26] After he rescues Kavanagh from a dangerous attack, they become fast friends and "the Chief," as he was known, convinces Kavanagh to immigrate to Upper Canada (where he too has old connections) while awaiting a Chancery decision concerning his claim upon a nearby family estate. A second Irish thread, promising plenty of vernacular humour, involves the Irish servant named "little Tim" who has loyally served Black Hawk.

The plotting is typical; there is much ado about pure love and troubled family relationships among the gentrified white characters. But in chapter 9, just as the narrative is about to make its promised return to the Rice Lake-Peterborough area, it breaks off. Thus, it disappoints in its failure to engage closely with the land and the indigenous peoples of eastern Canada. Like most such fictions, it dedicates attention to backroom villainy and the genteel love relationships between men like Kavanagh ("our young adventurer" and "hero") and sweet young women like Olive Mornington.

Why McCarroll failed for a second time to complete "Black Hawk" is a puzzle. In his desire to place the serial before the public he had managed to find a second publisher. Relatedly, it is worth noting that there was a similar hiatus in the appearance of the Terry Finnegan letters in the early 1860s. In fact, Terry's letters ceased for a year and a half – from 28 June 1861 until 5 December 1862 – before he continued the series in the *Grumbler*. The failure of *Momus*, the short-lived Toronto magazine in which the first eight Finnegan letters had appeared, certainly played a part in this disruption. Adding the case of "Black Hawk," however, one wonders if there was some emotional breakdown on McCarroll's part or a loss of interest in the project. Perhaps he had come to a dead end with the narrative before bringing it back to its Canadian setting. Perhaps the illness cited by the *Sentinel's* editor was of greater substance than it appeared. No doubt he and his *Cobourg Sentinel* readers were disappointed – the novel was their big subscription initiative for the year.

Retrospectively, "Black Hawk" would certainly have added lustre to McCarroll's literary reputation had he finished it. "The New Gauger" had won him many followers only a few years earlier. In reviewing this situation, I posit two other factors.

First, the grim darkness of his poem "February" (placed in the *Cobourg Sentinel* on 8 February and dated 1 February 1862) offers what might be a glimpse into his depressed state of mind that winter. It begins darkly and proceeds toward a "chill … anguish":

The famished sun crawls through a flaw in night,
And blurs the hissing tempest into morn,
Spreading a misty pool of sickly light
That widens till the ghastly day is born.

The phrasing may imply that he was grappling with a bout of depression that had temporarily derailed his creative energies. In the poem he deplores the storms and the severe cold characterizing Canada West in February and summons up images of extreme poverty and death in the streets of Toronto to bolster the dark mood.[27] He completes the six-stanza poem with these two verses:

And, now, the blue-lipped orphan treads the street,
With naked shoulders pressed against her ears;
Washing the red stains from her bleeding feet,
At every trembling pause, with bitter tears:

While, 'mid the gloomy waste that ' round her lies,
Nor sight nor sound to cheer her can she trace;
For the dumb earth, before her sunken eyes,
A huge, chill ball of anguish rolls through space.

The image of "the dumb earth" as a "huge, chill ball of anguish" suggests a depressed state of mind during the winter of 1862. McCarroll may have needed many months to recover his usual equanimity and resilience.

Second, he received a letter from Charles Dickens dated 28 February 1862. Dickens was writing in response to a letter from McCarroll asking for help in finding a London publisher.[28] Dickens began his reply by firmly stating that he had always been unsuccessful "in inducing any publisher to accept a book on my recommendation." Then he turned to "the abstract merit of your writings, and the probability of their finding a London publisher." About both issues he found it "very difficult to arrive at a sound conclusion." His final two paragraphs read as follows:

The pieces in verse that you have sent me, appear to me to be more original in thought, and more strikingly expressed, than the prose tale. And yet I should deceive you if I concealed my belief that there are many writers of fugitive pieces who write as well, and yet who do not find it feasible or remunerative to collect their productions. In the prose tale I observe some very good description; I have not the means before me of judging of its merits in point of character or story, – but I have no doubt whatever that on this side of the Atlantic the Indian would scarcely interest any more, though he were in the hands of Scott himself.

On the whole, I fear you have not yet done what would make its way here, or what would make way for a poem of two thousand lines. But I can honestly add that your cultivation of literature evinces an earnestness of spirit, and a love and knowledge of nature, and a purity of taste, all very interesting and suggestive of advance.

Clearly, McCarroll had sent Dickens some early chapters of "Black Hawk," perhaps in print form, along with a selection of his poems.

Dickens's frank response may have played a part in the hasty termination of the "Black Hawk" serial. The long-range hopes that McCarroll had for it, in the mode of Richardson and Cooper, might have been squashed by Dickens's firm view that the London marketplace would not be interested in another "Indian" tale. If McCarroll was struggling at this time with his own health and energy, Dickens's advice – that he should focus on his poetry, which he described as "suggestive of advance" – may have led him to abandon his Black Hawk project.

At least three of McCarroll's *Daily Leader* poems of this period (1858–62) merit special attention for non-poetic reasons. The first was "Madeline"; decades later, it became the title poem in his only published volume.[29] Thomas D'Arcy McGee read the poem in the *Daily Leader* (6 February 1858) and decided to publish a shortened version (eight of its twenty-one stanzas) in his new Montreal newspaper, the *New Era*. In reprinting it, McGee paid him a welcome compliment in noting that this "fine poem [is] from the pen of a man of true genius."[30] It was the only McCarroll poem to appear in the *New Era* during its one-year run; indeed, McGee's flattering commendation is the only known instance in which he commented specifically on McCarroll as a poet, although he would certainly have seen many examples of his later writing.[31] The two former Irishmen, living and writing in different Canadian cities, had first become acquainted in Toronto at a lecture given by McGee a year earlier.[32]

There is, however, no evidence of a sustained friendship between them, despite McCarroll's cheeky audacity in addressing his Terry Finnegan letters to him.

The second is "Lines, Inscribed to His Royal Highness, The Prince of Wales. On the Occasion of his Visit to Canada" in 1860. The occasion was indeed auspicious. The young prince had apparently received the poem with favour during his much-publicized visit to Toronto that September. However, after the poem's appearance in the *Daily Leader*, the Duke of Newcastle, who was in charge of the prince's engagements and correspondence, chose not to acknowledge its receipt. Thus, the poem was not used in the welcoming ceremonies as McCarroll had hoped and he lost his chance to receive public recognition during the hoopla of the royal visit.[33]

Still, he was involved in several of the vice-regal activities in the city: he attended the Anna Bishop Promenade Concert in the prince's honour; he joined the delegation that waited upon the prince to invite him to attend a concert on 10 September to support the purchase an organ for St John's Church, York Mills;[34] and he attended the prince's levee a day later. Two weeks after the visit he arranged for a "Personal" column in the *Daily Leader*, designed to make clear that his poem had been important in the prince's eyes. It reported that the Duke of Newcastle had in fact sent the prince's thanks to "Mr McCarroll, Surveyor of Customs" for his lines addressed to His Royal Highness "in the *Leader* of the 8th instant." The column added that McCarroll had "just issued a prospectus of a book of Poems and one of Prose to be published *immediately*." The puff concluded on a still more self-congratulatory note: "Those who have perused the manuscript of [the poems] assure us of its high character; while the continuous endorsation of the Press generally of all that he has hitherto written is a further and broader guarantee of his eminent success."[35]

The ironies embedded in the stifling of McCarroll's royal tribute would magnify within a few years, especially as his own support of British rule diminished. In 1860 he was still a strong supporter of the queen and her family; however, within a few years his attraction to the Fenians would reduce his admiration of Britannia's warm "clasp" and "apostolic zeal," as well as "thy Royal Mother's matchless heart and head." Three years later he would put forward strongly pro-Irish, anti-English views as he embraced an outlook that would have been an anathema to the prince, the queen, and Newcastle. Newcastle had been prescient. McCarroll's reference in the poem to "the sturdy Saxon and the fiery Celtic child" might be seen to signify the Irish fire burning strongly in his own heart, a fire that, under certain circumstances, would wither "the sturdy Saxon" within him.

The third poem, "The 'Bridge of Sighs,'" was his response to one of Canada's earliest railroad tragedies – the crash into the Desjardin Canal in 1857. A train travelling between Hamilton and Toronto plunged into the canal near Hamilton, killing thirty-eight passengers, including Samuel Zimmerman, one of Canada West's most successful financiers. Zimmerman, who had been an influential detractor of McCarroll in his Port Stamford days, appears negatively in the poem as one of "the men of gold." His old musical acquaintance, Dr Macklem, was injured in the crash. McCarroll wrote the poem under the suggestive pseudonym "Professor Pike, UCD," and dropped it off at the *Daily Leader*.[36] Envisioning the train as an "iron horse" with "a strange, long fiendish [neigh]," he described the gruesome deaths of several passengers before ending the poem with this stanza:

Oh, God! who built that bridge – that fatal bridge of sighs? –
Who placed the pitfall there, before our very eyes?
Was it some rail-way man who, in his sordid strife,
Thought more of a piece of gold than he thought of a brother's life?

It was typical of McCarroll to keep an eye on important public events in and near Toronto. Train accidents, balloon travel, the condition of inmates in the Don River Prison, and images of those struggling with poverty and loneliness caught his attention.[37] In "The Bridge of Sighs," he vividly captured the power, speed, and (sometimes false) confidence associated with train travel and progress in the late 1850s while weighing in against the profiteers who placed monetary gain above matters of safety and responsibility.

Giving Birth to Terry Finnegan: An Irish Voice for Toronto

Savvy about his newspaper connections, James McCarroll was imagining new ways in which he could draw on his Irish heritage. Having penned his Leitrim novel, "The New Gauger" (1855), to much acclaim, he continued to write short poems in the Irish vernacular for the *Daily Leader*. One such poem, "Impromptu" (27 August 1859) captured his response upon seeing a large balloon named Europa ascend "to a great height" above Toronto at the beginning of its flight to Boston. An exercise in punning, it announced his economic hopes for Ireland and the strength of his Gaelic pride.

Why! In commerce, ould Ireland, I'm glad you're beginnin'
Just to hould up your head, and to "never say die,"
For, begorra, I'm sure that your beautiful linen
Never went off before, half so quick or so high.

Oh! thin, won't they be glad, from Coleraine up to Kerry
At its rapid and most unaccountable *sale*?
And, machree, it's no wonder they all should be merry,
For to see that so much can be done by the *Gael*.[38]

Such poems were Celtic *jeux d'esprit* – comic romps that spoke of his fond memories of Ireland.[39] Another was the delightful "Kitty Fitzgibbon" (6 January 1860), a "love'" poem dramatizing "young Paddy Casey's" courtship of "Charmin' Kitty."

In all, six new McCarroll poems appeared in the *Daily Leader* in 1859 and another fourteen in 1860. There was no slackening in his output during these years. Despite his Church of Ireland and Anglican pedigree, he was acutely sensitive to the challenges faced by poor Irish Catholics not only in famine-plagued southern Ireland but also as struggling immigrants in Canada. Perhaps as a sign of his growing identification with Irish Catholics, he began to alter the signature he usually attached to his poems; once simply "James McCarroll," his name now more frequently appeared as "James M'Carroll."

In 1857 McCarroll, alert to the need for effective leadership from Irish politicians in the Canadas, joined many Irish Canadians in hoping that a newcomer to Montreal, Thomas D'Arcy McGee, would fill that leadership gap. As a young man McGee had famously participated in the Rebellion of 1848 in Ireland, barely escaping from the English authorities by sailing in disguise to the United States. But after being convinced to leave the United States and try Canada, he seemed primed to become an Irish force for political good in the colony. McCarroll had kept a close watch on the political careers of Protestant Irishmen like Michael Foley and Ogle Gowan,[40] but over the years and for differing reasons, those hopes were disappointed. In McGee, a fervent Catholic and charismatic speaker, he felt he had found that rare Irishman who could rise above mundane issues and provide effective leadership for the Irish people in British America. McGee's history as a Catholic rebel from Wexford and his acknowledged journalistic skills made him a highly attractive presence in his new home of Montreal. In Protestant Toronto, he was welcomed more cautiously when he visited as a lecturer. However, many Irish Catholics in the city were anxious to hear him speak and to support him. When McGee came to Toronto on 5 March 1857 to speak on "the Late Presidential Election" in the United States, McCarroll was a member of the platform party that gave him an enthusiastic welcome.[41]

The irrepressible, chatty Terry Finnegan, who emerged full-blown from McCarroll's creative mind in 1861, was closely tied to his sense of Thomas D'Arcy McGee's potential as an Irish-Canadian leader. As Terry put it in his first letter to his "cousin," "There's somethin in you and we want to get it out." McGee was still a relative newcomer on the Canadian political scene and thus, in McCarroll's and Terry's mind, in need of guidance from members of the Catholic constituency. Born of at least one previous experiment in comic letter writing, Terry Finnegan became a literary phenomenon in Toronto that soon took on a life of its own; his letters in the brogue to McGee were full of cheeky fun and amusing wordplay as well as immediate political commentary.[42] Appearing in various humour magazines published in Toronto during the five years leading up to Confederation (1861–65), Terry's letters gave McCarroll a satiric platform for expressing his affection for Ireland and his wry views on current political issues affecting Toronto and Canada West.

Brazenly, McCarroll introduced Terry as McGee's "lovin' cousin."[43] With his wife Biddy, Terry was a Catholic living in largely Protestant Toronto. But, of course, he had no familial connection to McGee; moreover, his loose standards of behaviour were a far cry from McGee's closely guarded sense of personal respectability and intellectual acumen. The high-spirited Terry was a resident of a shabby ghetto, notorious for its unkempt and misbehaving Irish residents. "Stanly Street" was a degraded thoroughfare comprising mostly drinking establishments, brothels, and tenement houses in Toronto's downtown.[44] In his weekly letters Terry passed along social observations, creative effusions, and political advice to McGee, even as he made light of his cousin's swarthy features and provided advice about some of the political quandaries that McGee was facing in the shifting alliances of the day. On a less serious note, Terry often begged "D'Arcy dear" to respond promptly to his letters and send along writing supplies. Always short of money, Terry did not hesitate to beg for small favours like parliamentary stationery, envelopes (preferably unmarked), and the sealing wax needed for his own correspondence. At the same time Terry always held out the hope of sharing a cup or two of "Irish tay" with McGee when they were able to get together. Terry himself was a rather heavy drinker and his frequent lapses in decorum, including his involvement in an occasional "Stanly Street" donnybrook, often followed upon a night of heavy drinking.

In all, just over fifty of Terry's letters have survived, thirty-eight of which were published in what McCarroll called "the first series" of *The Letters of Terry Finnegan*.[45] This small book – his first! – was hastily prepared and published late in 1863 by the Toronto News Company.[46] In fact, Terry's popularity with city readers seems to have trumped McCarroll's plan to find a publisher for the two volumes he had earlier announced. The book contains Terry's letters from 14 March 1861 to 5 November 1863. "The second series" began soon thereafter in the *Grumbler*. As with the first volume, the appearance of these letters depended on certain little magazines in the city; at least one of those – the *Latch-Key* – was published by McCarroll himself during two consecutive autumns (1863 and 1864). Regrettably, the final Finnegan letters are no longer extant. They vanished along with William Halley's short-lived magazine *Pick* (1865), where they appeared with some regularity during that year.[47]

Allowing for several gaps, the Finnegan letters follow the political doings of D'Arcy McGee from 1861 to 1865. McCarroll was particularly attentive to what Maurice Careless called "the days of successive coalitions and shifting party fronts,"[48] which, from 1861 to 1864, were disturbing to residents of the colony and affected the ways in which McGee had to position himself polit-ically. Certainly, these were "days of anxiety" for him as a politician.[49] With "five administrations during the previous two years," he was often left in an uncertain position as a result of those "internal constitutional difficulties."[50] His political position was vulnerable, depending on which leader was in and which was out. However, Terry was there, offering weekly advice on how McGee should conduct himself both in Parliament and in relation to his leading political adversaries.

McCarroll was watching over and worrying about the slow dance toward Confederation, an initiative that McGee fully supported. McCarroll was less than enthusiastic about "this Confederrashun scheme," especially as it would affect the interests of the Irish. Despite recent demographic information that revealed the numerical dominance of the Irish in Canada West, he feared that he was witnessing an erosion of public interest in and support of the Irish situation; indeed, he detected a significant reduction in sympathy for and political interest in the needs of Irish Catholics in Canada West. Thus, as McCarroll's angst and frustration continued to increase in the aftermath the loss of his customs position in September 1863, Terry Finnegan's high-spirited letters became somewhat less humorous and more acerbic, his ebullience showing signs of aggravation and bitterness. The low-life, hard-drinking, sporting, music-loving, vernacular "janius" that Terry had been in 1861 became grumpier over time. In the wake of his loss of employment and his outrage at the insensitive treatment he was receiving from government officials, McCarroll inevitably darkened Terry's creative sallies and joie de vivre. But humorists are typically Janus-faced in pursuit of a good laugh, leaning first one way and then another while eschewing a consistent point of view. Hence, the "incomparable Terry" maintained sufficient bonhomie and buoyancy despite his creator's darkening perspective.

Regardless of the tonal and emotional shifts evident over Terry Finnegan's five years of letter-writing, individual missives would prove to be not only James McCarroll's most focused literary achievement in Canada but also an indirect record of his evolving personal views. As a whole, they provided a "racy" and unconventional look at Canadian life and politics from an unlikely centre – the notorious "Stanly Street" – and they delighted readers who enjoyed an unconventional take on Irish-Canadian life and a relief from the dull and polemical newspaper accounts of Canadian politics in the early 1860s. They brought the brogue into everyday Toronto life.

Terry's letters did not belong in the conventional press: their natural home was within the counterculture of Toronto's little magazines. Occasionally some of their content was quoted or commented upon in major papers like the *Daily Leader*. Terry's opinions as an outspoken Irish Catholic and his shrewd political observations made him an attractive and interesting voice even when he was at his most self-serving. McCarroll delighted in letting Terry have his say and using his letters to speak out on social life of Stanly Street and the city as whole. The letters were creative exercises in comic writing and expression; in their sustained exuberance and occasional insightfulness they held the attention of many readers and they certainly gained the admiration of McCarroll's fellow Irish journalists in the Canadas.

After he lost his customs position, McCarroll's discomfort with Canada slowly escalated from displeasure to anger to despair. In parallel, the Confederation movement gained increasing purchase in the colony in part because, south of the border, the Civil War was drawing toward its brutal close. Distressed about the lack of say for the Irish in the emerging power structure of the would-be nation, McCarroll was convinced that something striking had to be done by and for the Irish. Hence, Terry began to question McGee's ability to be an effective spokesperson for their people.

As early as 1863 McGee had taken an aggressive stand against the folly of Fenianism in Canada, thereby alienating some of his long-time supporters. The once-great Gaelic hope, the brave rebel of 1848, attacked and utterly dismissed Fenian aspirations in Canada in favour of what former supporters like McCarroll viewed as the misguided and unnecessary attempt at confederation and the tacit acceptance of Anglo-Saxon/Scots dominance in politics.

As McCarroll's disappointment with McGee increased, his connections with Toronto Fenians became his refuge. Nevertheless, in Terry's letters, images of pre-Confederation Toronto and Terry's voice are closely linked, both imaginatively and politically. They call out for recognition and attention today. To date, despite the availability of the first series of Finnegan letters as a (rare) book, cultural historians have made few attempts to explore the insightful glimpses that Terry provides of Toronto life in the early 1860s. *The Letters of Terry Finnegan* has never been reprinted and what remains of the second series has never been collected. The challenges of the brogue (at least at first sight) is one reason for this eclipse; nevertheless, it remains surprising that later Canadian historians and literary scholars have ignored Terry's once-popular letters.

The Power of Vernacular Humour

Terry Finnegan emerged in Toronto from the rich tradition of vernacular letter writing that flourished in early nineteenth-century newspapers.[51] McCarroll read and enjoyed such popular letter writers as Sam Slick, Artemis Ward, Yankee Doodle, and Terry Driscoll.[52] Of these, Terry Driscoll's Irish letters had the strongest influence. Originally written for the *Dublin Warder*, they were often reprinted in colonial newspapers and enjoyed popularity with readers in the Irish diaspora. In Canada West they were reprinted in papers like the *Cobourg Star* and the *Niagara Mail*. John Jackson of Kilrush, Ireland was the creator of Terry Driscoll (or Terry O'Driscoll as he was sometimes called). Jackson's "Terry" wrote from Stoneybatter, Ireland (near Dublin) to his friend Thady O'Donohoe who lived in St Giles, London. The *Cobourg Star* editor, H.J. Ruttan, republished a number of Jackson's letters; as well, in an obituary that appeared in 1857, he summarized the lively literary effects that Jackson regularly achieved: "No Irish writer, [William] Carleton not excepted, exceeded 'Terry Driscoll' in his peculiar style – his spontaneous humour, sly sarcasm, graphic portraiture of character, vivid pictures of life and manners, and his succinct and pointed allusions to the political and local events of the day."[53]

Ruttan's description can be applied to the voice of Terry Finnegan. Terry Driscoll, whose motto was "Ireland for the Irish," commented on politics, passing events, and social gossip, and was especially sensitive to the effects of the Great Famine on the Irish people.[54] But, as Ruttan implies (using Carleton as his measure of success with the vernacular voice), such journalistic writing aligned itself with the larger, revitalized tradition of nineteenth-century Irish fiction. Carleton and other popular novelists like Gerald Griffin, John Banin, Samuel Lever, and Samuel Lover, along with playwright Dion Boucicault, were in the vanguard of this major change. Collectively, they have received the lion's share of literary attention for the Irish revival in the mid-nineteenth century; however, journalistic incarnations of the Paddy figure – that talkative, opinionated, and attractive Irish voice – likely had a more immediate effect on readers than did the novelists.

In measuring literary achievement, what ought to matter most about James McCarroll is not his personal need to align himself with the rising tide of Fenianism in the 1860s; rather, it is his creation of an Irish-Canadian voice designed to amuse Toronto readers and to raise issues of social, political, and literary significance. His Terry Finnegan was a masculine, energetic, ungram-matical, unapologetic, epigrammatic, teasing, and worldly-wise son of the sod. He could be kindly or pugnacious, wise or bombastic, assertive or coy, but he was always observant, resilient, and pragmatic; as well, he was good-humoured and amusing in his excesses. He was a poor-in-purse resident of a Toronto slum who accepted his position in life without fuss and was undaunted by what many would have viewed as inescapable social limitations.

His palaver was marked by the standard stage-Irish tags – words and phrases like "begorra," "pon my sowkins," "ma bouchal," "mavourneen," and "blur an' agers." By sheer verbal exuberance and high spirits he cast a charm over his readers, many of whom were Irish-born and nostalgic for the Ireland they had left behind. A number of Canadian editors showered superlatives upon Terry, whether or not they were aware of his creator's identity. They described Terry as "irrepressible," "incomparable," and "inimitable." The *Daily Leader* assured its readers that Terry's letters had "the unmistakable stamp of genius about them," while a *Hamilton Times* correspondent wrote that "Canada could boast of having at least one real wit whose genius, force and fine imagination are a happy blending of the leading characteristics of Dickens and [Samuel] Lover." As such praise suggests, in both his Finnegan letters and the vernacular poems for his "Irish Anthology," McCarroll had emerged as an accomplished literary craftsman in Canada West; he was an Irish-Canadian writer worth celebrating in the moment and well worth watching in the future.

Certain scholarly difficulties follow from Terry Finnegan's letters. Tracking them is a challenge. Their home was not the conventional press; rather, they belonged to small Toronto literary magazines. The contributors, many of whom

THE GRUMBLER.

| VOL. 1. | TORONTO, SATURDAY, MAY 1, 1858. | NO. 7. |

THE GRUMBLER.

" If there's a hole in a' your coats
I rede you tent it ;
A chiel's amang you taking notes,
And, faith, he'll prent it."

SATURDAY, MAY 1, 1858.

PROVINCIAL SPOUTING APPARATUS.—No. VII.

During the past week the House has been engaged in brewing the small beer of legislation in the shape of Surrogate and water course bills. We are happy to see this little exhibition of industry after nearly three months' unmitigated sloth ; the mental calibre of the house is better suited by petty law-tinkering, and we almost think that half a dozen City Councils fully equal to our Toronto Corporation might be made out of the honorable body.

I. LOTBINIERE AGAIN.

We record with becoming thankfulness the fact that we have seen almost the last of the Lotbiniere examination. O'Farrell's defence was quite characteristic ; he did not attempt any contradiction of the damaging evidence given against him, but merely retorted upon his opponent in the tu quoqui style. He tacitly admitted that he had gained his seat by fraud, but pleaded as a defence that Noel had mobbed one of the polling places. We certainly never heard of so notable an effort to transmogrify two blacks into a white before. We should like to know, now that the investigations are about over, what the government is going to do with Fellowes and O'Farrell ; are they to be allowed to sit in the House in the face of frauds now proved to every body's satisfaction, or shall the indignant honesty of public opinion succeed in driving them back to their constituents ? Nous verrons.

II. THE USURY LAWS.

A very fiery debate on the Government measure on this subject, took place on Tuesday night, ending in a nice little squabble between MacKenzie and Mr. Speaker. The latter gentleman has made himself quite famous for the neatest and most unexceptionable little dodges under the cover of order and precedent. This time, without any call from the House, which is usually waited for by the Chair, he took it into his sage head to summon the members to vote, when Lemieux was actually on his feet to move an amendment. The particular joke in this trick was, that Mr. Brown had been called away by an alarm of fire, so the noble Frontenac desired to take a vote forthwith in the Grit's absence. This procedure naturally caused a little breeze, and the dignified Speaker at length gave way. We earnestly admonish him to consider the dignity of his office, and not sit with a pen in his mouth like a skewered pullet, or continually splautering like a tobacco-chewing

Yankee, into that odious American spittoon: We have no desire to be severe, but we have actually heard the head of our Canadian Parliament, compared to the Mock Duke in the Honey Moon.

III. PARLIAMENTARY JOKING.

Ghastly attempts at the funny are sometimes made in the House; we do not think it proper that these should be lost. We give a sample. By the Premier—" Like the soldier in the Gospel, he (Mowatt) came when he was told, and went when he was told. He would have made an excellent recruit for the 100th Regiment."

Mr. Mowatt's intended retort—" The Hon. Attorney General on the other hand, is very unlike the soldier, &c., for though Upper Canada has been bidding him to go for the last six months—" he goeth not." Very good for the Chancery bar.

Mr. Robinson made a very vigorous offer on behalf of his arrested friend Angus Morrison, who, he said, had been "looking after a sick man McDougall" in Oxford. If our memory serves us, we have some slight recollection that the late august Czar made a similar joke about Turkey ; the coincidence is no doubt accidental, for no one could accuse Mr. Robinson of plagiarism, he is so perfectly original.

By the way, we have not heard McKenzie's joke about " O'Gimlet's finger post" this session, we suppose he is reserving it for poor Cayley when the Public Accounts come up. Mr. Hogan's joke also about Dissolving Views, which in justice certainly belongs to himself alone, has not been heard since his blushing maiden oration.

There are many other members who might emulate the fame of the late Joe Miller, if they would only read the funny column of the N. Y. Ledger, for a month or two ; and by way of encouragement THE GRUMBLER offers a premium for the most barren joke of the session. Prize : An elegantly framed portrait of the Speaker, the prince of practical jokers. Messrs. Powell and Ferres stand an excellent chance in the competition.

A Wrinkle.

—— Dr. Mackay told us in his last lecture that the national poet of Ireland had to be born. We must say that we are not the only distinguished individual in the world who laboured under the delusion that Ireland has produced some very excellent poets before now, who by some unaccountable fatality had been looked upon as national poets; but we hasten to recant our opinion and to consign Goldsmith, Moore, Lover, Griffin, Carlton, Davis, Lever, and a host of such small fry to Orcus. We hope that the coming infant will soon make his appearance, and that the learned Doctor will lend his experience to make him increase to the proportions of a first-rate national poet. By the way Lalla Rookh is about to give way, in public opinion, to Down the Mississip.

ENGLAND'S NECESSITY IS OUR OPPORTUNITY.
Wrenched from a wicked old Song.

As recruits in these times are not easily got,
And the Crown Prince must have them—pray why should we not
As the least, and we grant it, the money we can do for him—
Ship off the Ministry body and bones to him.
There's not in all Canada, we'd venture to swear,
Any men we could half so conveniently spare ;
And though they've been helping the French for years past,
We may make them of use to the nation at last,
Nay, we do not see why the great Speaker himself,
Should in times such as these, stay at home on the shelf,
Though through narrow desires he's not fitted to pass,
Yet who could resist if he bore down en masse
And though oft at a fight he might frequently prove,
Like our gallant policeman, able to move ;
Yet there's one thing in war advantage unbounded,
Which is, that he could not ith ease be surrounded.

NEWSPAPER WANTS.

1. An editorial from the Colonist, in which the inexplicious name of Brown is not mentioned twenty times.

2. An editorial from the Leader, from which one can gather the drift twelve lines before its termination, or even then.

3. An editorial from the Globe, in which any body but the senior member for Toronto gets credit for anything, or in which "corruption" and "speculation" do not occupy a prominent place.

4. An editorial of the Message, (if such a thing as an editorial in the paper can be found,) in which Sir F. Head and 1837, are not raked up for public edification.

5. An editorial from the Citizen, without a smart rap at the "bloody Saxon."

Sabbath Desecration.

—— Mr. Brown's attention is called to the fact that a small craft yclept the "Fire-fly," breaks the Sunday calm by sundry trips to the Peninsula and back, on the Sabbath. It might be well, before endeavoring to extract the beam from the Welland Canal, to look after the mote (mote) traversed by the Fire-fly.

" Hitting Him on the raw."

—— We learn with surprise that some of our Western cotemporaries, who innocently copied some of our strictures on Rankin, have been prosecuted by the " monument" for libel. We can readily imagine twelve honest jurymen returning a verdict in favor of the pirate who has set all law at defiance, and about whose misdeeds not half the truth has yet been told.

A Sight for a Father.

—— Poor Ferres, (the man wot blushes,) had a spasmodic fit of independence on Dorion's Bill, relating to " Les Sœurs Grises :" he actually objected to the bill, but overcome by the effort, "trailed resolution" by voting in its favor. He has been in bed ever since.

6.2 Front page, *Grumbler* 1, no. 7, 1 May 1858. It was the leading Humour magazine in the city before Confederation. It was edited and published first by Erastus Wiman and then by John Ross Robertson. The lead column, "Provincial Spouting Apparatus," was a recurring feature from the magazine's inception. Robarts Library Media Commons, University of Toronto.

remain unknown to this day, and the publishers of these magazines formed a small group of literary types – an artistic in-crowd in Toronto – who were bent on criticizing and making fun of the leading political and corporate figures of the day. Always maintaining their anonymity, these elusive scribes would become the first set of alternative and countercultural, arts-oriented writers and humorists in Toronto's brief history. McCarroll may well have been pegged by some as "the man who was afraid to be known,"[55] at least in print during his Toronto years. Some magazines were so short-lived as to be forgotten today, and some have simply disappeared. As a result, these path-breaking little magazines have been mostly ignored by scholars of nineteenth-century Canadian cultural history, even though they provided a literary place for "racy," satiric, un-genteel, and notably off-centre writing in convention-bound, Victorian Toronto.

The best known and most durable of the little magazines was the *Grumbler*, published first by Erastus Wiman (1858–59) and later by John Ross Robertson (1862–65). Though many of its issues have survived, it has been little studied to date. A number of similar ventures, including the *Poker* (1859), *Momus* (1861), and *Pick* (1865) have also been overlooked; the latter two featured Terry Finnegan's letters.[56] Of these three, only the *Poker* is available on microfilm. As well, two other magazines – the *Latch-Key* (1863, 1864) and the *Growler* (1864) – were McCarroll's own handiwork. To date, these magazines have also been neglected by scholars of pre-Confederation life.[57] Despite the financial troubles that beset McCarroll after he lost his customs position, he remained hopeful that he might yet create his own humorous magazine, one that would ride in part on Terry Finnegan's vernacular coattails, thus allowing him a freer voice and a means of meeting some of his growing debts. Since he could do his own printing and typesetting from home, he needed only a small infusion of capital from a friend or two to undertake production of such publications.[58] However, without a sufficient number of subscribers – always a challenge in the short run – and with only limited backing, the life of his little magazines was always brief.

An Irish-Canadian "Paddy" for Toronto

Maureen Waters has identified four types of the "comic Irishman" to be found in nineteenth-century writing. In her book of the same title, she identifies the descendants of the stage-Irish reprobate (and villain) who was popular in earlier English dramas and political cartoons.[59] Waters argues that these later Paddy figures constitute a reversal of the negative stereotype belonging to early English drama. Her four types are the rustic clown or omadhawn,[60] the rogue or outlaw, the stage Irishman, and the comic hero.

In creating Terry Finnegan, McCarroll drew freely on these types, all of which were available to him in contemporary newspapers and novels. In describing an Irish brigade that Terry was thinking of creating in Toronto, he showed his colours by pledging "that the divil a sowl would be let into it that wasn't as ginuine a Paddy as ever kicked a fut ball or danced a jig" (Letter 19).[61] In McCarroll's hands Terry is a sport and a spontaneous dancer; he is neither a fool nor a reprobate. Rather, he is a breezy, rough-edged, and opinionated Torontonian whose views are irrevocably Irish. Perceptive and warm-hearted, he is surprisingly well connected for a poor chap living in a city slum. Above all, he has the gift of the gab and loves to celebrate the glories of his homeland and himself. He often waxes nostalgic about "ould Ireland" and he celebrates both "rale Celtic blood" and the "janius of the anshent Irish," while offering McGee a string of observations about Toronto's cultural life and the complexities of Canadian politics. Particularly proud of his own "janius" – rooted, of course, in his pure Finnegan blood – he occasionally offers his "cousin" a poetic effusion of his own creation, knowing full well that McGee saw himself as a serious poet and would have been appalled by the connection.

Terry's home was on "Stanly Street." A number of poor Irish immigrant families called Stanley Street home.[62] Its reputation for "housing a world of Catholic poverty, indolence and brogue-laden Irishness" was there for McCarroll to observe on his cross-town walks as a customs officer.[63] However, the sordidness of its reputation did not bother Terry. Indeed, the place and the man came to seem symbiotic. McCarroll chose Stanley Street as a deliberate "nudge-nudge" to McGee who, despite owing his continuing electoral success to the voters of lowly Griffintown in Montreal, was vigorously committed to maintaining his upper-middle-class identity.[64] McCarroll knew that, as a poet and a politician, McGee was loath to be linked to the low-life vitality of the Paddy tradition. Those stereotypes were to him demeaning, offensive, and reprehensible. He favoured a higher social and intellectual tone along with a pronounced respectability of purpose. In his own poetry and prose he sought to embrace his place within the high standards of the English literary tradition. In effect, then, "cousin" Terry's voice and assumptions were very much at odds with McGee's Irish-Canadian identity and his Irish sensibility. But that very inappropriateness made for satiric fun and amusing word games. Little wonder that Terry's letters were not placed in the mainstream newspapers where accounts of McGee's speeches and activities appeared in copious detail. The first series of Terry Finnegan's letters to the Honorable Thomas D'Arcy McGee was published in Toronto late in 1863. He dedicated "this trifling volume to every Irishman under the sun no matter his creed or country." In his "Advertisement" he wrote as follows:

The following letters were, from time to time, and without permission, addressed, through the columns of a humorous publication, to the Honorable Thomas D'Arcy McGee – a statesman of broad and generous views, an Orator of transcendent abilities, and a Companion at once, instructive, agreeable and refined. At the solicitation of a few literary friends they are now thrown into book shape, with a view, amongst other things, of extending a knowledge of some of the peculiarities of the Irish Character among those who may not have had an opportunity of studying it, in all its purity, on the other side of the Atlantic; and in the hope of beguiling a spare half hour on the part of such as are not the irrevocable victims of transcendentalism or sound, common sense.

The first Terry Finnegan letter appeared in *Momus* on 14 March 1861.[65] It was almost exclusively concerned with parliamentary doings "down at Quabec" and it advised McGee on how best to adapt to the religious and political pressures of the moment. Here it is in full:

Oh! Then bad cess to you, but you're the nice boy for thratin me this way. The last time we took a cup of Irish tay here, didn't you tell me you'd write afore you'd go down, and let me know what coorse you intended to purshue durin the sisshun? Whin you tould me it was your detarmination to give Brown, on the first occashun, "a left handher" for his thratemint of the Clargy, you recollect we took "another" on the head of it; but, begorra, if this will be like you're promise of writin, I'm afeered we'll not squeeze much out of you.

Pon my conshins, I can't help thinking but that little Frinch Attorney Gineral has been the cause of all your throuble. If both himself and his collague had common sinse, they'd have jumped at you, like a cock at a blackberry, the day they had a chance up in the ould hospital here. But you see the Frinchman thought you bein Irish wouldn't do from Monthreal; and besides, you know he tould you that you weren't long enough in the country. Wasn't that cute, and didn't you remimber it to him since?

God knows if you had the "ace and five fingers" in your hand you couldn't bate and remain where you are at present. Like the thriangular jewel in Midshipman Aisy, you have to fight your rale innimy and a fellow that belongs to your own squad. First you fire acrass the House at Attorney Gineral West, and thin you take a crack at Brown at your elbow; for you know you must give him a polthogue, no matther how soft, the moment he touches the soutane, digger mavourneen: – have a little more of the bird of passage in you, and step acrass the Spaker on the first dacent opportunity. You can't work the Pope and John Knox with the same sthring. Be independent, as they say – sich as Jim Smith was, long ago, whin he slipped his cable; and sich as John Cameron, Ogle R. and others are today. That's the way to make money. Always keep one leg loose on the flure. *Animus vesther ego.* – "mind your eye," as poor Mulloy of the "Sthrawberry Beds" used to say – the Lord rest him. You're not like Joe Goold or Tom Short. There's somethin in you and we want to get it out. Take care of that Frinchman. I'll write regularly. Let me hear from you at wanst.

Your lovin cousin,

Terry Finnegan

P.S. – What d'ye think ould Mullany sez to me jest now? "Terry," sez he, "I'll hould ye a tasther that it will be sometime afore Darcy takes tay wid the *Thrue Witness.*" Isn't he an ould rake?

Each Finnegan letter is striking in the fluidity of its brogue, its allusiveness, and its easy, familiar language.[66] They twinkle in their informality and sassiness, though, read in the light of David Wilson's biography of McGee, they provide a set of glimpses that often belie the real complexity of McGee's motives and his pragmatic strategies as a sometimes isolated parliamentarian. McGee's motives were on the whole more intellectually principled and more nuanced than the pragmatic Terry was willing to allow. Very much of its particular moment, each letter requires the reader to know something about the political players and the specific issues of the day in order to respond to the jokes while recognizing the facts that underlie Terry's allusions, images, and advice.

Key to Terry's first letter, for instance, were McGee's problematic relationships with the three influential Georges of the day: George Brown, George-Étienne Cartier, and George Clerk. George Brown, the influential Scottish-born politician and founder of the *Globe* newspaper in Toronto, was a Scottish Protestant and an unyielding critic of the inordinate influence exerted by the Catholic Church in Canada East. On this occasion he deserved "a left-handher" for what Terry saw as his betrayal of McGee on the political stage. In a surprising coalition, the two men had become political allies for a time in 1860–61, but then Brown cut McGee loose, apparently because of their strong religious differences. Cartier, "the little frinch Attorney General" who, like McGee, represented a Montreal riding, exercised a great deal of political influence in Canada East. Initially, he had been dismissive of McGee as a newcomer to Canada and Quebec; in fact, an Irish Catholic was for him a figure of considerably lesser significance than a genuine French Catholic. By 1861 they were at best uneasy allies, despite their shared religion.

The outspoken George Clerk was the editor of the *Montreal True Witness*, the city's ultra-conservative English Catholic newspaper. In recent issues he had chastised McGee for having abandoned the true Catholic faith, especially by fraternizing with dour Protestants like George Brown who were, in Clerk's view, little better than the devil's disciples.[67] In the spring of 1861, as McGee shifted his alliances and consciously tried to speak for a more liberal approach to politics and religion in the Canadas, Clerk, who was an uncompromising ultramontanist, questioned the kind and quality of McGee's faith. How could a serious Catholic align himself with a dogged and unsympathetic Presbyterian like Brown? And how could he desert his own previously declared ultramontanist beliefs for more liberal views? Like George Clerk in Montreal, Terry kept a very close watch on McGee; by contrast, however, he offered McGee cousinly council rather than acute religious criticism. One piece of Terry's advice speaks succinctly to the matter – "You can't work the Pope and John Knox with the same sthring."

The fun of Terry's letters resides in the jocular observations and the tongue-in-cheek, vernacular comments. Misspelled words ("innimy," "wanst," and the added "h" to "t" in words like "Vesthur" and "sthring"), the brogue and stage-Irish tags, conspicuous grammatical infelicities ("like you're promise of writin'"), and Terry's jaunty images and phrasing all contribute: indeed, Terry commands a range of colloquial idioms that are often surprisingly modern; they connect with the attentive reader and provide a stream of verbal amusement that has vibrant appeal, regardless of the reader's nationality. McCarroll had a good ear for the well-turned phrase ("Irish tay" for a whiskey cocktail, "like a cock at a blackberry" for trying hard but achieving little, and "Animus vest(h) er ego" for "mind your eye"); as well, he delighted in including references to notable Irish locales such as the Strawberry Beds, which are located near Dublin on the north bank of the Liffey. Overall, the verbal exuberance vies for attention with the political name-dropping and strategic advice that Terry persistently offers McGee.

Letter after letter followed the doings "down" in "Parlemint" and the shifting alliances that characterized legislative control in the unsettled pre-Confederation years. Terry often urged McGee to avoid taking sides at tense moments. His standard metaphors for political survival included tightrope walking and gymnastic manoeuvres like somersaults. "Look to number one, even at the expense of a few summersets," he advised. Or, be "a tumbler" and "step into office with the agility of a mountebank."[68] Or "you must bring your experience on the tight rope into requisition" (Letter 16). Terry saw no point in being moralistic or high-minded; a politician's goal was to stay in office – "beware of principle and consistency; for a divil a two worse brickbats a man ever carried in his hat. Have your legs as soople as an eel" (Letter 14).

What Irishmen wanted from McGee, according to McCarroll, was evidence of his commitment to issues of importance to them. The Irish needed an effective voice at important moments. There was no question that McGee was blessed with "the gift of the gab" (Letter 9) and commanded a "profound eloquence" (Letter 22). Terry's advice was to apply those skills effectively and only when required. Don't overplay your hand or become too committed to any high-sounding issue like representation by population (Rep by Pop) or the schools question. On 21 June 1861 (Letter 7) Terry offered McGee a typical, tongue-in-cheek piece of advice about the upcoming election: "I wish you luck in your canvas, and would advise you not to be over particular as to the manes you use in endeavourin to resume your sate. Get into parliament honestly if you can; but get into Parliament. The divil a one of thim but does the same. Keep your spirits up – accordin to the recognized institutions of our ancesthers – Go to mass regularly, and be sure to confess to a Priest that doesn't undherstand a word of [E]nglish; and bedad you'll be likely to pass musther."

At times Terry discoursed on extra-political matters in Toronto. He was, for instance, excessively critical of the weather in Canada; indeed, it likely had a dampening effect on his own irrepressible spirit at times: "Ah! Mavourneen, I have been here in this cowld counthry for minny a long, long year; and this much I can say, that I niver yet saw in it what I could call a rale summer's even-ing wid the bewtiful, blue haze that the sun stained with cathedhral light as he lay on some far off golden sand bank on the verge of the horizon. Oh! But this is the dhreadful place! Nine months winther and three of cool weather, barrin the odd hot whiff from some ethayrial furnace or other, that's no more the rale thing itself than Joe Gould's like Lord Brougham" (Letter 6, 12 June 1861).

Much as McGee was proud of his own poetry, so was "cousin" Terry of his. On occasion, he commented disdainfully on McGee's poems and fired off shots at other contemporary poets who were receiving public attention. With a nasty "left-handher," he dismissed Alexander McLachlan, who had received "a [public] certificate of character" from McGee himself; he was one of the "long winded hucksthers … who lies a very Lazarus at the gates of true poesy." For Terry as poet, "The art of poetry is not the throwin of a few handfuls of prose into a bag, and the shakin of them up till they jingle" (Letter 8). Rather, it involves an imaginative exploration of emotions sometimes related to the body and aspects of sexual attraction. Such attention was, of course, conspicuously avoided by most poets in the colony. What McLachlan – and by implication McGee himself – lacked was a sensitivity willing to probe such subject matter freshly and imaginatively. As poets they failed because they offered "No glimpse of the sunny instep, pink nails or delicate ankle of an idea, affordin the reader the exquisite pleasure of supplyin the remainder of the nude figure, and afterwards drapin it accordin to the tints of his imagination." McCarroll's phrasing here is both delicate and vivid. Terry knew that, in the high-minded and often stuffy realm of colonial gentility and Victorian manners, "rale" poetry was misunderstood and undervalued. Hence, the serious and sensual poet had to proceed through indirection.

Terry also took aim at the praise heaped upon Isadore Ascher in the *British American Magazine*, where, not coincidently, some of McCarroll's own poems were then appearing.[69] The magazine's editor, Henry Youle Hinds, was "two good natured for a critic."[70] Seeing Hinds as a man who had "mistaken his vocashun" in trying to write insightfully about poetry, Terry asked if "such criticisms [as his] are jest and calculated to enhance the cause of littherature in this Province." Then he explained his position: "In my opinion, the pursuits of Mr Hind and the constitushun of his well-stored and educated mind, unfit him for a thorough appreshiashun of the florid and ethayreal bewties that pervade the ragions of thrue poethry, and separate them from those of prose. People who are prone naturally to the dhry details of science are unsafe guides in this connexion, and verify the sayin: 'Those who are fond of mathematics are not given to the Gods.'"[71]

By way of promoting his own "janius," Terry sent McGee a poem entitled "Peggy Morin." McGee "might study [it] with profit," he suggested.[72]

You may talk as you plaze, Peggy Morin,
But this much you know to be thrue;
That 'tis you I am always adorin,
And the divil another but you.

And you know, besides, by the law Harry,
That at Nenagli, that's near Roscrea,
Ooney Gallagher's niece I could marry,
While Miss Grady herself axed me to tay.

Yis! – nobody less than Miss Grady;
For didn't she ax me herself?
And wasn't she, oh! the rale lady,
Though a thrifle too long on the shelf.

But didn't the pair look fulloren,
When I axed – like the bouldest of min –
If they ever knew one Peggy Morin
That lived at the foot of the glin?

"And," sez I – and I spoke at my peril,
They were gettin so wild, do you see –;
"Now, I'm not goin past that same *girl*;
And I think she's not goin past me."

Delightfully breezy in its language, the poem affirms Terry's democratic outlook while dramatizing the struggles of an eligible young man in a society dominated by talkative, socially prominent women. Having offered up his own poem, Terry posed a cunning question to McGee: "Now, yer sowl you! what do you think of that? Is that rale stone turf or sodhoch! Och! Me darlin! There's a sthrake of bog dale in me that lights like a candle whin the time comes; and that's the raison I know I don't belong to that unfortshunate class of ferrits berried up to their eyes in an iclaya-burrow, and bringin to the surface every thin that even a pawnbroker could minshun, except the rale rabbit itself" (Letter 15).

McCarroll regularly sought to unearth that "sthrake of bog dale" in his inner being and bring the "rale rabbit itself" to the surface. Terry Finnegan gave McCarroll a public voice that allowed him to explore the edges of his challenging literary quest and make a case for what he believed was the essential goal of poetry. In "Peggy Morin," as in other "Irish" poems like "Biddy McGuire" and "Kitty Fitzgibbon," McCarroll wedded the vernacular and the comedic to provide a zesty blend of wordplay and emotion. A lightness of touch and a commitment to the sensory and sensual were, he knew, missing from the work of most colonial poets. But Ireland was "the land of song" (Letter 13) and Terry regarded himself as one of its natural exponents; his was an exuberant voice rooted in that heritage and actively at odds with Victorian restraint. McCarroll's long-standing affection for the poetry of Thomas Moore was the root of his sense of cultural heritage.

Furthermore, Terry was an Irish nationalist. As he put it, "No matter how the game goes, all I care about is that ould Ireland will carry the day in the prisent row, no matther whether she is in the right of it or not" (Letter 30). He insisted on browbeating McGee on this premise, even as he realized, with increasing regret, that his "cousin'" was developing a more Canadian and continentalist vision the longer he resided in the colony. In that way McGee was distancing himself from the primary issues of Irish political and social identity that increasingly preoccupied McCarroll.

But while the "etherial" essence of poetry engaged Terry, so too did his love of music. In an 1863 letter Terry waxed eloquent about the "great singer, Madame Anna Bishop," who had recently appeared on a "balmy August evening" at the Horticultural Gardens in Toronto. The experience of hearing her sing in the park moved him deeply.

Bad luck to me but I thought I was fairly in the ragions of the Arabian Knights, or whatever you call thim. Did you ever hear a thrush in the blue haze of a warm summer evenin – in a hazel brake by the side of some purple sthrame in the ould sod? If you did, you may just console yourself wid the conviction that you harde the countherpart of Madame Anna, barrin that you might throw in a couple of black birds and a dozen or so of nightingales besides. You won't believe me, I suppose, whin I tell you that I had to go out undher a tree and cry when she sung "The Beggar Girl," and the next morning the only shillin I had in my pocket I gave to the first poor woman I met on the sthreet. Oh! there's nothing for pickin the lock of a fella's sowl like thrue music, for wheniver I hear it, I feel as if I could almost commit murther without exactly knowing the raison why, or inquirin into aither. (Letter 31)[73]

In Letter 13 (30 January 1863) Terry issued a sharp attack on the double standard of proper Torontonians in their treatment of the city's black residents. In a British colony where slavery had been abolished for decades and the principle of equality was publicly celebrated, McCarroll provided a frank piece of social observation, especially in the context of the Civil War still raging to the south. While excessively wrought in its style, the piece cut to the core of the social hypocrisies too often practised in the "land of promise" by apparently progressive white citizens:

Darcy, dear, some of our frinds up here are greatly disthressed about naygers – some of the nasal chaps and white chokers, wid faces the linth of a fiddle on them. Oh! such a pack of hypocrites niver bruk the bread of life. They, in abaydiance to scripther, as they say, induce the colored man to lave his southern home, as their enslaved brother; and beckon him to this land of promise, where he is to be free, and form part and parcel of our soshal compact. They ought, every mother's son of them, be brought undher Dick Martin's Act: for, when the poor sable dupe casts aside his hoe and cotton trowsers, and stands in our midst, he finds he has but exchanged them for rags and a white-wash brush, and the education offered his little ones must only serve to make them comprehend to the fullest extent the depth of their degradation. He has no more fair play among us than he had in the South. What is his liberty to him, whin no man opens his pew door to him – whin no man asks him to tay – whin no man will walk the streets wid him – whin no man will give him his dauther in marriage – whin no man will shake hands wid him, or permits him as an aqual under his roof? Are we not liars and hypocrites of the first wather, to call this man brother, when we thrate him like a brute? By the mortial, I'm sick of Christianity and the min that profess it. Down wid slavery, I say; but hang the false pretences we use in relation to it. (Letter 13)

The Finnegan letters loosely follow McGee's political and spatial move-ments, though their appearance was irregular; in that sense they followed from McCarroll's work schedule, health, and the availability of publishing outlets. As noted earlier, there was a hiatus of a year and a half between Letter 8 (28 June 1861) and Letter 9 (5 December 1862) of volume 1, after which the letters begin to appear again, about once a week. The long hiatus can be partially explained by the failure of *Momus* and the loss of a site of publication. But, as previously noted, McCarroll's entire literary output slackened in 1862, owing to either an illness or a struggle with depression. When the letters reappeared in 1862, their new home was the *Grumbler*, a larger alternative magazine already well established in the city, despite a law suit that had temporarily terminated its publication schedule for several months.[74]

Among the most enjoyable features of Terry's letters are its running jokes. Terry is an uneducated but poetic spirit devoted to "the ould sod." He coyly admits that "this pin I have doesn't spell well" (Letter 14), but persists in turning out phrases and images that cleverly violate linguistic standards even as they create vivid pictures and evoke chuckles. Not surprisingly, Terry is a drinking man, a lover of "Irish tay" or "pottein," and he delights in referring to McGee's well-known weakness for the bottle. Liquor was a pleasure that neither cousin could resist.

Relatedly, after numerous tumblers, Terry could become a brawler. Donnybrooks – almost always involving Irishmen – frequently occurred in the vicinity of "Stanly Street" in the 1860s. Terry was sometimes a participant, sometimes a victim. But as an Irishman, he was keenly attentive to "donnybrook style" (Letter 14). He writes, for instance, of a pugnacious friend named "ould Lanty Cummins," who "couldn't behave himself for a single quarther of an hour if he even had a whole townland in Paradise to himself" (Letter 28). In one letter Terry describes a true Irishman as one who "can burn a haystack, 'hoch' a cow, or shoot a 'tithe procther.'" While scarcely a prescription for social deportment, such men were valued in southern Ireland. Still, with a knowing wink, he recognizes that sort of pugnacious spirit on the streets of Toronto. His "little vein of good humour" (Letter 16) is at play in such contradictory descriptions.

Terry's letters are so rife with colourful oaths that his wife, Biddy, occasionally chastens him about his profanity. Ever the quiet swaggerer, however, he does not hesitate to offer McGee advice on how best to treat his wife, or women in general. To Biddy's displeasure, Terry also finds reasons not to attend Mass and "do his [Catholic] duty" (Letter 15). With a rough-edged acuity, however, Terry on occasion probes his own inner nature, linking his letters to the famous "Confesshuns" of "Jane Jack Rooso." Remarking on the duplicity typical of politicians and men in general, he informs D'Arcy, "It's the thruth I'm telling you. Nearly all male persons are double – a blaggard and a gentleman – the latter bein the husk and the former, in most cases, the kernel; and, begorra sometimes I feel it in myself; although, like the rest of thim, I'm always inclined to put the best fut foremost and keep, if possible, the wake ankled lad in the back grounds" (Letter 24). That inner "blaggard" is always present in Terry. McCarroll linked it to "the strange inner fatality" rooted in the Irish character. It led men like Terry to value emotion over reason and often make bad choices, if sometimes for the right reasons. Politically, however, he would not be taken for a fool or, in stage-Irish vocabulary, an "ommadhawn" (Letter 13).

Terry also responded to such ongoing civic matters as the annual St Patrick's Parade in Toronto. In the early 1860s the parade had been cancelled because of fears of rioting, but in 1863, it was revived. Even as he kept an eye on the doings of the leaders of the Orange Order and the aspirations of Toronto Catholics, Terry urged a resumption of the parade. At the same time news of the horrendous events of the American Civil War served to heighten his negative view of the democratic republic of "un-united" states to the south.

Racialized Realities in Toronto and the Canadas

Terry Finnegan's letters were written in the context of the rival racial identities that informed the thinking of politicians and citizens in pre-Confederation Canada. Being proudly Irish, Terry held strong views concerning the dominant races in Canada and the complicated tensions their interactions fostered. At times he despaired of the French political control in Canada East and worried about the continuing effects of "the unmixable natshure of the Frinch and English elements."[75] "Sure, allannah," he told McGee, "as long as it's English and Frinch and Frinch and English, yez will niver get along. Jean Baptiste will niver play succond fiddle to yez or us up here durin secula seculorum."[76]

With a major decision pending about the future location of the seat of the "Canadian" government, there was a sense that the French would do all they could to keep the parliament in Quebec City, despite a prior agreement to shift it back to Canada West. Then, too, there were the tensions generated by the "Rep by Pop" issue forcefully put forward by George Brown. Nevertheless, Terry Finnegan was surprisingly sympathetic to the needs of those in Canada East; hence, he wrote, "And, whin I come to look into it, I think it's mane of some of us, now that we have got a thrifle more people in this seckshun of Kinnada then the Frinch have below, to want to take advantage of it to disturb the equipose which has existed so long and so happily" (Letter 17).[77] While the political demands of Canada East sometimes frustrated him, Terry took comfort in the current balance of power and recognized that a shift in population numbers in favour of Canada West created a new vulnerability for the French; more personally, he likely anticipated reasons that might incline Irish Catholics to align themselves with the French Canadians.

Beyond the definitive French-English tension, Terry was irritated that English control of Canada West persisted unchallenged. Together the English and the Scots had far more say concerning political matters than their numbers justified. Hence, he was ready to voice his mistrust of the Scots, those "sons of oatmeal," as he characterized them. As a poet with his own reputation to promote, McCarroll was particularly prickly; he did not hesitate to make Terry "a rale poet" while dismissing lesser writers, be they Scots or English, who received what he felt was unjustified attention.[78] Politically he viewed the Scots as deceptive and untrustworthy: they masked their cunning and backstabbing with an air of intellect, seriousness, and racial superiority.

Terry, however, did several somersaults of his own in assessing the political leadership and manoeuvres of leading Scots-born politicians like George Brown, John Sandfield Macdonald, and John A. Macdonald. In fact, having early on expressed admiration for the political doings of John Sandfield Macdonald and George Brown, he had, by the summer of 1863, come to regard both men as arch-enemies of the Irish. By contrast, John A. Macdonald, about whom he had at first expressed distrust, emerged slowly from the conservative side of the political ledger to earn Terry's praise and admiration. Underlying this change was the fact that, likely in 1862, McCarroll became an occasional drinking partner of John A. Thereafter that personal connection led Terry to offer kindlier and more sympathetic responses to Macdonald's political doings. "Don't make John A. your implacable innemy," he advised McGee early in 1863 (Letter 16), "and keep rubbin a friendly shouldher against George Brown – although, be gochhins, if a sartin peculiarity of his counthry be taken into considejashun, it is he that should be rubbin against you." As the primary spokesman for the emerging Grits, Brown's stridently anti-Catholic views distressed McCarroll. Increasingly, Terry saw him as "a savage." It was best to approach "Le Brun" cautiously, given his evident wildness.[79] By early September 1863, Premier John Sandfield Macdonald had become McCarroll's *bête noire* among elected politicians. After eliminating McCarroll's customs position, he sank like a stone in Terry's estimate. McCarroll's poem "Three Loaded Dice" (1863) epitomizes his scorn.

Overall, Terry's letters (in both series) provide a dramatic commentary on McGee's changing relationships with John Sandfield Macdonald, George Brown, and John A. Macdonald, all of whom were in and out of the premiership of Canada West during these difficult years. One of McCarroll's ongoing jokes was to have Terry boast of his friendship with Lord Monck, the new governor general of the Canadas. Claiming that he had access to privileged government thinking through Monck, Terry set about passing on insider information to "cousin" D'Arcy. After McGee was made a member of Sandfield Macdonald's cabinet in 1862–63 and thus placed in what appeared to be an influential position, Terry wrote positively about the premier. In Letter 10 (12 December 1862) he praised his "cunning" and claimed to have no "sarious objection" to him. Still, he continued to advise McGee to look out for himself politically, always attending to the long-range interests of the Irish. However, when Sandfield

Macdonald "betrayed" McGee, first by denying him the immigration portfolio (to which McGee aspired) and then, during the spring of 1863, by leaving him out of crucial cabinet discussions pertaining to the upcoming election, Terry's view of the premier became as hostile as McGee's. McGee felt that he had been badly used by the ministry to which he ostensibly belonged. Neither had he been supported in his initiative to develop the Intercontinental Railway project. That projected line joining Quebec and the Maritime colonies would have facilitated trade between them and was crucial, McGee believed, to the future possibility of confederation among the Canadian "provinces." Indeed, Sandfield Macdonald's mistreatment of McGee was in step with McCarroll's dismissal from his customs position. In both cases, the dour and commanding Scot was seen as the man who betrayed the legitimate hopes of the Irish in Canada.

An Anglo-Protestant by birth, McCarroll had long sought to align himself with Irish-Catholic interests. His inclusive view was not a goal that many would have publically attempted at that time. As he later told John A. Macdonald, he hoped to speak effectively to both sides of the Irish religious-cultural divide, thereby nurturing the possibility of Irish unity. In unity, the Irish would certainly have more power and more political heft. In his Peterborough days he had been an active Orangeman as would have befitted his circle of friendship there. By the 1860s, however, he was projecting his own Catholic sympathies through two humorous voices – Terry Finnegan in Toronto and Lanty Mullins in Peterborough. In the process he was implicitly distancing himself from Orange and Protestant connections in Toronto and the province. In 1864, he remained a cautious supporter of the Orange.

At John A.'s specific request, he inserted a column in the *Daily Leader* on "The Thugs" of India. John Sandfield Macdonald had compared those eastern "Thugs" with the Orange Order in Canada (*Daily Leader*, 14 May 1864). He had argued that he was merely repeating an earlier remark made by D'Arcy McGee, but his excuse was dismissed and mocked by many Toronto observers. McCarroll's role was to pinion the premier for his "intemperate and ill-considered language," and label him as "thoroughly unscrupulous." The criticism was yet another small nail in Macdonald's political coffin.

McCarroll's attempts to encourage unity were conducted for the most part undercover, by means of journalistic anonymity or through his stage-Irish alias. Increasingly, he aligned himself with the *Irish Canadian* and, in the guise of Terry Finnegan, he distanced himself from Protestant Irishmen like John Hillyard Cameron, Michael Foley, Ogle Gowan, and the increasingly politicized operations of the Orange Order. Terry warned McGee, as if there was any need, not to become "entangled in the meshes of Orangeism" (as he might have to do through his new connection with John A.). He wrote off the increasingly notorious Gowan as a once-useful Irishman, both because of his aggressive Orangeism and the sexual scandals that had begun to discredit him. Much as he liked Michael Foley and wished him well, he continued to be disappointed by him.

Lanty Mullins in "Petherboro"

Having recovered from his "illness" in the spring of 1862, McCarroll was once again spreading the net of his influence as widely as he could. In addition to resuming the weekly Finnegan letters, writing reviews and columns in several Toronto newspapers, contributing to the *British American Magazine*, and publishing his own magazine the *Latch-Key* (in 1863 and 1864), he began a new series of "Irish" letters for the *Peterborough Examiner*. The *Examiner* editor, Alex Graham, welcomed the initiative and, from 18 July to 10 August 1863, he printed four letters from Lanty Mullins (then residing at "Toronto, Park Lane – That Was") to "Paddy Mahony, Ould Dinny's Son" (in "Petherboro, Kinnada West"). They ceased abruptly when Graham wrote McCarroll on 11 August to say that he had to cancel the column because of hostile responses from his readers, who particularly disliked his treatment of George Brown.

The Graham letter, which is a part of the John A. Macdonald Papers, is of interest for both its substance and its tone. He wrote as one editor to another and as a fellow journalist aware of McCarroll's earlier connections with Peterborough. "Dear McCarroll," he began,

> I am sorry to say that you will have to stop writing your letters to me as I find they are not going to pay me[;] besides there is no interest taken in such things here that I thought would be taken. You gave Brown a hard Rub in one of the letters and it had a very bad effect. You know the kind of people I have to deal with here, you will therefore oblige me by not writing any more of them until you hear further from me.
>
> Yours, &
>
> Alex Graham

Graham's conservative readers had little taste for such hard-hitting literary playfulness; influential literalists balked at the outrageousness of McCarroll's freewheeling scenarios. In addition, sloppy typesetting at the newspaper may have created difficulties for Peterborough readers trying to make sense of Lanty's brogue in print form.

There were problems in Lanty Mullins's insistence on a democratic view of sorts and the sly crudity of his cosmopolitanism. Casting himself as a former Peterborough resident who once walked the sixty miles from Port Hope to Toronto (because there were no trains on a Sunday), he focused on his Toronto experiences. Being a democrat at heart, Lanty expressed a desire to befriend as many "servants of the principle people here" as he could manage; "then, of course, I'm as good as in every house in the city." Like Terry Finnegan, Lanty was hostile to rank and presumption, and expressed empathy with those living in depressed or marginal circumstances.

At the same time, he and Paddy Mahony shared an acquaintance with "our ould frind" Thomas D'Arcy McGee. The four letters covered themes such as the upcoming government session (set to begin on 13 August), the strength of monarchical support among Canadians, the ongoing campaign for Rep by Pop, the future seat of government, relations with the Americans during their "little family quarrel," and current British and Canadian attitudes toward both sides in the Civil War. Lanty managed to refer to McGee's doings in each letter, be it his promotion of his new book on Ireland or his visit to Toronto during which he told Lanty that "Rep. By Pop. and the sait of Governmint question [are] goin to puzzle John Sanfield terribly."

Lanty's most outrageous comedic set piece was a bizarre drinking party hosted by the Honorable George Brown. Having befriended George Brown's servant Sandy MucIntire, Lanty learned that Brown, the arch anti-Catholic, not only "goes to confession as regular as the sun" but often "takes an odd taste with the [Catholic] Bishop here." Lanty then described a "jovial" evening at Brown's home, attended by such unlikely colleagues as Bishop Lynch and Egerton Ryerson. After the bishop toasts "the Church, the Press and the Educational interests of the country" (which, he asserts, "are in good hands at laste"), Brown bragged about his improvements in the *Globe*'s printing operations by purchasing a "double sillandher driven by steam." Despite his bravado, however, Brown could not contain his cynicism; he bragged that he could now put in print much more quickly "any kind of rubbish you want to stick on the public." However, when Brown allows that "the *Layther*" has the same level of equipment, he reflected McCarroll's loyalty to James Beaty and his newspaper. Either the bizarre drinking party or Brown's cynical remarks may have been the "hard rub" alluded to by Graham.

Losing It, 1863–66

The "Outing" of James McCarroll: A Bitter Downturn

John Sandfield Macdonald's treatment of McGee and other Irish politicians during his premiership in 1862–63 created political trouble for his administration, even as his actions incensed James McCarroll. In his re-election campaign, McGee criticized the premier at every possible turn during the summer of 1863. But when Terry Finnegan made pointed criticisms of both Macdonald's ministry and the premier himself in his weekly letters, it is probable that the overly sensitive Macdonald took special note. At the same time Albert Brunel and Thomas Worthington likely passed on to the premier their concerns about McCarroll's testy and uncooperative behaviour during their investigations into the ports of Port Credit and Collingwood.

In the end it matters little which of McCarroll's actions had the most telling effect on Macdonald. As premier he was in a position to make a straightforward executive decision under the principle of reducing the costs of the Customs Department and improving public efficiency. On 6 September, he announced the elimination of the second outdoors surveyor's position at the Port of Toronto; for public information, the government simply reported that McCarroll's duties were unnecessary for the efficient operation at the port.

That announcement landed like a bombshell in McCarroll's busy world. In his mind he had suffered a grievous personal injustice at the hands of the callous, Anglo-Scots establishment. Within a month his exasperation reached a fever pitch. Volatile by nature, he found it impossible to be patient or quiet. Angrily, he wrote columns about his dismissal for the newspapers with which he was connected, condemning both Macdonald's ministry and the Brunel-Worthington Commission. The *Daily Leader*, the *Irish Canadian*, and the *Canadian Freeman* all provided editorial support for his case and urged redress. But, to no immediate avail.

Six months later, when John A. Macdonald had been installed as the premier of Canada West, McCarroll sent him a series of letters, presuming on their friendship and making his case. In effect, he was begging for help. At this early stage, however, he still hoped that he might regain his old position or be named to a similar post in another government department. In his letter of 29 April 1864, he defined his "case … in a nutshell":

Injudiciously or otherwise, I permitted the Hon. Mr Sandfield Macdonald to become aware that I wrote in the public press against him. My *nom de plume* and a peculiar style in which I sometimes indulged betrayed me. On the 27th of last August I wrote censuring his conduct on more than one point. On the 6th of the following month my connexion with the Port of Toronto was severed; and I have been ever since unattached; and am possessed of the power of seizing only. This foul move was accomplished in part by two enemies of mine, who acting in conjunction with the late Premier, reported that one Surveyor could do the business of this Port, and that I being the junior might be dispensed with.[80]

He felt at this point that his Terry Finnegan letter of 27 August in the *Grumbler* had tipped the premier against him.

That letter (32) was indeed critical of the premier but primarily on the grounds of his conspicuous neglect of McGee, the only Irish-born member of his cabinet. Here he was reiterating McGee's own criticisms of Macdonald during his re-election campaign that summer. In the letter Terry congratulated McGee on his parliamentary speech of 24 August in which he had "disturbed the grit in John Sandfield's gizzard" and "astonished the brigade of dhrivellers" supporting him. In addition, Terry criticized Sandfield's dictatorial attitude toward immigrants – he was "virtually applyin' the term emigrant as a reproach to any man who has honestly stepped in among us to form part and parcel of our yet highly impressionable Commonwealth."

On the face of it, Terry's criticisms in this letter were not particularly strident. Nevertheless, a few bits of name-calling, like "drhivellers and "whipper snappers," may have irked the premier's brittle sensibility. In contrast to attacks made against him in later Finnegan letters, they were not excessively mean-spirited.

Regardless of what led Sandfield Macdonald to dismiss McCarroll, he let loose a Celtic tiger. McCarroll attacked the premier relentlessly, either in his own voice or in Terry Finnegan's. His poem "Three Loaded Dice" stands as a low – or high – point in his campaign against the premier. It first appeared in the *Latch-Key* on 10 October, but was actually dated "Toronto, 9th September 1863"; that is, just three days after the public announcement of his dismissal. It was then reprinted in the *Daily Leader* (14 October) under the heading "Clippings from the *Latch-Key*":

Shrivel'd, ugly and hard – sharp, repulsive and thin;
With no body wi'hout, and no spirit within;
With the face of a fox, and a heart made of ice,
Every number he throws is with three loaded dice.

Without h'nor or pride – low, vulgar and vain;
With a mountebank's tongue and a driveller's brain;
With a troth only pledged to be snapped in a trice,
Every trick that he wins is with three, loaded dice.

Though the fingers of friendship grow warm in his grasp,
Yet his touch is the poison that lurks in the asp;
And his smile, but a traitorous empty device,
And his Faith, Hope and Charity, three loaded dice.

And should History e'er glance at so worthless a name,
Only known as an infamous huxter to Fame,
He'll be dragged from the tomb, an example of Vice,
With his skeleton hand shaking three, loaded dice.

After Finnegan's 27 August letter, McCarroll went silent for a few days. Thereafter, he wrote a string of withering evaluations of the premier and the two customs investigators. While McGee was battering Macdonald in Parliament with his rhetorical "left-handhers," McCarroll delivered his own punches in editorials and in Terry Finnegan's voice. Often playing upon Macdonald's thin-faced, cadaverous appearance, he called attention to the "filthy and acrid scum of his dwarfed sowl and narrow understandin'" and described him as "a politician unjust, contemptible, and imbecile in the exthreme" (Letter 33). He was "a disreputable and dishonest huxther" (Letter 35) whom Terry wanted to take "by the nape of the nick and the sate of the britches and sind … into the atmosfare, like a flyin squerrel, if the windy was thirty feet from the ground – the miserable cratshure" (Letter 34). His venom nearly overwhelmed Terry's comic spirit.

Six months later he offered a different explanation for his mistreatment in another letter to Attorney General John A. Macdonald. He now realized that the customs imbroglio in which he had been tested by Worthington and Brunel had likely played a larger role than he had realized in his loss of position.

A customs officer since 1849, McCarroll had risen through the ranks to become one of two outdoors surveyors at the Port of Toronto. In the early

1860s, however, he began publicly to criticize some of the changes being implemented by the two-person Customs Commission appointed to review operations in Canada West and make recommendations about the closing of less profitable ports. Such an investigative commission was new in Canadian government operations; it bothered McCarroll that the commissioners were given the arbitrary power to challenge conventional practices and to remove those collectors deemed to be redundant and incompetent.

Initially, McCarroll had been optimistic about the assignment given to Brunel and Worthington. He knew Brunel as an influential engineer with a famous English father and a political presence of some note in Toronto. He was more familiar with Worthington, having worked with him for several years. However, as the months passed and certain recommendations of the commission were made public, he began to have doubts about the commissioners' competence and judgment. When in the summer of 1863 he was seconded to take part in two ongoing investigations, he began to describe in print his concerns about those investigations and to defend beleaguered colleagues who were, as he saw it, fine fellows of the old school.

Matters intensified over that crucial summer. Invoking their new powers, the commissioners co-opted McCarroll to help them with their investigation into the messy books at Port Credit. Thomas Cotton was the collector at McCarroll's former post. Under orders, McCarroll spent several weeks at Port Credit studying the manifests and accounting books, and requesting missing documents from local companies like Barber and Brothers. After a few weeks of waiting, however, the commissioners became impatient, deeming his reporting too tardy and his excuses unsatisfactory. McCarroll argued that certain documents necessary to complete his report were not available to him. At the same time he became increasingly exacerbated with the commissioners themselves. Indeed, in Terry's letters he began to speak out against their tactics. By this time his relationship with Worthington had become obsessively antagonistic.

Later that summer, the commissioners suddenly appointed him to take over the Port of Collingwood temporarily after they suspended the collector, John McWatt, and his small team of supporters. An angry McCarroll was not long in getting into more hot water.[81] Under commission orders, he journeyed to Collingwood, but once there, according to his own account, he received conflicting orders from Worthington on the one hand and Commissioner Bouchette on the other. Following receipt of a telegram from Bouchette advising him to leave the port and return to Toronto, he promptly did so even though his wife Ann was travelling to Collingwood to join him. A panic set in at headquarters when no one could locate him; he was now apparently refusing to answer telegrams. When he left Collingwood, he left the port without a customs officer in charge. As a result he was suspended for ignoring the commission's orders. Always an able letter writer, he defended his actions by return post. He did so effectively enough that the suspension was rescinded and he was restored to his Toronto position – for the moment.

The cumulative effects of the Port Credit and Collingwood incidents weighed heavily against McCarroll, despite his letters of self-defence. By summer's end Worthington and Brunel had come to view him as volatile and recalcitrant; indeed, it is possible to interpret the Collingwood episode as a trap deliberately set for him, knowing he would overreact to being sent away from Toronto against his will. They may well have also suspected him of posting anonymous critiques of their work in the Toronto press. In those articles Thomas Worthington was the object of McCarroll's spleen. As the commissioners became more frustrated by his behaviour, they saw him as an expensive employee who could readily be dismissed on cost-cutting grounds. No longer did McCarroll have a supportive Francis Hincks at head office, Bouchette notwithstanding. He had become to Worthington and Brunel an obnoxious and expendable employee.

Hence James McCarroll and his $1,400 salary were cut loose.[82] Terry Finnegan had been right in a much earlier assessment – John Sandfield Macdonald was "cunning as a fox" (Letter 10). At that time there was no hearing available for a disgruntled employee nor was there any formal means of appeal. Like Nathaniel Hawthorne in his preface to *The Scarlet Letter* (1850), McCarroll had become a "decapitated surveyor"; he was, in fact, Canada West's most public example of autocratic government action. In his case, however, "the political guillotine" did not fall as a result of the "spoils system," a fate that could not be avoided once a government was voted out in the United States. The guillotine fell because of the outdoors surveyor's uncooperative actions and covert criticisms. In large part, McCarroll was the victim of his own actions, though he was loath to admit it. Even more disturbing, he found that no matter how much he complained in print, no matter how justified he felt in making specific accusations, there was no form of redress for the wrongs he had experienced. He could pile word on word, article on article, accusation on accusation, but to no avail.

McCarroll intensified his counterattack in several print outlets that autumn. The *Daily Leader* continued to provide space for him as did the *Grumbler*, and he launched his own weekly magazine, the *Latch-Key*, in August 1863. For nearly three months he printed his Terry Finnegan's letters there and continued to

THE LATCH-KEY.

VOL. I.—No. 8.]　　　　　TORONTO, SATURDAY, OCTOBER 24, 1863.　　　　　[PRICE 3 CENTS.

THE LATCH-KEY

Is published every SATURDAY MORNING in time for the first trains and early delivery throughout the city, at the yearly subscription of One Dollar. Single copies Three Cents each—to be had of the principal News Dealers.

All communications to be addressed, pre-paid, to the Editor of "The Latch Key," P. O., Toronto.

THE LATCH-KEY.

"OPEN SESAME!"

SATURDAY, OCTOBER 24, 1863.

TO THE SEA.

Unfathomable waste of winds and waves,
And stars that tuft the purple woof of night,
And pin it shadowed, down amid thy depths,
How great art thou in all thy twofold strength !
Whether one, vast, unbroken sheet of calm
Where the long finger of the lonely mast
Points through the azure solitude, to God !
Or whether from out thy solemn slumbers roused,
Shaking thy dripping hide and awful crest,
Thou goest forth to meet the fierce typhoon
That, plumed with darkness blur'd with fire and flame,
Scatters thy fleets 'mid shoals and sunken rocks,
And leaves them like dead sea-fowl drifting there !

How great art thou !—at morn !—or noon ! or eve
When through the crimson portals of the West
The huge, red furnace of the dying day
Pours out its lava o'er thy radiant floor,
Till thou art as the vestibule of heaven
Leading to the great llanos of the sun
That carpets the dread space before His Throne
And till the earth clasped in thy glowing arms
In emerald splendour 's borne along its path
And thou doest seem a giant ruby set
In the broad chasing of a thousand shores
Where thou dost meet the sea-shells and the sands—
A rim of golden dust, and pearl and rose.

PSEUDO CRITICISM.

Society, from one point of view, may be considered a reflex of the criticisms it pampers or tolerates. A tacit submission to any injury thrust upon it in this relation, is, therefore, criminal. To be just, it must reward or punish. Every individual who assumes the pen of a critic, virtually steps out from the masses and lays claim to an exalted position. Consequently, when an instance of this character occurs, it is the bounden duty of every man of taste and judgment to look narrowly into the qualifications of what may be, after all, but a self-constituted censor. We are led to these observations from the recent advent, through the columns of the *Leader* newspaper, of a certain H.M., who, after having graduated on the Organ in a neighbouring village, taken a few lessons in drawing from Mr. Bull of Upper Canada College, and spent six months in England studying Ruskin and the Hartz Mountains, has taken Literature, the Arts, and everything else in

steps out before the public as a veritable Crichton, and plays with us as a cat does with a mouse. As observed, upon a former occasion, a cursory glance will satisfy any one of ordinary abilities, that the criticisms of this modest gentleman are written mainly with a scissors, and are only original to the extent of the stupid ligaments which tie down their incongruous articulations. On the subject of painting, he gravely informs us, that the "old masters" are very fine indeed ; and that Raffaelle was born on Good Friday, and Titian in the year 1477, for all which information he is indebted to "Maunders." In addition, in one of these ligaments, he finds fault with some of our drawing masters here for not being able to sketch "a coal scuttle *from nature*," and urges upon lovers of the Fine Arts, the necessity of first examining the body of any strange picture before they turn their attention to the frame! And thus, while insulting the common sense of the age, he heaps up his interminable twaddle, and registers his own presumption and incompetency in the most slovenly dabs of slip-shod English. His knowledge of either drawing or painting, however, may be gathered from the simple circumstance of his selecting " dead game," and difficult " fore-shortenings" for the earliest lessons of his own pupils : and from the fact, that he has chosen for one of his accomplished protege's a professional gentleman, who, in copying the Falls of Tummel, from a picture of J. D. Harding, took the liberty of introducing two deer, frightfully out of perspective, and a boy with a fish, which do not belong to the original. But to do the professional gentleman in question justice, he is at least possessed of gratitude ; for he has made a Pegasus for his Mecaenas, with ears of unobjectionable length, although the hide appears to be covered with a species of languid, porcupine quills instead of hair. Nor has H. M. succeeded better in relation to Music ; for, here, notwithstanding his columns of statistics, which are to be found in every library, we perceive him drifting about helmless, and closing a late criticism on a waltz by Charles Fradel in the following words :—

" It must be played with taste and correctness, or the full merit of the piece will not be shown !"

The note of admiration is ours ; and is it any wonder that we should have placed it where it is, when we find this profound critic gravely informing us that a mutton chop should not be boiled ? This is really clever ; and we take the liberty of directing the attention of our able cotemporary of the *Leader* to the fact that it is so.

But as we have neither painting nor music

quote his own words, and thus effectually nail the rap to the counter. In a paper of the third of September, to which our attention has just been directed, we find him tossing about in his awkward paws the celebrated and philosophic exclamation of, we think, Beranger—"Let me make the ballads of a nation and I care not who makes its laws," regarding which, he observes—" We quote this worn out saying, not because we believe it, but because we don't," and " which no body believes," and " which next to no body ever reflects on for a moment." This is rather rough usage for a poet and a philosopher whose glorious emanations have stirred the heart of the whole civilised world. And here we find that H. M. lies grovelling in the dust ; for it is obvious, his shallow understanding does not comprehend, even remotely, that this splendid expression is based upon the unassailable fact, that the ballads of a nation themselves shape and determine its laws. Who shall dare to say that the songs of Dibdin have not worked silently among the musty parchments of the Admiralty, or that " Rule Britannia," " The Marseillaise," " A Man's a Man for a' that," or their counterpart, have not influenced the legislation of England, Scotland and France, respectively ?" Out upon the dunce who festers a very Lazarus at the gates of all his genius, then, in this relation, he quotes from our columns the following verses as unworthy a place in any publication, and highly indicative of weakness and folly on the part of the author :—

SONG.

I ask no joys but those you give—
　No joys but those you share ;
No lips but thine to bid me live,
　No smiles but those they wear.

No morn but what o'erspreads your cheek,
　No light but from your eye ;
No music love, but what you speak ;
　No language but your sigh.

No pillow, darling, but your breast,
　No curtain but your hair.
To fall in clouds around my rest,
　And shade my sannan there

editorialize about those responsible for his dismissal.[83] He also managed to get self-supporting articles into the *Canadian Freeman* and the *Irish Canadian*. He had been involved in both since their inception.

The *Daily Leader* provided a series of supportive accounts of his situation. On 8 September, an editorial in language that he himself might have mustered denounced his firing. Casting him as "a hard-working and zealous public servant," the article denounced the "summary" dismissal as "the merest shadow of an excuse for the perpetuation of one of the grossest acts of personal malevolence and party spleen that the present Government has yet been guilty of."

Then, on 26 September, the *Daily Leader* published a long letter by McCarroll to Luther H. Holton, the minister of finance in the Sandfield Macdonald government, detailing his role in the commission's inquiry into the financial records of the Port Credit Customs Office. He described the "official acquaintance" that had existed between the commissioners and himself, before documenting how he had been co-opted as an agent in their investigation. Following their orders, he spent weeks sorting through Collector Thomas Cotton's books and attempting to gather up a number of missing documents. What he discovered turned him firmly against the commissioners. They were, he argued, not only wrong in their assessment of the Port Credit bookkeeping but they were unwilling to accept an alternative explanation for Cotton's situation based on the past practices of collectors in Canada West.

McCarroll claimed that he had discovered that Thomas Worthington himself had made "false entries" in the record and that he had asked him point blank about the disappearance of important documents, but was met with stubbornness, rebuffs, and "unpleasantnesses." As he saw it, "The Inspectors were totally in the dark in relation to the true condition of Port Credit." While he accused Worthington of "occasional fits of unenlightened stubbornness," the commissioner responded by chiding him both for his tardiness in completing his assignment and his lack of cooperation. In taking such a stubborn line, McCarroll was ready to admit that "my office trembled in the balance"; still, he opted to "stand by Cotton to the last." His final words in the letter emphasized the moral high ground he had taken, regardless of the consequences: "I have lost my office, but preserved my integrity," he concluded.

While the *Daily Leader* remained generally supportive of his embattled situation, there were occasional signs of resistance. In a *Latch-Key* column that took aim at the series of music columns in the *Leader* ("Familiar Notes on Music and Musical Matters") written by H.M. [Henry Martin], McCarroll accused Martin of plagiarism.[84] The *Daily Leader*'s editor defended Martin's originality and called attention to the occasional borrowings of Terry Finnegan himself, citing a recent instance in which he had stolen phrasing from the American humorist Artemus Ward.[85] More pointedly, the *Daily Leader* editor warned McCarroll of "the necessity of curbing his Pegasus when he grapples with an opponent." While Terry's comic letters "overflow[ed] with the best of wit and sarcasm, and deserve[d] to be read by everyone," there had to be limits to his ad hominem attacks. Nevertheless, the *Daily Leader* continued to take friendly notice of the weekly issues of the *Latch-Key*, praising the "ability and literary talent" of its "principal writer." True to form, however, the uncurbed Pegasus in McCarroll's personality would work against him for months to come.

Another column in support of McCarroll appeared on 23 October. Under the headline "The Worthington-Brunel Commission," the *Daily Leader* suggested that the government, which was now reconsidering its "retrenchment policy" regarding the elimination of certain customs posts, might also turn its attention to "the lucid letter of Mr McCarroll, of this city." Rehearsing the charges that he had preferred against Worthington and Brunel, and alleging that "serious mischief has been done to the country through the work of the Commission in question," the editorial hoped that "All this cannot be permitted to slip into one ear and out at the other."

Then on 18 December the "Late Surveyor of the Port of Toronto" directed a second public letter to the minister of finance. The *Daily Leader* prefaced its text by noting the ministry had so far failed to answer McCarroll's complaints about the government's handling of the Port Credit case. Rehearsing those charges, McCarroll called special attention to both Worthington's general ignorance and certain specific errors he had made. While ready "to produce oral and documentary evidence of [the commissioners'] corruption [and criminal negligence]" for the minister, he remained deeply frustrated by the government's silence on the issue.

As the months passed, it became clearer that James McCarroll was snookered. Convinced of his "honest and correct view of the case," he could only hope that "some member of the Legislature will, as a last resource, move for a committee to investigate it." That did not happen. He was thus ensured of fulfilling a grim public role – in becoming Canada West's "decapitated surveyor," he also suffered the curse of Swift, which he had striven to avoid. Meanwhile, Tom Worthington and Albert Brunel continued their administrative work unimpeded.

Despite his frustration, McCarroll did not slow down very much. Confident in his own voice and the influence he wielded in the newspapers, he kept up his connections with city editors. As well, he remained publicly prominent. When D'Arcy McGee spoke on "The Future of Canada" in Toronto on 26 November 1863, McCarroll was one of the dignitaries on the podium. He was also present at a well-attended dinner for the opposition party and its leader, John A. Macdonald, at St Lawrence Hall on 17 December 1863.

When the *Latch-Key* ceased publication (for the second time) in early November 1864, McCarroll once again began to place his Terry Finnegan letters with John Ross Robertson's the *Grumbler*. More significantly, he increased his involvement with the *Irish Canadian*. Owned and edited by Patrick Boyle, the city's Hibernian, or pro-Fenian, newspaper had begun its weekly publication on 7 January 1863. Initially, McCarroll contributed as a poet. His poem "Resurgam!" appeared in its first issue, commemorating the newspaper's motto. It celebrated the "glorious years" of Ireland's heroic past and offered a vision of a unified and revitalized "young nation" in the future.

> Come! let us form a solid square,
> No matter what our creed or clan,
> And plant our drooping standard there,
> Beside some wounded Dalgais man.[86]
>
> Till all its emerald folds unfurled
> O'er yonder sea of kindred sheen,
> Shall mid-way meet before the world,
> Its other half of living green.
>
> Then shall a rainbow span the skies –
> A pledge of countless glorious years –
> The light of a young nation's eyes
> That flashes through her joyous tears.
>
> While in his ancient glory decked
> Beneath the arch of dazzling rays,
> The haughty Celt shall stand erect,
> As once he stood in other days.

His second signed poem, "Oh! Sainted Shannon," appeared on 25 February 1863.[87] It celebrated the historic river and its "emerald waters," which he had known from childhood, but did so by evoking "dreams of glory long since passed away." Seven hundred years of martyrdom had to be answered for and a fettered nation freed. The poem held out the hope of a return to the grand old days of Celtic superiority.

Given the anonymity of the prose contributions to the *Irish Canadian*, it is challenging to track McCarroll's work with the paper. He was certainly active in 1863 and later in 1864–65. However, the *Montreal Herald* (8 May 1868) retroactively identified him as an early editor of the paper at a time when the joint stock company that owned it had appointed no single editor. The *Herald* further reported that McCarroll served as editor for a period to time in 1863 "until he quarrelled with some of the proprietors." Patrick Boyle took over the editorship soon thereafter and served in that capacity for the rest of its operation.

Another of his "Irish" poems, "Insula Sacra" appeared in the *Daily Leader* on 27 January 1864. Written in nine triads, it lamented the "sad music" now characterizing Ireland's once "sainted" beauty and its children ("Now a wretched alien band"). Increasingly he viewed his native land with a "broken heart." With the romance of his Celtic ancestry brimming over in his saddened present, he became more hostile to the outspoken views of D'Arcy McGee, who, in an 1863 speech in Peterborough, began publicly to proclaim his anti-Fenian views. Nevertheless, as McCarroll continued to review his roster of Irish voices in Canada, he had to admit that McGee still remained the best hope for meeting the needs and interests of the Irish in Canada. Perhaps he might be convinced to moderate his negative views on Fenians in North America. As well, it was increasingly evident that support was mounting for John A. Macdonald and his "Liberal-Conservative" coalition party. John Sandfield Macdonald still clung precariously to power, but a future alliance between John A. and McGee seemed a stronger possibility, and one worth backing in prospect.

Music and Writing in the 1860s

During these stressful months, McCarroll stayed busy as a musician and a poet, though neither activity brought home much income. He performed numerous times in the early 1860s, including in several Grand Concerts at St Lawrence Hall. Typically, he contributed a flute and piano duet to such events, accompanied by his daughter Mary. John David Sale has listed three appearances by the McCarrolls in 1860, four in 1861, one each in 1862 and 1863, three in 1864, and one in 1865.[88] Their repertoire included pieces by Verdi, Rossini, Donizetti, Martini, and Mozart.[89]

Beyond the weekly Terry Finnegan letters for the *Grumbler*, McCarroll wrote seven original poems for the *Daily Leader* in 1863 and three for the *British American Magazine*. He weighed in as a literary critic of Isadore G. Ascher's *Verses from the Hearth*, recently published to acclaim by John Lovell in Montreal. His review of Ascher's book in the *Daily Leader* accorded with earlier comments made by Terry Finnegan and challenged several overly positive notices that the book had received.[90] Defining "true poesy" as "the language of passion or vivid imagination imbued with a sort of florid or mystic logic," he examined Ascher's poems in terms of rhythm, rhyme, euphony, and their quality of imagery. While noting several captivating passages in the book, he found much of the poetry "replete with false quantities, strange misconceptions, weakness and faded imagery." Overall, Ascher's unmusical effects and lack of precision regarding nature led to obvious poetic flaws that McCarroll deemed "beyond remedy." As a serious poet, he was by the 1860s seldom hesitant to pass severe judgment on a "Canadian" peer.

Another of McCarroll's winter poems was among his most startling and musical. Its precise and vivid imagery of the "wind-singer" at play captured the beauty of a weather-changing winter "gale"; such a storm suddenly descends upon unsuspecting nature, turning all to ice, "marble," and stasis in its wake. Its arresting power anticipates the close attention to the natural world later practised by the painters in the Group of Seven. "Winter" first appeared in the *Daily Leader* and then in the *British American Magazine* in the spring of 1864.[91]

Through the pines of the north the dark Wind-Singer strode
As he hummed the first notes of the gale;
While a ghastly, white cloud of cold dust swept the road,
Rushing downwards to smother the vale.

Though each note that he chaunted was hollow and drear,
Still with mystical sweetness it rung;
For the rivers all paused in their headlong career
Just to list to the lay that he sung.

And a streamlet that over a frowning cliff fell
Like a long, jewelled tress of bright hair,
Caught the magical strain, in its leap to the dell,
And stood suddenly still in the air.

Slowly turning to marble along the lone way,
Here and there, too, a worshipper bowed;
Till the last, feeble pulse of his heart ceased to play,
As he vanished within the white cloud.

All nature seemed strangely deprived of its pow'rs,
As the Wind-Singer hurried along,
For the woods and the waters, the birds and the flow'rs,
Fell asleep till he finish'd his song.

In 1864 McCarroll twice stretched his own wings in the small-magazine business. In fact, within a year's time (summer 1863–summer 1864) he launched no less than three magazines in Toronto, none of which lasted more than three months. The *Growler*, which appeared in only four issues in 1864 (22 July–19 August), was both his most temperate literary effort of the time and pictorially his most ambitious. It included illustrations and cartoons on almost every page. Though no name (editor, owner, or illustrator) was attached to the magazine, there are several McCarroll poems in the four issues.[92] The *Growler*'s masthead image was a fierce bulldog that promised to be "more amiable than he looks"; indeed, the growler enjoyed a drink as much as his creator. An introductory quatrain made light of the connection:

When I die, as needs must hap
Then bury me under the good ale tap
Cheek by jowl let us lie
Both together, my dog and I.

The *Growler*'s contents were meant to be amusing and satiric; they included comedic attacks on George Brown, John Sandfield Macdonald (a man of "melancholy aspect" and "native insignificance"), William McDougall, and D'Arcy McGee. The latter, as minister of agriculture, had not issued a ticket to the brilliant "Editor in Chief" of the *Growler* inviting him to join the press's all-expenses-paid trip to the Maritimes. The magazine includes several other examples of McCarroll's comic letters (by Ham Junks, Sambo Lively, and Elizabeth). There were also columns on the summer weather, local manners, and in praise of Anna Bishop in concert, etc.[93]

One column of particular note was entitled "Poetry and the Press" (1:3). Here McCarroll argued that poets who publish in the press should be granted the protection of anonymity. Not only were there few newspaper readers capable of appreciating "what is exquisitely hidden in true poetry," but poets themselves were typically sensitive and shy about "parading their work under their own name." Given the delicacy of such exposure, he deplored the tacit requirement of the press that poets should attach their names to their work. "A more damning rule has never been obtained in relation to letters," he wrote. It allowed "a class of barefaced huxters" to eclipse "those finely strung natures" who hesitate to present their "effusions" for fear of being ridiculed or misunderstood. He believed that if poems were published simply for their individual merits, "we will have a new and improved spirit pervading the newspaper literature of the day." This argument helps to account for his own inclination to seek anonymity, though his personal concerns about privacy would also have to do with self-protection in the market place.

In a similar vein, his *Latch-Key* caught considerable public attention; its weekly appearances were often noted and favourably commented upon in the *Daily Leader* where he still exercised some weight in editorial commentaries. Regrettably, only five issues from the two appearances of this important magazine have survived.

While the 22 August 1863 issue of the *Latch-Key* contains his doggerel poetic exercise "Rep by Pop," extant issues for 17 and 24 October reveal more about his satiric inclinations and targets, especially in the wake of his lost position.[94] The 17 October issue includes two letters by Pierre Lafontaine to "Da Hon. Mr George Le Brun" "redacteur de world – de *Globe*," written, amusingly, in fractured English. Calling Brown a "villain politician," Pierre writes, for example, "SARE – Vat is your politique? Vell, it is no vorse, I am suppose, den John A. who makes the Clargy Reserve and ozzer questions scatter to the vinds for his purpose. It is to me possible to have de conviction, dat all politique is much of de same ting, and dat it comes into de one important leetle vords, monnaie! office! Certement, Monsieur – office! Dat's de grand final of all de speech – all of de patriotism – all of de profession of dose who make up de 'great sacrifice' in going into Parliament 'for de general good.' It is drole. It is funny – very funny, and it is Upper Canada."

Such letters – playful and "droll" – tapped into the racialized outlook and taste so dominant in Canada in 1863. On occasion, as here, McCarroll revealed his deepening cynicism about the political process. But not yet fully committed to John A.'s emerging political grasp, he lumped him together with George Brown, Canada West's arch anti-Catholic. The future he predicted here would likely involve "a shipwreck" as politicians peered into the dark, like cats searching for mice.

The two surviving *Latch-Key* letters of 1864 reveal a many-sided humorist. Each contains a Finnegan letter (numbers 11 and 12 of the second series) and includes letters (in what were ongoing series) by such figures as Jemimah, Pierre Lafontaine, and a Scots political observer named Logie O'Buchan. While continuing with his editorial indictments of Worthington and Brunel, McCarroll also waxed analytic about the nature of the ideal heroine he would create should he ever undertake to write a novel. She would be robust and healthy, not a fainting milk-sop. He also offered the opening chapter of a serialized prose piece, "Pippin: by Himself: or, the Autobiography of a Lean Man." Whether he saw himself as fat or lean, the narrator of the preface to "Pippin" argued for a personal leanness, juxtaposed to "the bully corpulence" of so many of his contemporaries. Calling forth fatty allusions to Falstaff and Horace, he raises challenging questions about the authorial desire to "tell" one's life. McCarroll writes of sitting "content in [one's] own carcass" and of being "a man of importance [who] ought to write his own memoirs provided he has honesty enough to tell the truth." Such a premise begs the question of how far he was prepared to go (in specific detail and personal honesty) in telling either Pippin's story or his own. McCarroll certainly could have done so about himself had he been so inclined. However, lacking the opportunity, he left many fragmentary hints about the story of his own multifaceted, yet frustrated life as an Irish writer in pre-Confederation Canada.

Notices in the *Irish Canadian* confirm that the *Latch-Key* continued for a few weeks into November. Significantly, reports of those issues reveal that McCarroll was becoming increasingly hostile to and critical of McGee's recent political manoeuvres. On 2 November, for instance, the *Irish Canadian* provided this observation: "in the present number, he [Terry Finnegan] unburthens his mind a little to his cousin, the Hon. T.D. McGee, whom he accuses of pie-crust promises and a most treacherous memory."[95] As an instance of the "cold shoulder" tendency of his cousin, Terry cites the case of a young Catholic gentleman, a former employee of the Toronto Post Office, whose claims to preferment while in the service of the government were so shamelessly neglected that he felt it his duty to tender his resignation. "For this young man, who again seeks a just recognition of his claims on the Postal Department, Mr McGee promised to intercede with the Postmaster General; but up to the present nothing, so far as we can learn, nothing has been done in the matter. We are thoroughly conversant with the case particularised on this occasion by our friend 'Terry,' and we venture to say that a grosser act of injustice was never perpetrated in the Post Office Department."

The Aftermath — Struggling into 1865

Overall, 1864 was a quieter year for James McCarroll. Having elected to wait as patiently as possible for the help promised by now-premier John A. Macdonald, he stayed in the city. Strapped for money and concerned about Ann's failing health, he did what he could to make his living by his pen, writing newspaper articles that brought small payments. With the aid of his own printing press, he was able to produce the second incarnation of the *Latch-Key* and the short-lived *Growler*, magazines likely bankrolled by friends.[96] He was also able to take on printing jobs for businesses and acquaintances, and he could typeset newspaper copy to submit to editors of his acquaintance. As he later told John A. Macdonald, "it was with this little office that I fought the battles of the Hon. Mr McGee when Sandfield cut his throat. It was from this little office that 'Three Loaded Dice' was issued when you were on the opposition benches."[97]

In the long term, however, his situation was unsustainable. He had many debts and too often had to rely on loans from friends and colleagues who remained supportive of his talents and upset at the treatment he had received. Nevertheless, he had to realize that substantive redress was unlikely: there was no apparent interest among government officials to help him, while for their part Worthington and Brunel ignored the criminal charges that he repeatedly voiced against them. They anticipated that his bluster would pass. What John A. could do for him remained a question for the future, though it was a non-starter for others.

What followed was an inevitable downward trajectory. McCarroll was not by nature a man to be silent, but he had realized that silence might better serve his hopes for some form of reparation. During the two-and-a-half years following his dismissal, his letters to John A. Macdonald provide a useful source of information about his daily activities and aspirations. In addition, some of his doings can be traced in the pages of the *Daily Leader* and to a lesser extent in the *Canadian Freeman* and the *Irish Canadian*. All three papers supported his claims for redress. For his part he placed his last hope in the general assurances made to him by John A. His friend's growing political stature and power could, he hoped, be his support in the long run. However, when John A. first became the premier in the spring of 1864, an intervention was not immediately practicable because he faced an uncertain period of adjustment in establishing his government's power base; in part as well, Macdonald needed to quiet the *cause célèbre* that McCarroll had managed to stir up. A year and a half later, however, it became clear to McCarroll that the promised help was not forthcoming.

McCarroll's letters to Macdonald in 1865–66 are acts of desperation, confession, personal reportage, and begging – in themselves a mini-autobiography, they project "the decapitated surveyor" narrative from the perspective of the Irish in Protestant Toronto. McCarroll had to admit that his "campaign" had not been effective, especially in the minds of Irish Protestants. The durable and feisty Terry Finnegan was his most important voice in this undertaking, but Terry was often guilty of special pleading on his creator's behalf.

Still, creative spirit that he was, James McCarroll remained busy. His poems continued to appear, he penned music reviews for the *Daily Leader*, and he began to plan a promising new venture – he would perform his own one-man show in cities and towns across Canada West and in Montreal.

His poems cover a wide range of themes. They include a tribute to Shakespeare on his birthday ("Impromptu: Hail Monarch of Three Hundred Years"), and four that celebrate the seasons in Canada: "Why Dost Thou Tarry?," "At Last! At Last!," and "Winter," which had first appeared in the *British American Magazine*. Poetically the most interesting is "The Rainbow" (16 May 1864), which first appeared under Terry Finnegan's name and was written in the brogue. McCarroll later included it in *Madeline* (302–3), but there he stripped it of the brogue while still grouping it among his "Humorous" poems. What began in the *Daily Leader* with the line "Blur an' agers! How I hate to hear those ballad mongers sing" was later sanitized to read:

Oh! how I chafe whene'er I hear those ballad-mongers sing
Of the wedding link that binds the golden sunshine to the showers;
Which of them has ever christened it the skipping-rope of Spring,
Or the handle of the landscape's balmy basket full of flowers?

Which of them has ever fancied it a swing on yonder plain,
Just inverted, by some frolicsome celestials in their mirth,
With a swoop that had upset the blessed angel of the rain,
Till his stock of liquid jewellery came tumbling to earth? –

Or believed it but the engine-hose stretched o'er the sultry sky;
Or the bell-rope pulled by nature when she wants to wash her face;
Or the clothes-line upon which the dripping clouds are hung to dry;
Or a thousand other names that I can't mention in this place?

Oh how I hate to hear those sorry ballad-mongers sing;
Of the gold and purple comb, with all its showery silver teeth,
That among the emerald tresses of the beautiful young Spring,
Pins the violet and the primrose and the daisy in one wreath.

With characteristic panache, McCarroll continued to celebrate "rale poetry."
"The Rainbow" vividly catalogues images of spring that defy the conventional
clichés applied by the "sorry ballad-mongers" of the day. Ever playful, he had
not yet fully evolved his Terry Finnegan voice into that of Terry Fenian, though
that feisty Irish nationalist was looming just off stage.

A week later (23 May) McCarroll offered "Why Dost Thou Tarry?" to his
Daily Leader readers. It offers a sensuous picture of "the maiden of Spring,"
delayed in her march from the south to "this cold, reluctant sod of ours." The
poem rises above its own conventionalities through its richness of imagery and
its sustained musicality.

Among the fragrant blossoms of the South
That blow the golden orange from their lips,
And where from the sweet jasmin's amber mouth
The honey-bee its subtle nectar sips,
While, burning through the halo of his wings
That murmur round him like an unseen lute,
The humming-bird in sudden glory swings
From dewy bells, like some enchanted fruit;

And where beneath the cool o'erspreading vine,
Tangled with light the purple shadows sleep,
And emerald waters tremulously shine,
Or down the dell the jewelled laughter leap,
While through the damasked gloom, on every blast,
A thousand censers all their perfumes pour;
And Echo, like some memory of the past,
Sings the sweet songs that wake her, o'er and o'er,

Why dost thou tarry, maiden of the Spring?
Think'st thou that there are Northern lips and eyes
That can supply the roses thou would'st bring,
And compensate us for thy absent skies?

Or think'st thou there are silvery voices here
That speak the music of those fairy vales,
And balmy sighs whose treasures are as dear
As the pure incense of thy softest gales?

Come! shining loiterer, come! nor longer stay
And let thy leafy gems and opening flowers
Be spilled, like stars along the milky-way,
Upon this cold, reluctant sod of ours.
Come with thy zephyrs and thy sparkling streams,
And feathered throng of every throat and plume;
Come with thy coronal of buds and beams –
Come, fragrant-footed angel of the bloom.

Although his poems often belied his personal angst, 1864 was clearly a year of particularly bitter disappointment and frustration for him, one in which he struggled to maintain his usual sunniness of disposition while feeling "the cold hard gripe of the world."[98] Trapped in a condition he was inclined to blame on others, he was trapped nonetheless. He saw himself as a victim of political and social forces at work in Toronto; he was a conspicuous instance of the underappreciated and overlooked Irishman of the day. By contrast, a poem like "Reverie" reveals a man given over to hope and joy, whatever his despair.

As 1864 gave way to 1865, McCarroll renewed his attempt to reach out to a wider audience. Recalling a scheme first envisioned in the 1840s, he planned to take a one-man variety show, keyed in part to the popularity of Terry Finnegan, on the road across Canada West. He would seek out audiences large enough to help him meet his current debts. He billed the show as an evening with "James McCarroll, The Celebrated Flautist, Humorist and Poet" and "The Famous Terry Finnegan." The evening promised an amusing potpourri of vernacular comedy, witty political commentary, and musical interludes. It included a humorous lecture entitled "The House That Jack Built," making light of the dominance of the English influence in Canada.[99] Then he would read a couple of Terry Finnegan letters in the brogue along with some of his "Irish Anthology" poems. Accompanied by his daughter Mary on piano, he would play a few classical pieces and popular songs on his flute while offering stirring examples of aeolian showmanship to please and astound his audiences.

McCarroll enjoyed a number of successful performances during his year-long tour. However, given the costs of living on the road, he usually had to return to Toronto after each performance. Members of the press were unanimous in praising "The House That Jack Built" and they delighted in Terry's letters, while lauding McCarroll's virtuosity as a flautist. However, over many months, the grind proved exhausting, especially as audiences were often disappointingly small. Despite his efforts to arrange advance publicity, some performances were poorly attended or fell victim to inclement weather. Having to act as his own advance agent, he was by mid-year exhausted and dispirited. The convenience of rail travel and the free notice provided by newspaper colleagues across the province were not enough to counter the depressing reality of inadequate ticket sales, endless travel, and generally uninformed audiences. In a letter to John A. Macdonald, dated 19 January 1866, he summarized his frustrations.

> I have borrowed from my friends in every direction until I am ashamed to look them in the face; and, besides, I am in debt in almost every second town in the Province; from my attempt to lecture through them without any aid save the repeated thunders of meagre audiences and the Unanimous voice of the press. There was more wanting, – I had no money to work things up – there is too small a number of people in our towns and villages – and I did not deem it advisable to pay a large salary – or rather to promise a large salary, to an agent to precede me a week or so wherever I went. Our population must increase materially before *we* can support even *one* literary man or paper. Negro Minstrelsy and the cheap trashy literature of our neighbours have run us into the ground in this relation, and driven the genuine article out of the field. This is the true state of the *bill*; and here am I and others the living witnesses of it.

It was a painful admission. Despite offering up a critically acclaimed, amusing and entertaining evening, he could not generate sufficient income over the course of the tour. Nevertheless, he took the show to many places – Toronto, Montreal, Ottawa, Peterborough, Lindsay, Barrie, London, Windsor, Hamilton, and smaller towns along the way like Yorkville, Kennanville, Adjala, and Dunnville. All in all, 1865 was for him "a year of strange probation."[100]

By year's end he realized that his efforts were mostly wasted, his energy and spirits worn down. As a public performer, he was a man ahead of his time. Seeking to entertain citizens of the rural centres of Canada West, he came up against the hard fact that people had little time for leisure activity and little money to spend on such entertainment, unless it was to enjoy the amusing fun of the travelling minstrel shows he deplored. His Finnegan tour was a good idea, but the results only contributed his mounting frustration.

Battling fatigue, disillusion, and debts, it is not surprising that in 1865 he shifted his ground more fully toward his Hibernian friends in Toronto. There he continued to enjoy warm fellowship. Patrick Boyle and Mike Murphy had been acquaintances since 1862 and Boyle's newspaper, the *Irish Canadian*, increasingly became a place of refuge where he could operate quietly behind the scenes.

Meanwhile D'Arcy McGee had created an increasingly problematic situation for the Irish in Canada by his outspoken attacks on the "Fenian pestilence" in British America. In the same vein he often criticized the aggressive, pro-Fenian tone of the *Irish Canadian*.[101] With John A. Macdonald now premier and McGee his minister of agriculture, immigration, and statistics, McCarroll was caught in a dilemma: he continued to hope for a government intervention on his behalf, but McGee's anti-Fenian stance disturbed him as deeply as did John A. Macdonald's silence on the matter. In one letter to the premier, he urged him to do what he could to make McGee tone down his rhetoric. McGee would have none of it, however, and he continued to denounce the Fenians. His hostility culminated in his famous Wexford speech in May 1865. McCarroll reminded Macdonald of the number of Irish votes available to him in coming elections and warned that McGee was not only alienating many Irish colonists but also hindering McCarroll's personal attempts to argue for a unification of Catholic and Protestant interests in Canada West. There is, McCarroll reported, "an under current of feeling [that] runs, to some extent, through the united mass, which is secretly unfriendly to the doctrines propounded by Mr McGee in relation to Irish affairs." "In whatever I have done for the [*Irish Canadian*]," he added, while implying his close connection with that newspaper, "I have always endeavoured to keep within constitutional bounds, and to smooth down the asperities existing between the Catholic, and the Orange body. I have done much in that direction; but I can't do anything more, if Hibernians are to be denounced as rebels. I am not a member of their Association; nor do I sympathize with their existence; but a large number of them here are *voters*, and I want to see them right when the time comes."[102] His assertion of his distance from the Hibernians is certainly open to question. As usual with John A., he was playing both sides of the issue, keeping an eye out for what best served his own interests.

In another letter (16 February 1865) McCarroll promised Macdonald that he would be "silent if you desire it." Still, he was having difficulty stifling his indignation and frustration after so many months of waiting. It was a function of the kind of man he was, especially as his uncertain probation persisted.

If I am as poor as a church mouse and as reckless as a highway man, I am as proud as Lucifer and as consistent a friend or enemy as ever breathed. I know I'm an honest man; and that's the end of it. How must then I feel when I find myself embarrassed by a person [Worthington] who has done more to injure the revenue of this province and the morality of the Department outside, than any man that has ever existed; and who is inferior to me in everything connected with the practical workings of the Customs – or with humanity?[103]

With his bitterness bubbling over, his Fenian leanings were growing stronger by the day. So too was his long-standing empathy with Irish Catholics. While on tour with his one-man show in Kennanville, a village northwest of Toronto, he wrote a poem under the provocative pen name of "Terry Fenian.'" It appeared in the *Irish Canadian* on 20 September 1865. It addressed long-standing Irish-Catholic complaints in Ireland and celebrated the leadership of "peaceful" Daniel O'Connell. In this poem Terry Fenian advocated support for Fenian military action in the United Kingdom. As such, it articulates the Fenian desire to seek redress by violent means. Catholic Ireland continued to be sneered at, repressed, and degraded. However, the poem made no mention of Canada as a Fenian target, though *Irish Canadian* readers might well have made the connection.

The Great O'Connell sought in vain
Our rights, by peaceful Agitation:
What did that mighty Chief obtain?
Naught but a mock Emancipation.
The poor disenfranchised by the Act,
The rich to office elevated;
But the Fenian's [*sic*] now proclaim the fact
That Ireland must be liberated.

That Gallant Tribune, we confess,
By peaceful means and strong persuasion,
Sought long our grievance to redress –
Alas, 'twas all hallucination.
The Saxon sneered at honest Dan,
His "moral force" and peace orations;
But the Fenians boldly now tell "John"
That Ireland's rank must be with Nations.

Some worthy men oppose our cause,
Whilst other knaves, for peace and pension,
Will eulogize the British Laws,
But Ireland's wrongs they seldom mention.
Let such, their country's cause desert,
Leave her in woe and degradation,
But Fenians fearlessly assert,
That Ireland must soon be a Nation.

We're well aware of Britain's power,
Her wealth and strength and vast resources;
But we're prepared at any hour,
With will and might, to meet her forces.
Our Isle has been, for centuries long,
The scene of blood and desolation;
But Fenians vow to avenge the wrong,
And swear their Isle must be a Nation.

A roadblock hinders the tracking of Terry Finnegan's letters in 1865. No copies of *Pick* are extant. However, through puffs and notices in the *Daily Leader*, it is clear that Terry's letters appeared in many of its issues. Charles Pelham Mulvany reported that *Pick* was published by William Halley with whom McCarroll had a long-standing connection. Halley had published the *Home Journal* in 1861, delivered speeches on subjects like "The Irish Race at Home and Abroad," and, with John O'Donohoe and Thomas McCrossan, had financially backed D'Arcy McGee in Toronto and James Moylan's the *Canadian Freeman*.[104] Regrettably, there is little additional information about Halley and *Pick* other than Mulvany's brief notice. It is tempting to think that McCarroll might have had some involvement with this new magazine; however, his troubled finances, the demands of his one-man show, and the absence of any mention of the magazine in his letters to John A. Macdonald make that unlikely. He was, however, a regular contributor. The loss of his final Finnegan letters is significant, as much for their importance as comedic prose as for what McCarroll had to say about the ongoing consequences of McGee's hostility to Fenianism, the implications for Canada of the end of the American Civil War, and the hovering prospect of confederation.

To the end of his days in Canada, McCarroll continued to see himself as a "representative man" among the Irish. By birthright a Protestant, he now kept a careful distance from the Orange Order and the Anglican Church. In imagination he was more Catholic than Protestant in a city that was avowedly much more Protestant than Catholic. He liked to think that he had earned the trust of conservative Catholics and activist Hibernians alike; he continued to see himself as well positioned to do crucial work in bringing the Catholic and Protestant interests of the province closer together.

In reality, however, he had far less influence than he imagined and certainly he had no effective base of power in Toronto or Canada West as a whole. The futility of his position must have been galling for him even as he kept up his begging letters to John A. In political and civil matters he was entirely without protection or support; moreover, his more subversive literary activities left him, if not exposed, then vulnerable. Financially, his debts were overwhelming and, politically, his prospects were desperate; the kind of governmental goodwill that had supported him in the past was no longer available to him.

John A. Macdonald could find no feasible way to provide him with a new position or salary. Neither was he willing to personally loan him $100 when, early in 1866, McCarroll asked for a monetary gift. He needed the money, he said, to travel to Boston where, he hoped, with help from fellow poets Oliver Wendell Holmes and Henry Wadsworth Longfellow, he might find a publisher for his two manuscripts.[105] Meanwhile, Ann lay very ill at their home. Nevertheless, in late February 1866, a trip to Buffalo and the prospect of putting on another evening of humorous entertainment was one more positive action he planned to undertake during that winter. But, as usual, he had other plans a-brewing.

The Curse Fulfilled:
Escape to Buffalo, 1866–69

WHEN JAMES MCCARROLL LEFT TORONTO in the dead of winter in 1866, his apparent plan was to make arrangements to perform his one-man show in Buffalo. On 28 February Patrick Boyle's *Irish Canadian* offered him a positive send-off:

> We learn from Buffalo exchanges that our talented fellow countryman, James McCarroll, Esq. – the inimitable "Terry Finnegan" – is at present in that city, where he intends to lecture in the course of the coming week. Mr McCarroll's abilities as a poet and *litterateur* are too widely known to require any mention in our columns; while his character as a flautist is unapproachable in these Provinces, or indeed on this continent. Better still, he is one of the few Protestant Irishmen, with whom we meet in these distant parts, who have not yet forgotten the land of their birth; and it is for this latter shining quality, more than any other, that we bespeak for him a cordial reception at the hands of the Irishmen of Buffalo. An overflowing house should greet him on his appearance, which will amply be repaid by a lecture at once sarcastic, serious, comical and musical.

The "lecture" took place on 7 March. It is not known whether his daughter Mary accompanied him on piano.

The *Buffalo Courier* reported that the evening of entertainment was attended by a "moderate sized" audience at St James Hall. Unable to attend the event himself, the reviewer described the audience as "highly pleased with the musical feature of the entertainment." As always, McCarroll's performance as a flautist was "unapproachable." However, the reporter said nothing about his political humour, slanted as it likely had to be toward an Irish-Canadian perspective. Still, the verdict was positive: "With such a speciality, there is no reason why Mr McCarroll should not make it profitable to himself in this country."[1] Making money was, of course, very high among his priorities; however, the crusade of Fenianism was the major attraction for him.

Such a tepid welcome was better than nothing and certainly better than the sense of despair and failure that had marked his final months in Toronto. His dream of literary success and becoming a cultural and political influence in Canada West was in shambles; at the same time, he opposed the direction in which the colony was heading, believing that the changes that followed Confederation were bound to diminish the hopes of the Irish as a people.[2] As well, he had finally to admit to himself that there would be no help from his friends in government. While he remained hopeful that his two manuscripts – one of poetry and the other of prose writing – might be sold to a publisher in Boston or New York, he now had to admit that neither of them would see the light of day in the near future. His literary capital remained "on the shelf," like himself. His Toronto friends now were mostly Irish Catholics like Patrick Boyle, Mike Murphy, John O'Donohoe, and James Moylan, though he maintained some Orange connections; acquaintances of a literary-musical bent still valued his friendship, mostly for old time's sake and in the name of artistic expression.[3] By contrast, many saw him now as an angry and obsessive figure, whose crankiness too often overwhelmed his natural ebullience, wit, and charm.

Having been locked in a limbo of frustration for two difficult years, McCarroll was no longer able to provide for his family. His wife was dying, he was broke, and his spirits were at a low ebb.[4] Ann McCarroll returned to her mother's home in the company of her daughters. She died and was buried in Peterborough on 13 July 1866 in her forty-ninth year while her husband of nearly thirty years sought to develop his Fenian connections in Buffalo; much later, her remains were moved to the McCarroll plot at St James (Cathedral) Cemetery in Toronto that he had purchased years earlier.[5] Three of the McCarroll girls stayed on in Peterborough after their mother's death, where they were watched over by old friends like William Cluxton, who had established himself as one of the town's most successful businessmen. They worked there as music teachers. In fact, in 1871 Emma and Clara were still living and teaching in Peterborough. By then, Mary had moved back to Toronto to live with Kate and Fred Menet.[6] Kate had married Menet in St Catharines in January 1871.[7] In the meantime McCarroll was not long in finding a new partner of his own. Likely in 1867 he married a widow named Julia Dolmage in Buffalo; they had probably first met in Toronto.

Slipping down the road to Buffalo for a one-off concert offered a brief respite from McCarroll's Toronto pressures. But he had another plan in play. In Buffalo he could tap into Toronto-bred connections with Fenian leaders while seeking out new sources of employment. With Fenian excitement on the rise in several states along the American border, he found himself much more open to the prospect of American life – its bustle, enterprise, and self-reliance – than he had been in the past.

A thriving, fast-growing manufacturing town, Buffalo was one of the major transportation hubs for northern New York State and the Great Lakes. By 1850 "the Queen City of the Lakes" had become "the world's largest grain-shipping center," while its position as the western terminus of the busy Erie Canal gave it major advantages for inland trade and travel. Moreover, the city's large Irish population was far more Catholic than Protestant.[8] In 1865, McCarroll had mentioned to Macdonald that, in his increasing frustration, he was thinking about abandoning Canada: "I am desirous of leaving the country for many reasons," he reported, without providing a specific rationale.[9]

Friendships with prominent Toronto Hibernians helped to develop his sense of Buffalo as a promising new base for his Irish hopes and aspirations. Fenian traffic between the two cities was frequent. His own trips to Buffalo were thus partly his personal effort to connect more closely with Irish nationalists living there; several had Toronto connections and many were spoiling for a fight on behalf of Ireland's "national'" interests in North America. In 1866 Buffalo was also swarming with Irish-born soldiers, fresh from the Union Army's victory in the Civil War. Many who were not war-weary or wounded were still in a military state of mind. Moreover, a couple of "Fenian Centres" in Buffalo were eagerly stirring the pot.[10] One was auctioneer Patrick O'Dea's business office on Pearl Street. The much-rumoured Fenian plan to invade Canada that year was generating plenty of press in Buffalo, while in Canada West the growing concern and anxiety was reflected in newspapers like the *Globe*. Such an attack, which might be three-pronged, promised increased military engagement and camaraderie for those Irish-American soldiers not yet ready to return to domesticity and their social roles.[11] Meetings and lectures were frequent, local saloons had become dens of heated talk, and drilling exercises were taking place in and around established Fenian centres.

To the Fenian leaders in Buffalo, McCarroll was prepared to offer not only his journalistic experience but also his knowledge of Canadian ports and

THE USUAL IRISH WAY OF DOING THINGS.

7.1 Thomas Nast, "The Usual Irish Way of Doing Things," *Harper's Weekly*, 2 September 1871, 824. The Irish were often mocked and degraded for their militant propensities in satirical cartoons, as in this representative Thomas Nast cartoon. Microfilm Room, Firestone Library, Princeton University.

the operations of Her Majesty's Customs. The last letters he wrote to John A. Macdonald provide a picture of his eager but unsettled state of mind early in 1866. Always ready with a Plan B if Plan A failed, he found fresh camaraderie and support from prominent Buffalo militants like Patrick O'Dea and B.F. Gallagher. Among them he could feel relief from his financial difficulties and engagement in a bracing anti-English, pro-Irish agenda. The advice he had offered to D'Arcy McGee five years earlier – keep one foot firmly on the floor and the other ready to move quickly when necessary – certainly applied to himself as he cut his Toronto ties and took up residence in Buffalo.[12]

McCarroll wrote three letters to John A. Macdonald from Buffalo in February and March 1866; the third was his last. The first, written on 18 February, reveals a man much impressed by the city's lively business world. He reported that he had spent his first "few days under the American flag" where he found a friendly reception and an outgoing populace whom he described as "powerful and enterprising beyond all conception."[13] He again urged Macdonald to lobby Finance Minister Alexander Galt on his behalf. The second letter, written three days later, was completely different in tone and content. It was a darker, begging missive. Finding himself in "my extremity in another land," he reported that he was "without one shilling" in his pocket. Perhaps exaggerating his need as was his wont, he begged Macdonald to "Lend me or send me $50, out of your own private purse," if only to pay him back for journalistic work he had done on the premier's behalf in May 1864. "Must I not be driven when I write a note like this? – Oh, Yes!" he concluded dramatically.[14] In emphasizing his own desperation, however, he made no mention of the dire situation of his wife and daughters. Nevertheless, he continued to imply that he would return to Toronto after his concert.

His final letter – dated 18 March, nearly two weeks after the concert – was longer and climactic.[15] After rehearsing his several grievances against the Canadian government, he announced his "final adieu to all my hopes in relation to my claims on you and the Government." Having now crossed a kind of Rubicon in his own mind, he was set to enter upon a newspaper campaign of self-justification and revenge from Buffalo. For "two long years" his friends in government had promised him some help or compensation; despite the encouragement received in private notes from Macdonald and Galt, no support was forthcoming.[16] The result for him personally had been "penury" and "the systematic ruin of both myself and my family."

Buffalo provided him with "the proper moment" to speak out in the American press about the injustices he had experienced. His "mission" was clear and his threat two-fold. First, he was prepared to publish ministerial letters revealing the ill-treatment he had received at the government's hands; second, he remained bent upon indicting the man most responsible for his ill-fortune, Thomas Worthington. He assured Macdonald, however, that "I have no bitter feelings regarding you."[17] His justification was a "duty to myself, my family and the people of Canada."[18]

For the time being, he would feel his way forward. "You behold me, not your enemy, but a man constrained in self-defense to apply the knife to every fibre of this injustice, and bare it to the gaze of the province at large."[19] That image

RIDGEWAY

AN HISTORICAL ROMANCE

OF THE

FENIAN INVASION OF CANADA

By SCIAN DUBH

"On our side is virtue and Erin;
On theirs is the Saxon and guilt," - MOORE

BUFFALO:
McCARROLL & CO., PUBLISHERS,
CORNER OF SWAN AND PEARL STREETS

1868

7.2 The title page of *Ridgeway* announced its author as SCIAN DUBH (Black Knife), but also states that James McCarroll published it from his Buffalo office. Source: Michael A. Peterman, *James McCarroll, alias Terry Finnegan: Newspapers, Controversy and Literature in Victorian Canada*, Occasional Paper 17, published by the Peterborough Historical Society, November 1996.

anticipated the penname "Scian Dubh" that he chose in writing *Ridgeway: An Historical Romance of the Fenian Invasion of Canada.*[20] In that book, despite his earlier assertion of continuing friendship and respect, he attacked John A. in personal ways for his failure to provide the help he had often promised.

It is characteristic of McCarroll's obsessively romantic sensibility and his ad hominem scorekeeping that, in his final letter to the premier, he persisted in his need to bring down Tom Worthington. He continued to see himself as the wounded, much-abused Irish gentleman implacably pursuing a justifiable course of retribution against his villainous foe. His was a classic case of the Irishman mistreated and ignored. The fact that Worthington had been favoured by the government in recent appointments and had once, as McCarroll knew, written a letter meant to expose an instance of Macdonald's secretive manoeuvring while he was a minister of the Crown, stuck like a needle deep into his craw. It was crucial evidence of his duplicity and treachery. "I must place Worthington in his true light before the people," he told Macdonald.

Feeling his grievances so strongly, he failed to see how irrelevant his personal complaints must have seemed to others. He appears never to have asked himself whether people in Toronto – other than his Hibernian friends – would care a jot for civil servants like Tom Worthington or himself. The rantings of a disgruntled customs employee could scarcely fire the interest of a people who were deeply concerned with the immediacies of their own daily needs and the ongoing hostilities between Catholics and Protestants in the city. For Torontonians, the looming threat of a Fenian invasion from the south, related worries about American threats to Canada and the future of the Reciprocity agreement, and the ongoing excitement about a possible confederation of the Canadian provinces were of more vital concern. Nor did he seem to realize that once he formally aligned himself with the Buffalo Fenians, few Canadians would see him as worthy of attention; he had made himself a traitor to their valued British heritage.

McCarroll's plan was to itemize his complaints through the American press and to begin to make himself a significant player on the larger American stage. Hence, he warned Macdonald that "I'll shortly be in a position" to write for the Buffalo press "with which I shall soon be identified intimately." He imagined himself filling a position of importance within the Fenian media; from the new editorial seat he had been promised by Patrick O'Dea, he would be able to influence Irish-Canadian thinking on matters of importance to their future. By March his optimism about his Buffalo prospects revived his sagging spirits.

One report on McCarroll in Buffalo provides a detailed look at a man already engaged in his Fenian connections. Written by Alexander McLeod in his capacity as a spy for the Canadian government, the letter is dated 19 March 1866.

James McCarroll is here, he has been a Collector of Customs in Canada, and I believe has been connected with the press there. He is now a prime Fenian – lectures among them on the weakness of Britain & Canada, etc. He said to my employer [Patrick O'Dea] a few nights since that I was a dangerous man to have about these head quarters – an incorrigible Tory and pensioner, and just the man to take notes for the Canadian government. Gallagher says – I said to McCarroll that you [McLeod] knew nothing about the Fenians movements that was not known all around. I had just written the above when in walks Mr G[allagher] and James McCarrol [*sic*] [who] was introduced to me, and said oh I have known Mr McLeod since 1832 when he kept store in Toronto. He remained ½ an hour – says that the Canadian Govt discharged him for his liberal independent principles, and owe him $2000 which they refuse to pay – altho he has a letter from the Attorney Genl admitting to his claim, etc. etc. I think he is a needy adventurer.[21]

As McLeod's report notes, there was some truth to McCarroll's assertion about his growing connections in Buffalo. He believed that he would soon have a new "field battery at [his] command." Part of that battery would spring from his privileged position with the Fenians and his access to his own printing press, which was being transported to Buffalo.[22] Meanwhile he was immersing himself in Fenian activities. By October 1866 reports began to reach Canada that he was indeed editing a new Fenian newspaper called the *Buffalo Globe*. It was published from the business office of Patrick O'Dea (O'Day), the head of one of the city's most influential Fenian centres. Several months earlier he had become an intimate in O'Dea's "hall on Pearl Street." That hall "was no insignificant venue."[23] For business purposes, it was an auction room, but it functioned as O'Dea's personal centre for Fenian rallies and meetings; its basement was given over to gathering and storing munitions, and for drilling Fenian recruits. Before and after the infamous Ridgeway raid of 2–3 June 1866, McCarroll busied himself in developing connections with and passing information on to influential Fenians in the city. O'Dea, B.F. Gallagher, and Barney O'Donohoe helped to connect him with other sworn Fenians. That year as well, Mike Murphy, one of Toronto's leading Fenians and an old friend, moved to Buffalo to set up a saloon.

Though I have found no home address for McCarroll in Buffalo until 1869 – his last year in the city – he no doubt lived close to the First Ward, located just north of the Buffalo River, the Erie Canal, and the Lake Erie waterfront. He did so for financial and political reasons. This "hidden away community, just south of downtown Buffalo,"[24] an area "akin to a small industrial town,"[25] had a high density of (poor) Irish-Catholic labourers and, relatedly, a strong level of communal support for Fenian goals. Many returning Civil War soldiers called the First Ward home. Near the waterfront there were seasonal jobs in the grain elevators and boat-building docks, in addition to dock work itself. Here too he was close to O'Dea's business headquarters and the site of his Fenian *Globe*. The First Ward "neighbourhood" teemed with cheap wooden buildings, boarding houses, and saloons.[26] His 1869 residence at 343 Ninth Street was close to the First Ward boundary; so too was his own printing company, McCarroll & Co., at the corner of Swan and Pearl.[27] No account exists of his perceptions of life in the First Ward, though some thoughts and views would have appeared in both the *Globe* and its successor, the *Fenian Volunteer* (1867).

One of McCarroll's special resources as a Fenian convert was his knowledge of the vulnerabilities of the Canadian ports to which he had been connected. Canadian watchdogs along the border, like Alexander McLeod, followed his movements closely. Another such glimpse (dated 11 April) came from Charles Treble, a border agent reporting to Thomas Worthington, the same man whom McCarroll so deeply loathed.[28] After predicting that a Fenian invasion from Buffalo and other border cities would likely occur in late May, Treble turned his attention to news he had received about Mr James McCarroll. His source was a clerk with active business connections in Buffalo (possibly McLeod himself). Treble wrote, "McCarrol ('Terry Finnegan') [*sic*] has tendered his services to the 'General' stating he has resided in Canada for 29 or 39 years, for sixteen years he occupied a position in Her Majesty's Customs & has a complete knowledge of the people and the country. Although a protestant he is a dear lover of his native country and deeply sympathises with her in the wrongs endured from the powerful arm of a tyrant and has sufficient documentary evidence in his possession to prove the fact."[29]

While Buffalo was bristling with Fenian excitement, the split in the leadership of the Fenian Brotherhood in the United States was also garnering much media attention. The O'Mahony and Roberts wings of the Brotherhood were at odds about what sort of campaign to launch into Canada. A raid across the border was at the forefront of the Roberts wing's plans, especially because of the recent influx of Irish-born Civil War veterans and anti-English sympathizers

in Buffalo. That infamous "raid," which lasted less than three days, took place
at the beginning of June. Closely watching were the O'Dea circle, including
James McCarroll, and Buffalo journals like the *Courier*, a widely distributed
newspaper that paid regular attention to the meetings and movements of the
local Fenians.[30]

Ridgeway: The Battle

The actual invasion into Canada occurred on the night of 1 June 1866, just three
months after McCarroll moved to Buffalo. Under the leadership of General
John O'Neill, about 600 Fenian troops crossed the Niagara River by barge near
the town of Black Rock, just north of Fort Erie. The invasion was shocking
but short-lived; in its wake, McCarroll would busy himself gathering personal
accounts of what is now known as the Battle of Ridgeway for his *Buffalo Globe*
columns and would later write a historical romance about those still-luminous
events, the better to contribute to the local publicity campaign supporting the
first and only Fenian "victory" to date. Within eighteen months, *Ridgeway: An
Historical Romance of the Fenian Invasion of Canada* appeared in Buffalo. It was
self-published and distributed by McCarroll & Co., Publishers, of Buffalo.[31]

To this day the Battle of Ridgeway remains one of Canada's least known
military engagements. From a Canadian perspective it has usually been viewed
as a gallant but flawed defence of Canada's border by ill-prepared troops summoned to deal with the sudden invasion by battle-ready Irish-American soldiers.
More recently, Peter Vronsky in *Ridgeway: The American Fenian Invasion and the
1866 Battle That Made Canada* (2011) has probed the ways in which Canadians
over the years have signified that battle, arguing that its enduring importance
lies in the fact that this was the first time that Canadian troops operated on
their own, and with some success, in a dangerous border conflict. With British
leadership unavailable, the inexperienced Canadian volunteers successfully
managed to recover from their initial losses and, over a couple of days, forced
O'Neill's soldiers back across the Niagara River. The battle itself and, more
importantly, the rather pathetic retreat of the Fenians at Fort Erie on 3 June,
illustrated that Canadian volunteers and their leaders could effectively rally
to their country's aid, thus preserving Canada's pre-Confederation border and
engendering fresh pride in the colony's future. Vronsky further argues that the
invasion led the Canadian government to create a secret service operation for
the country.[32] As well, after Ridgeway, Canada began to direct more money
and attention to the preparation and arming of its militia units. In these ways

– and it was certainly an ironic result from James McCarroll's Fenian point of view – Ridgeway "Made Canada."

In certain inescapable ways the Battle of Ridgeway proved a failure for both sides. For the Fenian Brotherhood, what had initially been designed to be a bold and impressive first strike against the British in Canada was soon seen as a harbinger of the Brotherhood's weaknesses and failures. On the afternoon of 2 June, the Fenians, under General John O'Neill, met and defeated several battalions of hastily summoned Canadian volunteers from Toronto and Hamilton at the Ridgeway site, some ten miles into Canadian territory. Short-lived as it was, the victory initially signalled great promise for the Fenian Brotherhood campaign in the northern United States. This was, of course, the interpretation that McCarroll put forward both as the editor of the *Globe* (1866) and in his later novel. The reality, however, was deeply tinged with failure. O'Neill's troops soon found themselves in need of the backup support promised by Fenian headquarters in Buffalo and New York. However, those reinforcements were not forthcoming.

By contrast, as Vronsky makes clear, the Ridgeway encounter can be seen as a positive response, if not a clear victory, for Canadian soldiers who showed courageous resilience in the face of the sudden invasion. In regrouping after their initial defeat, they pursued the Fenian troops back to Fort Erie and forced them to retreat across the Niagara River, thus helping to establish a new military identity for the country. Mostly inexperienced and poorly armed, the Canadian troops arrived by train from Toronto without adequate supplies; they were sent immediately into action under the inept command of Lieutenant Colonel Alfred Booker. At "the ridge road" they fought doggedly against a battalion of experienced Civil War veterans and suffered the loss of nine young volunteers, several of whom were University of Toronto students. Though they were routed at first, they managed to regroup in a few hours. Aided by reinforcements who soon joined the defense under Lieutenant Colonel George J. Peacocke, they drove the invaders back to Fort Erie; there several units of Canadian volunteers closed in on the exhausted Fenian soldiers, forcing O'Neill to order a retreat across the Niagara River.

Once on the river, the Fenians were arrested by American border troops on the battleship *Michigan*, then stationed in Buffalo. Though initially slow to respond to the first signs of invasion, American officials now charged the troops with violating the Neutrality Laws then in place. This action, apparently unanticipated by the Fenian War Office, put an end to the immediate operation. It did not, however, silence Fenian rhetoric; the war talk and military planning would continue for several years, especially in cities along the Canadian border. Rumours of several major invasions circulated over time, raising alarm bells in Canada with each burst of rhetoric. For his part, McCarroll, now seen by many in Canada as a traitor, would play a notable part in helping to heat up that Fenian rhetoric, especially in his work as the editor of O'Dea's *Globe*. He himself did not participate in the raid, though at least one journalist accompanied the Fenian troops to Ridgeway.[33]

Under the auspices of Patrick O'Dea, the *Buffalo Globe* made its first appearance on 6 October 1866, four months after the Battle of Ridgeway. It lasted about three months, ceasing publication that winter.[34] Word of its birth and polemical purpose soon reached Canada West. As editor, McCarroll delighted in sending copies to journalistic friends and acquaintances north of the border. On 19 October, Patrick Boyle of the *Irish Canadian* (Toronto) wrote a column in support of his old colleague, whom he deemed the agreeable Protestant Hibernian also known as Terry Finnegan. Boyle fully supported the reconquest of Ireland by the Fenians, but he had refused to take a stand for or against the Fenian Brotherhood south of the border.[35] However, he published McCarroll's poem "National Music," reprinted from the *Buffalo Globe*, identifying its author by his new pseudonym, "The Irish Wolf." It was a moniker McCarroll no doubt relished.[36] Boyle also provided his readers with this description of "The *Buffalo Globe*" and its editor:

Under this caption comes the first number of a well-gotten up, neatly printed, and ably edited weekly newspaper, published, as the heading implies at Buffalo, N.Y., by Messrs. P. O'Day & Co. [*sic*]. In the leading editorials and the "poet's corner," we detect the vigorous and *musical* pen of an old friend, lately resident in Toronto. The editorial chair of the *Globe* could scarcely be filled by a gentleman more versatile and talented, and our contemporary may count it fortunate in securing the services of so ripe a scholar as James McCarroll, Esq. We wish the *Globe* all success in the wide domain which it has chosen as the field of its labor in the cause of Ireland and of truth.

In the enthusiasm of the moment, what McCarroll, O'Dea, and Boyle could not foresee was the *Globe's* lack of influence beyond its coterie of Fenian readers in the Buffalo area. It was a small-scale production, handsomely got up (by Boyle's account), but with very limited distribution in New York State and even less in Canada.[37] The paper was undercapitalized, lacked sufficient subscribers, and was specifically tied to Irish pride following the Fenian "victory" at Ridgeway. Like McCarroll's own independent publishing ventures in Toronto in 1863–64,[38] the paper died a quiet death within a few months. But O'Dea was eagerly making plans for a promising successor.

In the *Globe* (and later in *Madeline*), McCarroll prefaced "The Irish Wolf" with this epigraph: "Some years ago, the *London Times* used the above epithet ('The Irish Wolf') in designation of the Irish upon their native soil." The poem reads as follows.

Seek music in the wolf's fierce howl
Or pity in his blood-shot eye,
When hunger drives him on the prowl
Beneath a rayless northern sky;

But seek not that we should forgive
The hand that strikes us to the heart,
And yet in mockery bids us live
To count our stars as they depart.

We've fed the tyrant with our blood;
Won all his battles – built his throne –
Established him on land and flood,
And sought his glory next our own.

We raised him from his low estate;
We plucked his pagan soul from hell,
And led him pure to heaven's gate.
Till he, for gold, like Judas, fell.

And when in one, long, soulless night,
He lay unknown to wealth or fame,
We gave him empire – riches – light,
And taught him how to spell his name.

But now ungenerous and unjust,
Forgetful of our old renown,
He bows us to the very dust;
But wears our jewels in his crown.

Revisiting the litany of Irish complaints about English tyranny throughout the centuries and Ireland's ancient claim of superiority in language and religion, McCarroll created a kind of anthem and vision for the Fenian movement in America. There was "music in the wolf's fierce howl" and its powerful crescendo would soon be heard in "the northern sky." Extreme in its view but sharply chiseled in its lines, "The Irish Wolf" is, interestingly, the one James McCarroll poem that currently lives on for twenty-first century readers. Patrick Crotty included it in his new edition of the *Penguin Book of Irish Poetry* (2010).

"National Music" is another Fenian diatribe. It draws on a choral metaphor to distinguish the kinds of mistreatment and tyranny that the English have practised in Ireland.[39] It emphasizes the famines and related deprivations endured by Ireland's "decent poor" at the hands of "the great of the land."

> In mansions built of the mouldering bones
> Of those who died from the want of bread,
> The great of the land, blend their happy tones
> As their festal halls they gaily tread.
>
> Grim skulls are the lamps that hang around;
> Their oil is the widow's tear;
> And the dust of the orphan strews the ground
> That's made from the houseless stranger's bier.
>
> While the cup's red draught, from the heart is trod,
> A nation's sighs dims the jewel's blaze,
> That hangs on the breast of some noble clod
> Who reels through the dance's giddy maze.
>
> But, is not the music sad and wild?
> It falls on the ear like a dying shriek;
> The ALTO's sung by a hungry child,
> With a scalding drop on his pallid cheek.
>
> And the TREBLE's sobb'd by the decent poor
> Who tried to conceal their hapless fate,
> 'Till the Landlord drove them to the door,
> And bared to the world, their wretched state.

And the TENOR's raved in a mother's pray'r,
As she wildly clings to her starving boy,
While angels weep o'er the ragged pair
Who had never tasted a moment's joy.

And the BASS is an old man's feeble groan,
Who toils here below with sighs and tears,
For a piece of a coarse brown loaf, alone,
Though bow'd with the weight of three-score years.

And the CHORUS bursts in wild despair,
From the bloodless lips of a countless throng,
While a heart-string breaking here and there,
Beats sullen time, to the mournful song.

But the dancers still move gaily by;
Or turn to the helpless, famish'd band,
To ask who it is, that dares to sigh
When he sings for the great of a Christian land.

McCarroll's newly minted Fenian poems found only a few readers in Canada. As editor of the *Buffalo Globe*, he had a free hand in emphasizing English tyranny and injustice in Ireland, but he had limited reach. As well, given the success of the Ridgeway raid, he had what he and his fellow Fenians believed was a compelling narrative to build on.[40] In nearby St Catharines, where he was still remembered with some fondness from his Port Stamford days, the *Evening Journal* at first referred to the American Fenians dismissively, but with a firm nod to McCarroll, as the "Finnegans."[41] Influential and "super-loyal" papers like the *Toronto Leader*, *Canadian Freeman*, and *Montreal Gazette* were quick to denounce McCarroll in his new and outspoken Fenian guise.

Still, not all Canadian responses to his new identity were negative. In the *Canadian Freeman* of 15 November 1866, James Moylan, now turned severe critic of his friend's "firebrand" polemics, printed an article by SACERDOS calling attention to the *Buffalo Globe* as "The New Fenian Organ." While SACERDOS prefaced his piece by providing quotations from the *Toronto Leader* and *Montreal Gazette* assailing the *Globe's* editor,[42] he argued that McCarroll was being unduly censured by an ungentlemanly and forgetful Canadian press. Such newspapers now chose to overlook a man of special talents. "Mr McCarroll

is an accomplished flautist, and a classical English writer ... His English for
purity of diction – vigor of style and loftiness of sentiment, has never been
and never can hope to be equaled by anything that has emanated from either
the *Gazette* or *Leader* offices." While he had been wrong-headed in aligning
himself with a Fenian (and American) newspaper, "there his offense ends." It
was just as wrong to condemn him for such actions as it was to pronounce
the Rev. Mr McMahon guilty of Fenian crimes against England in Canada.[43]

Buffalo gave McCarroll a fresh working environment, a new set of challenges attuned to his Celtic identity, and a busy Irish-Catholic population to
mingle with. True to form, he now opted to look forward rather than backward,
ignoring as best he could the obligations and discomforts – financial, familial,
and moral – that he had left behind in Toronto. Better to throw himself
into his new propagandistic role, better to show Canadians their error in not
attending more closely to the great Fenian crusade for Irish retribution and
recognition in North America, better to oppose Confederation north of the
border from an American perspective. The *Buffalo Globe* gave him a new pulpit
from which to trumpet his ideas and enthusiasms; at the same time, though
he was loath to admit it, he found himself occupying a narrow editorial seat,
one that protected him from the antipathy that most Upper Canadians felt
toward Fenian extremism, especially in the context of ongoing fears of American
aggression and annexation.

Given his Fenian politics and his circumscribed finances, it is unlikely that
McCarroll had any opportunity or desire to return to Canada during these
months. Writing in the *Canadian Freeman* on 14 February 1867, James Moylan
confidently opined that he "would hardly have ventured to visit Canada."
His name was now "odious throughout the province" because of his writing
for "Mr O'Day's firebrand Fenian sheet"; he would risk "tar and feathering"
should he return. Moreover, he was being watched closely as a turncoat spy.

Although Patrick O'Dea closed down the *Globe*, he was keen to continue
publishing a Fenian newspaper in Buffalo. The *Globe's* successor was more
evocatively named the *Fenian Volunteer*. Its first issue appeared in the summer
of 1867 and it continued as a weekly into 1868. McCarroll again took up the
editor's role from the beginning, but resigned in October 1867, presumably to
devote himself to his novel about the Fenian invasion and to find better-paying
opportunities for his journalistic work. He had already been working for some
months as a stringer for a popular New York City periodical called *Frank
Leslie's Chimney Corner*. His Leslie assignment was to write biographies for that
magazine's "Self-Made Men of Our Times" series. One example, reported in

the *Buffalo Evening Courier and Republic* (1 August 1866), was his biography of the Honorable William G. Fargo, a well-known Buffalo citizen whose accomplishments included co-founding the Wells Fargo Express Company.[44]

Information about Patrick O'Dea's three Fenian newspapers is still very limited today. There is no mention in city directories about the short-lived *Globe* and only a couple of references to the *Fenian Volunteer*. However, twelve issues of the *Fenian Volunteer* were recently purchased by the National Library of Ireland; alas, only two of them date from the period before McCarroll resigned as editor.[45] Neither is there any evidence to suggest that McCarroll was connected with O'Dea's third paper, the *United Irishman* (1869), which was published from the same location as the *Volunteer*. Nevertheless, a few salient details about McCarroll do emerge from local newspaper reports and documents. The *Fenian Volunteer* changed its address in 1868. One wonders if that move implies that O'Dea needed to relocate the operation because he lost the use of McCarroll's personal printing press.[46]

In Canada some attention was paid to the *Fenian Volunteer* as word of McCarroll's new editorial position became more widely known in the province. But, except for an aggrieved editor like James Moylan, who had a burning reason to be angry with McCarroll, such recognition was short-lived. Rather, he plodded along at the *Volunteer*, underpaid for his services and still scrambling to make ends meet. In 1868, the *St Catharines Evening Journal* delighted in reporting that the *Fenian Volunteer* had applied to Buffalo City Council for a grant of $1,000 to help meet publication costs. Council rejected that application on 9 September.[47]

On 6 October 1867 he ended his working relationship with Patrick O'Dea. In a genial note, the *Buffalo Courier* (8 October) reported that McCarroll had formally relinquished the editorship of the *Fenian Volunteer*:

It will doubtless be a matter of regret to the readers of the *Fenian Volunteer* that Mr James McCarroll's no longer connected with that journal, as whatever success has been attained by it is mainly attributable to his vigorous pen, and the inflexible manner in which he excluded all American party politics from its columns. His loss to what may be termed the Fenian or Irish newspaper literature of the day, could not fail to be felt severely, had not the authorities of that organization determined that his long experience in the press and patriotic record shall be made available in other quarters where his pen will have a larger scope in the cause of Irish freedom than it possessed recently. His connection with the *Volunteer* terminated on

Tuesday Inst., with an able leading article, "The New Era." Amongst the Irish nationalists and literary men of Canada, Mr McCarroll has held a very high position for the last twenty-five years.[48]

The squib suggests that, having tired of editing a weekly Fenian paper for insufficient remuneration, McCarroll was now ready to devote himself to what he hoped would be a more profitable and resonant Irish project – a "historical novel" celebrating the Fenian "victory" at Ridgeway. The *Courier* column suggests that he was repurposing his writing time with the approval of "the authorities of that organization" who had heretofore done what they could to support him. Still, it is possible that his insistent focus on anti-English politics and his refusal to address American points of view made him replaceable in the eyes of those same Fenian authorities. But, in practical terms, he needed to reclaim his printing press in order to earn sufficient income for himself and his new family.

There had been earlier rumours that McCarroll would soon terminate his editorship of the *Fenian Volunteer*. On 24 April 1867, the *St Catharines Evening Journal* reported that "the notorious James McCarroll, better known as Terry Finnegan, has resigned as the editor of the *Fenian Volunteer* (Buffalo)." While this rumour may have involved a confusion between the *Buffalo Globe* and the *Fenian Volunteer*, underfunding and the lack of capital behind O'Dea's newspapers was a daily reality from the outset.

While McCarroll's Fenian activities in Buffalo led many in Canada to view him as a traitor, by far the nastiest attack on him came in Toronto on 14 May 1868 from the pen of his old friend James Moylan of the *Canadian Freeman*. By this time Thomas D'Arcy McGee lay dead and buried in Ottawa, having been murdered on 7 April by a late-night assassin's bullet. Long a fervent McGee supporter, Moylan was livid about the disrespectful and partisan treatment that his friend was continuing to receive posthumously, especially in Fenian newspapers. In his 14 May editorial entitled "The Fenian Organs and the Assassination," he reasserted his charge that "Fenianism was at the bottom of the murder." Troubled by "the tone and spirit" of such writing, he took aim at the *Irish People*, the *Irish Republic*, and "an infamous print published in Buffalo, known as the *Fenian Volunteer*." Moylan's condemnation of the Buffalo paper and James McCarroll merits a lengthy quotation, if only to measure the white heat of Moylan's anger and his need to condemn his "lewd and dissolute" former friend. For the full text, see Appendix B.

The sentiments which find expression in the columns of this last named journal, are, unexceptionably, the most atrocious and diabolical that we ever saw published. In no other country of the civilized world would the abomination be tolerated. There is no subject too sacred, no personage too venerable or exalted, by sanctity of life or dignity of character and position, to escape the coarse and defamatory malevolence of the lewd and dissolute creature, who – after having made Canada too hot for himself by debauchery and every species of rascality – now so worthily fills the editorial chair of the 'Fenian Volunteer.' This person, after having assigned reasons for the murder of Mr McGee, which have no other foundation than the prompting of his own filthy and impure mind, enters upon the vindication of [Patrick] Whelan, urges the creation of a fund for his defence, and threatens Sir John A. Macdonald and sundry journalists in Canada with 'swift and certain destruction' should 'a hair of Whelan's head be hurt.'

No personal attack on James McCarroll had ever been so vitriolic or sustained. While many of its assertions were patently false, particularly the notion that McCarroll was a sycophant of McGee and a Tory partisan, Moylan made it clear how completely he had managed to earn the scorn and hostility of some of his old journalistic colleagues in Toronto. The fact that he had ceased several months previously to be the editor of the *Fenian Volunteer* escaped Moylan's knowledge, though it is possible that McCarroll continued to contribute to the newspaper, especially when Canada, D'Arcy McGee, and John A. Macdonald were the subjects of the moment.

Certainly, McCarroll had shifted from his Protestant roots and early Orange connections to a more Catholic and integrative view of Irishness, a view that he hoped would speak to a more united, less politicized future for all Irish Canadians. He had as well, like many Irishmen in Canada, grown to mistrust McGee and to regard him variously as a turncoat, a job seeker, an anti-Fenian, and an Anglo-sycophant. His Terry Finnegan letters had initially placed great hope in McGee's political capacity to act on behalf of the Irish in Canada, but, after witnessing alterations in his views and feeling the shock of his famous Wexford speech in 1865, his hopes had been undercut.[49] Certainly, he continued in Buffalo to seek journalistic opportunities to attack Canada's first prime minister, the now knighted Sir John A. Macdonald.

But had McCarroll, who was closely tied to the Reform platform of the 1840s, once been "a violent Tory partisan"? No. Had he for a time been "an extreme anti-Fenian?" Not likely. Was he a "lewd and dissolute creature," well known for his "debauchery" and "rascality"? Perhaps, but not likely. And should he have been more "grateful" for the "beneficial" treatment he had received from McGee and other government officials prior to 1864? Again, not likely. Had he played a part in McGee's assassination? No. As well, was he wrong in urging a fair trail for Patrick Whalen when partisan journalists like Moylan argued that, given his unquestionable guilt, he should be executed at once and without a trial? Moylan's diatribe rode roughshod over many facts, so strong was his anger at McGee's assassination. For its part, the *St Catharines Evening Journal* now concurred with Moylan, making special note of his attack on the "notorious" ex-Gauger, and accusing McCarroll "of all crimes known to man" in editing that "infamous sheet," the "Fenian Volunteer."

Ridgeway: The Book (1868)

Published eighteen months after the invasion, *Ridgeway: An Historical Romance of the Fenian Invasion of Canada* documents the evolution of Fenian militancy in Ireland and North America and highlights the victory at Ridgeway as the most recent achievement of the Fenian Brotherhood in America. It includes the names of a number of current leading Irish Catholics and Fenians in Buffalo. Recently, it has been seen as one of the earliest works of fiction about the city of Buffalo. D.M. Doolin has argued that, though "the Fenian raid did not fit neatly into those ... emerging cultural expressions of ... [the] newly found confidence in Irish identity on the global stage," "Mr O'Carroll's" [sic] *Ridgeway* contains "subtleties and complexities of Irish American Fenianism" that should not be overlooked.[50] Peter Vronsky recognizes it as the only American literary perspective on the famous invasion.

The book views the United States of America, fresh from its own Civil War, as Ireland's new partner in the campaign to redress her centuries-long suffering at the hands of the English. McCarroll hoped that "the great, Irish national idea which now so moves this continent" would expand in influence (17). He saw his new Buffalo home as a representative part of the land of opportunity, an expanding nation offering Irish newcomers "the sublime lessons of the great American people, and the generous sympathy they evince invariably in regard to nations deprived of the blessings of freedom" (xvii). America's lessons are founded on democratic principles and a "broad platform of justice and common sense" (xviii); it has made freedom readily available to its citizens and succeeded in ending preferment based on accidents of birth. "The open arms of free America" (xiv) have generously welcomed the Irish into its midst. In this spirit McCarroll argued that, while "the terrible war cloud of Fenianism has fill[ed] the whole west," it was surcharged not only with vengeance but also "the great, broad lightnings of American freedom" (xvii). His optimism was, however, a wishful misreading of events, a misreading in tune with the thinking of most Fenians: "the whole west" was not moved by the Fenian "war cloud" nor was the American government of the day willing to support its agenda, however evasive in certain instances.

England's systematic suppression of Ireland and the undermining of its economic and cultural potential over the centuries had been one of McCarroll's abiding themes since the late 1840s. In editorials he had celebrated Ireland's early record of linguistic and religious achievement, rooted in the Catholic monasteries, and had praised the purity of Celtic blood, while deploring England's long record of suppression and its mean-spirited refusal to address the sufferings and losses of the Catholic peasantry during the catastrophic Famine years. What he had seen as a Protestant youth in County Leitrim fed his growing frustration with the indifference and callousness of "Saxon" authorities. The sufferings of the Famine years, the failed Rebellion of 1848, and the ineffectiveness of Daniel O'Connell's Catholic reforms had deepened his anxiety about Ireland's future. By 1866, having left behind the many frustrations of his later Toronto years, he had sharpened his Fenian rhetoric – a rhetoric at once melodramatic and aggressive – and adopted a "Catholic" view of history that admitted neither qualifications nor rebuttals, even as it managed to avoid the kinds of issues that most concerned the Church itself.[51] He wanted to believe that the time had come for a definitive change in Canada: Confederation was not the answer and England must finally suffer its well-deserved reckoning at the hands of the Fenians in North America.

Ridgeway's *Introduction*

Ridgeway has three parts, an introduction, the narrative, and an appendix, all designed to lionize the Fenian invasion and applaud its future objectives. Its polemical epigraph, taken from McCarroll's mentor Thomas Moore, sets the tone:

> On our side is virtue and Erin;
> On theirs' is the Saxon and guilt.

The introduction describes the development of Fenianism in Ireland. McCarroll
confidently declares that "Heaven has decreed [the coming hour]" (xvi; xiii).
He argues that it is inevitable that the Irish will at last succeed in freeing
themselves; only then will its noble cultural heritage be recognized by the world
at large. At the same time the Irish will exact their long-awaited revenge on the
"stolid" Saxons who for so long had oppressed the country and its people.[52]
He imagines a groundswell of moral justice sweeping forward with the force
of an "avalanche," "rolling down the steep of seven successive centuries" in its
"resistless course" (xx).

A "disunited" Ireland (vii) had been forced to accept "the most frightful
bondage" for centuries (xx). From Pope Adrian's gifting of Ireland to Henry II,
to the early invasions, to the Pale and the Union, England's tyranny had taken
many forms, worsening during the reign of Elizabeth I and through the years
of the Protestant Reformation. Elizabeth I emerges as a particular target of
McCarroll's anger – he sees her as "that lewd monster [who] disgraced her sex
and the age" [vii]; while on the English throne "she combined the courtesan
with the assassin" (x), and was "absolutely satanic" (x) in her treatment of
Ireland. The litany of abuses continues not only through "the atrocities of the
Georges" but into the present day under the "cruelties" of Queen Victoria,
whom he labels "that traitress to humanity" (xiv).[53]

McCarroll stresses the "annals" of Ireland's cultural superiority, calling
attention to "the profound learning and noble chivalry of the Irish from the
earliest periods" (vi). In fact, Erin should be seen historically as England's "*Alma
Mater*" [iii]. She was a "learned, philanthropic and chivalrous" country (iv),
far advanced in religion and the linguistic arts at a time when the mongrel
Saxons wallowed in Paganism, backwardness, and illiteracy.[54] Why then did
the Irish fail to live up to their cultural eminence? His answer is romantically
ethnic and facile. While the Saxons were crude, barbaric, aggressive, stolid,
and vulgar (freebooters and tradesmen at best), the Celts were too chivalric
and high-minded;[55] sometimes to their peril they were lacking in unity and
organizational skills.[56] Rather, they were governed by "a spirit of knight-
errantry, which disdained to take an enemy unawares" (vi), and by the purity
of their Celtic blood. He chooses the legendary O'Neills of Aileach, Ulster, and
Tir-Eogain (x) to represent that chivalric spirit at its best. Despite England's
attempt to suppress and "blot out a nation" (xviii), the pure Fenian spirit of
the Irish always persisted, awaiting its proper moment to assert itself.

After centuries of abuse and neglect, the Irish are ready to "grind their
enemy into pulp" (vi) and to relish "their debt of vengeance," in the name of

"the blood of [their] martyrs" (xi). Celtic purity becomes a persistent, though unexamined, motif in the introduction. The Irish were never conquerors; rather, they were at their best in resisting from within; hence, their desire for revenge on their tormentors has grown in intensity over the centuries. Only in passing does McCarroll glance at the religious tensions that have characterized Irish disunity for so long or the vexed nature of the Irish character, which he often wrote about on other occasions. Instead, he emphasizes Ireland's distinguished chivalric history and the ability of its Catholic citizens to endure mistreatment and pain.

As McCarroll well knew, it is the victors who write history. In his optimistic vision, the Fenians were, by the summer of 1866, preparing for a large military victory that they imagined was theirs by moral right, patient suffering, and intelligent endurance. His heady optimism was blind on the one hand to the (limited) organizational skills and abilities of the leaders of the Fenian Brotherhood in America, and on the other to the enormous resistance that the Fenian invaders would face from the majority of Canadian citizens and (belatedly) the American government. He seemed unaware of the deep "indignation" felt by most Canadians in addressing the "wanton injustice" of such an invasion.[57] Though he completed *Ridgeway* a year and a half after the raid, his romance is a history written in glowing superlatives, dismissive negatives, and great expectations. The English are his villains – they are mongrels and merchants who lack the pure and high-minded values of the Celts. His Fenians are disinterested in their motives while the tyrannical English continue to practise "the blackest ingratitude, the vilest injustice, and the direst oppression" (ix) known to humanity. Hence, a militant corrective was inevitable. "History," he argued, "does not record a more daring and chivalrous project" than the Fenian invasion of 1866 (135).

Ridgeway's Appendix

By way of objectivity, *Ridgeway* does offer a muted sense of moderation in its final section. Structurally, its third part is a document, an "AUTHENTIC REPORT OF THE Invasion of Canada, and the Battle of Ridgeway, By the Army of the Irish Republic, under General O'NEILL, June, 1866."[58] Biased as that report is, Vronsky deems it a reasonably accurate account of events; notably, it makes clear that both sides suffered major failures during the actual invasion, notwithstanding the high-hearted leadership of General O'Neill and the exemplary conduct of the Fenian soldiers under his command. Here, the galloping optimism of the introduction is tempered by actual details, most designed to support the groundless hope that the Fenian initiative might still be welcomed in Canada and the claim that the gallant John O'Neill was too noble to ever surrender to the Canadian forces that cornered his troops at Fort Erie. However, the report does criticize those Fenian soldiers who deserted O'Neill on route to Ridgeway. It also acknowledges the conspicuous failure of the Fenian War Office to provide the support that O'Neill's invaders required once they had won their first skirmish on Canadian soil. Then came the surprising arrest of the retreating Fenians by American authorities on the Niagara River. Charged with violating international Neutrality Laws, O'Neill's troops made a sad and pathetic spectacle as they huddled together on "a large scow attached to a tug boat [and] hauled into American waters." The image of those 200 men, left for four days on the scow's deck in sun and rain, represents the dramatic comeuppance experienced by the Fenian invaders at the hands of their own American government. McCarroll tried to make a convincing case for the Fenian retreat and the subsequent arrests, but he was unable to paper over the grim realities of the retreat and the subsequent embarrassment experienced by the exhausted Fenian troops on that dirty scow.

The Romance/Novel Itself

Ridgeway's narrative is a conventional, nineteenth-century romance of the sort that McCarroll often wrote on a smaller scale for commercial purposes. Set against the background of O'Neill's invasion, it comes complete with hero, heroine, supportive female friend, "dastardly" villain, groups of Fenian supporters on both sides of the border, and a number of n'er-do-wells in the pay of the English villain who voice deplorable English thoughts. While it has the bones of a serviceable melodrama (including the kidnapping of the heroine, betrayals, and disguised identities), the narrative is so heavily awash in Fenian rhetoric and self-congratulation that it severely undercuts reader interest in its story.

Presented in a realistic mode and set on both sides of the Niagara River, the narrative gave McCarroll many opportunities to criticize the Canadian government for what he deemed its spineless support of English values and biases, and to applaud, by contrast, "the pure atmosphere of this free continent" (18), meaning, of course, the United States. It also sanctioned a prolonged poke at English spy operations in Canada. The duplicitous English spy, Edward Lauder (aka Philip Greaves, but actually Edward Philip Darcy), could be a veiled portrait of either Gilbert McMicken, the head of spy operations in Canada, or one of his leading agents, like Thomas Worthington. McCarroll had known and mistrusted McMicken, an Englishman by birth, since his Port Stamford days in the early 1850s, perhaps in part because McMicken had received patronage favours from his friend John A. Macdonald in 1864.[59]

The narrative draws affectionately on McCarroll's Irish background. His central romantic figures, Kate McCarthy and Nick Barry, share his County Leitrim upbringing; they spent their formative days "on the banks" of the "noble" Shannon River and in "the sweet little town of Drumsna" (20). Indeed, they owe their Irish identity and purity of spirit to the legendary atmosphere of Connaught (5). Their exemplary courtship springs from this rural and storied realm, and their youthful beauty and "good blood" mark them romantically as a worthy couple. Circumstances, however, force them to separate while they are still in Leitrim: the beautiful Kate has to emigrate with her family to North America while, the "dashing" Nicholas, hemmed in by poverty and family, has to enlist, much against his will, in the English army he despises.

Nick arrives in Canada with his regiment early in 1866, ready now to buy his release from military service. After a frustrating two-year posting in Malta, his regiment is now garrisoned near Fort Erie on the Niagara River, just as the Fenians are preparing to launch their invasion of Canada. Meanwhile Kate, who has patiently awaited Nick for four years, is currently living near Buffalo after stays in Quebec City and Toronto. In Buffalo she is kidnapped by her disagreeable admirer, the villainous Edward Lauder, and taken by his henchmen, Black Jack and the Kid, to a house in the Canadian countryside near the border. Lauder also serves as a spy for the English, assigned to the Niagara area. He works out of Dublin Castle under the name Philip Greaves. When Nick Barry's hopes for a discharge are ruined by Greaves's double-dealing manoeuvre, Nick is forced to desert his regiment without gaining the official permission he had sought. Escaping across the border, he joins the Fenian force under General O'Neill. By linking Nick with the Fenian army, McCarroll aligns the novel's plot with the actual events of the invasion and the Battle of Ridgeway.

In fact, Nick, ever the pure and good-hearted Irishman, moves with remarkable ease from his English barracks in Canada to Big Tom O'Brien's tavern, the Harp, in American territory. O'Brien, who is "a [Fenian] Centre here" (93, 96), is brimful of "native eloquence"; he speaks in "a style somewhat uncouth" (16) – that is, much in the vein of Terry Finnegan.[60] At the Harp, Big Tom quietly encourages Fenian support among his guests. Amid the flowing tankards, cigar smoke, and smack of billiard balls, Ireland, America, and Canada are regular subjects of discussion. In particular, Canada is seen not as the enemy of the Irish but as the imminent beneficiary of Fenian objectives and American expansion. Most Americans, we are told, have "a fixed impression … that the Canadas belong of right to the great people who now rule the continent" (127). At the same time, most Irish-Catholic Canadians will be ready, once given the opportunity, to rid their country of the scourge of English control at the far-lesser cost of becoming a part of America.

Confederation is firmly dismissed as an English plan "forced upon the people of the Canadas, through falsehood, bribery and the vilest fraud" (46). In effect, the new Dominion of Canada is merely "the new despotism" (46–7) of the English in British America. Dismissing the popular view that Confederation would be the means of saving the country, McCarroll declares that "Canada is doomed, whomsoever her conqueror may be" (183). Big Tom asserts that "Canada beneath the skull and cross-bones of St George, must ever remain a poor, puny starvling" (147). As a political entity the country lies too far north and is too "frozen" to be significant in its own right (141). Moreover, its government is currently rife with corruption, which McCarroll links directly to John A. Macdonald, "the Scotch thricksther at the head of the governmint here" (15). Among such scandals he points to the ongoing saga of financing the Grand Trunk Railway, the corrupt dispensing of Crown Lands, and the ruinous cost of John A.'s "pet Parliament Houses" (145–6).

Fenian thinking, governed by "the purest motives" in the world (65), had for the time being darkened and blurred McCarroll's view of his adopted country. Thirty-five years in Canada West now amounted to little of value in his personal accounting. Inspired by the Ridgeway victory, he compares the Fenian soldiers with the Spartans at Thermopylae (190). He imagines a relatively painless takeover of Canada once the Fenians get their act together in America. The plan is all "so reasonable and so logical" (10), he argues, skating blithely over the realities of day-to-day life as experienced by most Canadians. Seduced by gaudy rumours, overheated Fenian bravado, and a romanticized kind of wish fulfillment, he wanted against all reason to believe that "Canada [wa]s evidently tired of British rule" (22), and that nine-tenths of "the loyalty of Canada towards the British Crown" was "superficial and terribly unreliable" (50–1).

In fact, most Canadians were far less at odds with English rule than McCarroll and the Fenians wanted to believe; most did not see themselves in the thrall of "a pack of government officials" and "a subsidized press" (21).

The Protestants and the Orange Order were well organized in cities like Toronto and they were avowedly anti-Fenian, while most Irish Catholics, in Toronto and elsewhere, dutifully aligned themselves under the guidance of Archbishop John Lynch and the sacred power of their Church. In fact, a large majority of Irish Canadians had little time for the heated promises put forward by Fenian rhetoric.

McCarroll adopted the rather cavalier view that, if Canadians had to suffer from invasion and war because of legitimate Irish interests, it was for their own good. He saw Canadians as complicit in "the wrongs inflicted by the British Government upon Ireland" (10), whether they realized it or not. Furthermore, he dismissed the conventional pro-Irish views espoused by the popular St Patrick's Societies in Toronto and Montreal. They were themselves "the very sthrongholds of England" (13), not of Ireland; they were "simply whited sepulchres" (14), "filled chock full of a pack of miserable toadies to the government" (13) and "pseudo patriots" (16), almost as devoted to "the English sintimint of the counthry" (15), and as loyal as members of the many Orange Lodges.

Ramping up his campaign of dissatisfaction with Prime Minister John A. Macdonald, McCarroll belittled him for his infamous weakness for alcohol, citing the "prolonged and fearful drinking bouts" in which he engaged (67) – "a whirlpool of the most deplorable intemperance" (68) – that rendered him useless for days on end. He enumerated several instances of fraud that had occurred when Macdonald held various government positions. Still smarting over his treatment in Toronto, he could not resist rehearsing again the charges he had so often proffered against "the present Assistant Commissioner of Customs and Excise" – aka Thomas Worthington – whom he twinned with Macdonald, noting sarcastically that "these two worthies" "are still in the pay of the Canadian people" (145). Never one to forget a personal affront, he presented his readers with a picture of a "most wretched government" (144), hopelessly corrupt and inept. It was much in need of restoration through a union with "this mighty Republic" (148) where, he implied, corruption had ceased to exist in the pure air of democracy and civilization that flourished everywhere under the American flag.

I know of only one pre-publication notice and one review of *Ridgeway*, both in Upper Canadian papers. The first appeared in the *St Catharines Evening Journal*, a newspaper that had followed McCarroll's movements with interest but now saw him as a traitor. Responding to an announcement of the book's publication, its editor wrote that it "no doubt will distort facts and glorify the

great 'Gineral' O'Neill, of which we could not complain, but such a work from
the pen of Mr McCarroll no one could anticipate. For years he ate the Queen's
bread, and so long as the supply kept up, he was one of the most blatant in
his loyalty … The moment he lost place and pay he commenced abusing his
benefactors, winding up turning traitor to his country. The work, coming
from the pen of Mr McCarroll, will be well written, but we fear will contain
as many untruths and lies."

The review appeared in the *Irish Canadian* (13 January 1869), where, for
months, McCarroll continued to advertise his new book for sale.[61] Deliberately
skirting Fenian politics, the review focused on the novel's love story. It praised
"its very simplicity and beauty," and commended its celebration of "the con-
stancy of Irish affection in humble circumstances." The reviewer also paid
close attention to Nick Barry's heroics as an Irish soldier who had to carry on
under great pressure during the invasion. In passing, the reviewer noted that
James M'Carroll is a former Torontonian "well known in this city and … ever
deemed a patriotic Irishman."

Cultural Groundings in Buffalo

There are only a few details available concerning McCarroll's musical activities in Buffalo from 1866 to 1869. As well, there is little information about
connections he may have made with other newspapers, though he told one
interviewer that he had done some "journalistic gypsying" in northern New
York State. The Buffalo City directories are only marginally helpful in tracing
his movements. Curiously, he was approved for membership in the Buffalo
YMCA, but that came in 1871, after he had resettled and was working in New
York City. But he did become involved with one promising cultural venture
during his early months in the city. In a column dated 7 August 1866 the *Buffalo
Daily Courier* commended him for the poetic address he wrote to commemorate
"the opening of the first Museum and Opera House" in Buffalo. A local actress,
Cora Jefferson, read the poem. Here is its first verse:

> In this fair land of genius, every hour
> Lends some bright feature to the busy age,
> And clothes the bar, the pulpit and the stage –
> That classic triad – with new pomp and power;
> 'Till Virtue, Truth and Pleasure, all combined,
> Alike enchant and elevate the mind.[62]

The repurposing of the Buffalo Opera House, erected in 1861–62, was an ambitious arts project for the city, but it hung on the abilities and financial resources of an actress named Mrs English (formerly Annie Fox) and her husband. The building combined a museum on the ground floor and an opera house/ theatre on the upper floor. As the moving force behind the plan, Mrs English hoped to present dramatic performances by her own theatre company while encouraging citizens to gather socially and to attend musical performances on the museum premises.[63] McCarroll honoured her in his poem's seventh verse:

And thus, sustained by your approving smiles,
This temple of the Muses yet shall stand
A sculptured pillar in this favored land;
While its fair priestess with her gracious wiles,
Shall place it on the eminence sublime
Where not one other step remains to climb.

As in Toronto, McCarroll was always ready to seek out theatrical and musical opportunities. A further newspaper notice about the Museum and Opera House reported that "Mr James McCarroll, the well-known Canadian musical and literary celebrity is, we hear, to be connected with this great enterprise, in both a critical and musical aspect – in the latter as a soloist."[64] Mrs English's plan called for a group of resident musicians, including a harpist and McCarroll as flautist, who would perform regularly for Buffalo audiences. However, no further press squibs followed. The theatre changed hands several times over the next few years before it was renamed the Adelphi in 1874. McCarroll buried his disappointment by throwing himself into editing the *Globe* and then the *Fenian Volunteer* while he fomented Fenian propaganda.

McCarroll was a keen collector of autograph letters and documents of cultural interest. One such letter had early theatre connections in Buffalo. It was a missive from the well-known actor and writer John Howard Payne (1791–1852) to Thomas N. Parmelee, the editor of Buffalo's oldest newspaper, the *Commercial Advertiser*.[65] Payne asked Parmelee to give preferential treatment to Miss M.A. Tyrrell, an English-born actress who was coming to Buffalo from Washington: he wrote, "you will oblige me much if you will favor her with the sort of aid in the press & in society so essential to the recognition of a strangers worth." As it turned out, Miss Tyrrell's time on the Buffalo stage was painful for her. While Parmelee himself was "civil," Mrs Parmelee made no effort to introduce the actress to her friends in society. Tyrrell thus suffered the curse of actresses off the stage, telling Payne in one letter of the cold reception she had received and complaining about the refusal of the Buffalo theatre manager to pay her salary. Whether McCarroll knew any of this earlier story, especially Payne's epistolary pursuit of Miss Tyrrell to be his mistress, is unknown. But he certainly recognized the value of a John Howard Payne letter written to Buffalo's best-known editor.

The other event of major significance during McCarroll's time in Buffalo was highly personal and not at all evident in newspaper reports about his doings. The details, however, are suggestive and of interest. He had likely begun his relationship with Julia Ellen Dolmage in Toronto. English by birth, Julia had immigrated to Toronto with her husband, Henry Sr, and their four children, Henry, Allen, Florence, and Jessie. The Dolmage family then moved to Buffalo. After Ann's death in July 1866, McCarroll was free to marry Julia. Her husband, who had become blind and deaf, had by then died as well.[66]

McCarroll and Julia married in 1867, thus greatly improving the quality of his personal life, but apparently imposing another notable burden on him in terms of her family's financial needs. Julia's four children lived with them during their Buffalo years. However, when McCarroll and Julia moved to New York City in 1869, it appears that none of her children went along. By then Henry, who was twenty-two, had found full-time work as a printer in Buffalo. He had likely begun as an apprentice working for his stepfather at McCarroll & Co., then through other connections found work as a printer for the *Buffalo Commercial Advertiser*. Through his stepfather, he was likely involved in the printing of the text of *Ridgeway*. Julia's other children probably stayed on with Henry. His sister Florence served as housekeeper for the family.[67] The enduring relationship between McCarroll and his stepson is confirmed by his warm inscription to Henry, "my dear Step-Son … with the affection and love of the Author," in presenting him with a signed copy of *Madeline*.[68] Years later, in 1892, Henry was able to provide a home for his widowed mother in the wake of James McCarroll's unanticipated death in New York that April.[69]

By the time McCarroll left Buffalo he had likely begun to ween himself of his passion for Fenianism and for partisan politics in general. Certainly, he realized that non-partisan journalism paid better and provided a steadier opportunity to make a living in the United States. What is more, he had before him New York, America's most populous city. Here he could direct his talents and energies to the expanded range of journalistic opportunities and the wealth of theatre and music available to him.

New York, New York!
1869–92

THE FIRST EVIDENCE OF JAMES MCCARROLL'S PRESENCE in New York City is an Irving Hall concert bill for 31 March 1869. This was Madame Mina Geary Fitzpatrick's Annual Vocal and Instrumental Concert held under the patronage of "The Knights of St Patrick."[1] McCarroll was a special guest on the occasion and performed a flute solo to "repeated applause."

The event was more than the pleasing mix of Celtic ballads and light musical pieces that made up a typical Geary concert.[2] It was also a celebration of Fenian aspirations and spirit. While Mina's own songs included Thomas Moore's "The Harp That Once through Tara's Halls," her husband, Randolph (James) Fitzpatrick (1841–1907), transfixed the audience with a stirring recitation of John Savage's "splendid" poem, "Shane's Head," a tribute to ancient Irish heroism.[3] Some months earlier, Fitzpatrick had been a Fenian spy and had served as Colonel O'Neill's assistant secretary of war (Senate Wing). John Savage had been an active rebel supporter since 1848 and had been formally accepted as a Fenian by the Brotherhood in 1867. Like Fitzpatrick, he remained active in promoting Fenian interests and raising financial support through his readings and addresses. No doubt McCarroll felt quite at home in such company; he had met both men during his Buffalo days and had mentioned "Rudolph" Fitzpatrick in the final chapter of *Ridgeway* (168).

There is, however, no further evidence of his continuing attachment to the Fenian cause. By 1869 he could see that the movement was weakening in the wake of ongoing internal squabbles, the absence of American government support, and the mounting evidence of failure to awaken enthusiasm in Canada. He was ready to move beyond his recent role as Fenian writer and publicist. And he was happy to escape Buffalo's First Ward. More to the point, he now had the opportunity to pursue journalistic employment and his own artistic interests in the liveliest centre of cultural activity on the continent. For the next twenty-three years – that is, for the rest of his life – he would live in New York with his second wife, Julia Ellen (Dolmage). They were joined there in the 1870s by the second of Julia's sons, Allen Dolmage, who died in August 1879 at their residence on 83 East 10th Street.[4] Though the McCarrolls lived in a number of flats and boarding houses, they always stayed in the vicinity of Irving Hall, Washington Square, and the centre of the entertainment and publishing business in the city.

During these early, heady days in the city, McCarroll was imaginatively caught up in the wide spectrum of human activity he witnessed while strolling down Broadway and its adjacent streets. Gilded-Age New York was alive with energy, building projects, and cultural activity; while embracing that excitement, McCarroll was also struck, as he had been in Toronto, by the chilling evidence of poverty and misery in city streets and byways, especially as winter settled in.[5] He responded positively to the gospel of progress and the vitality of the arts world flourishing around him, but he remained attentive to the visual evidence of America's social shortcomings.[6] In prose and poetry he grappled with the inequities in opportunity and the evidence of personal despair he saw around him. At other times he would harken back to his former life in Canada to reconnect with friends and to recast some of his earlier experiences into print. Always, however, he remained at heart a pure-spirited Irish writer who set out to write a perfect poem and who wished to articulate publicly poetry's significance as an art form. One aspect of his new fate was to see himself in the vanguard of social change during the Gilded Age, even as he remained a devotee of the poetic excellence achieved by the poets he most admired –Thomas Moore, Edgar Allen Poe, Tennyson, Longfellow, and Oliver Wendell Holmes.

Music and Musicians

Once settled in New York, McCarroll freelanced while seeking out full-time editorial work. In short order he found such a position, first with *Watson's Art Journal* and then with the Frank Leslie Publishing House, for whom he had worked part-time while in Buffalo. He began to dabble in playwriting with the hope of finding outlets for his work on stage and in print; doubtless he attended the rollicking Irish plays of Dion Boucicault that were drawing large New York audiences in the 1870s. He also renewed acquaintances with or befriended famous musicians, actors, and literary figures, some of whom, like soprano Anna Bishop and violinist Ole Bull, he had known since the early 1850s in Canada. In April 1870 Ole Bull played two (more) "Farewell" concerts at the Association Hall and was highly praised in *Watson's Art Journal* for his distinguished career, the warmth of his personality, and the extraordinary tonal variety of his violin playing.[7] Earlier, a brief note in that same magazine described a pleasant social visit made by owner Henry Watson and McCarroll to Madame Bishop's New York flat where she was teaching singing and preparing for a series of concerts in Canada, including two at the Horticultural Gardens in Toronto.[8]

A music lover, a connoisseur of classical music, "a composer of rare talent," a gifted performer, and a reviewer who hobnobbed with "a host of famous [musicians and singers]," McCarroll knew – or came to know – "Jenny Lind, Lucca, Sir Julius Benedict, [Henri] Vieuxtemps, [Henri] Wieniawski, Ole Bull, Catherine Hayes, Maurice Strakosch, Arabella Goddard, Madam Anna Bishop, Herr [Frederick] Griebel, [and] Carl Formes," among others.[9] He wrote about many of them during their New York appearances.[10] He also performed as a flautist in concerts or at private functions in the city. One was a Madame Varian Hoffman concert at Association Hall on 15 February 1871. In its review, the *New York Evening Post* paid tribute to his skill "in producing a tone not everyone would suppose dwelt in the recesses of a flute." He also earned "a spontaneous encore for a Mozart air with brilliant variations." Overall, however, given the emphasis on vocal performance then dominating New York concerts, there was less opportunity for him to perform than he would have liked.[11]

McCarroll sought other ways to make personal connections with the city's classical music community. A musical "note" in *Frank Leslie's Illustrated Newspaper* on 30 October 1875 (perhaps inserted by McCarroll) reported that "James McCarroll recently delivered the first lecture of the season at the Grand Conservatory of Music, Fifth Avenue. Subject: 'A Glance at the Origin, Early History and Influence of Music.'"[12] Finding information about McCarroll's particular interests and actual performances remains a challenge despite the fact that more and more nineteenth-century New York newspapers are now becoming available on line; happily, some are indexed. But there are many gaps still to fill. Some later biographical sketches report that McCarroll worked as a reviewer of music and theatre for newspapers during his New York years. However, because reviews were generally unsigned and because he left no precise information about which newspaper(s) he wrote for and when he did so, it is very difficult to track his contributions.

Knowing that he worked for *Watson's Art Journal* (1869–71) and the Frank Leslie Company (1871–80), one can at least identify or conjecture about some specific pieces. One noteworthy article appeared in *Frank Leslie's Chimney Corner* on 27 July 1872. Entitled "Handel and the Irish," its information about musical and Irish history suggests McCarroll's pen. Robert and James McCarroll had hoped to teach Handel's music in the Upper Canadian backwoods. Drawing on a number of supporting documents, the column describes Handel's gratitude at being recognized for his musical genius in Ireland during a period when responses in England were tepid. Determined "to appeal to another tribunal, and one of a very refined and enlightened character at that period," the composer moved to Dublin in 1741, where he was celebrated as "the Shakespeare of music" and "a colossus in everything." His compositions met with large, enthusiastic audiences at Dublin's Old Music Hall. A year later he directed the first performance of his oratorio, "The Messiah," and was once again heartened by the thunderous applause of Dublin audiences. Though the author admitted that Handel returned to England in his later years, he insists that the great composer met his warmest critical response in Dublin.[13]

"The Test of a Man of Letters"[14]

McCarroll continued to seek a publisher for his serious literary efforts. To that end he sought help from Oliver Wendell Holmes and Henry Wadsworth Longfellow in Boston, hoping that the two eminent American poets might be able to interest Fields and Ticknor in his work. Nothing came of that plan. Only two of his books were published during these years. The first, which appeared in 1874, was a light-hearted play, *Nearly a Tragedy: A Comedy*, in five acts, published by John F. Trow & Son. It is now a very rare book. His second, which proved to be his most important book, took nearly two decades to reach the public. *Madeline and Other Poems* was published in 1889 by Belford, Clarke & Company. It pulled together many, but certainly not all, of the poems he had written since the early 1840s. In the introduction, his friend and colleague Charles Lotin Hildreth called attention to his abilities as a poet, the breadth of his literary output, and his distinguished career as a writer and editor. Indeed, Hildreth ventured to say that he "probably has the honorable distinction of having edited or been connected with more newspapers, journals, and magazines than any other man in America" (v). That remark reminds us that his continental range is an important element in considering his literary life as a whole.

One of the most important connections of McCarroll's final years in New York was his renewed friendship with publisher Robert Belford. Along with Charles Hildreth, he held a valued editorial position with *Belford's Magazine* from 1888 to 1892. The relationship among the three men certainly led to the publication of *Madeline*; moreover, it brought to full circle a friendship begun in Toronto in the 1860s when Robert Belford was a young boy fresh from Ireland and McCarroll an active poet and journalist.[15]

Henry Cood Watson (1816–1875), the owner and editor of *Watson's Art Journal* was another of McCarroll's early connections in New York.[16] Born in England into an impressive musical family, Watson had immigrated to New York in 1840 where he took up editorial work and music criticism.[17] In 1845 he co-founded the *Broadway Journal* with Charles F. Briggs and Edgar Allen Poe, and a decade later he served briefly as editor-in-chief of both *Frank Leslie's Illustrated Newspaper* and *Frank Leslie's Lady's Magazine*.[18] By the 1850s Watson had established himself as an influential art and music critic in America.[19] He gave McCarroll his first full-time position in the city. *Watson's Art Journal* began publication in 1862; its office was located at 746 Broadway near Astor Place, not far from Greenwich Village. Billing itself as a weekly magazine devoted to Music, Theatre and the Visual Arts, *Watson's Art Journal* promised its readers "Criticisms, Biographies, Tales, Anecdotes, Etc." Fancying himself a poet, Watson published several of his own pieces in his magazine.

McCarroll's first contribution appeared on 15 January 1870. His poem "Maud" made the first page and was followed by an essay entitled "The Wolf." Celebrating "the priceless heritage of sound" achieved by the best musicians, "The Wolf" argued that "musicians as a class" and "among themselves" are "the most inharmonious and disagreeable people imaginable." Having described "the wolf" of rivalry and envy so active in the lives of leading musicians, he then looked at prevailing national biases, pointing out that German musicians as a group frequently heaped scorn on "the Italian School." While recognizing "the thunders" and the masculine outlook that characterized so many German compositions, McCarroll declared his personal preference for melody, which he called "the veritable soul of music." He found melody most deeply rooted in the Italian tradition. Siding with "the soft, dreamy echoes of balmy, dark-eyed Italy," he declared, "I am no stranger to the melodic charms of Mozart, Schubert or Bartholdy [Felix Mendelssohn], but I am still inclined to the opinion that not one of them has ever sympathized with pure and simple melody so largely as Rossini, Bellini or Donizetti."[20]

V.—No. 2.   NEW YORK, SATURDAY, NOVEMBER 12, 1870. $4.00 Per Annum.
shed 1863.   Single Copies, 10 Cts.

8.1 Front page, *Watson's Art Journal* 14, no. 2, 12 November 1870. McCarroll worked as the managing editor for Henry Watson's magazine in 1869–70. The masthead here includes McCarroll's poem "The Silver Lining" in the third column. A bound copy of the 1869–70 year is held by the New York Public Library, Lincoln Center Division.

For over a year – from January 1870 until the end of March 1871 – McCarroll's poems, stories, and columns appeared often in *Watson's Art Journal* (WAJ). In fact, on 29 January 1870, Henry Watson glowingly described his presence as a freelancer with the magazine:

We have enjoyed the pleasure of a visit from Mr James McCarroll whose recent contributions to our columns have given intellectual delight to our readers. He is almost an "admirable Crichton" in his varied talents. He is a poet, musician, and literateur. He possesses a wonderful facility with his pen, which, with his extensive and general information, enables him to write ably upon almost any subject, from a political editorial to a humorous item. His stories or novelettes are distinguished by elegance of language, cleverness of construction, and interest of plot. His short stories are singularly striking and felicitous. His poetry is of a high order, both in thought and diction. In Canada, his *nom de plume* was a home word, so universally was [*sic*] his brilliant, sarcastic, but humorous letters read by the people.[21]

He is also an admirable lecturer, both in the humorous and serious vein, while, as the sailor says, "he plays on the flute like an angel."

We welcome Mr McCarroll to New York, and recommend him to the editorial fraternity, of which, by the by, he is a distinguished member, and hope to see his fine, available talents in speedy prominent use.

Given such support, it is not surprising that on Saturday, 9 July 1870 Watson named McCarroll his "Associate and Managing Editor" while keeping for himself the role of "Editor." In that issue Watson wrote that "We have been induced to offer this position to Mr McCarroll from an intimate knowledge of his thorough ability to fill it in every relation." McCarroll would stay on as associate and managing editor until the end of March 1871 when, without notice, his name was dropped from the masthead. By my count, he contributed twenty-five poems and four stories, as well as numerous unsigned but often stylistically identifiable columns on music, theatre, and writing.[22] After his appointment was announced, he began a signature series of wide-ranging articles; calling them "The Pepper-Pot Papers" he adopted a new penname, K.N. Capsicum, Esq. As if to confirm his use of that pseudonym, he published a few of his own poems under the Capsicum *nom de plume*.[23] Given Watson's esteem for his story-telling abilities, some of the other unsigned stories in WAJ may have been by McCarroll.[24]

McCarroll's writing for *Watson's Art Journal* was typically confident and wide-ranging – from informed observation of current events to artistic criticism. It provides a revealing look at many of his ideas, enthusiasms, and pet complaints. In fact, few periods of his lifelong writing are as fully available for study today as those in the pages of WAJ. The twelve papers in the Pepper Pot (PPP) series gave McCarroll a platform from which to speak his mind, playfully or seriously, along with space to present some of his own poems.[25] He began the series using a loose narrative structure likely borrowed from Oliver Wendell Holmes; he positioned young Capsicum in debates of opinion and taste with his elderly uncle, Arthur Grainger of Grainger Hall, New York. Described as "a hale old bachelor" of fifty-nine, Grainger is "an accomplished critic and an educated enthusiast." In the first column, "American Yellow-Covered Literature, etc." (16 July), Uncle Arthur sets the agenda by deploring, as McCarroll himself often did, "the inferiority of much of our periodical and newspaper literature." What is lacking is "a true standard of letters and taste among us." The blame must fall on both inferior printing offices run by incompetent editors and the absence in America of editors and publishers of real taste and judgment who can see beyond "the torrent of trash" they face daily.

Watson's Art Journal gave McCarroll a cultural pulpit from which to speak out on many matters. Though he dispensed with the table-talk format after the first two PPP columns, he has K.N. Capsicum reveal himself as a practical man with spiritualist interests and a muted Christian faith. "Not born to wealth and leisure," he is democratic in his beliefs and fundamentally at odds with social pretension ("the brownstone standard"); he deplores the misuses of power based on social position and a false sense of superiority.

But achievement in the written word was of the highest importance to McCarroll. In PPP #2, "Spurious Currency," he praises those rare poets in America who truly deserve the name; "amongst the foremost" he places Oliver Wendell Holmes who, "through originality, exquisite conception, beauty of finish, and harmony of numbers," has achieved indisputable greatness. Though less prolific than many of his contemporaries, Holmes is a poet whose "genius" is evident when his verse is studied "line for line." In this column McCarroll included two of his own poems; "Dawn" serves as a short example of writing vividly and accurately about nature, while "Cede Majori" is an indictment of those "organ-grinders and their abettors, who have now overrun the territories of the muses."[26] The latter poem deplores the "gorgon-triad" that ignores Genius because it is unable to recognize it.

> Oh! How shall we escape that triple curse –
> The stupid critic, publisher and bard,
> Who leave true Genius with an empty purse,
> And make the way of Poesy so hard.

In PPP #5 ("Only Goosequill Recreations") he laments the lack of genuine artistic understanding among most writers. Few seem able to "steal into the inner life of poetry"; instead they pay to have their third-rate books copyrighted rather than striving to explore real "feeling and eloquent truthfulness."[27]

In PPP #7 he lists Moore and Holmes, Byron and Swinburne, and Tennyson and Longfellow as artists who are able to flesh out "the perfect embodiment of the divine embryo" in a poem. The great poets, he theorizes, strive to achieve an originality that is able to "sing any essentially new strain in relation to light, the rose or the rainbow." They work closely with the natural world to ground their original connection. Poetic genius aims to approach "the sublime earnest" through an inspired conjunction of language, image, idea, and at times humour. In that spirit Capsicum/McCarroll offers an example of "my originality," just as Terry Finnegan offered examples of his "janius" to D'Arcy McGee. McCarroll's poem "The Rainbow," is framed by the line "How I hate to hear those sorry poetasters sing." It offers, with tongue in cheek, to ring the bell of real poetic expression by offering a string of extravagant but vivid images. The full text of this poem appears in chapter 6.

As social critic McCarroll adopted a satiric position that allowed him to criticize both social pretensions and the attitudes of the servant class. In "Advice to Maids of All Work" (#3, 3 July), he colourfully criticized the pretensions and vices of the master class while duly noting the problems generated by ambitious and grasping servants. Capsicum's general advice to "Maids of All Work" is to control or quietly manipulate your master as best you can. In PPP #12 his poem "Lady Julia" offers a rollicking look at social hypocrisy, showing how nasty criticisms of a hard-working and attractive young woman of the lower class are transformed once she becomes the admirable wife of a "handsome millionaire."[28]

The fourth Capsicum column (6 August), "Adrift without Helm or Compass," is one of his most disturbing pieces, expressing his critical sense of a world gone wrong despite all the improvements and amenities enjoyed by the upper classes. Focusing on the state of religion in the Western world, he argues that "the moral and religious perceptions of Christian nations, as well as the world at large, are so absurd and contradictory as to defy comprehension or analysis." Sweeping through history's endless, blood-spattered battles, he concludes that "When possessed of numbers, wealth and power, what scoundrels we become, and how religiously we always endeavor to make the Divine Being a party to our rascality." No wonder, he concludes, that "murder and robbery are the distinguishing characteristic[s] of [our] age." Religion and politics have always been forces at work in the world, he notes, while "poor humanity has been ground into dust to the tune of the Ten Commandments." Men and women are mostly adrift and vulnerable to the social conditions that control their lives. Yet McCarroll is not a determinist; rather, he is a realist staring down inescapable facts. When "cold or hungry, [people] will steal" and "when wronged, oppressed or outraged [they] will kill," he writes. There seems to be no force or idea sufficient to bring about spiritual improvement in the human condition. How then, he wonders, can God's "infallible" word be effective in a world dominated by rascality, money, and woe? Furthermore, he asks, "is man in his essence capable of spiritual insight and betterment?" "I want to see better," he concludes, though his frustration is evident.

Subsequent columns are less dark and more assertive. In PPP #4 (24 September 1870) he writes on the folly of overvaluing "a sound classical education." The classics, he argues, have little connection to "the useful relations to life." English has "greater power, idiomatic grace, and more fervid eloquence than Latin or Greek." Accordingly, "The test of a man of letters, and that of different professions apart from their specialties, should be a thorough knowledge of the leading living languages, with English at their head, together with a most profound acquaintance with history, geography, mathematics, and the natural sciences generally." Here he positions himself as a literate, well-informed man of his times, at home with language, history, and the sciences. In a powerful epigram he concludes, "he who would live by the light of the ancients must go to bed at sunset."

A final element of McCarroll's work with *Watson's Art Journal* involved the controversy initiated in part by Henry Watson over the quality of Christina Nilsson's voice. The famed Swedish soprano arrived in New York in September 1871, backed by an impressive set of English and European reviews. Under the watchful eye of musical impresario Max Strakosch (1835–1892), the publicity preceding her arrival was Barnumesque – in short, extraordinary. As the successor to Jenny Lind, as the new "Swedish nightingale," she had the America cultural community agog long before she reached the city. As an arts editor, Henry Watson himself was very much caught up in promoting her arrival, offering his readers weekly reports on her doings and a full biography of her life. He even offered his subscribers a celebrity "portrait" of Nilsson, the first such "gift" in the magazine's history.

When Nilsson finally appeared at Steinway Hall on 19 September 1871, her singing and deportment disappointed Watson. Likely she was not in good voice as a result of travel and a lingering illness, but, holding her to the high standards he expected of such a celebrated European star, Watson expressed his displeasure in considerable detail (24 September). As well, he was indignant to see that Strakosch was demanding $4 a ticket to see her in person! The "$4 ticket scandal" became one part of the general displeasure and disappointment that greeted Nilsson in New York, at least among serious critics. This negative response and disappointment persisted in many newspapers in the eastern United States for several months.

For his part, McCarroll was supportive of Watson. He made it his business to attack members of the newly formed Lotus Club in the city, which had begun its operations on 15 March 1870, just a few months before Nilsson's arrival. Dubbing its members the "Lotus Ring" for their unqualified support of Strakosch's smothering advertising and his shocking level of pricing, he attacked the Lotus Club as a "nefarious organization"; he mocked their feeble attempts to assemble furniture for their clubhouse and challenged their submissiveness to Starkosch. His familiar style of attack is evident, especially in describing Mr Andrew Wheeler, a writer for the *New York World*, as an "addle-brained word-spinner" who specialized in "inane drivel" and "evasion."[29] Though they were unsigned, his two columns, "The Lotus Club Critical 'Ring'" and "The Lotus Club Prepares to Receive Nilsson" (both on 10 September), smack of his familiar mode of mockery and his penchant for dismissive ad hominem attacks. While Henry Watson kept up a brave, impartial face as an independent-minded critic during the Nilsson firestorm, McCarroll likely made no friends among the writers, journalists, and critics who had recently founded the Lotus Club. It didn't occur to him that the Lotus Club would soon become a staple of New York's cultural world and would grow in prominence into the twenty-first century.

Why and how McCarroll left *Watson's Art Journal* is not evident in the magazine's pages.[30] The editor-poet whom Watson had welcomed so effusively in January 1870 disappeared completely from its pages at the end of March 1871. Likely the answer can be found in two different directions – the rivalry between Watson and McCarroll as poets and Henry Watson's personal enthusiasm for Frank Leslie and his influential publishing house.

Frank Leslie

Frank Leslie's Illustrated Periodicals

The Frank Leslie Publishing House began in the mid-1850s in New York. Born Henry Carter in Ipswich, England, Leslie had developed an expertise in making engravings for woodcuts and had been employed by the *London Illustrated News*. In 1848, however, he changed his name to Frank Leslie and moved to New York City with his young family. Once there, he set up his own small engraving shop on Broadway, but in 1850 he was hired by Phineus T. Barnum to produce woodcut illustrations of Jenny Lind and her musical entourage during her highly publicized tour of American cities. Leslie thus became part of Barnum's large promotional team. This led to further work for Barnum and Beach's *Illustrated News* in New York and (Frederick) *Gleason's Pictorial* in Boston. As a close observer of Barnum's grandiose schemes, he was attentive to new possibilities for the publishing world.

Seeing an opportunity to branch out on his own, he broke free of Barnum and opened his own firm in New York in 1854. With *Frank Leslie's Lady's Magazine and Gazette of Fashion* as his initial publication, he added an illustrated story paper to his operation that same year.[31] His abiding aim, however, was to create an illustrated, sixteen-page weekly newspaper for New York, modelled on the *London Illustrated News*. It would offer a more aggressive and American brand of news coverage both national and international in scope. He planned to support his flagship newspaper with a number of specialty magazines, designed to appeal to emerging sectors of the American reading public. All his publications would be illustrated and would share his name; all would be published and distributed centrally. His team of editors and illustrators in the head office would work on several of his periodicals at any time.

Frank Leslie's vision was prescient and timely. He knew the heavy costs of preparing engravings for print, but he was willing to invest heavily in the growth of his business, often taking on debts that put pressure on his equity and capital. Barnum had taught him much about the possibilities of connecting with the large and fast-growing audience of American readers; he realized that they shared "a growing demand for news" and that there were now "unprecedented opportunities for pictorial reporting."[32] With the development of railroads across the country, there was a new wave of travellers, many of whom had time on their hands as they journeyed from place to place. His challenge was to make timely, illustrated material available to those with money to spend and time to read. Through subscription offers and newsstand sales he was able to meet the large costs of production and, in turn, buy more advanced printing machines. Overcoming many financial bumps along the way, he had built his publishing house into both a New York City success story and a national phenomenon by the time McCarroll joined his editorial team.

While in Buffalo, McCarroll had served as a stringer for the Leslie Company, but, as importantly, Henry Watson had worked in the late 1850s as editor-in-chief of Leslie's two flagship weeklies, *Frank Leslie's Illustrated Newspaper* and *Frank Leslie's Lady's Magazine*. In fact, Watson wrote a very positive article, "What Is an Illustrated Paper?," for WAJ on 26 February 1870. Having listened often to Watson's reminiscences, McCarroll took special note.[33]

Watson argued that Leslie's illustrated paper was "the most perfect news-paper in the world." Leslie was both a path-breaker and a "business genius." As Watson astutely noted, "the world to-day demands news of the hour – of the minute." That was 1870. Leslie's "high mission" was to satisfy that demand in as timely a way as possible: he offered readers up-to-the-week journalistic reporting and evocative picture making, supplemented by "original" literary selections. Speaking of the literary aspect, Watson argued that Leslie had engaged "some of the first writers of America ... permanently to supply that element of universal interest" to his readers.[34] For Watson, Leslie was a visionary who had been willing to gamble everything he had in pursuit of "the true meaning of the title 'Illustrated Newspaper.'"

Leslie's business required an expensive, centralized operation; there had to be paid draughtsmen (both in New York and on location around the world), engravers, correspondents, editors, editorial assistants, printers, and marketers to gather the news of the day, transform it into woodcuts, and deal with literary contributors. What distinguished Leslie from his competitors was his keen sense of "the wants of the public" and his "broad and comprehensive grasp of the [work involved in putting pictures to newsprint]." Moreover he had "the indomitable pluck" and "persistency" needed for success in the increasingly competitive news world. On occasion, he had to risk much of what he had in order to further the development of his journalistic products and expand his readership. By the late 1860s his success was so striking that his *Illustrated Newspaper* sometimes sold more than 300,000 copies in a week. He catered to subscribers, railroad travellers, and newsstand readers while increasing his advertising revenue issue by issue. His newspaper's quick response to particular events – the various battles of the Civil War, for instance, and the famous Heeney-Sayers prize fight in London, along with his crusade against public health issues like the sale of "swill milk" – gave his name a dramatic luminosity during that decade, even as the swill milk campaign earned him death threats. "Scarcely an event ... worthy of record" was omitted from his newspaper. Calling *Frank Leslie's Illustrated Newspaper* a kind of "archives of the nation," Watson deemed it "beyond question the most perfect newspaper in the world."

By the time that James McCarroll left Watson for Leslie, likely in the spring of 1871, Frank Leslie had firmly established himself as the most visible and, on occasion, the most flamboyant publisher of newspapers and magazines in the United States. But controversy and scandal were beginning to mark his public image even as the battle to grow bigger while staying profitable was creating financial strains for his firm's overall operation.

FRANK LESLIE'S
ILLUSTRATED
NEWSPAPER

No. 1,410.—Vol. LVI }   NEW YORK—FOR THE WEEK ENDING APRIL 28, 1883.   [Price, 10 Cents.

NEW YORK.—COMPLETING A GREAT WORK—LASHING THE STAYS OF THE BROOKLYN BRIDGE.
FROM A SKETCH BY A STAFF ARTIST.—SEE PAGE 155.

8.2 Front page, *Frank Leslie's Illustrated Newspaper* 56, no. 1410, 28 April 1883. From his publishing house on the corner of Park Place and College Place (a point of pride for Leslie and what he called "The Home of Illustrated Literature"), Frank Leslie issued more than fifteen publications weekly, monthly, or annually. One example is his popular *Illustrated Newspaper*. This issue depicts work on the Brooklyn Bridge while ships of various sizes pass underneath. Microfilm Room, Firestone Library, Princeton University.

As a matter of policy Leslie did not provide the names of the editors on his various publications. Only his name was used, and used prominently. In laudatory articles summarizing the firm's scale and range of operations, the names of a few editors were mentioned in print. No report contains McCarroll's name.[35] But while no information is available about his rank, salary, specific editorial duties, or years of employment, there are many indications of his presence and involvement in three of the leading house periodicals, *Frank Leslie's Illustrated Newspaper*, *Frank Leslie's Chimney Corner*, and *Frank Leslie's Sunday Magazine*.

The document that led me to the McCarroll-Leslie connection is a letter written on company stationery. On 12 May 1873 McCarroll wrote to his old Toronto friend, Charles Lindsey.[36] The letter (see Appendix A) offered an explanation of why a "biography" and portrait of Lindsey had appeared that very day in *Frank Leslie's Chimney Corner*. The column was part of the magazine's regular "The Self-made Men of Our Times" series.[37] McCarroll wrote as follows: "You must have been astonished at not hearing from me before, in relation to your portrait and biography ... They appear to-day, and would have appeared long since were it not for the immense amount of matter which has so long embarrassed our portrait gallery. I hope you will not only recognize a fair likeness in the engraving, but an honest and kindly hand in the letter press." More personally, he added:

> I have been in this office for some time now, and filling, you may be assured, no very secondary position. You may form some idea of our establishment when I assure you that we have the largest engraving [plant] in the world, and that, as I am informed, we keep forty power presses running day and night throughout the year.
>
> You will, I am sure, be glad to learn that I am quite comfortable, and that I am at last far from being absolutely penniless. In fact, although, on my first arrival here, I had some hard tussles, I have succeeded in clearing the road before me, and aided by my own right hand only.[38]

Confident and buoyant, he made it clear to Lindsey that he was comfortably settled and employed in New York City. The phrase "for some time now" and the fact that he had worked himself up "to no very secondary position" in the Frank Leslie Publishing House suggest that he was well established in his work. Moreover, he clearly relished the fact that, having endured prolonged financial struggles before and after leaving Toronto, he was now a

well-regarded editor working for North America's most progressive and influential publishing operation.

It is intriguing to note that, in information that he later provided to biographical scribes, McCarroll chose not to mention the years he worked for the
FLPH, even though they were crucial in the regaining of his financial balance
and the remaking of his literary career. Frank Leslie was a name to be reckoned
with. As Joshua Brown notes in his study *Beyond the Lines: Pictorial Reporting,
Everyday Life, and the Crisis in Gilded Age America* (2002), Leslie's importance
has often been dismissed by academics as low-brow and pedestrian, given his
attention to merely popular publishing operations. However, that view is now
being challenged as "high-brow" misrepresentation, especially by a new breed
of cultural historians who have been actively re-evaluating Leslie's contributions
to illustrated journalism and American cultural activity.

Why, then, did James McCarroll choose to omit this significant part of his
editorial work in New York?[39] Was the omission a deliberate obscuration on
his part or simply a case of neglecting one kind of detail in order to include
another? It is possible that he became disenchanted with Frank Leslie and his
infamous wife after several years of employment. Indeed, by the early 1870s
Leslie had earned a reputation as an employer who was often unreliable and far
too caught up in self-promotion. McCarroll may have come to dislike aspects
of the autocratic FLPH operation, including the flamboyant public behaviour
that Leslie shared with his second wife, Miriam Squier, under whom McCarroll
worked as an editor and writer for the *Chimney Corner*. Whatever his reasons,
he opted to exclude any reference to his Leslie years from the personal record he
left behind. But then, he did so as well with *Watson's Art Journal* and presumably
with other parts of his New York literary career.

McCarroll's years with the FLPH paralleled Leslie's much-publicized travels
and adventures with Miriam Squier. In part through his own publicity machine
and with Miriam's help, Leslie had made himself a national celebrity by the
early 1870s. In 1861 he had left his first wife, Sarah Ann, and their three children
in order to live with his chief editor Ephraim G. Squier and his wife, Miriam.
Miriam, who was already employed by the firm, was the main attraction in an
arrangement that soon became a much-publicized ménage à trois, American
style.[40] Ephraim Squier, who suffered several setbacks during the 1860s, would
later leave the publishing house while his talented wife emerged as a major
force at Frank Leslie's side. She took the editorial lead of both *Frank Leslie's
Lady's Magazine* in 1863 and his new story magazine, *Frank Leslie's Chimney
Corner*, in 1865. After divorcing her husband, she married Leslie in 1874, but

only after Leslie's wife had received a large financial settlement in court and the mentally troubled Ephraim was forced to enter a Long Island sanitarium. Salacious publicity tracked the Leslies through the decade.

While the couple was much in the news, reports on the extent of Leslie's personal debts began to circulate in the press. Still, though he often dipped into business capital to meet personal expenses, the publishing house continued to grow and flourish. Reports of the day suggested that each year close to half a million issues of Leslie's illustrated periodicals were in print. Leslie quietly sought to meet the demands of his creditors and reposition the company for the future. In fact, by the time of his death in 1880, he had managed to retire many of those debts. In his will he named Miriam to run the company, ignoring the claims of his sons. Miriam then had her name legally changed to Frank Leslie in order to preserve and celebrate the firm's distinctive publishing image and achievements.

As one of Leslie's new hires in 1871, McCarroll found himself assigned to both the weekly *Illustrated Newspaper* and the popular monthly *Frank Leslie's Chimney Corner*. Working in the large editorial room, he was initially in awe of the scale of the operations. In the 1870s the FLPH had twenty-eight periodicals in print, including a German illustrated newspaper. By late in the decade, however, that number had proved too unwieldy and unprofitable, especially in the face of mounting company debts. The number of periodicals was significantly reduced after 1880.

McCarroll was one of some three hundred office employees in the early 1870s and for several years he seems to have worked comfortably within the Leslie empire. Moreover, he appears, at least on occasion, to have exercised a relatively free editorial hand within the firm's house rules, though his working relationship with Leslie himself and with Miriam, his immediate boss at the *Chimney Corner*, remains a mystery. Frank's "flamboyance and [his] exploitation" of his employees were legendary by the 1870s and must have been a trial to salaried employees. Joshua Brown reports that he "ran through a succession of chief editors and young artists" year by year.[41] Nevertheless, *Frank Leslie's Illustrated Newspaper* remains an important publishing endeavour not only because of its scale and circulation but also because of its contributions to the history and development of illustrated journalism prior to the integration of photographs into the printing process. As Joshua Brown notes, many highly skilled artists, including a young Thomas Nast, worked for Leslie during these years. But the company also sought out and promoted stories that lent themselves to pictorial representation, while catering to America's middle-class reading habits and values. For years a writer of "exciting" stories, McCarroll could select and edit the formulaic narratives that the FLPH received by the bagful. Stories needed to be full of action and incident and written in a dramatic way that favoured pictorial representation. They might tend toward the sensational, but they were never to challenge or undermine basic American social values.

Given its formulaic nature as well as its conventionality and conservatism, such "railroad reading" has limited "literary" value today. For many working writers, however, it had a singular appeal – it paid reasonably well and promptly. Moreover, once accepted, such work was publicized and widely distributed. Writers could range in their choice of subject matter as they appealed to and aroused the interest of "railroad" readers. One notable practitioner in the 1860s was Louisa May Alcott of Concord, Massachusetts. Sometimes using a pseudonym for her Leslie stories, she wrote more than twenty tales and short serials for him, at first earning $25 a story and later $100 or more. Knowing the value of her name, Leslie urged her to send more contributions and invited her to become a regular contributor to the *Chimney Corner*. In her journal, she noted that her "thrillers" appealed to Leslie and his "readers of sensation rubbish."[42] In one wry journal entry in 1865, she commented, "Sewed, cleaned house & wrote a story for Leslie,"[43] implying that such writing required neither intellectual effort nor emotional input. Other popular Leslie authors included Mrs Jane G. Austen, Etta W. Pierce, Amanda M. Douglas, John de Forrest, Annie Thomas, Amelia Barr, W.O. Stoddard, Bracebridge Hemyng, and Ella Wheeler.

When a story or a serialized novel arrived at FLPH, especially from an unknown author, it was registered in the company's manuscript ledger and assigned to a sub-editor for evaluation. While works by proven writers were welcomed, a manuscript by a new author had to earn a recommendation from the editor assigned to it; it would then be accepted on her or his say-so. The duties of a house editor included overseeing the story's production and publicity, especially if it were a serialized narrative. However, as an operative principle, FLPH did not identify the editor of a specific story. Even the names of the lead editors of the various periodicals were not mentioned, with the conspicuous exception of Miriam Squier. Such anonymity makes it a challenge to detect an editor like McCarroll at work for Leslie since only a few of his editorials or columns were signed.

A Not Quite Invisible Hand

Despite his requisite restraint, James McCarroll left a few clues (and patterns) in his editorial work for both the *Illustrated Newspaper* and the *Chimney Corner*. Of course, his hand is evident in many of the weekly "Self-Made Men of Our Times" columns in the *Chimney Corner*, though they were unsigned. Having gathered and written profiles during his freelance days in Buffalo, he now oversaw the column. His weekly profiles included a number of Buffalo leaders of his acquaintance and, more evidently, several Canadian figures he knew well.[44] In addition to Charles Lindsey, two of his oldest Peterborough friends, William Cluxton (23 October 1875) and William McDonnell, recently living in Lindsay, Ontario (14 February 1874), appeared during his tenure. Like Lindsey, each received a congratulatory letter from McCarroll when the profile was set to appear. He may also have renewed correspondence with them earlier in seeking out a photographic likeness for the engraving department.

One can, for instance, see McCarroll's hand at work in the profile of Henry Buckingham Witton. Witton's profile (15 March 1873) preceded Charles Lindsey's appearance by two months.[45] He was an English immigrant and self-made man who rose to the position of head painter for the Great American Railroad in Canada West before entering politics as a member of parliament for Hamilton (1872–74). In writing that profile, McCarroll used his editorial privilege to begin the column with a paean to America and a critique of newly confederated Canada. Witton himself is nowhere mentioned in the first two paragraphs.

One of the most notable evidences of the powerful influence of this great Republic over the politics and destiny of Canada, or the new Dominion, is to be found in the fact that the importance of what has been called and considered the privileged classes is rapidly disappearing before the principles of democracy, and that the road to the highest positions under the Government is being steadily opened up to the workingman, who had previously not dared to aspire to anything beyond the narrow limits of his calling, not to speak of a leading voice in the councils of the state.

Time was, and not so long ago, either, when the whole of what was then termed Upper Canada was in the hands of the famous Family Compact, composed of the Sherwoods, the Joneses, the Boultons, and other aristocrats, who ruled the Province with a rod of iron, monopolized all place and power, and whose unjust exactions led to the Rebellion of 1837, and nearly to the loss of the Colony to the British Empire. At that period, the Upper

Canadian Parliament was filled with half-pay officers, and the creatures of
the few, to the utter exclusion of every liberal and healthy element. In such
hands, backed by English bayonets, the masses were completely powerless,
and hence the backward condition of Canada to-day, and the want of life
and energy which has so long characterized her history.[46]

In accord with his increasingly negative view of Canada and his memory of
the Reform agenda he actively served in the 1840s and 1850s, McCarroll opted
to picture the now-confederated country as not very far removed from the
"backward condition" of the colony in the 1830s and 1840s. He asserts this
backwardness despite having before him the example of the rise of Witton from
humble immigrant to working man to elected political official.

A more subtle sign of McCarroll's presence – this time in the pages of
Frank Leslie's Illustrated Newspaper – is a serialized novel by a young Ontario
writer named Isabella Valancy Crawford (1850–1887). Entitled *Wrecked! or,
The Rosclerras of Mistree*, it appeared weekly in the *Illustrated Newspaper* from
26 October 1872 until 29 March 1873. A new writer on the Canadian scene,
Crawford had just begun to have her work published. She was only twenty-two
and living in Peterborough, the town where McCarroll had spent fifteen happy
years and where, in 1843, he had set up his first newspaper.[47]

Though Crawford was too young to have known McCarroll during his
Canadian days, she likely knew about him either through his writing or her
acquaintance with one or more of his daughters, three of whom were living in
Peterborough in the early 1870s. Crawford and the McCarroll sisters were drawn
together by musical interests and proximity in age, for all three McCarroll girls
taught music and Crawford was in the early 1870s the organist at St John's
Anglican Church.

No letters or documents support this connection, but the fact that McCarroll
was working at the FLPH when Crawford's novel appeared in the pages of the
Illustrated Newspaper suggests the link. For his part McCarroll provided his
own editorial hints for watchful readers. Four of his unsigned poems appear
in close proximity to four of the final instalments of *Wrecked* in 1873. These
poems, which served editorially as column fillers, can be seen as phantom
signatures, at least to those in the know. They are found on 22 February 1873
("The Angels of the Blind"), 8 March ("Tee Weet"), 15 March ("The Magic
Mirror"), and 29 March ("The Husbandman"); this last accompanied the
novel's final instalment.[48] They hint at the supportive older editor overseeing
one of the young author's first works.

McCarroll continued this practice, positioning several of his unsigned poems in alignment with chapters of Mrs Oliphant's serialized novel *Innocent: A Tale of Modern Life* (1873), which for a few weeks ran simultaneously with *Wrecked*. He thus appears as the house editor shepherding *Innocent* through its publication. These poems included his popular "The Gray Linnet" (8 March), "At Sunrise" (5 April), "The Bethesda of the Heart" (19 April), "National Music" (10 May), "Our Work" (17 May), and "To the New Moon" (7 June). Datelined New York, "Our Work" had first appeared in *Watson's Art Journal* (6 August 1871). It emphasizes his freshened optimism about America while projecting an up-and-doing attitude couched in a Christian view of hearty work and natural renewal. He printed it a second time in the *Illustrated Newspaper* on 22 November 1873; on both occasions it was unsigned.

Good people, quit your weary knees,
Your drowsy prayers and useless sighs,
And leap to your feet and seize
The present moment as it flies.

God fixed the destiny of men,
From the first hour that saw their birth,
A brawny arm and tongue and pen
To deal alike with heaven and earth.

We want no maudlin, lazy crowds,
With lengthened face and upturned eye,
Communing with the empty clouds
That float above them two miles high.

An honest heart and sturdy hand,
These are the implements we want
To till the heart and till the land
Instead of all this wretched cant.

Those who aright would worship God,
Must leave a record of their creed
Upon the expectant soul and sod,
In sowing both with proper seed.

And when the work's securely done
Within the heart and on the plain,
No fear but He'll supply the sun,
No fear but He'll supply the rain.[49]

Serializing Stories for the Illustrated Press

After several decades of literary experience McCarroll had come to believe that selling stories or serialized fiction to North American periodicals was the best way for an author to be paid for his efforts, especially during difficult economic times. Much as a writer might wish to have a book published, the many story magazines and illustrated newspapers in operation in the 1870s not only paid for the work they published but usually paid promptly. There was little fussing about rates and no need to gather subscribers to appease a cautious publisher. In that spirit, he may have encouraged young Isabella Valancy Crawford to submit *Wrecked* to Leslie. If she did so on her own, he made it his business to work with her, shepherding her chapters through the publication process. The success of her first submission to FLPH led to the appearance of ten short stories in the *Chimney Corner* from 1874 to 1879, and several more in the 1880s. A second Crawford novel, *Hate*, also appeared as a serial in the *Chimney Corner* from 1 May to 11 September 1875. While there are no subtle signatures on this occasion to indicate that McCarroll was still functioning as her house editor, he continued to be a Leslie employee and thus was well positioned to do so.

There is, however, an earlier link between Crawford and McCarroll that preceded their connection at FLPH. It can be found in the pages of a short-lived Montreal story magazine. Seeking to tap into the burgeoning short-story market already being aggressively tapped by Frank Leslie and others, George-Édouard Desbarats (1838–1893) purchased a floundering city magazine called the *Hearthstone*. In the issue of 13 April 1872, he included a story by Crawford and a poem by McCarroll. Crawford's "The Hospital Gondola" was likely her first published story. McCarroll's poem was entitled "A Royal Race." In light of the disguised Crawford-McCarroll connection in *Frank Leslie's Illustrated Newspaper* a few months later, this earlier pairing may be more than coincidental.

Later in 1872, because of debts incurred by the former owner of the *Hearthstone*, Desbarats shut down that magazine and began the *Favorite* in its place. In the second issue of his new story magazine, he began the serialization of Crawford's novel *Winona: or, the Foster Sisters* (11 January to 29 March 1873). McCarroll likely knew about this publication in his editorial position at FLPH.[50]

Thus, young Isabella Valancy Crawford had serialized novels appearing simultaneously in two leading story papers – one in Montreal and one in New York. It is certainly possible that the hand of James McCarroll was quietly at work in both instances of her literary debut. In the initial issue of the *Favorite*, the editor spoke of having received a considerable amount of literary material from "Peterboro" Ontario. Among the authors whose work might soon appear in the pages of the *Favorite* were Crawford, Susanna Moody (*sic*), and Mary Muchall. Muchall was not only Catharine Parr Traill's daughter and Susanna Moodie's niece, but a friend of Crawford and by extension the McCarroll sisters. These young women shared not only familial and literary connections but also, in the case of Crawford and the McCarrolls, an enthusiasm for music. Two Muchall stories appeared in Leslie's periodicals during the early 1870s though not under her name; that connection again suggests the editorial hand of James McCarroll.[51]

Other McCarroll poems appeared sporadically, usually as fillers, in subsequent issues of *Frank Leslie's Illustrated Newspaper*. One in particular merits attention. "Every Inch a Man" was published under his own name on 29 August 1874. It can be seen as a companion piece to "Our Work," offering a kind of manifesto of personal self-evaluation and the deliberate repurposing of his life "in the [early] sunset of his years":

Who does and says, with all his might,
All that he might do and say;
Who is as pure and good by night
As he appears to be by day.
Who stands approved in his own sight,
But never doubts God's glorious plan,
And goes on battling for the right
That man is every inch a man.

He makes no lazy, loud appeal
While struggling through the sloughs of life;
But claps his shoulder to the wheel,
And triumphs in the noble strife.
At every step his way he clears,
Till he is foremost in the van,
And, in the sunset of his years,
Comes, right out, every inch a man.[52]

As part of his duties, McCarroll wrote editorial columns and short squibs for both the *Illustrated Newspaper* and the *Chimney Corner*. Because of his interests in music and theatre, he likely wrote profiles on various performers and celebrities, some of whom were his acquaintances; as well, because of his connections to Canada, he would have been assigned or perhaps would have chosen to write on Canadian subjects. In scrolling through both periodicals during these years, one notes a number of unsigned pieces that might be his; such speculation is unnecessary, however, given the amount of his writing that can actually be identified.[53] Thus, by 1874, McCarroll was well established in the editorial department of Frank Leslie's Publishing House. But, as a man of many parts, he pursued several other interests, particularly the theatre and music, along with certain kinds of scientific inquiry.

A Hunger for the Stage

The year 1874 saw the publication of McCarroll's play *Nearly a Tragedy: A Comedy*. A five-act drama, set in rural Kent, near London, it was published by John F. Trow & Son, 209 East Twelfth Street, New York and registered with the Library of Congress. He would register two more drama manuscripts with the Library of Congress in subsequent years. While there is no record that *Nearly a Tragedy: A Comedy* was ever performed, he must have entertained modest hopes for his comedy and for several other plays that he worked on during these years. It is the least known of his four published books. The play, however, reveals another side of McCarroll's literary range and confirms his desire to succeed in a genre he loved as a playgoer and theatre critic. During his Toronto days and in his work for Henry Watson, he was respected as an informed observer of dramatic and operatic stagecraft[54] and one biographical sketch noted that he "was engaged as a musical and dramatic critic on New York daily papers" though it named neither the newspapers nor the dates involved.[55]

In *Nearly a Tragedy: A Comedy* McCarroll adapted the durable model of Eugene Scribe's "well-made play" to his purposes. In the 1870s the form still remained popular among English and European theatregoers, though it was increasingly viewed by younger playwrights as an outdated, artificial, and restrictive form.[56] In setting his comedy in rural England, McCarroll sought to appeal to the continuing interest of American theatregoers in old-world drama.

Following Scribe, his plot is carefully constructed and meticulous in its use of detail. Nothing extraneous or romantic is allowed to impinge on the action, which presumes that a good deal of pertinent activity related to the story had already taken place. There is, however, a portentous secret in the air that is unknown to the characters on stage; the audience, by contrast, is immediately aware that "summat's up" (43). The good people of Gray Cliff Manor are in a terrible quandary as Sir Reginald Howard, the estate's arrogant heir-apparent, is within days of taking over the property. Once in control, he promises to dole out punishments to all its denizens, regardless of social rank, and to take special delight in seeing many of them exiled from their beloved home. The plot then oscillates between the grimness of the immediate situation and the desperate hopes of the Gray-Cliffers as events further confirm Sir Reginald's villainy and the good-heartedness of the vulnerable tenants.

The prescribed happy ending unfolds in act 5. The secret of the plot hangs on a case of mistaken identity that followed from the vaccination of two boys in France during the Napoleonic Wars. When, after her ward's vaccination, the maternal protector of "the good boy" finds herself incarcerated as an English spy and cut off from help in a French prison, the villainous youth is launched on a course that will see him eventually become heir of the manor. The ending is designed to restore social order and to condemn the villain to his rightful place in jail. In act 5, Stanhope Travers, the clever and "handsome" tutor at the nearby Grange (whom the audience first meets in act 1), is identified as the innocent victim of the hospital switch. Unaware of his own early history, Travers has bettered himself through his own intelligence and education. Having by act 4 won the heart of and married Alice Mortimer, who has lived for years with her father in the manor house (the courtship occurs in acts 3 and 4), he takes his rightful position as Gray Cliff's owner in act 5. He ends the play by pledging to restore the old and happy order to the estate.

A conventional melodrama, *Nearly a Tragedy: A Comedy* involves little by way of social criticism or character development, despite its clever adaptation of the vaccination device, a newish medical trope for altered identities. Travers Stanhope sets himself up in act 1 as an authority on theatre and class values, arguing that the theatre has the ability to bring the realities of life before less educated people. He also forthrightly defends the value of the working man. The latter theme is validated in the play; its real vitality lies not in the aristocratic or upper middle-class realms, but in the lives of those who work for a living on the estate. These characters include Old Capon, the "landlord" of the White Hart, and two servants, Irishman Mike O'Grady who works for Capon, and Dick Whiting, who is the Mortimers' retainer.

The play's liveliest scenes involve these three in dialogue. Mike's brogue stands out as colourful and candid. Besides the usual stage-Irish tags ("me bouchal," "be the mortial," and "be me sowkins"), he has the gift of creating vivid images. He describes Sir Reginald, for instance, as "look[ing] like a hap'orth of soap afther a hard day's washin" (5) and "as kantankerous as a mule, and as sour as a gallon of vinegar sharpened down to a pint" (7). Speaking to the temperamental Sir Reginald during the latter's arrest in act 5, Mike says, "What are you raisin' sich ructions for, … Take it aisy, man! take it aisy! Sure, afther all, you were only changed at nurse! – a thing that happens nearly every day wid us over there in Ireland!" Mike's comment leads to "merriment and laughter" (53) on stage.

A bachelor who relishes snaring rabbits illegally and musing about life's misfortunes, Mike is deeply Irish and conspicuously uneducated. Over many a pint at the White Hart, he bemoans his lost "Limerick girl," claiming she deserted him, but he is at heart a jolly and adaptable fellow. In the end he happily changes his story about his lost Irish love – asserting now that it was he who left her. In the spirit of the happy ending, Mike announces that "The millaynium is come!" Feeling inclined in his happiness to "turn a summerset like a showman," he acknowledges that he has plenty of room in his "soft heart" for the "handsome servant girl now hanging on his arm" (55).

Other than Mike O'Grady, McCarroll's play lacked the rollicking, high-spirited comic elements of his popular contemporary Dion Boucicault (1820–1890) who, since 1860, had been enjoying great success in New York with his refreshing brand of Irish comedy. The success of *The Colleen Bawn; or, The Brides of Garryowen* that year and *Arrah-na-Pogue; or, The Wicklow Wedding* in 1864 earned him large and enthusiastic American audiences. Both plays were successes when he took them to London and Dublin as well. By contrast, McCarroll's Scribean comedy was dated – stiff, subdued, melodramatic, and conventional, despite the conversational leaven of Mike O'Grady and his pals.

Boucicault's plays must have been a great joy for McCarroll. After a lengthy and checkered career in the English theatre, the Dublin-born Boucicault had come to New York in 1854. As an actor and playwright, he had led a colourful life in the theatre; along with a few early successes – such as his English production of *London Assurance* (1841) – he spent time in France reworking French plays for English audiences; he survived two bankruptcies and lived through a couple of well-publicized affairs and marital controversies. However, by the 1870s he had established himself as the durable voice of Ireland on the American stage. Having adapted Gerald Griffin's novel *The Collegians* into *The Colleen Baun*, he continued to give New York audiences the joy and exuberance of the stage-Irish character in an era characterized by Victorian restraint and English sobriety. In focusing on the vitality and cleverness of his Irish heroes and by playing those roles so compellingly himself, he became a great favourite with the New York theatre audiences, even though the plays themselves were still governed by the usual melodramatic plotting.

With *The Shaughraun*, which appeared in the same year as McCarroll's play, Boucicault once again tapped into warm feelings for his native Ireland and in Conn, he brought to the stage his liveliest incarnation of "the Irish rogue-hero." According to David Krause, Conn enjoyed a significant theatrical pedigree. He sees him as "the theatrical descendant of the parasite-slave of Plautus and Terence, and the prototype of Synge's peasants and O'Casey's Dubliners."[57] As McCarroll himself had done earlier in his serialized novel, "The New Gauger: or, Jack Trainer's Story" (1856) and then reprised in the irrepressible voice of Terry Finnegan, Boucicault cleverly reworked and countered the negative tradition of the Stage Irishman that had thrived for two centuries as a staple of English drama.

In those English plays the stereotypical Irishman was often a despicable buffoon, blowhard, and petty criminal. In reversing that stereotype, Boucicault was following the lead of popular Irish novelists like Samuel Lover and Charles Lever. In the mid-nineteenth century, they had created a roster of likeable "comic-rogue heroes" who were able to outwit the arrogant and falsely superior English figures. In Lover's 1837 novel *Rory O'More*, for instance, Rory as rogue hero became the comedic centre of the action. So too in his later plays Boucicault's Conn figure triumphed over his English adversaries. Krause delineates the process by which that reversal of Irish inferiority came to be:

At the time [Boucicault] wrote and acted the role of the comic vagabond – the *shaughraun* or wanderer – the Stage Irishman had long since been a stock caricature in English drama. This buffoon was merely a figure of ridicule, the absurd Irishman making a fool of himself among the English; his hard drinking and over-ripe blarney made him the butt of comedy, and he was usually relegated to the sub-plot. But Boucicault altered this image by making his Irishman the clever and attractive central character in a play set in Ireland, in which the absurd Englishman, or Anglo-Irishman, makes a fool of himself among the Irish. His hero is the wise fool, the master of mischievous revels who is the inevitable occasion of hilarity in others as well as a natural humorist himself. To be sure he is a blathering rogue, a cheerful liar with a powerful thirst, but he is also a liberated playboy who cavorts outside the ordinary restraints of society, a picaresque clown who ingeniously rights all wrongs with an instinctive sense of justice and bonhomie.[58]

In 1874 Boucicault's *The Shaughraun* opened at Wallack's Theatre to great acclaim. He starred as Conn, the amiable Irish layabout who wins the audience's heart and outwits the English squires. McCarroll's Mike O'Grady in *Nearly a Tragedy: A Comedy* belongs to that same tradition, though he remains a downstairs player who does little to influence the main plot. Rather he serves as a colourful commentator on the action, occasionally anticipating what is about to happen within the mode of the well-made play.

While there is no known link between Boucicault and McCarroll, they shared a love of the brogue and its dramatic attractiveness on stage. Moreover, they both lived in the Washington Square area in the 1870s. But Boucicault was a celebrity at the high point of his theatrical career while McCarroll was, as a workaday editor, hoping to catch a break and move forward his own theatrical ambitions.

In occasional newspaper squibs, biographical sketches, and copyright registrations, there is further evidence of McCarroll's attempts to make his way as a playwright. Patched together, they trace both his ambition and futility. He formally registered two dramatic pieces for copyright during these years. The first, described as "An Afterpiece in One Act" (21 March 1874), was called *The Bohemian; or, Taking Time by the Forelock*. The other was a full-length play, registered on 13 March 1876, entitled *A Queen without a Crown: A Sensational and Historical Drama in Five Acts*. No copy of either has been found nor is there evidence of a production. Furthermore, in a "Musical and Dramatic News" column in *Frank Leslie's Illustrated Newspaper* (13 May 1876), there is reference to another play he was preparing. The column announced that "Mr James McCarroll, of this city, is engaged in the preparation of a three-act drama, founded on incidents in the Revolutionary War. It is to be produced immediately upon its completion at the Third Avenue Theatre, in this city." McCarroll may have planted this item himself, as he so often did, anticipating that he would complete the play as promised.

One signed column in the *Chimney Corner* (24 July 1875) must also be noted. In "Some Thoughts on the Creation of American Drama" McCarroll mused on the evolution of drama and the state of American theatre. Emphasizing the lack of "homogeneity" or a "common whole" characterizing current life in America, he concluded that, with the country's centenary (1876) approaching and "the tide of emigration still flowing," "there is yet no American people, pure and simple" to be clearly identified, defined, or dramatized. Rather the United States is "a gibbet-pie," flavoured by "some rigidly cherished transatlantic memories" from many countries. For all its innovative experimentation and sheer energy,

America will need two or three more generations before "our nationality" can define itself clearly in theatre and art.

Overall, theatre had moved from the Pagan (ancient) era to the Christian (modern), but it still awaited a new kind of drama and energy keyed to the vital American present. It may even grow, he speculated, "out of the loins of the Spiritualism of the present day." America, however, still lacks a "grand central figure to rally around" in part because "Uncle Sam is a Down-Easter whose influence is not gracefully acknowledged very far south of Baltimore." Given the persistent sectionalism of the country, theatrical achievement, for the time being, "must be accomplished in the footprints of the English drama, with a few local dashes, to meet the necessities of a purely American audience, until the time for the appearance of the latter shall have arrived." In 1875 America still awaited "a concrete and homogeneous nationality" that could serve as a foundation for the theatre of the future.

McCarroll's analysis of the growth of American nationality fits nicely with the English-Irish subject matter of *Nearly a Tragedy: A Comedy* and his other known titles. The play on the revolutionary war would presumably have relied more on those "few local dashes" of American colour that were evident in present-day dramas about the country. Nevertheless, his personal identification with America and its "genius" is clear. Indeed, he opted to become a naturalized citizen of the United States during that centennial year.

Freelancing and Editing

Judging by the number of his pieces that appeared in the *Chimney Corner* from 1875 to 1877, McCarroll maintained close connections with FLPH into the late 1870s, even as Leslie's financial troubles led him to fire large numbers of employees or leave them hanging uneasily in their positions. Indeed, McCarroll may have sought freelance work as a new kind of security. A freelancer could make submissions to FLPH and be paid without having to be engaged in workplace duties and uncertainties. It seems likely that he did what he could to keep up his Leslie connections as a freelance author and editor while taking up work elsewhere. His independence as a writer and editor is evident by 1877–78.

In 1877 McCarroll published seven stories under his own name in the *Chimney Corner*. This was a surprising burst of signed writing on his part. Relatedly, the editor of Frank Leslie's new *Sunday Magazine*, where several of McCarroll's essays and poems appeared in 1877–78, described him as "our excellent contributor."[59] After 1878, however, his contributions to, and perhaps his connection with, the FLPH ended, although he may have taken on occasional editorial assignments for the company.

At the same time, there is passing evidence that McCarroll either freelanced for other publishers or took up other temporary editorial positions. In 1876, for instance, two pieces appeared in *Appleton's Monthly*. About this time, he also began writing and editing for *Appleton's American Cyclopedia* and the *People's Cyclopedia of Universal Knowledge*. On the title page of the volume of the *People's Cyclopedia* published in 1884, he was identified impressively as "James M'Carroll, Composer and Musician, Editor and Literatteur."

"American" Sensational Stories

McCarroll's seven stories for the *Chimney Corner* were typical adventure tales written in the highly wrought vein of "Her Own Executioner," which had appeared in two parts in the *St Catharines Evening Journal* in 25–26 April 1872.[60] Why this sudden burst of signed stories in the *Chimney Corner* at this particular time – and not before or after – constitutes another small mystery. But taken together these "American" stories make it clear that he was still connected to the Frank Leslie Publishing Company and that he was a master of such narratives.

His *Chimney Corner* stories are as follows, in order of appearance: "The Hurdy-gurdy Man" (14 October 1876), 339–41; "The Red Nun" (18 November 1876), 14–15; "The Poor Scholar" (17 March 1877), 289–91; "The Ruby Cross of Oulart" (2 June 1877), 33–5; "The Young Padre of San Salvador" (9 June 1877), 53–7; "The Two Spies" (30 June 1877), 405–8; and "The Red Lasso" (15 September 1877), 294–5. Three served as cover stories in their respective issues.[61] As well, one signed poem, "God Help Her," appeared in the magazine on 3 February 1877.

The stories have a sameness and simplicity that follow from their commitment to the conventions of "the sensation narrative." In a letter to John A. Macdonald written while he was still in Toronto, McCarroll described the literary material he had on his desk, the least of which were a number of "the blood thirsty American sensational stor[ies] where the author is never satisfied until he has his heroine hanging by the hair, <u>of her head</u>, over some gloomy precipice ten thousand feet in depth." Aware of such excesses, he readily mocked them, even though he knew they were a freelancer's stock in trade. However, his stories also show a commitment to realism and the use of local colour.[62]

Typically such stories had at their centre an "aristocratic" love match between an exceptionally beautiful and good young woman and a virile and handsome man, who on occasion had an intellectual bent. One or both belong to wealthy, or once-wealthy, families. But circumstances or misunderstandings conspire to keep them apart, even as a villain – a cruder, more covetous and vulgar character in terms of manners and rank – is positioned to make venomous threats against the lives and fate of the principals. A mood of mystery and fatedness prevails, abetted by disguises, assumed identities, withheld information, and a feeling of desperate vulnerability in the face of such treachery and power. In the end, the swooning heroine (she always swoons at the most terrifying moment) is rescued from the brink of despair and imminent death. Order is restored, values are reasserted, and the villain receives his just desserts.

In his Leslie stories McCarroll's individuality lies in his vivid use of particular settings and his ability to present informed historical situations. Often he employed an articulate and knowledgable narrative voice, be it omniscient or in the first person. As well, he deftly plays with matters of carnality in describing his villains; they respond far too eagerly to the natural sensuality, and even the unintended voluptuousness, of the attractive heroines. In "The Young Padre of San Salvador," for instance, the narrator offers this description of the pirate villain who has boarded *The Falcon* and tied up those in the crew who are still alive after the attack. When the heroine, Isabella Lopez, and her maid Marguerita emerge from below deck, "the devil seemed to take possession of the eyes and features of the pirate, who was a fellow of gigantic stature and the most repulsive appearance. He gazed on his hapless victims with a terrible sensuality which was dreadful to contemplate." Typically, McCarroll grants a beguiling sensuality or a mild voluptuousness to his heroines, though their attractiveness is never at odds with their chaste and pure natures; neither is that sensuality a matter of particular note to their prescribed partners. The sexual element functions as a means to draw in, tease, and titillate both villains and readers.

Designed for an American readership, these stories reflect a conspicuously aristocratic or European bias. Little attention is given to American values or social goals. Only the servant class seems democratic in their outlook, though they are loyal to their masters and mistresses. Were the grasping villains not designed to be so completely monstrous and covetous, they might well have been reconstituted to reflect those upward-striving and driven figures who were helping to feed the myth of American success that was then very much in play. However, no such thinking was permissible in the sensation-story formula.

Two of the stories drew on McCarroll's Irish roots. "The Poor Scholar" is set in Roscrea, Tipperary and begins near one of the round towers that even in the nineteenth century attracted the attention of visitors and historians.

The second dips more deeply into Irish history and the rebel tradition that so interested him. "The Rose Cross of Oulart" is set during the United Irishmen Rebellion of 1798 in County Wexford, near Carnsore Point on the Irish Sea. In his general account of the rebellion, McCarroll makes clear not only his sympathy with the rebels but the value of their guerilla attempts to defeat the royalist forces, even after the tide had turned against them. Noting the invocation of martial law in the county earlier that year, he celebrates the rebel victory at the Battle of Oulart Hill in May 1798, but alters the actual details to his purpose by creating a Robin Hood narrative to replace the facts of the bloody battle and by allowing a steep and dangerous gorge to replace the landscape of Oulart Hill. A royalist militia detachment, known for its brutality and besotted commander, stands in for the infamous North Cork Militia of the actual battle; as well, the defeat of the royalists is celebrated by the spectacular fall of their detachment from a bridge into the 300-foot gorge. The event, so interpreted, made for a sensational cover illustration. After the massacre, McCarroll allowed the rebel leaders to escape by boat to America rather than face the inevitable reprisals awaiting them for their unexpected military success. Still a Fenian sympathizer at heart, McCarroll made heroes of the band of United Irishmen known as the Rose Cross of Oulart and villains out of the English forces.

Frank Leslie's Sunday Magazine

While McCarroll's personal contributions to both the *Illustrated Newspaper* and the *Chimney Corner* appeared to end in mid-September 1877 with "The Red Lasso," he was also writing for *Frank Leslie's Sunday Magazine*. It had begun in January 1876 under the editorship of Charles F. Deems, a prominent New York minister and theologian. From February through October several signed poems and essays by McCarroll appeared in its pages. This minor deluge may suggest that he had undertaken sub-editorial duties during this period in support of the busy Deems. However, since most of his submissions appeared in 1877–78, it seems that his freelance work for the company ceased completely late in 1878. Several of his stories would be reprinted in later years in both *Frank Leslie's Popular Monthly* ("an inexpensive family miscellany" that ran under that title from 1876 until 1905) and *Frank Leslie's Pleasant Hours*.[63]

Leslie must have paid Deems a handsome fee to lend his valued name to the *Sunday Magazine*. According to the magazine, Deems "conducted" it and offered readers some of his sermons. But he was a busy and famous man of the cloth. One of the best-known and most respected ministers in the city, he was a friend of many rich New Yorkers, including Cornelius Vanderbilt, and he had become the "Pastor of the Church of the Strangers" where he enjoyed a strong connection with nearby New York University. Earlier he had been associated with several southern universities and schools, and had established himself as a leading religious scholar. His *Life of Jesus* stayed steadily in print while he continued to edit a respected religious periodical entitled *Christian Thought*. Because Leslie's *Sunday Magazine* functioned well below his usual level of religious discourse, the magazine had to be overseen in the Leslie editorial office by lesser lights who adopted a liberal Protestant, non-denominational outlook. Not surprisingly, a portrait and description of Deems had appeared in *Frank Leslie's Illustrated Newspaper* on 18 November 1876. Listing his attributes and achievements in the platitudinous manner typical of the "Self-Made Men of Our Times" series, it may well have been written by McCarroll himself in his capacity as temporary sub-editor.

McCarroll's contributions to the *Sunday Magazine* included twelve signed poems, the majority of which were reprints, and four essays, some of which were of a scientific bent.[64] Two of the poems focused vividly on the poverty and despair witnessed by many city dwellers. His "February" aligns the despairing cold of winter with death and hopeless anguish (see chapter 6).[65]

His most unusual prose piece was the lengthy lead article for the October 1877 issue. "A Glance at Jerusalem and Portions of the Holy Land" is a detailed account of Jerusalem past and present, written to accompany selected illustrations. He compares the modern Jerusalem of the 1870s – "a mass of ruin, filth, bad smells and all but impassable streets, and no municipal or other available government," according to the Rev. Dr William Hanna[66] – with its historical significance as "a centre of sublime religious revelations – as the theatre of glorious and unparalleled events." Never having been to the Holy Land himself, he relied on the impressions of religious tourists like Hanna, the Rev. Norman Macleod, Dr Thompson, and Augustus Lyne.[67] Adopting "the royal we" as tour guide, he takes readers on visits to Jerusalem, Bethlehem, Nazareth, and the port of Jaffa, while concentrating on the well-known biblical sites in and around Jerusalem and Bethlehem. At the same time he puts the story of Jerusalem into a detailed historical perspective, emphasizing the heterogeneous composition of its citizenry and the fact that it had been the site of many battles for control. Currently governed by the Turks, the city was in 1877 a lively mix of Arabs, Jews, Turks, Armenians, and others.

Mr McCarroll — Where Are You?

Following his periods of employment under Henry Watson and Frank Leslie, James McCarroll stayed busy in New York on several fronts. However, a precise tracking of his movements and places of employment — a detailed summary of his working days and literary activities — presents numerous challenges. Biographies offer few specific details about his many years in New York. One particularly striking anomaly is the list of contributors to *Appleton's American Cylopedia* (revised edition, 1879). Here he is described as "James McCarroll, Montreal, Canada."[68] The reference is startling for there is little evidence to support his return to Canada (the Montreal city directory does not list him for 1879); indeed, it is uncertain whether he would yet have been welcome anywhere in the country, only a decade after his Fenian days in Buffalo. He did work for Appleton's and the *People's Cyclopedia of Universal Knowledge* in various editorial capacities in the late 1870s and early 1880s. These periods of employment, either full time or part time, may have provided his main income for a number of years.[69]

Trow's *New York City Directory* is unhelpful for some periods. It gives no city residence for him in 1878–79 or from 1881 to 1884. Thus, for a couple of periods, questions about where he lived and whom he worked for, be it as an editor or freelancer, remain. So too, nothing is known about his use of the printing press which he had managed to keep in his possession, or where and how he undertook his scientific research and experiments. Only by 1887 does his path become clear, because by then he had begun to work as an editor for *Belford's Magazine*. But what he was doing and where he was working from 1878 to 1887 remain unclear; only fragments of information are available.

Science, Songs, and Other Pursuits, 1881–88

James McCarroll saw himself as a scientist and an inventor, a kind of nineteenth-century Ben Franklin figure. However, his work seldom achieved the public recognition he sought, despite his engagement in scientific debates and his pursuit of practical strategies to solve engineering challenges. His theories about the gyroscope, for instance, led to public controversy in the 1870s.[70]

On 18 December 1874, he had given a lecture for the Polytechnic Association of the American Institute at the Cooper Union on "A Brief Glance at the Snow Plough and Some of the Effects of Snow upon the Trade and Travel of this Country." With an eye to historical information about both Canada and the northern states, he cited evidence of the inadequacy of snow removal on both roads and railways, emphasizing the losses suffered by business operations because of snow.

Another indication of his inventive pursuits in the early 1880s is found in the annual reports of the commissioner of patents for the United States. The reports for 1882, 1883, and 1884 track his submission of patents for better fireproofing and safer elevators. In 1882 he patented two "self-acting elevator safety apparatus[es]"; the first was designed to prevent fires and to admit light and air through wooden walls and partitions; the second aimed to prevent "elevators from falling in case of accident to the rope, chain, or other contrivance by which the platform or carriage is suspended." The latter was a kind of safety pulley attached to the side of the elevator shaft to prevent the elevator from suddenly plummeting in case of equipment failure. But, as wooden elevators were being replaced by metal constructions, he came forward in 1883 with another patent for the use of wire gauze in the construction of elevator floors and partitions. By December 1884 he reported in his patent application that the "McCarroll Fire Preventive Manufacturing Company" was now in operation. As its "assignor," he applied to patent "a fire shield for roofs" and elevator carriages.

The potential significance of these patents is difficult to estimate today. Certainly he held on to them for their potential value and, as one of his New York obituaries noted, he was preparing to sell them in the months before his death. No doubt, he faced sharp competition from Elisha Otis and the Otis Elevator Company, among others, as independent inventors and manufacturers raced against time to provide improved building materials and techniques for elevators now being used in mining shafts, industrial factories, and multi-storey public buildings. Changes of this kind were occurring at a rapid pace during the Gilded Age, and the time was ripe for technical improvements and better safety measures, given the recognized need for taller buildings in cities like New York. When he died in 1892, his pursuit of "secret things" was work still in progress. In its obituary, *Belford's Magazine* paid tribute to another of his inventions, a means to "doubl[e] the light of gas while halving the quantity used" in chimney burners of various kinds. The magazine also asserted that his ingenious work on elevators "will one day be better known and of great value."

But to return to the New York City directories, they contain a few references that help to amplify McCarroll's life there. For instance, his residence from 1878 to early 1881 was 83 East 10th Street. This was no ordinary boarding house; rather it was the long-time home of Claudio S. Grafulla (1812–1880), the well-respected military bandleader and composer. Born in Minorca, Spain and an American resident since 1838, Grafulla became ill in 1880 and died that December during what would have been the McCarrolls' third year as his tenants. Grafulla was the bandmaster of the 7th Regiment Band of New York (formerly the 27th Regiment) which he had developed into "one of the finest musical organizations in America."[71] He was also the respected composer and arranger of numerous grand marches and quick steps which were published as sheet music during his lifetime.[72] "From all accounts Grafulla was a superb musician and had 'a remarkable talent for organizing, governing and disciplining' his musicians."[73] A quiet and modest man deeply devoted to his music, he never married, but he rented out apartments in his house to fellow musicians like McCarroll.[74]

Always a musician either at home or on stage, James McCarroll shared Grafulla's interest in composing and publishing sheet music. He wrote for voice and piano. Three of his songs can be found in the "Music for the Nation [Collection]: American Sheet Music, 1870–1885." "I Can't Sing for Gold" (words and music by James McCarroll) was published by the Boston firm of Oliver Ditson and Company in 1877. The other two, "O, the Rapture o'er Me Stealing" and "Don't Nelly Dear," were published by Richard A. Saalfield, 839 Broadway, the latter composition in 1881. Such pre-Tin Pan Alley sheet music likely brought him a little ancillary income and added to his musical credentials.

"O, the Rapture o'er Me Stealing" and "Don't Nelly Dear" are light fare, marrying the piano to the male (Irish) tenor voice. They are love songs, the first caught up in the vision of the beloved and the other a plea that Nellie (Mavourneen) not break her lover's heart by being indifferent to his attentions. McCarroll's playful poetic skills are evident in both songs. He lightly defines rapture as the "deeper depths of love" that fill the "bright phantom of my soul"; as musical direction for the performance, he suggests "Andante apassione." "Don't Nellie Dear" is written in an "Allegretto" tempo and pleads playfully with the young woman. The last four lines beg her to take his plea seriously:

Oh! My darling, 'twas only in jest, you declare,
Just to see if I loved you, ah, Nell, that's not fair
But come let me breathe it once more in your ear
And don't teaze me that way, Oh don't Nellie dear!

The most musically interesting of the songs is "I Can't Sing for Gold." It requires a slower, more classical accompaniment appropriate to the genesis of its theme, which McCarroll, ever the close observer, summarizes in a brief

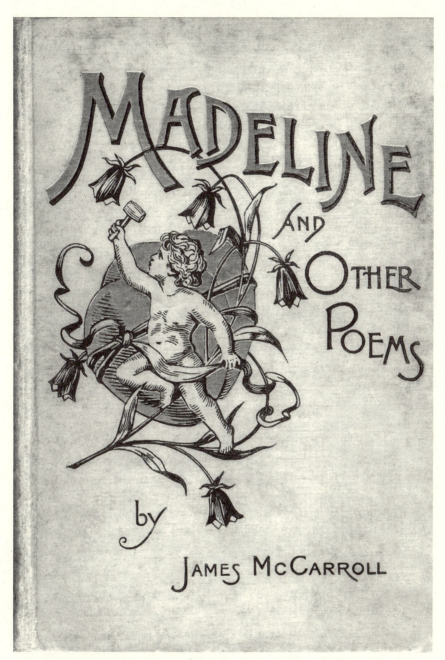

8.3 The title page of McCarroll's only published book of poetry, *Madeline and Other Poems*. New York: Belford, Clarke and Company, 1889.

preface. "A distinguished American contralto being asked to name her terms for singing some soothing melodies to a heart-broken young lady, a great lover of music, while seated before the coffin of her husband, to whom she had been but recently married, exclaimed, 'I can't sing for gold here, but I'll sing for love!'" The song uses a refrain that concludes both stanzas, emphasizing the contralto's antipathy to gold in the face of the widow's sorrow:

> I can't sing for gold, I can't sing for gold
> But let my poor song fall for love on your ear,
> Oh! Let my poor song fall for love on your ear.
> I can't sing for gold, I can't sing for gold, I can't sing for gold.

There is very little information about McCarroll's employment in New York from 1884 to 1887. The Trow Directory places him and Julia Ellen in several lower Manhattan locations – 119 East 15th Street (1884–87), 21 East 18th Street (1887–88) and 438 West 32nd Street (1888–89). During these years (1884 to 1887) Trow also lists him as an editor working at 56 Bible House or, simply, Bible House. That large and impressive building, between 3rd and 4th Avenues, and fronting on Astor Place, had been the home of the American Bible Society since 1852; from its premises bibles were produced for national and international distribution, along with several religious periodicals. However, in surviving biographical sketches no mention is made of any connection to Bible House. Such employment might be seen as consistent with the more conservative and conventional religious outlook he had adopted in his later years, even though some of his later writing suggests his continuing fascination with spiritualist matters.

His final New York residence was 99 Clinton Place, and it was here that he died in April 1892. Shortly after moving there in 1888, he took up an editorial position at *Belford's Magazine*, a new periodical begun a year earlier by Robert Belford.

The Belford Brothers and *Belford's Magazine*, 1889

James McCarroll enjoyed a special status at *Belford's Magazine* through his longstanding connection with its owner. His poetic tribute to Robert's wife – "Lines. On Viewing an Exquisitely Painted Portrait of the Beautiful Mrs Robert Belford" – was included in *Madeline*.[75] Beginning in 1889, he and Hildreth served as co-editors of the magazine's book section and regularly reviewed books themselves.[76] They were conservative readers who offered lively takes on the books they read. As well, McCarroll wrote a number of articles displaying his range of literary, musical, scientific, and Canadian interests. His numerous contributions suggest a multi-faceted writer and an engaging personality, still very much in his prime at age seventy-five. Indeed, until his death three years later, he continued to think of himself as young in spirit and as a man who relished the literary life he was now able to lead in some comfort. After his death, *Belford's* recognized his "intimate" connection with the magazine in a tender obituary, praising him for having "contributed many valuable articles and much intelligent editorial work" to the magazine. The piece further noted that he "endeared himself to his proprietor [Robert Belford] and his fellow workers as a brother laborer in the field of literature and a true Irish gentleman of the old school."[77] The commitment to Ireland linked McCarroll and Robert Belford, belying the view, recently put forward by Eli McLaren, that Robert (and his older brother Alexander), who had emigrated with their family from County Kerry in 1857, "had no memory of Ireland and would grow up wholly oriented to the new world."[78] Indeed, though it is not clear whether Robert was born in Ireland or in Toronto (his birth occurred about the time of the Belford family's arrival), it is evident that he shared in the family's pride in its southern Irish roots.[79]

The *Belford's* obituary was well informed and heart-felt. It confirmed that McCarroll's Irish heritage and pride remained an attractive aspect of his personality and outlook until his death. He maintained his distinctive Connaught accent over the years and loved to regale friends with Gaelic stories, Irish songs, and historical lore. His "happy, sanguine temperament" and "genial, wholesome nature" appealed to male and female friends alike.[80]

McCarroll had known the Belford family from their earliest Canadian days: they arrived in Toronto about the same time and they shared a connection to James Beaty's *Toronto Daily Leader*.[81] Robert, the youngest of the three brothers, was still a boy in the 1860s.[82] Even today relatively little is known about him as an individual, despite the collective notoriety of the three brothers as newspapermen and publishers. The eldest, Charles (1837–1880), got into the newspaper business early, serving from 1862 as an assistant editor at the *Daily Leader* before being appointed editor in 1867, one year after McCarroll decamped to Buffalo. Charles was also busy on various literary fronts including the Ontario Literary Society. As recording secretary (1860–62), he arranged speakers for society meetings and worked closely with local writers like William Alexander Foster, a friend of McCarroll and an occasional contributor to the *Leader*.[83]

Led by the precocious and venturesome Aleck (1854–1906), who had a genius for start-up projects, Charles and Robert joined him in creating Belford Brothers Publishing Company in Toronto in 1872. That "house" proceeded to exploit the prevailing limits of copyright protection for British and American authors and publishers outside their national jurisdictions. Belford Brothers specialized in publishing cheap "pirated" books in Canada soon after their appearance in London or New York.[84] Although the firm faced numerous lawsuits for their pirating ventures and developed a somewhat suspect business reputation, it prospered. Inexpensively reproduced works by well-known authors like Mark Twain became important staples.

In 1875 the Belfords established a new partnership with another enterprising Irishman named James Clarke. With Clarke on board, Aleck, ever the opportunist, moved the firm, now called Belford, Clarke and Company (BCC), to Chicago, where he was able to obtain strong financial backing and begin to experiment with new sales tactics.[85] Robert stayed on in Toronto to keep their Canadian publishing arm alive and publish *Rose-Belford's Magazine* there. Then, with the American operations of BCC flourishing in Chicago – the firm was doing over a million dollars in business a year in the early 1880s – Robert moved to New York to oversee the expansion of their operations there. In 1888 he set up *Belford's Magazine*, the major aim of which was to promote the interests of the Democratic Party. By the late 1880s, however, the two parallel streams of Belford operations – in Chicago and New York – had to negotiate a legal separation following a devastating warehouse fire in Chicago in 1886 and the near bankruptcy of that wing of the firm. By 1888, when Robert renewed acquaintances with McCarroll, he was running his own publishing house in New York. Their reunion proved mutually advantageous.

Humanity and Health, 1892

McCarroll's editorial reputation was called upon during his brief engagement with another new New York magazine, *Humanity and Health*. Initially *Humanity and Health* set up its office at 18 Clinton Place, down the street from the McCarrolls' flat (this may have been the address where he housed his printing press). In fact, he had undertaken on his own to print the first two issues of *Humanity and Health* for its editor and driving force, Dr Ella A. Jennings, a progressive medical doctor and feminist dedicated to women's health issues and providing aid to the poor.[86] Interestingly, her roots were Canadian: she was born in Norwich, Upper Canada.[87] Years earlier she had challenged current practices by setting up "The Twenty-Five Cent Provident

Dispensary for Women and Children," first at 42 University Place and then at 13 Clinton Place. Here female practitioners provided inexpensive advice and courteous help to women, especially self-respecting but poverty-stricken women in medical need.[88]

The first issue of *Humanity and Health* appeared in January 1892. For the second issue in February, Dr Jennings engaged McCarroll as her co-editor. However, as her subsequent editorials reveal, that February issue would be his first and last as co-editor. For that issue the magazine called 93 Clinton Place its home; it was a mere two doors from the McCarroll residence.

As a supporter of the magazine, McCarroll had written a letter of "Greeting" for the February issue, praising Ella Jennings and her social objectives while slyly calling attention to his own contributions in editing and printing the first issue.

When an educated woman with noble aspirations and a clearly defined purpose sets about her work she is irresistible. The aggressiveness which would not be tolerated in a man is, through the charm of her sex, accepted at her hands as not only apposite but indispensable. This is where a good deal of her power lies, and where we have strong indications of her fitness for missionary work. In this handsome and artistic magazine of yours ... I perceive you with the lamp and broom in your hand visiting the dark and unswept corridors of our hearts and of society, and can see in advance how benign and elevating the results in the near future. Failure in your case seems to be impossible; for, surely, your publication will be a welcome visitor to every chimney-corner and educated coterie in the land. Both young and old will consider its well-stocked, well-printed and well-edited pages a public boon.

McCarroll provided three essays and two poems for *Humanity and Health* during his brief connection. Some appeared posthumously in the magazine's third and fourth issues (May and June). The poems included the previously published "Meum and Teum" and what was likely his last poem, "The Missing Link." The latter presents through images some of the "scientific" (inductive) thinking and social philosophizing that characterized his later essays.

All essences are under lock and key;
Yet, comprehend one atom through and through,
And Nature holds no secret then from thee,
For in that atom thou hast found the clew.

However varied things may be in name
Do they themselves a difference express?
Or does their seeming not to be the same
Come simply to our inner consciousness?

Behold that mighty octopus, the Sea,
Whose flowing arms are twined around the globe,
Does it involve a greater mystery
Than the dew-spangle of the lily'd robe?

In opposites all things appear arrayed,
Yet how harmoniously are they bound up;
How deftly half in light and half in shade
The Earth lies like an acorn in a cup.

But we so long have worn our self-wrought chains
That in the dust our finer sense lies prone;
Nor dream we that whatever light obtains
Is but the shadow of the Great Unknown.

But though our quest be deep, or near or far,
What travail to unveil the mystic plot
That will not grant one glimpse of what we are
Unless we can suggest what we are not?

And yet that glimpse has ever been revealed
To those who seek it on an open plain –
Who cast their bulrush-spears aside, and wield
The two-edged logic of the heart and brain –

Men whose philosophy is not all eyes –
Men who are modelers in more than clay –
Men who grasp Earth and its sequential skies
In some such sense as we grasp night and day.

With a confidence born of his scientific musings, personal philosophizing, and spiritualistic optimism, McCarroll argued for the essential unity of the Earth and all human experience. In the atom lay "the clew." The pursuit of meaning defeats our normal senses because we don't know where or how to look.

That meaning is mirrored in the twined oceans and answers to all profound human inquiries of the heart and brain. His idea about ether echoes a similar romantic and spiritual sense of unity, which we can seek to understand through metaphors, but must accept as a glimpse of essential matter. The essay "Bread and Butter" blends a kind of cultural anthropology (the known and unknown history of bread) with a historical and pre-historical sweep that acknowledges ages past and forgotten and "the powerful logic and impressive revelations of the Darwinian theory." An aging McCarroll viewed with deep awe the long, known history of humanity and reminds the reader of "the awful space that stretches beyond."

Dr Ella Jennings was not the only woman flattered and charmed by the elderly James McCarroll. A Texas writer, Belle Hunt Shortridge (1858–1893), published a collection of poems entitled *Lone-Star Lights* with the Belford Clarke Company in New York in 1890, in part through McCarroll's agency.[89] The volume included a brief introduction by him – he called the collection a "volume of unusual excellence" that "pulsat[es] with exalted poetic fervor" – and a poem that Shortridge dedicated to him. A wise mentor, he was her "King of Song," her "Sage," her "sweet familiar in the realms of Art." The poem is dated 25 October 1890.

> Thou gentle, helpful friend,
> Whom God hath left to keep watch on this shore.
> Nor let thy sweet life end
> Till thou hast helped a timid wanderer o'er!
>
> O wise, divining heart,
> That comprehendeth great things, yet doth smile
> To see the pale blush start
> That promiseth the full rose, after-while!
>
> Thou friend of Poet, Sage;
> Thou sweet familiar in the realms of Art;
> Thou King of Song thyself,
> With youth perpetual in thy regal heart! –
>
> What can death do to thee,
> But waft thy brightness to a brighter land,
> To shine eternally?
> I kneel, and kiss thy toiling, aged hand.

Belford's Again: Some Final Revelations

The best writing of James McCarroll's final years appeared in *Belford's Magazine*. His first article entitled "A Familiar Mystery" was the lead piece in the May 1889 issue. In it, he took a personal look at the nature of dreams, arguing that "the wild incoherence and the irrational essence of our dreams play a most important part in our physical and mental economy" (810). Because we are never quite unconscious in our dream states, we can learn much from that "wild incoherence." At such times we "revel" in a state of "uncontrolled freedom" that helps to refresh and restore us.

Alluding to mesmerism and spiritualism, he attacked conventional academic science (and debunked the "privileges that attach to 'a degree'") for both its devotion to Lilliputian methods and its insistence on "turning up its nose at the occult" (809). A religious zeal underlay his enthusiasm. Dreams, he argues, take us "to a plane so mysterious and exalted as to set all logic and speculation at defiance" (804). As he had done in the past, he defended spiritualist inquiries, while drawing together diverse supporting references from Louis Agassiz, Professor Zollner ("of Leipsic"), Archbishop Berkeley, Goethe, Coleridge, Swedenborg, and his own experience. Highly rhetorical in its language, the article is socially inclusive, open-minded, allusive, speculative, and anti-institutional. Although Freud was looming in Vienna, gentility was still very much in the saddle for both McCarroll and *Belford's Magazine*; the article does not mention sex in its consideration of dreams and their meanings.

The most important of his final essays was a tribute to his old political friend and belated enemy, John A. Macdonald, who, after an extraordinary career in Canadian politics and two stints as the prime minister of the new dominion, had died in 1891. Having publicly attacked him in *Ridgeway* (1868), McCarroll now sought to replace that criticism with high praise. "Some Social and Other Characteristics of the Late Sir John A. Macdonald" appeared in *Belford's Magazine* in August 1891. McCarroll praised Macdonald's vision for Canada, his statesmanlike adroitness, and his sense of fairness, even when dealing with his political opponents. However, he could not refrain from recalling his old grievance and calling attention to services he himself had rendered on John A.'s behalf.

First, he recognized that the "charge of insincerity and a reckless making of promises" was often levied against John A. in the years before the Civil Service Act was put in place. While describing occasions in which Macdonald

BELFORD'S MAGAZINE.

VOL. II. MAY, 1889. No. 12.

A FAMILIAR MYSTERY.

STARTLING as the proposition may appear at first sight, it can be asserted with some degree of reasonableness that for nearly one-third of its existence the whole human family is the victim of a most pronounced and incurable species of insanity! From the harmlessness of the affliction, however, and the frequency and regularity of its recurrence, we accept it as simply a peculiar feature of our normal condition; but that it means infinitely more than this may be deduced from the fact that, upon adequate investigation, it will be found to involve not only one of the most benign provisions of nature, but a condition indispensable to the continuance of the harmonious relations that obtain between mind and body—nay, more, to the very maintenance of life itself.

The mind or soul *per se* is, I venture to believe, never unconscious for even a single moment. This would seem to be a foregone conclusion, from the fact that its consciousness is its life, and that any lapse here would be tantamount to absolute extinction. The mere circumstance of its deserting, from time to time, the outposts of our physical being, and abandoning the citadel of reason itself, affords no conclusive evidence of its not being active in its own separate domain, so to speak. Overtaxed by its drudgery in the workshop of the brain, it is constrained to lay down periodically all the implements of its material craft, and to seek refuge and recuperation in a state of existence intangible to physics.

In the depths of the most profound slumber, or those of trance, it seems only possible for the spirit to relieve itself of its material fetters, or renew its jaded energies. If influenced in any degree

8.4 First page, *Belford's Magazine* 2, no. 12, May 1889, featuring McCarroll's story "A Familiar Mystery." Microfilm Room, Firestone Library, Princeton University.

belatedly, but genially, delivered on such patronage promises, he was now willing to sympathize with the pressures Macdonald so often faced from aggressive "office-seekers": "That under severe pressure he may have made a promise to an important and importunate supporter that was never fulfilled may be true; but, then, let it be understood that throughout the whole of his long official career he was constantly pursued by a reckless pack of office-seekers, and that it would not be very unreasonable and should not be unexpected if, when run down and brought to bay by one of those sleuth-hounds, he saw no way for it but to clear his head at a single bound with some sort of promise, and trust in God for the rest." McCarroll, of course, never succeeded in "running down" his friend.

Second, he described a difficult political situation in which Macdonald showed "adroit diplomacy" and worked out an amenable solution with McCarroll's help. In 1855 Macdonald was faced with a potential religious controversy among the electorate just as the house was about to be dismissed and an election called. The issue involved the engagement of Lord Viscount Bury, the young secretary to Governor General Sir Edmund Head, to one of Sir Allan MacNab's daughters. MacNab was at the time the prime minister of the Canadas. Although MacNab himself was a Protestant, the daughter in question, was, like his wife, a Catholic. For his part, Macdonald was well known as an Orangeman who was expected to support Protestants over Catholics. The engagement had led to a blow-up between Head and Bury, the former charging Bury with "marrying a Papist."

What would the Catholics of the Canadas think of this charge if it became public? Had Bury quit his position or been fired by Head? As rumours circulated in the press, Macdonald "saw in a twinkling that, election or no election, it would be indispensable to take time by the forelock here." Hoping to avoid a potential controversy and the ire of Catholics, he asked McCarroll for help, "knowing that I had some influence with many of the Catholics of Western Canada, and with the *Catholic Citizen*, the bishop's organ." He carefully studied the letters of Bury and Head, and intervened through the *Catholic Citizen*, "set[ting] matters at rest far and wide among the faithful, should any false version of the viscount's resignation have reached them."

McCarroll completed the article with a couple of charming anecdotes about John A's congeniality and wit, concluding that he would "venture no further explorations at present." His phrasing implied that more of his Canadian political memories might be forthcoming. Now in his mid-seventies, he was aware that he had limited time. Recalling the long journey of his past, he felt an increasing urge to write more about his Canadian years, both out of nostalgia and by way of repairing the damage that his Fenian enthusiasm had generated in the 1860s.

That desire for home underlay a letter he sent to his Peterborough friend William Cluxton in March 1891. The *Peterborough Weekly Examiner*

(19 March 1891) published a summary of it under the title "A Distinguished Veteran." Among other things, McCarroll wanted to make clear that his loyalty to the Queen and colonial Canada was longstanding. The *Examiner* piece read,

Mr Cluxton has received a letter from Mr James McCarroll, who will be well and pleasantly remembered by older residents of the town as a genial gentleman, one of the best flautists of the day, and a litterateur of high order. Mr McCarroll states that he was fighting for the Crown in the disturbance of 1837–38. He was a member of the 7th Provincial Battalion. Mr McCallum [sic] is at present editor of *Belford's Magazine*, New York. He is a graceful and vigorous writer, has won his spurs by literary work of the highest order, and Peterborough people will be interested in knowing that Mr McCarroll is contemplating writing some sketches of Peterborough. Whatever Mr McCarroll undertakes in a literary way, is sure to be well done and worth reading.

While he was indeed a "veteran" of the 7th Provisional Regiment in Peterborough, it would be a stretch to regard his military service as "distinguished," since the regiment did nothing of positive note. However as writer, as editor, as musician, and as a high-spirited Irishman in colonial Canada, he did deserve the kind of recognition granted him by the *Examiner*. It was now important to him to try to review old accounts and reverse whatever negative memories still lingered about his engagement in the Fenian cause. To that end he hoped to write some new "sketches" of his early Peterborough experiences, much as he had done in remembering special moments he had spent with John A. Macdonald during the pre-Confederation years in Toronto. Regrettably, those Peterborough sketches never appeared. Neither did further pieces on John A. or Canadian politics. Pneumonia and time prevailed.

A Sad but Valued End

In late February, McCarroll suffered "a severe attack of the grippe." He struggled to recover his health through much of March, but on 1 April, he was diagnosed with pneumonia. Ten days later he succumbed to what was likely double pneumonia. In an obituary, which appeared in the third issue of *Humanity and Health* (vol. 1, no. 3, May 1892), Ella Jennings remembered the revered "senior editor." The delay in publication, she reported, was the result of two factors. First, on McCarroll's advice, and likely because he worried that his own energies

were waning, the magazine undertook to find a new printer. Then came the
news of his worsening illness, further delaying production of the third issue.

In remarks preceding the obituary, Dr Jennings reported that she and
others had taken part in a six-day vigil at McCarroll's bedside as his condition
worsened and death became inevitable. Still feeling his loss, she provided a
warm tribute to a generous and "all-round man," "a most gifted musician
and poet," and a patient, wise teacher. "His life was a practical sermon, full of
discipline and experience," she wrote. "We heard from his lips so many truths,
and were so much helped by his counsel, his advice, his loving example, that
we feel we have sustained an irreparable loss."

He possessed a deeply religious nature, intensely strong in his faith, hope
and love qualities. He was an optimist of the most pronounced kind; he
always saw the silver lining beyond the cloud; he could see goodness and
beauty all around him. He drew the best from others, because he gave
forth the sweetness that was in his own wholesome soul. He was a man
whose friendship extended beyond the line of duty into that of sacrifice;
he counted it a pleasure to do for others everything that lay in his power,
at all times and under all circumstances.[90]

James McCarroll was buried in Maple Grove Cemetery in Queen's, New
York, on 12 April 1892.[91] Only recently has his unmarked grave been "discovered" in the old Victorian section of the cemetery grounds by the Friends of
Maple Grove Cemetery.[92] The plot was owned by his friend Dr Ella Jennings,
under her married name Ella A.J. Macdonald, and she had made it available
to McCarroll's wife. The grave was likely left unmarked because Julia, bereft
and suddenly alone, left the city before arranging to have a gravestone erected
in her husband's honour. Rather, she returned to Buffalo to be with her son
Henry Dolmage, her daughter, and Henry's family.[93]

The McCarroll plot at St James Cathedral cemetery in Toronto, which
he had purchased in the 1850s, was forgotten at the time of his death. That
arrangement belonged to another life, another wife, and another country. Thus,
in death as in life, James McCarroll lacked a sustaining champion who could
foster a comprehensive view of his life's work and could persist in finding ways
to remember him and to celebrate his life. Dr Jennings and Robert Belford
did what they could in print at the time.

Indeed, McCarroll's obituary in *Belford's Magazine* offered readers a warm
final glimpse of this outgoing and multi-talented Irishman, who has been

– for over a century – lost to students of Canadian literary and cultural history. "Hardly shall we behold a man of such varied gifts and accomplishments, and of such a genial, wholesome nature," read the obituary. He was a bard, a minstrel, and one "of the nobles." He would have appreciated all three encomiums, but the latter perhaps most of all.

In rather grand fashion the tribute began as follows: "the last of the genuine Bards of Inisfodhla, the latest of the Seannachas of Eirinne, who held in their grasp the learning and the poetry of their nation, has left us for Tir-na-n-oge – the land of the young. James McCarroll, the poet, the musician, the inventor and the scholar, has departed." To the end he remained "a true Irish gentleman of the old school" and an "admirable Crichton" to all who knew him well.

It remains now to give him his rightful place in the development of nineteenth-century Canadian poetry and culture.

Appendix A

Letter to Charles Lindsey

Frank Leslie's Publishing House
537 Pearl Street, corner of Elm St
One block from Broadway
New York May 12th 1873

Dear Lindsay,

You must have been astonished at not hearing from me before in relation to your portrait and biography. The reason lies in a nutshell – not having written at once I determined to say nothing until both were published. They appeared to-day, and would have appeared long since were it not for the immense amount of matter which had so long embarrassed our portrait gallery. I hope you will not only recognize a fair likeness in the engraving, but an honest and kindly hand in the letter press. I felt a little annoyed that a biography and portrait that reached me from Hamilton after yours, appeared, through some mistake, before yours. Whillon, or something like that is the gentleman's name. He is a Canadian M.P. However, you are now afloat as you will perceive by the Chimney Corner, and let me say, that you will find your way into every civilized land on the face of the habitable globe – so enormous is the circulation of this journal.

I have been in this office for some time now, and filling, you may be assured, no very secondary position. You may form some idea of our establishment

Frank Leslie's Publishing House
537 Pearl Street, corner of Elm St.
one Block from Broadway,

New York May 12th 1873

Dear Lindsay

You must have been astonished at
not hearing from me before in relation to your
portrait and biography. The reason lies in a nutshell.
— not having written at once I determined to say
nothing until both were published. They appear
to-day, and would have appeared long since
were it not for the immense amount of matter
which had so long embarrassed our portrait
gallery. I hope you will not only recognize a
fair likeness in the engraving, but an honest
and kindly hand in the letter press. I felt a little
annoyed that a biography and portrait that reached
me from Hamilton. after yours, appeared, through
some mistake, before yours. Whitton, or something
like that is the gentleman's name, He is a Canadian
M. P. However, you are now afloat as you will
perceive by the Chimney Corner; and let me
say, that you will find your way into every

civilized land on the face of the habitable
globe — so enormous is the circulation of
this journal

I have been in this office for some time
now, and filling, you may be assured, no
very secondary position. You may form some
idea of our establishment when I assure you
that we have the largest engraving one in the
world, and that, as I am informed, we keep
forty power presses running day, and night
throughout the year.

You will, I am sure, be glad to learn that
I am quite comfortable, and that I am at last
far from being absolutely penniless. In fact,
although, on my first arrival here, I had some
hard tussles, I have succeeded in clearing the
road before me, and aided by my own right
hand only.

I should like to get a few more Canadian
selfmade men. Name some worthy persons with
whom you would like to be associated. Write
to me, and tell me how you like what I have
done, and believe me.

Most faithfully yours,

M. Carroll.

when I assure you that we have the <u>largest engraving one in the world</u>, and that, as I am informed, we keep forty power presses running day and night throughout the year.

You will, I am sure, be glad to learn that I am quite comfortable, and that I am <u>at last</u> far from being absolutely penniless. In fact, although, on my first arrival here, I had some hard tussles, I have succeeded in clearing the road before me, and aided by my own right hand only.

I should like to get a few more Canadian selfmade men. Name some worthy persons with whom you would like to be associated. Write to me, and tell me how you like what I have done, and believe me,

Most faithfully yours,

McCarroll

Appendix B

James Moylan, Editorial, *Canadian Freeman*, 14 May 1868

The sentiments which find expression in the columns of this last named journal, are, unexceptionably, the most atrocious and diabolical that we ever saw published.[1] In no other country of the civilized world would the abomination be tolerated. There is no subject too sacred, no personage too venerable or exalted, by sanctity of life or dignity of character and position, to escape the coarse and defamatory malevolence of the lewd and dissolute creature, who – after having made Canada too hot for himself by debauchery and every species of rascality – now so worthily fills the editorial chair of the 'Fenian Volunteer.' This person, after having assigned reasons for the murder of Mr McGee, which have no other foundation than the prompting of his own filthy and impure mind, enters upon the vindication of [Patrick] Whelan, urges the creation of a fund for his defence, and threatens Sir John A. Macdonald and sundry journalists in Canada with 'swift and certain destruction' should 'a hair of Whelan's head be hurt.'

It is with reluctance and loathing we refer to this alleged apostate Catholic, this ex-secretary of the Peterborough Orange Lodge, this rampant Tory whilst living on the good things of office in Canada. He is now the dastardly defamer of Thomas D'Arcy McGee in his grave; and, to our knowledge, and that of hundreds in Toronto, this self-same 'Terry Finnegan' was the most abject sycophant and toady to the late member from Montreal West until all hope of being reinstated in office died away in his breast. Then it was that he turned against the man he professed to admire and esteem. Then he began to pour forth the torrents of abuse and slander – of which 'The Fenian Volunteer' furnishes such unstinted measure, against one who had incurred the displeasure of many of his friends, and offended his political colleagues by his persistent efforts to serve the very ingrate who now seeks to defile his ashes. Of a piece with the treatment of the late Mr McGee has received from the quondam 'Gauger' of Toronto, is the deep and base ingratitude which Sir John A. Macdonald is experiencing at his hands.[2]

We have overcome our repugnance to advert to the 'Fenian Volunteer' and its worthy editor, for a two-fold purpose. First, to let the readers of that most respectable! sheet know something of the character and antecedents of the individual from whom they draw their newspaper inspirations, and who aims to shape and direct their views upon matters of the most vital importance. We would simply ask these people, can they have confidence in the sincerity of the person who supplies to them their weekly intellectual food? Can they bring themselves to believe that an ex-Orangeman, a violent Tory partizan, an extreme anti-Fenian, whilst a resident in Canada, could have so suddenly and completely changed his sentiments as he professes to have done in the columns of the 'Fenian Volunteer'? Those who know him well would say, 'Habet faenum in cornu,' – the expression the Romans applied to a wicked ox, of which there was need to beware; 'He has hay on his horn.'[3]

They would, further, considering his base ingratitude to poor McGee, and his heartless strictures since his assassination, say with Cicero, 'Ingratus animus odio damnatus rit' – 'an ungrateful mind should be condemned to the hatred of all men'; or with Syrus – 'Omne dixeris maledictum cum ingratum hominem dixeris,' – 'You will have mentioned every curse when you mention an ungrateful man.' But enough of the loathsome subject.

In the second place, we refer to the 'Fenian Volunteer,' as a specimen brick of that class of publications, to show that if the assassination of Mr McGee be attributed by any portion of the press in Canada and the United States to Fenianism, the views and utterances of such journals leave no other alternative. If then the Brotherhood – jealous of whatever good name and fame they may lay claim to – desire to escape the odium and obloquy which their organs are laboring to fix upon the organization, in connection with the murder of Mr McGee, they must promptly and distinctly repudiate and disavow all concurrence in the views published by such sheets as the 'Fenian Volunteer,' otherwise they will be held by the civilized world morally responsible in that they approve of the assassination and sympathize with the assassin. Has Fenianism the hardihood to brave this issue?

Notes

Introduction

1 *Irish Canadian*, April 1892.

2 Davin (1843–1901) was an Irishman and journalist, born into a Catholic family in Kifinane. He had recently immigrated to Canada from England where he had converted to Protestantism. In Canada he sought to hide his roots as an orphan and Catholic.

3 Mount, *When Canadian Literature Moved to New York*, 138.

4 *Irish Canadian*, April 1892.

5 Ibid.

6 Ibid.

7 Obituary – Editorial Department, *Belford's Magazine* 9 (June 1892), 137–8. This affectionate remembrance may have been written by either Robert Belford, the magazine's owner who had been a friend of McCarroll's from their Toronto days, or his New York friend Charles Lotin Hildreth. *Inisfodha* is Gaelic for long island; *seanachai* is Gaelic for traditional storytelling.

8 *Irish Canadian*, April 1892.

9 Quoted in the *Irish Canadian* from the *Hamilton Times* (28 December 1864).

10 The only exceptions are his numerous letters in the Customs Department files, written from the various ports at which he served. McCarroll's handwriting is clear and steady.

11 *Selections from Canadian Poets* included seven McCarroll poems. Dewart's brief biographical note about him suggests that he did not know him personally.

12 Many of McCarroll's poems in the *Leader* appeared under his own name but he also used several pseudonyms; in fact, he seemed to delight in the playful

use of pseudonyms. Consider, for instance, his use of "Professor Pike, UCD" in the *Toronto Daily Leader*.

13　The *Peterborough Daily Examiner* (18 December 1885). The article was no. 23 in the series. Although its author remained unidentified through the series, it is possible that it was Edward Hartley Dewart who had long-standing connections with the Peterborough area and a deep interest in poetry in Canada.

14　See Charles Lotin Hildreth's introduction to McCarroll's *Madeline and Other Poems*.

15　Charles Lindsey's name was often spelled "Lindsay." I have opted here for the spelling used in the *Dictionary of Canadian Biography*, vol. 13.

16　See *Susanna Moodie: Letters of a Lifetime* (1985) and *Susanna and John Moodie: Letters of Love and Duty* (1993).

17　Nickinson withdrew his advertising from the *Daily Leader* and fired off a number of letters to various city newspaper editors listing his objections to the detailed but, to his mind, unfair criticism levelled at his company and some of its actors. Many of the company claimed to be deeply wounded by the anonymous reviewer's critical arrows.

18　Patrick O'Neill has studied the record of Daniel Morrison's work as drama critic for the *Daily Leader*. O'Neill, however, did not know about McCarroll or his early connection with Lindsey's paper and their mutual interest in improving the level of theatre and music criticism in the city. In fact, O'Neill forthrightly admitted that he was puzzled by the distinct change of tone that he detected in Morrison's reviews during and after 1854.

19　See Jenkins, "Poverty and Place."

20　The Finnegan letters appeared sporadically from 1861 to 1865. They number more than fifty in all; however, the final letters that appeared in *Pick* in 1865 have been lost.

21　A rare book now, *The Letters of Terry Finnegan* was published in Toronto in 1864 by the Toronto News Company.

22　The *Grumbler* had runs in 1858–61, 1863–65, and 1867.

23　Only five issues of the *Latch-Key* (1863, 1864) have survived, while no issues of the *Pick* have been located.

24　William A. Foster was a young Toronto lawyer with a penchant for both humorous and serious writing. He later became a leading member of the Canada First Movement after Confederation. He was a close friend of Henry Morgan.

25　I was at work on the biography of Catharine Parr Traill for volume 12 of the DCB at the time.

26　I count David Wilson, Chris Raible, and William Jenkins among my most valuable research colleagues. Janet Friskney has been my loyal and creative researcher over most of the time I have worked on McCarroll's life.

27 With his first family – Ann and their four daughters – in Canada, there is some evidence of a normal family life, but there were also charges from his adversaries that he was licentious and hard drinking. That he left his family behind when he moved to Buffalo is still more problematical, his own financial problems notwithstanding, because Ann was very ill at the time. Unfortunately, no reminiscences have been found to throw light on these circumstances. Nor is there much evidence to provide perspective on his relationship with his second wife, either in Toronto (where they may have met) or in Buffalo or New York City.

28 In 2015 Carl Ballenas and Helen Day contacted me about an unmarked grave at Maple Grove Cemetery in Queens, New York. By comparing outdoor evidence with the cemetery's indoor records, they suspected they had found James McCarroll's resting place, but they knew little at the time about who he was. Since then, we have worked together both to confirm the gravesite and to search out many fresh details about McCarroll's life and death in New York.

29 Letters from Oliver Wendell Holmes to McCarroll, addressed to him at *Watson's Art Journal*, turned up for sale on the Internet and led me to that source.

Chapter One

1 Connaught (the anglicization of Connacht) includes the five counties of Roscommon, Leitrim, Sligo, Galway, and Mayo. As a province it contains the largest number of Celtic or Gaelic speakers in the country.

2 Kiberd, "Introduction" to McGahern's *Love of the World: Essays*, xv.

3 Henry Morgan was the leading cultural and political biographer in colonial Canada prior to Confederation.

4 Morgan gave McCarroll an extensive and well-informed treatment in his short biography. See *Sketches of Celebrated Canadians* (1862). Beginning with praise for McCarroll's many literary and musical talents, Morgan's description is the fullest source of information about his early life and was likely supplied to him by McCarroll himself. It was a particularly useful resource for "biographers" writing about McCarroll later in the nineteenth century.

5 Item 302, "Upper Canada Sundries." Robert McCarroll reported in his application that he served in the Leitrim Militia as bandmaster for twenty-one-and-a-half years.

6 I have found no information about the ship in which the McCarrolls crossed from Ireland to Canada

7 Robert McCarroll received a grant of one hundred acres in Emily Township (Newcastle District) – south half, 14, 19. The land grant was located to the north and west of Peterborough, but it held little appeal for either father or son.

8 Robert vanishes from the Peterborough-Cobourg area soon after he and his son abandoned the idea of a music academy in the early 1830s. The only advertisement for the school appeared in the *Cobourg Star* (14 February 1832). In a later biographical note about James McCarroll found in an essay entitled "Men of Irish Blood Who Have Attained Distinction in American Journalism" (*The Journal of the American-Irish Historical Society* 3 [1900]: 71), Michael Edmund Hennesay reported that "His father fell, fighting bravely for the Union, at Antietam." If this stunning account of his death could be verified, including his involvement in the American Civil War, Robert, who was likely born about 1780, would have been a very old soldier at the time. He may, however, have returned to military duty with the Northern army in order to serve as a bandmaster or fife player. The report implies that he left Canada for the United States sometime between the mid-1830s and the outbreak of the Civil War in 1861.

9 On James McCarroll's death certificate (New York, 1892) his mother's maiden name is listed as Kennedy.

10 Father John Corkery, "Some Forgotten Longford Exiles," 217.

11 It is possible that the McCarroll family had both Protestant and Catholic offshoots. The family of Varsay McCarroll settled in the Peterborough vicinity about the same time as James.

12 Why James was born in Longford rather than Leitrim is nowhere accounted for, but it is likely that there was some family connection between Lanesboro(ugh) and Carrick-on-Shannon; both were Protestant militia towns in southern Connaught.

13 In the McCarrolls' advertisement for their music school in *The Cobourg Star* (14 February 1832), they cited Logier and Briscoli as their teachers in Ireland and noted that they had studied with them for five years.

14 Logier lived in the Sackville Street area of Dublin for two periods in the 1820s. He was both famous and controversial for his invention of the Chiroplast, a machine for the correct positioning of the hands while playing the pianoforte, and he wrote several books, including *A System of the Science of Music and Practical Composition* (London 1828). His "scientific" assertions led to much controversy. See the *New Grove Dictionary of Music and Musicians*, 2004 and its earlier edition.

15 The full title of Briscoli's composition is "Three Grand Overtures Entitled The Conversation of Five Nations, Composed for Military Bands, etc." (1810). It highlights the flute. There is no entry on Domenico Briscoli in either edition of *Grove*.

16 See O'Neill, *Irish Folk Music, A Fascinating Hobby* (1910).

17 He became known, at times affectionately and at times with a certain disdain, as "Melody Moore."

18 In addition to Byron and Lord Lansdowne (Henry Petty-Fitz-Maurice, 3rd Marquess of Lansdowne), Moore's career was helped a great deal by Francis Rawson-Hastings, 2nd Earl of Moira. Byron in fact coined the phrase that defined one aspect of Moore's social life – "Tommy loves a Lord." Moore enjoyed the company of the well to do and often entertained at aristocratic mansions and country houses.

19 "To Moore" appeared in the *Peterborough Despatch* on 31 January 1849 and was one of a group of poems belonging to what McCarroll called his "Irish Anthology." Most of these were written in the vernacular – that is, the brogue.

20 Like many people of his time, McCarroll collected autographs of famous people he knew, especially those whom he sought out as correspondents. Moore autographs were part of his collection. In the last two to three years of his life, Moore was in ill health and rendered inactive because of "senility." There is no evidence of McCarroll's letters or of Moore's responses to him in the two-volume *Letters of Thomas Moore*, edited by Wilfred S. Dowden (1964).

21 The omission of "To Moore" from *Madeline* is remarkable. The poem is one of his finest and cleverest lyrics. Its sensual forthrightness is also striking.

22 Moore's sensual and sexual poems appeared under the pseudonym Anacreon. Moore was sometimes called "Anacreon Moore" in order to focus attention on his light, wine-women-and-song lyrics and sad love songs.

23 McGahern, "County Leitrim: The Sky above Us," in *Love of the World*, 19.

24 The novel was published in America as *By the Lake* (2002).

25 Flynn, *History of Leitrim* (1937), 94–5.

26 Ibid.

27 Boyle is a town in the county of Roscommon, located just eight miles from Carrick-on-Shannon.

28 "Captain Rock" was the name used by vigilante groups across Catholic Ireland during these years; the name made a strong impression on Thomas Moore, who read and heard many Captain Rock stories and reports. Such lawless actions usually involved a threatening letter signed by Captain Rock, with the mark of a (crude) drawing of a coffin. So strong was the Rockite presence in western Ireland in the early 1820s that Moore chose to celebrate Rock, granting him heroic stature in his book *Memoirs of Captain Rock* (1824). See also the new edition edited by Emer Nolan (2008). A recent study of Rockite letters by Gibbons, *Captain Rock, Night Errant*, points to "the pre-Famine agrarian disorder"(12) of southern Ireland and the culture of rural terrorism that functioned in part under the umbrella of Captain Rock's name and reputation.

29 The *Roscommon and Leitrim Gazette* called on occasion for the banning of ballad singers (see 19 September 1829), especially in the wake of incidences of local rioting, blaming them for inciting sedition and unrest.

30 "The New Gauger; or, Jack Trainer's Story" appeared in the *Anglo-American Magazine*, vol. 6, beginning in February 1855 and running through seven monthly issues until August.

31 "Rapperies" were men who made up a party of Irish fugitives, dispossessed and inclined to operate and sometimes steal in the night. The term grows out of the Irish "repaire" meaning a short pike. McCarroll's emphasis here is on roguery for roguery's sake rather than on vigilante action rooted in political injustice and vengeful purpose.

32 Susanna Moodie used the word "mania" as in "a Canada mania" rather than "rage" to define the flood of immigrants to Canada during these years (see *Roughing It in the Bush*, chapter 1).

33 It is possible that while James gave music lessons in Peterborough (to the north), Robert McCarroll moved to Cobourg (to the south), the better to offer musical instruction to the larger number of people living near Lake Ontario or "the Front." Peterborough and Cobourg are about forty miles apart and in that period travel between the two towns was irregular and slow.

Chapter Two

1 The McCarroll family included his parents (Robert and [Catherine?] Kennedy), young James, and at least one sister, also likely named Catherine. However, information remains scant on the extent and make-up of his immediate family. No Canadian census records were compiled when they were together as a family unit. There were other McCarroll families in the Peterborough vicinity in the 1830s, for example, the Varsey McCarrolls, but they may have been Irish Catholics. No familial connection has been established between them and Robert McCarroll's family

2 Morgan, *Sketches of Celebrated Canadians*, 757–8.

3 The various Peterborough histories dealing with the nineteenth century (T.W. Poole, C. Pelham Mulvany, F.H. Dobbin, F.M. de la Fosse, and Elwood Jones) mention James McCarroll only in passing, if at all. The broader record offered here is the result of the gathering of snippets of information from disparate sources and linking otherwise unconnected dots of information and community activity together. The results show a young man who eagerly became involved in many aspects of work and play in early Peterborough. Elwood Jones has been particularly helpful in providing suggestions and useful sources.

4 The backwoods are the second tier of townships north of Lake Ontario; the townships closest to the lake were called "the Front." They were settled first and had the readiest access to settlement and trade routes.

5 The *Peterborough Gazette* (18 April 1846) gave the population in 1846 as 2,430.

6 The village of Ashburnham ("the Scotch village") expanded simultaneously with Peterborough on the east bank of the Otonabee. The river was crossed

by scow, canoe, or ferry in the early years, since wooden bridges did not prove durable enough to resist the river's powerful currents and the downward rush of ice breaking up in the spring.

7   Frances Stewart (1794–1872) later wrote a family manuscript (based on her letters home and edited by a daughter) called *Our Forest Home* (1889), while her husband Thomas (1786–1847), a prominent landholder and early settler, served as the first elected member from the Newcastle District in the Upper Canadian House of Assembly. Samuel Strickland (1805–1867) wrote *Twenty-Seven Years in Canada West* (London, 1853) after his sisters had become well known for their accounts of pioneering and settling in Upper Canada: Catharine Parr Traill (1802–1899) wrote *The Backwoods of Canada* (London, 1836) and *Canadian Crusoes* (London, 1852), and Susanna Moodie (1803–1885) wrote *Roughing It in the Bush* (London, 1852) and *Life in the Clearings* (London, 1853). Anne Langton (1804–1893) kept journals that would be edited much later as *A Gentlewoman in Upper Canada* (1950).

8   Peter Robinson, the younger brother of John Beverley Robinson of York (Toronto), led a government-financed immigration of poor Irish settlers to Upper Canada in 1825; many settled in the Peterborough area.

9   McCarroll knew Sam Strickland as a proud, opinionated, and sometimes feisty Tory in Peterborough during the late 1830s. He met Catharine Parr Traill as a fellow writer in Peterborough or Ashburnham in the early 1840s and he would have read Susanna Moodie's poems and stories in the *Literary Garland*, a prominent Montreal magazine (1839–52) to which she became a regular contributor. The Moodies included two of McCarroll's own poems in the *Victoria Magazine* (Belleville), which they co-edited in 1847–48.

10 Raised in the Church of Ireland, McCarroll naturally became an Anglican in Peterborough where he attached himself to St John's.

11 The advertisement appeared in the *Cobourg Star* in February 1832. In this insertion "McCarrol" was spelt with one "l." Such variant spellings are found frequently in nineteenth-century newspapers and letters.

12 The ad was dated 14 February 1832.

13 Ferry boat service on Rice Lake and up the Otonabee River to Peterborough had begun by 1832. Catharine Parr Traill describes her first trip north across Rice Lake, then up the Otonabee River on the *Pem-o-dash* ("this apology for a steamboat") that same year. See *The Backwoods of Canada* (1836), Letter 5, 52.

14 Moodie, *Roughing It in the Bush*, 11.

15 *Cobourg Star*. See note 5.

16 Brief in the Queen's Bench; James McCarrol [*sic*] vs William Lepar Scobell, January 1842, Peterborough Centennial Museum and Archives. Hereafter referred to as Brief. This document offers important details about McCarroll's first decade in Peterborough.

17 William Cluxton, "Reminiscences of Peterborough, 1837–1887," *Daily Review* (Peterborough), 19 June 1887, 1.

18 Young men without families to support often lived in boarding houses, at least until they could afford to buy a home of their own.

19 See de le Fosse's *Centenary History of St John's Church, Peterborough 1827–1927* (1927) and Elwood Jones's *St John's Peterborough: The Sesquicentennial History of an Anglican Parish 1826–1976*. The Episcopal church of Peterborough was formally named St John's in 1881, but the actual church, using that name, was built between 1837 and 1839. Its services on the site began in 1837. For simplicity's sake I refer to the church as St John's in this chapter. Neither de la Fosse nor Jones records any early connection of McCarroll to the church.

20 In the aforementioned legal brief, McCarroll confirms that he served as the choirmaster at St John's Church.

21 James McCarroll's Longford-Leitrim connections may have been a factor in the working relationship between him and the Rev. D'Olier.

22 Jones, *St John's Peterborough*, 26.

23 George Haslehurst was born in New Brunswick. Susanna's maiden name was Haslehurst (Hazlehurst). The White Cottage was located near St John's Church and adjacent to the property of Charles Rubidge.

24 On the marriage list Ann Davis is listed as Anne. The shorter spelling is used here.

25 Dr John Hutchison of Kilcaldy, Scotland, was the first doctor resident in Peterborough. The citizens of Peterborough built his home, now called Hutchison House (270 Brock Street), to keep him with them as their resident doctor. Today it is a living museum and houses the doctor's record books and account ledgers. Those ledgers contain important medical details about James McCarroll and his family.

26 In the brief McCarroll reported that he had served as choirmaster at St John's Church. Cluxton later recalled that he himself had led the choir from 1844 to 1846. Eventually, Cluxton left the Anglican congregation and joined the Methodist church.

27 Jones, *St John's Peterborough*, 30.

28 The Rev. Samuel Armour (1785–1853) was the missionary in charge of the Peterborough-area Anglican community from 1826 to 1833. See Jones, *St John's Peterborough*, 99.

29 Jones, *St John's Peterborough*, 31. Robert J.C. Taylor was the rector of St Johns from 1841 to1852.

30 While he was teaching music and living in Cobourg after 1847, his wife and daughters stayed on in Peterborough, close to Ann's family. He returned often and did his best to keep up his journalistic and social connections in town. Several of his original poems appeared in the *Weekly Despatch* in the late 1840s.

31 De la Fosse, 52. The *Weekly Despatch* succeeded McCarroll's *Chronicle*. In his 1976 history of St John's Church, Jones notes an earlier bazaar and concert that was advertised in the *Cobourg Star* for 7 January 1846. On that occasion it was promised that "the distinguished Violinist Monsieur Blery" would perform. Though the music for the evening might have involved McCarroll, he was not mentioned in the advertisement. But then, no reports about the bazaar have survived in the broken runs of the two Peterborough newspapers of the time, McCarroll's *Chronicle* or its Tory rival, the *Peterborough Gazette*. See also Jones, *Peterborough: The Electric City*, 30. On this occasion in 1850 McCarroll performed with the St John's choir, Cluxton, Taylor, and a newcomer to town, Templeton Brown.

32 See the legal brief (1842).

33 Henry Thomas Strickland (1835–1908) recalled that McCarroll had been one of his early teachers at the Government school (Mulvany, *History of the County of Peterborough*, 397). Henry would likely have been boarding in town. The Traills had sold their bush farm near Lakefield in 1839 and in 1841 were living in Ashburnham (now East City), across the Otonabee River from Peterborough. The Stewarts, who were among the earliest settlers in the area, lived in relative comfort at Auburn, their villa to the north of town and on the east or Douro side of the Otonabee.

34 The Tory element in Upper Canada was first identified as "the Family Compact," especially in the Toronto area. In Peterborough Tory conservatism and loyalty flourished among the wealthier and more influential citizens of middle-class background, a number of whom brought family money and military rank and experience with them from Britain.

35 Articles and editorials in the *Backwoodsman and Sentinel* were unsigned. Hence, it is impossible to know if and when McCarroll wrote for Darcus. It is likely that he joined Darcus in the newspaper's later days, given his commitment to Reform and his desire to see his poems published. By 1841 he was beginning to publish poems in newspapers like the *Christian Guardian*.

36 Messenger and McCarroll preferred the shorter spelling of Peterboro in introducing their newspaper in 1843. How best to spell its name was likely an ongoing debate in the town.

37 As is the case with the *Backwoodsman*, only two issues of McCarroll's *Peterboro Chronicle* have survived. The fire that destroyed the *Chronicle*'s print shop in the summer of 1846 is the likely reason for the loss of two-and-a-half years of weekly publications, hence, of more than one hundred issues.

38 See Poole, *The Early Settlement of Peterborough County*, 34–5 for the list of appointments on 28 December 1838. The list was gazetted in Darcus's *Backwoodsman* on 11 January 1839. Captains for the six companies were J.G. Cowell (sometimes referred to as Major or Colonel Cowell), S.F. Kirkpatrick,

J.C. Boswell, John R. Benson, Thomas Murphy, and A.S. Fraser. Samuel Strickland and George W. Caddy were among the lieutenants appointed. Cowell had been a captain in His Majesty's 1st or Royal Regiment of Foot before immigrating to Canada. During the immediate post-Rebellion period, he was lieutenant colonel of the 2nd Northumberland Militia, a position that gave him clear precedence over Richard Birdsall when the officers of the 7th Battalion were officially announced. He died in 1840 at the age of fifty.

39 Carter-Edwards, "Promoting a 'Unity of Feeling.'" Carter-Edwards kindly shared with me the pay lists of the 7th Battalion, which include McCarroll's name and his rank.

40 Mulvany, *History of the County of Peterborough*, 314.

41 Poole, *The Early Settlement of Peterborough County*, 35.

42 Halkett to Bullock, 29 January 1839. Adjutant General's Office, 1837–39, RG9 1B1, vol. 31, NAC. Halkett urged that ongoing difficulties in the 7th Battalion be cleared up immediately. However, confusion and ill feeling seem to have persisted. In late February Birdsall wrote to officials in Toronto arguing that he had initially trained voluntary members of the battalion in good faith and at "my own cost and trouble." He urged them to confirm both his appointment and those of Lieutenant William Shairp and Ensign Fortune, "two active intelligent and meritorious officers." By 17 March 1839, Shairp was an officer serving with the 7th, but Birdsall's petition was overturned while Cowell was in command. As might be expected, Cowell was highly supportive of his men, regardless of evidence of misconduct or abuse of power on their part.

43 RG9 1B1, vol. 31, NAO. The various reports and letters cited here are taken from this file.

44 Captain A.S. Frazer. See Carter-Edwards, "Promoting a 'Unity of Feeling,'" 183–4.

45 Shairp, the son of a prominent British veteran named Major Alexander Shairp, was supported by Lieutenant Sam Strickland of Lakefield, Joe Dunlop, and Lieutenant George W. Caddy, who had recently become Shairp's brother-in-law. Major Shairp, a retired officer living in his Ashburnham villa (Endsleigh Cottage), later sought to bypass the facts of his son's heavy drinking and conspicuous misbehaviour. He wrote to the adjutant general of the province asking that William be considered for Colonel Alex MacDonnell's other regiment (the 4th), should the 7th Provisional be disbanded during or after its six-month service. MacDonnell was, according to Major Shairp, "a good strict officer"; his letter argued that his son, a lad of "good" family, would greatly benefit from firmer control. Hot-headed and hard-drinking, William Shairp was not an easy fellow to keep in line.

46 Susanna Moodie reported on the latter duel to her husband, who was away on military duty with the Queen's Own Regiment in the Niagara District. In

her letter, dated 6 March 1839, she describes Cowell as the "gallant" captain of the battalion (*Letters of Love and Duty*, 131). J.G Cowell and Edward Duffy (Duffie) had been partners in a Peterborough brewery, but the partnership had broken up. Duffy served as a justice of the peace in 1838–39 but left the area soon after these unsettling events; he was alleged to have mismanaged the funds in his role as treasurer of the new Peterborough Courthouse and Jail. Likely he had Reform leanings. His wife was the former Jane Crawford, daughter of a well-placed Anglo-Irish emigrant, Lieutenant Colonel Walter Crawford, who would later build a villa, Glenville Cottage, in Peterborough.

47 Carter-Edwards, "Promoting a 'Unity of Feeling,'" 186. Darcus is quoted in Upper Canada Sundries, vol. 220, p. 121.

48 Brief.

49 The *Weekly Despatch* evolved later into the *Examiner*. The *Gazette* was replaced by the long-lasting *Peterborough Review*.

50 Although no records are extant, McCarroll was, according to Moylan, the secretary of the Orange Order in Peterborough at some point during these years. Jones has also noted that he held a position managing local fairs in the Peterborough area.

51 Darcus's letter to Elliott was published in the *Cobourg Star* on 9 October 1839 as the new governor general, Mr Poulett Thomson (Lord Sydenham), was being attacked across the province by Tory editors like Chatterton for his alleged sympathies for Reform. A former grand master of the Orange Order in Londonderry and one-time president of the Prentice Boys of Derry, Darcus urged the Orangemen in Canada to hold to the strictures of the Orange constitution of 1688 that constrained them from following the directives of particular political parties. Elliott, who was a military officer and an elected member of the assembly for Durham, was playing politics in an unsavory way, and Darcus would have none of it. A further image of Elliott as a temperamental and hard-drinking officer while on military duty and a relentless Tory in politics emerges in a John Moodie letter of 22 June 1838 to his wife Susanna (*Susanna and John Moodie: Letters of Love and* Duty, 82–3). Elliott's letters to Darcus also appeared in the *Cobourg Star* on 9 October and in subsequent issues. Elliott accused Darcus of "breeding mischief" by attending a Port Hope meeting at which Elliott had sought to arouse Tory support among local Orangemen.

52 James Moylan became a friend of McCarroll in Toronto and was the editor of a Toronto newspaper, the *Canadian Freeman*. His description of McCarroll appeared in the *Canadian Freeman* in 1868.

53 *Cobourg Star*, 11 January 1843.

54 Poole, *The Early Settlement of Peterborough County*, 50, 53–4, 64.

55 "Peterboro Meeting," *Cobourg Star*, 31 January 1844.

56 Poole, *The Early Settlement of Peterborough County*, 54.

57 Mulvany reports that Darcus later committed suicide.

58 Ormsby, "Francis Hincks," 156.

59 The Rev. H.D. Dunsford.

60 There is no indication of any break in the *Chronicle*'s publishing schedule.

61 Ibid.

62 Ibid., 138.

63 Ibid., 106.

64 Reported in the *Toronto Patriot* (19 December 1843). A Tory paper, the *Patriot* held that the defeat of Baldwin, Hincks, and La Fontaine would be Canada's "salvation" (5 April 1844).

65 *Peterborough Gazette*, 17 October 1845.

66 Dunsford was a man of some wealth as well as religious reputation. In the published list of local donations for the victims of the horrible fires in Quebec, Dunsford gave 2/5 while McCarroll gave 1/5 (*Peterborough Gazette*, 15 August, 1845).

67 The McCarroll column has not survived – only the outraged responses it generated remain.

68 McCarroll was likely experimenting with poems or prose in the Irish vernacular by this time, hoping by means of that style to answer and upset G.

69 Cole, "Peterborough in the Hutchison-Fleming Era, 1845–46," 15.

70 Ibid. Cole writes, "The 1846 *Gazetteer* lists some 30 stores selling dry goods, groceries and hardware, as well as four butcher shops, five bakeries, four chair factories, a woolen mill, carding and fulling machines, 18 shoemakers, 12 tailors and at least two dressmakers who advertised in the newspapers" (5).

71 The lock at Whitla's Rapids on the Otonabee allowed direct access by water to Peterborough from the south. The bridge on Hunter Street (the first wooden bridge had been built about 1827) was a wooden structure that could not withstand the current and ice damage of the Otonabee River in the spring. It collapsed again in the spring of 1846. Hall's railway scheme, which included a bridge over a part of Rice Lake, was completed late in the decade.

72 As his newspaper indicated, McCarroll would insist on spelling Peterborough more economically as Peterboro.

73 Morgan, *Sketches of Celebrated Canadians*, 757.

74 McCarroll contributed at least one poem to the *Literary Garland*, but not as many as might have been expected.

75 See Moodie, *Roughing It in the Bush*, 417–18. Moodie published numerous poems in the *Cobourg Star* in the early 1830s but made her Upper Canadian breakthrough in 1837–38 when several of her patriotic poems, written for Charles Fothergill's *Palladium of British America* (Toronto) in the wake of the 1837 Rebellion violence, caught the eye of publisher John Lovell in Montreal and Lieutenant-Governor Sir George Arthur in Toronto.

76　Moodie had been born a Strickland and could point to her older sisters, Agnes and Elizabeth, who were well known in London literary circles. Five of the six Strickland sisters wrote and were published in the 1820s and 30s.

77　The *Christian Guardian* (17 November 1841). See also *Madeline and Other Poems*, 68.

78　Brown's *An Index to "The Literary Garland"* does not mention this or any other contribution by McCarroll. No explanation exists for his failure to write for the *Literary Garland*.

79　As the first anthology of poetry in Canada, Dewart's volume was a path-breaking collection. McCarroll's seven poems made him the third highest in terms of inclusions, behind Charles Sangster (15) and Alexander McLachlan (10). His poems were "To the Sea," "Autumn," "The Gray Linnet," "Impromptu on a Beautiful Butterfly," "Dawn," "Angels of the Blind," and "The Pearl." Incidentally, Dewart included four of his own poems in the anthology.

80　The poem appeared on Wednesday, 26 July 1843. He did not include this early poem in *Madeline*.

81　Young had a long and distinguished career as a poet, satirist, and dramatist. His friends were among the most famous literary figures of the time including Samuel Johnson, Samuel Richardson, and Alexander Pope, to whom he addressed a poem.

82　Poole, *The Early Settlement of Peterborough County*, 64.

83　Cole, "Peterborough in the Hutchison-Fleming Era, 1845–46," 6.

84　I have found no further reference to Lyman.

85　James Hall ran as the Reform candidate in the 1848 election and won the seat.

86　See *Madeline*, 98–9. The poem was written in the late 1840s and finds salvation in a meek natural response (like the "little flowers") and in God's beneficent succor. The fourth verse reads:

> And then I thought, in this fair land of ours
> How few who feel affliction's chastening rod,
> Are like the poor, pale, thirsty little flowers,
> With their meek faces turned towards their God –

87　Kate McCarroll was born in Peterborough on 11 August 1843 (see Dr Hutchison's records).

88　His two most prominent pseudonyms were CRUX and FAIR PLAY.

89　The issue appeared on 18 March 1847.

90　The *Weekly Despatch* appeared on Thursday while the *Gazette* was published on Saturday; the lag between dates allowed for the back and forth attacks.

91　The *Weekly Despatch*, 7 April 1847. None of the figures alluded to have been identified.

92　Such an allusion is lost since so few issues of the *Chronicle* have survived.

93　See chapter 4 for his angry response to Northey's dismissal of the Irish as an unworthy, impoverished people, despite their evident needs.

94 It is possible that Northey was alluding to John Darcus who had turned from Reform journalism to Tory support. But as Darcus's whereabouts after he lost his government position in 1844 are unknown, the reference remains uncertain.

95 *Weekly Despatch*, 29 April 1847.

96 A favourite phrase from Terry Finnegan's letters.

Chapter Three

1 Climo, *Early Cobourg*, 51.

2 The *Canadian Directory* for 1851 reported the population of Cobourg at "about 4,000." The census for 1849 gave the figure of 3,513. Peterborough had a population of 1,906.

3 Advertisement for the newly refurbished Globe Hotel, *Cobourg Star*.

4 Warm or hot drinks such as toddies, brandy, or wine. This Latin phrase was much in use in the nineteenth century both in public houses and in descriptions of such houses in popular novels.

5 Popular songs often sung in glees. The two songs express similar sentiments about the need to be merry in the face of life's challenges and the forces of fate. The first stanza of "Life's a Bumper" reads, "Life's a bumper, fill'd by fate, / Let us, guests, enjoy the treat, / Nor like silly mortals pass / Life as 'twere but half a glass." It is an English song, written by G. Colman with music by Richard Wainwright. "Fill the Bowl" begins, "Then fill the bowl – away with gloom." It's a shortened version of Thomas Moore's "Song: When Time, Who Steals Our Years Away."   .

6 "Molly (Bawn) Astore" was a popular Irish melody, often performed by McCarroll, though his stage-Irish spelling would have been "Molly Asthore." "Auld Robin Gray," "O Nannie, Wilt Thou Gang Wi' Me," and "Kinlock of Kinlock" ("Blow the Wind Southerly") are Scottish songs or jigs that were very popular as instrumentals (for flute, harp, or fiddle) or for group singing (glees).

7 Henry Jones Ruttan (1819–1879) had been taken on at the *Star* by R.D. Chatterton in May 1846. He was the son of Chatterton's influential friend, Henry Ruttan (1792–1857), a former speaker of the Legislative Assembly, the current sheriff of Cobourg (1827–57), and a prominent inventor. Henry's initial editorial challenge was to enlarge the paper to include a supplementary sheet "immediately upon the arrival of each packet from England" (20 May 1846). He served as editor from 1846 to 1855. For Ruttan and other Cobourg historical figures, see Daniel McAllister's pamphlet "Historical Reminiscences of Cobourg" (1903) and Edwin C. Guillet's *Cobourg 1798–1948* (Oshawa, 1948). McAllister would later become the editor of the *Cobourg Sentinal Star* and would publish in that paper the opening chapters of McCarroll's "Black Hawk" in 1861 (see chapter 6).

8 See the *Peterborough Weekly Despatch* (11 November 1847).

9 Climo, *Early Cobourg*, 116.

10 Guillet, *Cobourg 1798–1948*, 117.

11 Weller died in 1863 while serving his third one-year term as Cobourg's mayor.

12 The Hill property slopes down to Lake Ontario. Grandly built on the west side of the town (although the more exclusive and "established" Cobourg families lived on the east side) by James Grieve for a wealthy citizen named Wentworth Tremaine, it became the home of Weller's large family for many years. It later became the home of Nelly Grant Sartoris, daughter of the former American president Ulysses S. Grant, and of the daughter of Hugh Allen of the Allen Steamship Lines. Originally on Tremaine Street, its address is now Monk St. It became the home of the Sisters of St Joseph's Orphanage; now it is called Villa St Joseph Retreat and Ecology Centre (Guillet, *Cobourg 1798–1948*, 17).

13 Clark would later become the solicitor general for the Canadian Pacific Railway.

14 John Albro was a cousin of James Hall of Peterborough.

15 James Hall introduced the controversial Rebellion Losses Bill for citizens of Canada East (Quebec) in the Legislative Assembly. The bill was highly contentious and outraged Tories in both provinces. After it was passed into law, violence broke out in several quarters, directed in large part at Lord Elgin, the governor general of Canada, who signed it into law.

16 Only two issues of the *Newcastle Courier* have survived; both belong to the months after McCarroll resigned as editor. On occasion, however, his columns were quoted at length in the *Peterborough Weekly Despatch*; thus a few can still be accessed.

17 Hall #13 stood originally on the site of what is now the Masonic Hall on Reid Street.

18 The Dunsford reference is an odd inclusion since the *Gazette* was by then out of business; however, printing costs were likely still a competitive issue.

19 No review of the third Authurson concert has been found.

20 McCarroll was particularly devoted to Italian composers like Rossini, Donizetti, and Bellini. Giovanni Pacini (1796–1867) was another favourite; he composed seventy-four operas in his lifetime.

21 *Cobourg Star*, 20 March 1850.

22 Weller's stables and his carriage works were adjacent to the Globe Hotel.

23 Thomas Pope Besnard (1808–1878) has been dubbed by one historian "the mystery man" of early Toronto theatre. Born in Cork, Ireland of a well-to-do family that had fallen on hard times, he came to Canada after first immigrating to Australia. For about six years he was prominent in Toronto as an actor and promoter (manager lessee), of the Lyceum and then the Royal Lyceum Theatre. In the newly built Royal Lyceum he worked closely with the company

of John Nickinson. In 1847 he toured his one-man show, "An Hour in Ould Ireland," to towns like Port Hope and Cobourg. That show and others of a similar stripe became his staple performance pieces and made him popular on theatre stages and in saloons and music halls in Canada West. One Australian newspaper described the piece as "a national entertainment, consisting of recitations, songs, and anecdotes, illustrative of Irish customs, peculiarities, and eccentricities." See O'Neill, "Thomas Pope Besnard."

24 A popular farce of the day.

25 *Cobourg Star*, 6 June 1849.

26 For instance, Terry Driscoll letters appeared in the *Cobourg Star* on 5 September, 10 October, and 7 November 1849.

27 George Cruikshank (1792–1878) was the most famous English caricaturist of the day. A prolific artist, he had illustrated two of Dickens's early books. Thomas Hood (1799–1845) was a poet, author, and humorist who wrote for several prominent London magazines, including *Punch*. Early in his career he specialized in poetic caricature and incessant punning. In the 1840s McCarroll wrote a poem in the manner of Hood, which he entitled "An Easy Lesson in Humor and Versification" (*Madeline*, 287–9). He may have written it in honour of Hood soon after his death in 1845. Certainly, the poem is awash in puns.

28 In May 1851 McCarroll was appointed the collector of customs at Port Stamford or the suspension bridge near Niagara Falls.

29 *Victoria Magazine* (January 1848), 120.

30 See note 12.

31 *Cobourg Star*, May 1848.

32 Likely Henry Grattan (1746–1820), the Dublin-born Irish politician who opposed the Act of Union in 1800 and argued consistently for Catholic emancipation years before the rise of Daniel O'Connell. He was elected to the United Parliament in 1805 and, with another MP, Sir John Coxe Hippisley (1748–1825), tried by means of several published letters to convince the English to find a way to integrate the Catholic (and papal) view into a united England with a secure Protestant ascendancy. Admiral Lord (Cuthbert) Collingwood (1748–1810) was Nelson's second in command and famously took over the leadership of the British navy at Trafalgar upon Nelson's sudden death in battle. Of the four figures, Wolfe Tone (1763–1798) was the most influential in McCarroll's lifetime. He helped to form the Society of the United Irishmen in 1791 and led the Irish forces, hoping to remove the English from Ireland in the Great Rebellion of 1798. Though he died in prison before he could be executed as a rebel and traitor, he later became known as "the father of Irish Republicanism" to the leaders of the Rebellion of 1848. Tone saw England as "the never failing source of all our political evils."

33 With so few surviving issues of the *Peterboro Chronicle* to examine, it is difficult to know how many poems he self-published there between December 1843 and July 1846. So too it is impossible to know what poems he included in the *Newcastle Courier* in early 1848. His earliest known published poems appeared in 1841.

34 Another example of positive reader response is found in Toronto in 1860. McCarroll's "Kitty Fitzgibbon" in the *Toronto Daily Leader* (16 January) received a long poetic reply and commendation from "Whitby." See "On Reading 'Kitty Fitzgibbon'" (18 February 1860).

35 English-born Rhoda Ann Page (1826–1863) lived in Hamilton Township and wrote poetry for various newspapers and periodicals, usually under her initials R.A.P. Her only book, printed by the *Cobourg Star*, was entitled *Wild Notes from the Backwoods* (1850). Her father Thomas edited the *Newcastle Farmer*. George Coventry (1793–1870) was an English-born journalist, poet, and antiquarian who had written about William Lyon Mackenzie and Navy Island before becoming a clerk and secretary for William Hamilton Merritt in St Catharines. He came to Picton to edit the *Prince Edward Gazette* (1846–47) and in 1849 settled in the Cobourg area, becoming a custom's broker. Thus, for two years at least, he was a rival poet to McCarroll and someone he occasionally worked with at the custom's office. In 1857 Coventry returned to his work as a custom's broker in Cobourg. During his stay in the area he contributed prose and poetry to both the *Cobourg Star* and the *Cobourg Sentinel*.

36 The latter poem also later appeared under the title "Paddy Blake's 'Pinnance.'" See *Madeline and Other Poems*, 308.

37 The absence of an entire year (1848–49) of the *Cobourg Star* is a disappointment; however, it was heartening a few years ago to discover that a number of the missing years of the newspaper in the 1840s had belatedly been microfilmed and made available to researchers.

38 It may have been that McCarroll thought both poems were outdated by the late 1880s.

39 Sir James Bruce (1811–1863) was the 8th Earl of Elgin and the 12th Earl of Kincardine. A generation earlier, his famous father had brought the Elgin Marbles to England from Greece. Lord Elgin, as he was called in Canada, served as governor general of the colony from 1847 to 1853. His wife, Lady Mary Lambton, was the daughter of Lord Durham, the author of the Durham Report on the governance of the Canadas (1838).

40 Sir Allan Napier MacNab (1798–1862) was a Canadian-born veteran of the War of 1812 (at the age of fourteen) and the Rebellion of 1837. He was knighted in 1838 for his services to the Queen. As a lawyer in Hamilton and a land speculator, he made his fortune and built his home, which he named Dundurn Castle, before entering politics as a Tory. He would serve as the

premier of Canada from 1854 to 1856 and helped to finance the Great Western Railroad (Hamilton to Niagara Falls) along with Samuel Zimmerman of St Catharines. He was the leading Tory in the 1840s and 1850s, and received close support in his hostility to the Reformers from men like Henry Sherwood, Samuel Zimmerman, Prince and William Henry Boulton.

41 See chapter 1 for the full text of the poem.

42 The novels and stories of several popular Irish writers were available to North American readers either in book form or in newspapers. Among the writers McCarroll would have been reading were Gerald Griffin, William Carleton, the Banin brothers, Samuel Lover, and Samuel Lever.

43 A number of McCarroll's poems bore the descriptive tag "From the Irish Anthology" when they first appeared in newspapers or magazines. Clearly, he saw this group of vernacular poems as a singular part of his poetic oeuvre, though he never managed to publish them as a separate text. In *Madeline* he simply grouped many of these poems under the heading "Humorous" (267–321).

44 "Ah! Thin, take down that image that hangs near the althar" is the first line of a humorous poem later entitled "Paddy Blake's 'Pinnance.'" See *Madeline*, 308–9.

45 The poem in the *Cobourg Star* uses "iv" while in *Madeline* the preposition becomes "ov." This is one of the few "Irish Anthology" poems that use "iv" in presenting the Paddy vernacular.

46 In addition to Hall, Butler's chosen references were Ebenezer Perry, Thomas Scott, and A. Jeffreys. His petition was dated 30 November 1849. Ebenezer Perry was the town's most long-standing and successful businessman. His home, Woodlawn, on Division Street was one of the most impressive private residences in Cobourg. It is now a fashionable hotel. In addition to his store and his work in and on behalf of the harbour, he was on the building committee for Victoria College.

47 *Cobourg Star*, 26 December 1849.

48 Appendices to the Journals of the Legislative Assembly for 1850 and 1851 do not show McCarroll's promotion to acting collector and collector. Rather he remains listed as a landing waiter, though it is necessary to take note of his speedy progress through the ranks and his emergence as a sort of trouble-shooter for the Customs Department (1850 – Vol. 9, No. 1 A–Z Appendix C; No. 33 and 1851 – Vol. 10, Appendix B, No. 35).

49 Thomas Scott was the postmaster of Cobourg and one of the town's most prominent public men. Scottish-born, he had come to Cobourg as a merchant; the firm of Strong and Scott, dealers in dry goods, hardware, groceries, and crockery, was located on King Street. He died in 1866.

50 D'Arcy E. Boulton came to Cobourg in 1837, setting up as a lawyer in his uncle's (George Strange Boulton) office.

51 *Cobourg Star*, 17 July 1850.

52 See Customs Department papers, "Cobourg 1850," RG 16A Vol. 50.

53 Ibid.

54 See note 37 for Coventry. Thomas Eyre was a long-standing Cobourg merchant and businessman who lived in nearby Hamilton Township. He would serve as the clerk of the Division Court in 1857 but died a year later. He acted as one of McCarroll's two suretes in Cobourg just before he was appointed collector of Port Stamford in 1851.

55 See above for Customs Department papers, McCarroll to Dunscombe, 11 May 1850.

56 *Cobourg Star*, 15 October 1851.

Chapter Four

1 William Weller and Thomas Eyre had agreed to be his sureties while he was still serving at Cobourg. Those guarantees would suffice for a time, but McCarroll was required to provide two local sureties once he had settled in Port Stamford.

2 For McMicken, see the *Dictionary of Canadian Biography*, vol. 12.

3 Merritt, who lived in St Catharines, had gained fame for his financial commitment to the original Welland Canal. In 1851 he was the chief commissioner of public works for Canada West and one of the wealthiest men in the area.

4 Famous for its awning-covered balconies, cosmopolitan service, and luxurious facilities, the three-storey hotel had opened in 1835. It burned to the ground in 1895 and its successor opened in 1905. The local financier Samuel Zimmerman had bought the hotel in 1848 and "renovated and upgraded" it. See *Dictionary of Canadian Biography*, vol. 8.

5 Charles Ellet Jr was the engineer who built the pedestrian bridge while John Augustus Roebling took over the project in 1851, overseeing the construction of the upper or railway level of the bridge. Ellet left the project after a legal dispute over the control of tolls on the pedestrian bridge. After 1855 the completed bridge would serve three different railroad lines, all of which used different gauges. Samuel Zimmerman was one of the contractors employed to build the structure.

6 Ferries operated at St Catharines, Chippewa, and Niagara Falls.

7 Chippewa is four miles west of Drummondville (Niagara Falls), Canada West.

8 Once the bridge was opened in 1848, the Suspension Bridge Company collected passenger tolls. However, the Canadian government was slow to open a customs office, in part because the bridge was closed for an extended period due to legal disputes.

9 J. Hemphill had been the surveyor for the port of the Niagara ferry prior to his appointment as acting collector at Port Stamford.

10 A number of McCarroll's letters to Bouchette and Francis Hincks at customs headquarters are found in the National Archives (Library Archives Canada [LAC], Port Stamford file, RG 16, Series A. Vol. 335 (1851–53). They contain a great deal of information about McCarroll's struggles at Port Stamford and his changing attitude to his work at the bridge.

11 Samuel Zimmerman owned most of the land around Port Stamford and was planning to develop it at this time.

12 Letter to R.S. Bouchette in Toronto, 8 May 1851 (LAC).

13 Letter to R.S. Bouchette, 27 May 1851 (LAC).

14 Samuel Zimmerman was an active Tory and had previously supported the candidacy of his agent, Gilbert McMicken, as collector at the bridge. Francis Hincks would appoint McMicken to replace McCarroll after he was transferred to Port Credit. McMicken would later figure in McCarroll's life when he moved to Buffalo to join the Fenians there.

15 John Richardson used the adjective to describe Baldwin's government (*St Catharines Constitutional*).

16 Nora Lamb (1844–1911) was a singer of local note who occasionally performed with James McCarroll. She later married Henry R. Morton of St Catharines. Anna Lamb did not marry. She died in 1903 at the age of sixty-seven.

17 At this point McCarroll would have been in correspondence with the ailing Thomas Moore, who died in 1852.

18 McCarroll had two poems published in *Graham's American Monthly Magazine*, one in 1851 and the second in 1852. His poetry had also appeared in the *Christian Guardian, Canadian Gem, Victoria Magazine*, and the *Home Journal* in Canada West.

19 *St Catharines Evening Journal*, 28 August 1851. Lamb described CRUCIBLE as "our correspondent."

20 *St Catharines Constitutional*, 3 September 1851.

21 Lamb's salary was 75 pounds in 1851. By 1854 it had risen to 125 pounds.

22 The letter, written by "Denis Finnegan," was dated 23 September 1851 and appeared in the *Cobourg Star* under the title "From Our Niagara Correspondent" on 15 October 1851.

23 A thousand people paid at least $3 a ticket to attend the two sold-out Jenny Lind concerts in Toronto (Kallmann, "Frederick Griebel," 102–3).

24 Lamb described Jenny Lind's "forte" as "the Echo song and foreign operas," along with Swedish folksongs (*Evening Journal*, August 1851).

25 The *St Catharines Constitutional*, 26 May 1852.

26 Born in Limerick, Kate Hayes travelled with her mother and was often compared to the scrupulously moral Jenny Lind. Given the dubious reputation associated with a life on the stage for women, such behavioural credentials were essential in an unmarried female performer.

27 *St Catharines Constitutional*, 5 May 1852.

28 The town hall seated six hundred. At $1 a ticket, the proceeds could not meet the $700 requirement.

29 *St Catharines Evening Journal*, 22 July 1852.

30 *St Catharines Constitutional*, 21 July 1852.

31 No reviews have been found for either concert.

32 Griebel was often billed as a student of "the famed De Beriot." Kallmann, "Frederick Griebel," 102–3. His friendship with Dr Macklem was an important factor in his decision to stop touring and to take up teaching in Canada, first in Drummondville (Niagara Falls), then in Hamilton (1853), and finally in Toronto (1855). McCarroll became a close friend of Griebel while he was stationed at Port Stamford; likely they first met through Dr Macklem.

33 Kallmann, "Frederick Griebel," 102–3.

34 The Oakville concert took place on 23 June 1853 while the Hamilton concert (as part of the Provincial Exhibition) occurred on 10 October. The Toronto concert (23 August 1855) was a benefit in support of Stephenson House. Here McCarroll, Griebel, and Toronto baritone J.D. Humphreys received top billing. Reviews are lacking for all three concerts.

35 The story later appeared in the *St Catharines' Semi-Weekly Post* (23 November 1858) and was reprinted in several other newspapers across the province.

36 Lamb published his squibs based on quarterly reports to which he as a landing waiter had access. In this instance, he cited receipts from Port Stamford of 1,000 pounds, the port having been "separated for the last ten months from Chippewa." He deemed it highly credible frontier work on Collector McCarroll's part (12 February 1852). Again on 13 May he praised the revenue collection at Port Stamford, citing 750 pounds collected during the first quarter of 1852. Then in July 1852 Lamb noted that receipts at Port Stamford, after only a year of operation, were "equal to those formerly collected at the Bridge, the Ferry and Chippewa together during some periods of the year."

37 McCarroll to Francis Hincks, 15 March 1853.

38 The collector could announce of sale of seized goods after a waiting period of a month.

39 George F. Parsons ran a musical equipment store on St Paul's Street in St Catharines. He planned to set up a photography shop in his store and to bring in equipment from New York State while avoiding the border tax. McCarroll twice confiscated goods in 1851, and both times Parsons paid charges to have his seized goods returned (19 May, 6 December). The department decided that his goods should be returned to him without penalty.

40 McCarroll to R.S.M. Bouchette (commissioner of customs, Quebec) 15 March 1853. Wheaton had attended Hamilton College but had begun selling jewellery as a way of supporting his young wife and family. He claimed ignorance of

border duties and enlisted letters of support and character reference from such figures as Attorney-General Lawrence, President North, Professor Upson, and Mr Cook.

41 The department accepted Wheaton's claim that he was innocent of "any fraudulent intention" (affidavit submitted in September 1852). Bouchette argued that "the young man … makes out a good case for himself" and sought a departmental restitution to Wheaton even as he noted the "The Coll: at Port Stamford may have some objection to this arrangement."

42 McCarroll to Bouchette, 4 February 1853. He acknowledged "the merited severity of your letter" and promised to be "infinitely more cautious" in submitting future reports. It is likely that he assigned the task of completing his accounts to his brother-in-law, John Davis, who was living with his family at the time. In other claims to head office he had sought remuneration for John Davis's services, given the ready help he provided in meeting certain of the collector's duties.

43 McCarroll to Bouchette, 21 July 1851. Samuel Hamlin seems often to have located himself on the Canadian side of the bridge, the better to monitor the movement of his company's stages north of the border. McCarroll had most of his personal contacts with him.

44 Dubinsky, *The Second Greatest Disappointment*, 76–8.

45 McCarroll to Bouchette, 21 July 1851.

46 Ibid.

47 George Hamlin's petition against McCarroll was submitted to the Earl of Elgin and dated 11 October 1852.

48 William Fitch personally delivered Hamlin's memorial to the governor general in Quebec.

49 See the government report on the incident and Hamlin's claim (his document is dated 21 June 1852).

50 Like the first petition, this second one was carried by hand to Quebec by William Fitch.

51 The petition is part of the Port Stamford customs file for 1852. In it Hamlin claims to have been in operation in the region for seventeen years

52 McCarroll to Francis Hincks, 16 March 1853.

53 "The curse of Swift" is a coinage from Irish politician Henry Grattan that had by the 1840s come into popular usage. Jonathan Swift was thought to have suffered for his intellectual brilliance and eminence, and not through any fault of his own. Grattan wrote that it is often a grim and thankless fate "to have been born an Irishman and a man of genius" and to have used it for his country's 'good' only to find himself ignored and dismissed. In his novel *Charles O'Malley, The Irish Dragoon* (1841), Charles Lever wrote, "but to some luckless fatality of fortune, the great rewards of life have been generally withheld until one begins to feel the curse of Swift was less the sarcasm wrung from indignant

failures than the cold and stern prophesy of the moralist." McCarroll had certainly read some Grattan and enjoyed a number of Lever's popular novels. He was well versed in the popular Irish fiction and theatre of his day. As an ambitious Irishman he feared that the curse of Swift would apply to him. In the long run it could be said that it did.

Chapter Five

1 Clarkson, *Credit Valley Gateway*. There is only anecdotal evidence that Thomas Cotton was related to Robert and James Cotton.

2 James Cotton and Company bid on the contract to build the Toronto-Guelph Railroad but lost out to C.S. Gzowski in 1852. The railroad line would run from Toronto to St Catharines and on to Port Stamford.

3 There are only a few McCarroll letters in the Port Credit file of the customs papers (RG 16, vol. 64 (Port Credit, 1851–55), NAC.

4 8 October 1858. After the failure of the *Anglo-American Magazine* (1857), which MacGeorge edited, he continued his Laird's column intermittently in the *Toronto Daily Leader*. The line was quoted as a part of the Laird's latest epic.

5 Yedding to Bouchette, 12 March 1852 and 13 August 1852, Customs Service files, RG 16, vol. 64 (Port Credit, 1851–55), NAC. Further correspondence from the Port Credit Customs file is noted according to date and correspondent.

6 He had to choose quickly between Napanee and Port Credit.

7 McCarroll to Francis Hincks, 16 March 1853, RG 16 Series A–1, vol. 335 (Stamford, 1853), NAC.

8 The leave was granted and the McCarrolls returned to Port Credit from their St Catharines visit on 22 August.

9 See RG 16, vol. 64, NAC.

10 The words of SCRUTON BALMANNO, one of MacGeorge's imaginary Toronto correspondents, as reported in his newspaper, the *Streetsville Review*, 28 May 1853. Humphreys was sometimes spelled Humphries in newspaper reports.

11 Samuel Sawbones was the pseudonym of St Catharines resident Edwin Goodman. He was at the time attending Trinity College (Toronto) as a medical student and later became a doctor.

12 One man was killed in the riot, which took place at the workers' shanties near Port Credit. The fact that police took eight hours to arrive from Toronto was seen as a scandalous failure of duty (see *Daily Leader* reports 25 August, 30 August, and 1 September).

13 A small fleet of fishing vessels and boats that crowded Port Credit's harbour were used either for fishing or "stone hooking."

14 See Clarkson, *At the Mouth of the Credit* and the report on the "Dreadful Fire at Port Credit" in the *Toronto Daily Leader* (9 April 1855). Other Port Credit

businessmen suffering losses from the fire included James Clarke, George
Wright, and Robert Cotton's partner James Hamilton.

15 McCarroll to Hincks (4 February 1854), RG 16, vol. 64, NAC.

16 McCarroll to Bouchette (20 April 1855), RG 16, vol. 64, NAC.

17 McCarroll's other recorded visits in 1853 from Port Credit, accompanied by
Ann or one of their daughters, occurred on 25–26 August, 10 September,
23 November, 4 and 21 December. In 1854 he registered at the Wellington
Hotel on 11 January, 28 March, 26 April, 19 May, 21 and 30 August, 2 and 20–21
September. In 1855 he was there on 20–22 and 28 February, 2 and 5 March; and
in 1856 on 2 February, 29 March, 27 April, 10 and 24 May, and 1 and 13 June.
During some months this sort of notice did not appear in the *Daily Leader*.

18 See the *Daily Leader*'s advertisement for Ole Bull's upcoming concert (17
November 1853). The concert on 23 November was promoted as "the last visit
of the great violinist to America" (*Daily Leader*, 23 November 1853). Bull was
immensely popular in Europe and brought the nickname "petit" with him
to North America. It suggests that he was quite small in stature. Bull would
continue to perform "final"' concerts into the 1870s (see chapter 8).

19 Maurice Strakosch (1825–1887) was a Moravian-born pianist and impresario
(like his brother Max) who began working in Venice for the musical family
of Salvatore Patti. He married Patti's older daughter Amalia in 1852. Patti had
performed duets with Ole Bull while on tour and became Adelina Patti's first
manager and most important teacher, bringing her to America for the first
time in 1853. Strakosch's later career saw him organize American tours for and
performances by many of the great names of nineteenth-century European
music. McCarroll met and befriended him during visits to Toronto and later
New York City. Charles Hildreth listed Strakosch among his famous musical
friends: he added, "not a few of these acquaintances ripened into lasting
friendships" (see *Madeline*, vi).

20 Anna Bishop (1810–1884) was another of those famous musical acquaintances.
She was one of the finest operatic sopranos of her day. English-born and dogged
by scandals regarding her first husband, composer Henry Bishop, and her
subsequent musical partner and lover, Nicholas-Charles Bochsa, she endured as
the most travelled of nineteenth-century singers, avoiding France and England
for personal reasons, although she was invited to sing at the coronation of
Queen Victoria in 1838. McCarroll admired the brilliant quality of her voice
and saw her often in the 1850s and 1860s. Terry Finnegan waxed poetic about
her Toronto concerts in 1864. Later in New York City, McCarroll visited her at
her home (see chapter 8). So great was her fame that in 1873 she was invited to
be the first singer to perform at the new Mormon Tabernacle in Salt Lake City.

21 *Daily Leader*, 1854. Likely performed by the Sanford's Opera Troupe or the
Italian Opera Company.

22 A year earlier McCarroll had played a concert with Paige and his daughters in St Catharines. Paige and McCarroll shared a connection through St James Cathedral in Toronto; in 1856 he and his family attended services there and he purchased a burial plot through the church.

23 *Hamilton Spectator* (3 October 1854).

24 See David Sale's thesis. He compiled a list of all musical performances in Toronto and environs.

25 James Beaty and Charles Lindsey.

26 McCalla writes that "Beaty was important enough in boosting and, perhaps, financing Hincks in the 1840s to put the latter clearly in his debt." By the 1850s the two men were "bosom" friends and political allies in the Reform cause, according to their chief rival, George Brown of the *Globe*; clearly, they were Brown's political and journalistic critics.

27 *Toronto Leader* (3 July 1853): "We issue, this morning, the first number of the first liberal daily journal ever published in Canada."

28 On 26 January 1854, the *Daily Leader* announced its enlarged edition in response to increased circulation and advertising. It billed itself as "the largest and cheapest daily journal in Western Canada" with a circulation approaching 12,000. During the mid-1850s the *Globe* and the *Daily Leader* fought doggedly for subscribers in the Toronto newspaper market.

29 Rutherford's *A Victorian Authority* concentrates on the final third of the century. In fact, he gives short shrift to the *Daily Leader* and its competitive position in Toronto during what he calls "the heady 1850s" (13), despite the fact that, in that decade, the *Daily Leader* vied strongly with Brown's *Globe* for attention and circulation. Rutherford notes that the two papers were the leaders in making newspapers a mass medium and a popular phenomenon in Canada (4).

30 In *Mrs. King*, Gray describes Charles Lindsey as a "cautious Reformer" in politics and a sober, somewhat stuffy individual in his business and family life (36, 44–8). The fact was that his enthusiasm for Reform soon gave way to a more cautious conservatism in the editorial offices of the *Daily Leader* once "Responsible Government" had been achieved. I have adopted the Lindsey spelling here, though Lindsay was also used in the 1850s.

31 Dewart included seven poems by McCarroll in his path-breaking anthology *Selections from Canadian Poets*, the first such effort in Canada. Only Charles Sangster and Alexander McLachlan were better represented. That quantification suggests that McCarroll was a highly regarded though relatively new figure on the Toronto literary scene in the 1850s and early 1860s.

32 See *Madeline*, 90.

33 Mario (1810–1883) had been an officer in the Sardinian army. However, he had deserted and went into exile because of his involvement with Manzini's "Young Italy" party. Although he was patriotically drawn to support the Italian

cause during the Crimean War, he did not in the end return to active military duty. See *Madeline*, 275–7.

34 Trained under Meyerbeer, Mario made his debut in 1838. Having achieved a great success in operas by Rubini, Donizetti, Bellini, and Rossini, he went on to star with the Royal Italian Opera Company in Covent Garden for over two decades and enjoyed a well-earned reputation as one of the great tenors of the century. His operatic partner and later his wife, Giulia Grisi (1811–1869) (Donna Giulia), was an acclaimed dramatic soprano who had roles written for her by Donizetti and Bellini. Together they enthralled audiences and raised operatic performance to new levels. They toured the United States together in 1854 but did not formally wed until 1856 as Grisi had been married previously.

35 McCarroll did not include this short lyric in *Madeline*.

36 A number of McCarroll's published poems, as above, did not make it into *Madeline and Other Poems*.

37 "To Bacchus" appeared in the *Daily Leader* on 8 February 1854 and in the *St Catharines Evening Journal* on 9 March 1854.

38 Others include PROFESSOR PIKE, UCD. LATE IN THE DEI was another likely pseudonym for McCarroll, though I have not been able to connect the poems written under that name to actual McCarroll poems in *Madeline*.

39 A notice in the *Daily Leader* (16 December 1854) reported that the *Daily Leader* and the *Toronto Patriot* (then owned by James Beaty, who had founded the *Daily Leader*) were produced in close conjunction. As the article phrased it, the two papers were amalgamated under a common management; together they produced eighteen editions weekly. The *Daily Leader* published a daily morning edition along with semi-weekly and weekly editions.

40 McCarroll told biographers like Henry Morgan that he wrote music and theatre reviews for the *Leader* and the *Colonist* in Toronto, calling attention to his range of skills and accomplishments. See *Sketches of Celebrated Canadians*, 757–8, and *Bibliotheca Canadensis*, 254.

41 *Madeline*, Introduction, v.

42 The critical attack on "some colonial Mus. Bac." can be seen as characteristic of McCarroll's personal attacks on rivals in various spheres.

43 The references are typical of McCarroll. Belgium violinist Henri Vieuxtemps (1820–1881), German soprano Henriette Sontag (1806–1854), Austrian pianist Alfred Jaell (1832–1882), and Ole Bull had all appeared in Toronto in 1853. Jaell toured North America from 1851 to 1854, often performing with Adelina Patti and Ole Bull. McCarroll's admiration for Kate Hayes, "the Irish nightingale," is described in chapter 4.

44 The *Daily Leader* published no review of Bishop's concert but it may well have appeared in another edition of the paper.

45 McCarroll's reviews were unsigned.

46 It is known that Morrison moved to Toronto in 1852 to work with Charles Lindsey in editing the *Toronto Examiner*, but that same year Lindsey became the founding editor of James Beaty's *Toronto Leader*. Morrison joined Lindsey at the *Leader* some time in 1854. See Patrick O'Neill's "From Puffery to Criticism," 79, 81.

47 McCarroll reported on these two connections to Henry Morgan, though his reviewing for the *Daily Colonist* is difficult to track. Intriguingly, Patrick O'Neill notes "the similarity of writing styles within the reviews published in the *Daily leader*, the *Daily Colonist*, and the *Quebec Morning Chronicle*." McCarroll wrote for all three papers, likely in the 1850s or early 1860s.

48 *Nearly a Tragedy: A Comedy* was published in New York by John F. Trow & Son in 1874.

49 In 1854 the *Daily Leader* linked Charlotte Nickinson romantically with another actor in the company, Sir William Don. Whether this was an affection of the moment or a bit of gossip set loose by others or by McCarroll himself remains unclear.

50 McCarroll's theatre reviews were typically longer and more detailed than his concert reviews.

51 Eliza Nickinson was another of John Nickinson's daughters and part of his Royal Lyceum Company.

52 *Daily Leader*, 26 September 1854. The rebuttal likely alludes to *Jack Shepherd*, which was reviewed on 4 May.

53 See de Nie's *The Eternal Paddy*.

54 Sir William Don was a baronet who adventurously chose a career as a comic actor in America. He was a very tall man, "six feet and a half in height," whose "supple" capers on stage regularly proved amusing to audiences. Don's response to McCarroll's criticisms of him appeared in the *Patriot* and was answered by a "Reader of the *Leader*" (perhaps McCarroll himself), in a brief notice on 8 September 1854. See O'Neill, "From Puffery to Criticism," 80–1.

55 O'Neill, "From Puffery to Criticism," 81. Morrison replied – "tongue in cheek" according to O'Neill – by requesting that this "prince of critics" come forward and "administer a dose of his wholesome criticism, and the Theatre may yet be saved." Allowing for Morrison's ironic salvo, it is fascinating to think of McCarroll as a prince among Toronto critics in the mid-1850s.

56 *St Catharines Evening Journal*, 25 January 1854. The ZOD column was reprinted in the *Toronto Leader*, February 1854.

57 Thomas McQueen's two critiques of spiritualism appeared in the *Hamilton Canadian*, 17 and 26 January 1854.

58 Judge John W. Edmonds and Dr George T. Dexter co-authored *Spiritualism* (1853). Edmonds had been a supreme court judge in New York State.

Nathaniel Talmadge, the former governor of Wisconsin and a senator, wrote *The Healing of Nations* (1855). Edward Fowler and Susanna and John Moodie also found authority for their spiritualist experiments in these figures.

59 Pierre-Flavien Turgeon (1787–1867) was the highly respected archbishop of Quebec from 1850 until the year of his death. He had a distinguished career within the Catholic Church and was noted for his commitment to social causes and charities.

60 The *Toronto Daily Leader* (8 October 1855). YOD's letter is dated 6 October from Toronto.

61 Susanna Moodie, *Letters of a Lifetime*, 182. In the same letter (2 May 1858) to her London publisher, Richard Bentley, she described the experiments undertaken by her husband and herself, and her own delayed but passionate conversion to spiritualism: "I was not only, a sceptic but a scorner. Yet, so many strange things have come under my own knowledge, that though still doubtful on some points, I dare not now, exclaim, as I once confidently did, 'It is false. A mental puzzle. A delusion!' It is a mystery, strange, solemn and beautiful, and which I now believe, contains nothing more nor less than a new revelation from God to man" (179).

62 *Toronto Daily Leader*, 7 October 1854.

63 Gilbert Auchinleck wrote a popular history, *The War of 1812: A History of the War between Great Britain and the United States of America. During the Years 1812, 1813 and 1814*. It first appeared in 1852 and was published in Toronto by McClear in 1855.

64 The town of Streetsville was founded near the site of William Street's mill on the Credit River in 1825. It became an incorporated village in 1858 and today makes up a part of the northwest corner of Mississauga, west of Toronto. In 1854 it was a bigger settlement than Port Credit itself and boasted both a newspaper and an Anglican church.

65 MacGeorge was chaplain to the Orange Order and a strong advocate for the use of the Orange Order as a political tool. His numerous extracurricular activities led his Streetsville congregation and Bishop John Strachan to find him wanting in his pastoral duties. McCarroll must have had similar concerns about protecting his identity as a customs officer while carrying on with his creative writing and journalistic forays.

66 The *Anglo-American Magazine* and Dewart's anthology show Alexander McLachlan as a major rival of McCarroll for leading Canada West poet of the day. McLachlan's work is far better known today among literary historians, though, as this study shows, that view can be seen as uninformed in various ways. In their time both poets were highly thought of, though the lively McCarroll did not hesitate to label McLachlan's verse as heavy and dull.

67 "Lines" was written in Cobourg and first published in the *Cobourg Star* on 2 February 1851, then in *Despatch* on 6 February and in the *Toronto Daily Leader* on 29 March 1854.

68 The text used here is from *Madeline*, 62, rather than the *Daily Leader*.

69 See pp. 92–3. "Lines (how oft while wandering)" first appeared in the *Cobourg Star* (2 February 1851).

70 Interestingly, a McCarroll poem, "The Convulvus," appeared in the *Hamilton Gazette and General Advertiser* on 5 March 1855 and was described as having been composed in "Peterboro." It did not appear in the *Toronto Daily Leader*. Its place of first publication remains a mystery.

71 "On the Origin of Printing" appeared in the issue for January 1855 (vol. 1, no. 6). McCarroll's poems "The Storm" and "Finnola" appeared in the February 1855 issue (vol. 6, no. 2) and in March 1855 (vol. 6, no. 3).

72 *Anglo-American Magazine* 6, no. 2 (February 1855), 114.

73 Connaught is the large region of western Ireland which includes Leitrim and Roscommon. See chapter 1.

74 *Anglo-American Magazine* (June 1855), 103.

75 Ibid. 7, no. 2 (June 1855), 100.

76 Ibid., 114.

77 The *Anglo-American Magazine* in the *Streetsville Review*, 6 January 1855.

78 The *Toronto Daily Leader* (3 March and 7 June 1855); notices in the *St Catharines Evening Journal* are to be found in the papers for 11 January, 1 March, 7 June, 2 August, and 6 September 1855. The brief quotation is from the *Daily Leader* of 3 March.

79 *St Catharines Evening Journal*, 1 March 1855.

80 *St Catharines Evening Journal* 1855. The reference to Father Phelim is likely an error on Lamb's part, though he may be alluding to a well-known type of the Irish-Catholic priest in literature. Lamb also misspells "propria persona" which in Latin means "acting for one's self" or "on one's own behalf."

81 Ibid., 6 September 1855.

82 The "Editor's Shanty," *Anglo-American Magazine* 7, no. 5 (November–December, 1855).

83 *Toronto Daily Leader*, 3 March 1855.

84 Charles Dickens to James McCarroll, 28 February 1862. See *The Collected Letters of Charles Dickens*, vol. 12.

Chapter Six

1 See Greg Gatenby, *Toronto: A Literary Guide*, 115. Gatenby lists 54 Bay Street as McCarroll's address until 1864, but he likely lived there until early 1866. Earlier, while living on Church Street, he was a neighbour of Charles Lindsey

whose address was 171 Church Street. Frederick Griebel also lived on Church Street in the 1850s. City directories and newspaper references provide additional locations.

2 The Grand Trunk depot was at the East Don (River) Station. The terminals of the Great Western Railway and Great Northern Railway were at Union Station.

3 There were at least twenty bonded warehouses used by the Customs Department at the Port of Toronto in the 1850s.

4 Meudell soon rescinded the order and McCarroll was allowed to continue with his customs routes in the city.

5 Munro to William Cawley, 22 January 1858, RG 16 A1 Toronto, 1858.

6 The difficult relationship between McCarroll and his "aged" sister remains a significant family mystery. Munro was likely her married name. She is not mentioned in the few McCarroll family documents related to their immigration. Described in customs records as a widow with seven children in her care, she may earlier have sought her brother's help for her struggling family, only to be rebuffed. Whether McCarroll was seeking to injure his sister's family and young Munro by an act of "malice" or pettiness, or was simply hoping to antagonize Collector Meudell further, is not clear from the letters in the customs file. I would favour the latter alternative. However, in his letter Edward Curzon wrote that "I know many of the facts of the unhappy state of affairs between the two families, and I am quite satisfied that Mr Munro is deserving of your protection and patronage, or I would not write as I do." In the end Munro received his raise and business continued as usual in the Longhouse. Whatever the case, McCarroll's manipulative behaviour in this instance does not reflect well on him.

7 Meudell wrote in despairing terms that he was being moved from a first-rate to a fourth-rate port and was suffering accordingly.

8 On at least three occasions McCarroll reported on individuals who were presumed guilty either of drinking on the job, sporadic attendance, or fraud. See the Customs Fonds for Toronto for 1858.

9 In July 1859 Robert Spence approved McCarroll's application for a month-long leave.

10 See also the *Daily Colonist*, 10 May 1858.

11 McCarroll alludes here to the effects felt in Toronto as a result of the economic depression of 1857–58.

12 Kallmann, "Ferdinand (Frederick) Griebel," DCB, 8: 347.

13 *Toronto Daily Leader*, Friday, 20 February 1858. Griebel died at McCarroll's home on Church Street.

14 On 10 March in the *Daily Leader*, the Griebel Relief Committee announced that "sufficient funds have not been collected"; hence "the committee must carry on"

in its work. On 25 March Handel's *Messiah* was performed in honour of Griebel, who had played violin in its first performance in Toronto (*Daily Leader*, 25 March 1858). Other fundraising concerts took place in June (*Daily Leader*, 15 June 1858). See also related columns in the *Globe*. Concerts on behalf of the Griebel family continued into 1859.

15 The McCarrolls were practising Anglicans; St James Cathedral on King Street was the centre of the Anglican Church for Canada West; John Strachan was diocesan bishop. McCarroll's cemetery plot is Lot 21, Section G. As of 1996 the gravesite included Ann McCarroll (who died in 1866 in Peterborough and, likely in 1883, was removed to Toronto from her Peterborough grave); James McDonald McCarroll (1858); Frederick Griebel (1858); and daughters Mary McCarroll (1915) and Emma Hazlehurst (1920).

16 The Customs Department papers for Toronto (RG 16 A1, 1858) contain this letter dated 7 July 1858. Robert Spence immediately approved his leave and notified Commissioner Bouchette.

17 Michael Murphy was a Toronto saloon keeper who had become president of the Hibernian Benevolent Society. Patrick Boyle was the editor of the *Irish Canadian*, a Toronto newspaper that began publication in January 1863. Under his mask of anonymity McCarroll was involved in editing the newspaper on a couple of occasions during the early and mid-1860s.

18 Pseudonyms like MERCATOR and VOX appeared in the *Daily Colonist*. It is possible that McCarroll used one or both during the late 1850s.

19 McCarroll was very proud of his connections with the world of international music. He kept an autograph collection that featured many of the great nineteenth-century performers and writers. See the *Daily Leader*, 11 February 1863 when he announced that his collection for sale, or the list of his musician acquaintances provided by Charles Lotin Hildreth; these included Frederick Griebel, Ole Bull, Jenny Lind, Sir Julius Benedict, (Pauline) Lucca, Arabella Goddard, Carl Formes, and Henri Wieniawski (see *Madeline and Other Poems*, vi).

20 An Irishman by birth, Halley had his office on Colborne Street in Toronto. Claiming long experience in the publishing business, he saw himself as filling a significant void in Canada by offering in the *Home Journal* "the only literary publication" in the colony.

21 McCarroll's contributions included a poem ("Swallows" – see *Madeline*, 133), two stories ("The New Life-Boat: A Reminiscence of No. 108" and "Black Hawk"), and the aforementioned article.

22 *Cobourg Sentinel* (27 July 1861). The serialization of "Black Hawk" began for a second time here on 4 January 1862 under the heading "Canadian Literature"; it lasted through chapter 9 in this second attempt.

23 Halley argued in his "appeal" that there was plenty of Canadian talent (including McCarroll) to support "a native Canadian journal" and that the country

needed a new venue for its writers, especially given "the flood of trashy American sheets that swarm our periodical depots."

24 Puffs for the forthcoming serial appeared on 5, 12, and 19 October 1861 and 18 January 1862. The newspaper also published McCarroll's story "The New Life Boat," which had appeared in the *Home Journal* (14 and 21 December 1861). A dark poem entitled "February" (*Madeline*, 138) appeared in the same *Sentinel* issue of 8 February 1862, alongside chapter 6 of "Black Hawk."

25 A villain named Morton appears in both novels, though here, in clichéd form, Morton actually holds a mortgage on the widow Mornington's property. It is likely that McCarroll had read not only *Wacousta* but several of James Fenimore Cooper's popular frontier novels like *The Deerslayer*.

26 Roscrea is a historic market town in Tipperary County near Limerick. Recently it has been designated an Irish Heritage Town. McCarroll may have had a family connection in the town.

27 McCarroll wrote a number of sympathetic poems about the poverty and destitution suffered by people in the streets of Toronto during these years. Such depressing conditions weighed upon his sensibility even as he enjoyed the benefits of a good salary and a recognized social position. The text here is taken from *Madeline*, 138–9.

28 Storey et al., *The Letters of Charles Dickens*, 12: 40–1.

29 "Madeline" is the longest of McCarroll's published poems. He may have sent it to Dickens as an example of his poetry. However, there is no evidence that he was writing, or planning to write, a poem of two thousand lines; occasionally he would entitle a poem "a fragment," but his speciality was shorter lyric poems.

30 *New Era* (Montreal), 11 February 1858.

31 The *Irish Canadian* noted in its 1892 obituary of McCarroll that McGee had responded positively to the Terry Finnegan letters. I have found no such evidence.

32 The occasion was a lecture by McGee in Toronto on 5 March 1857. McCarroll was a member of the platform party organized by city leaders to greet McGee.

33 Newcastle's hostility to the Orange Order in Canada may have played a significant part in his original lack of response to McCarroll's poem; he was after all known to have been involved in the Orange Order in Peterborough in the 1840s and he was certainly identified as a Protestant Irishman. Newcastle wished to avoid any form of connection with or recognition of the Orange Order in Canada.

34 See "Amateur Concert," *Daily Leader*, 6 September 1860.

35 See "Personal," *Daily Leader*, 28 September 1860. McCarroll likely provided the material to the newspaper; he may even have written it for insertion, as he doubtless did on numerous other occasions. There is no surviving copy of the "Prospectus" issued by McCarroll that autumn for his two literary collections.

36 This was his first use of this pseudonym. The Pike name catches the anomaly between a University College Dublin professor and a man who might carry a wooden weapon into a battle or a donnybrook. The famous Bridge of Sighs in Venice joins the Doge's Palace to its adjacent prison. McCarroll did not have a university education; rather, he was a keen, largely self-educated reader. The poem is found in *Madeline*, 170–2.

37 See "The Prisoner" (*Madeline*, 91–3). The poem is set in the Don Jail, adjacent to "a sluggish river on which the jail in Toronto, Canada is built."

38 "Impromptu" appeared in the *Daily Leader* in 1860. It is included under "Humorous Poems" in *Madeline*, 310.

39 One such comedic love poem is "Biddy McGuire" ("I don't care for murther as long as it's fair") which appeared in the *Daily Leader*, 16 August 1860.

40 Michael Hamilton Foley (1820–1870) was a Protestant from Sligo who is mentioned often in the Terry Finnegan letters. A teacher and a lawyer, he was first elected to the Parliament of Canada West in 1854 as a "moderate Reformer"; his allegiances shifted from George Brown to Sandfield Macdonald and then to John A. Macdonald. Defeated in an election, he was appointed Postmaster General for Canada West in 1861. A heavy drinker by reputation, he seems to have been a particular friend of Terry Finnegan's, despite Terry's Catholic background. Originally from Wexford, Ogle Gowan was still an influential editor-journalist in the 1860s. In the 1840s he had served as Grand Master of the Orange Order and had been a supporter of "Responsible Government." In March 1862 he spoke on Ireland's warriors and poets at the St Patrick's Day dinner in Toronto and made special mention of James McCarroll as a fine Irish poet living in the city. (reported in the *Globe*, 18 March 1862 and passed on to me by David Wilson).

41 *Toronto Daily Leader*, 9 March 1857. The lecture took place at the St Lawrence Hall on the preceding Thursday and was chaired by Toronto's mayor, J.G. Bowes.

42 On 15 October 1851 McCarroll sent a comic letter to the *Cobourg Star* from Port Stamford. Its author was named Denis Finnegan, an early prototype for Terry Finnegan.

43 Each letter was signed "Your lovin' cousin, Terry Finnegan" (or "T.F."). At one point Terry described himself as "your Uncle Dandy's son." Although McGee was known as a "Waxford" boy, Terry occasionally alludes to their shared experiences in Leitrim and Roscommon; this was the world of McCarroll's own upbringing, not McGee's. The alleged connection reads a little like an early Irish travelogue.

44 Stanley Street, renamed in honour of Lord Stanley, was renamed for a second time – on this occasion as Lombard Street (1876), which is the name it bears to this day. It is a short thoroughfare running east-west between Church and

Jarvis streets, just south of Adelaide and close to St James Cathedral. Crime reports in the *Daily Leader* routinely cited many instances of donnybrooks, violent deaths, public drunkenness, and sexual impropriety on or near Stanley Street in the early 1860s.

45 The book actually contains thirty-eight, not thirty-seven, letters. In the botched editorial sequencing there are two letters numbered #13 – 23 January 1863 and 30 January 1863.

46 McCarroll had to wait until December 1863 to see his first book in print. It was a hurried and rather sloppy job (see note li), printed so late in 1863 that its publication date became 1864. The printing costs were likely paid in part by the Toronto News Company who sold the book at its office and distributed it to city residents.

47 Reports on the appearance of Terry Finnegan letters in *Pick* appeared in several issues of the *Daily Leader* and the *Irish Canadian* in 1865. Because *Pick* did not last a full year, copies were not bound for preservation. In similar instances no yearly record was preserved. There is a possibility that McCarroll himself was involved in the production of Halley's magazine. Certainly, he was one of its leading contributors. To date, however, no evidence has been found to verify that connection. Likely he was too busy with his travelling show and related duties in 1865 to have time and energy for such work. Allowing for the publication of ten Finnegan letters in *Pick*, the total of Terry's letters is likely closer to sixty.

48 Careless, *The Pre-Confederation Premiers*, 315.

49 Wilson, *Thomas D'Arcy McGee*, vol. 2, *The Extreme Moderate*, 231.

50 Ibid., 211.

51 McCarroll had sent a newsy and cheeky letter in the Irish vernacular back from Port Stamford to Cobourg on 15 October 1851. See note 42.

52 *Yankee Doodle* was an illustrated humour magazine published in New York. It began in 1846–47 and featured comic writing in various styles with many caricatures of well-known politicians. Comic letter writing was another feature; hence, the name "Yankee Doodle" could apply to numerous sorts of letter writing in the magazine. Artemus Ward (1834–1867) was a popular American humorist of the day; he lectured in Toronto in 1863. Born in Maine as Charles Farrar Browne, he became a humorist in newspapers and the lecture circuit, amusing audiences with his tall tales, puns, and conspicuous misspellings. He is sometimes seen as the father of stand-up comedy in America. McCarroll's debt to him was considerable. Canadian writer Thomas C. Haliburton (1796–1865) created his Sam Slick – and sketches of his sayings and doings – in 1835 as a way of making fun of sales-oriented Americans like Sam and criticizing the lack of enterprise and energy among his native Nova Scotians (or Bluenosers). These were published in newspapers and collected in several volumes.

53 See the *Cobourg Star*, 8 April 1857. Doubtless, McCarroll shared this evaluation of Jackson's epistolary achievements with Ruttan.

54 A tradition of Irish epistolary correspondence can be traced from John Jackson in Dublin through James McCarroll in Toronto to Finley Peter Dunne of the *Chicago Evening Post*.

55 From a letter written by "Truth" to the editor of the *Toronto Daily Leader* (18 December 1854). McCarroll often used pseudonyms to protect his identity. It might be more accurate to say that he was "hesitant" to be known publically for his various journalistic activities.

56 The *Grumbler*, edited first by Erastus Wiman and then by John Ross Robertson, had three incarnations – the first in 1858–59 (before McCarroll created Terry, though he was a contributor to its pages); from 1860 to 1865 (during which a number of Terry Finnegan's letters appeared); and in 1869 (after McCarroll had left the country for Buffalo). Other small Toronto satiric magazines included *Momus* (1861), the *Latch-Key* (1863, 1864), and *Pick* (1865). It is possible that McCarroll had a part in publishing *Momus*; the first eight Finnegan letters appeared here in consecutive weeks. Wiman (1834–1904) was a Canadian-born journalist, editor, promoter, and entrepreneur who founded the *Grumbler* as a "humorous weekly" while working as a commercial reporter for the *Globe*. He was a younger cousin of William McDougall who was then editing the *British American*, a newspaper in Toronto. Wiman moved to New York in 1866 where he became famous as a wealthy entrepreneur on Staten Island. (See DCB, vol. 13). John Ross Robertson (1841–1918) was a career Toronto journalist who was associated with the *Leader* in his early days; he edited the *Grumbler* from 1863 to 1865. (See DCB, vol. 13).

57 The *Latch-Key*, which had separate runs in the summer-autumn of 1863 and 1864, was McCarroll's own publication. He also published four issues of the *Growler* in Toronto in 1864, though he did not include any Terry Finnegan letters in the latter. While the four issues of the *Growler* have been preserved on microfilm, only five issues of the two *Latch-Key* runs have been saved in print form. See the Ontario Archives and the Fisher Rare Book Room at the University of Toronto.

58 McCarroll had his own printing press which he used to print his periodicals and to typeset articles for newspapers to which he was a contributor. He also did commercial job printing. See the John A. Macdonald letters.

59 Waters, *The Comic Irishman*.

60 An omadhawn or omadhaun is a foolish boy, a fool, or a simpleton. The word comes from the Gaelic *amadan* and came into usage in the early nineteenth century.

61 Letters are numbered according to their appearance in the first series (published in 1864).

62 See Jenkins, "Poverty and Place." See also his book-length study *Between Raid and Rebellion*.

63 Jenkins, "Poverty and Place," 498.

64 The *Irish Canadian* labelled McGee "the goula of Griffintown" once he began to issue his "strident anti-Fenian views." Wilson, *Thomas D'Arcy McGee*, 2: 225.

65 *Momus* lasted for only eight issues but each one contained a Finnegan letter. See note 56. Prior to its first publication the magazine ran a lively advertising campaign in the *Daily Leader*, boasting it would enlist 75,000 subscribers and set new standards for humour and political insight in Toronto. Letter 3 was reprinted in part in the *Daily Leader* (March 1861), likely because of its humour and topicality.

66 In many instances Terry Finnegan's allusions are so specialized as to seem opaque to a twenty-first-century reader. The "thriangular jewel of Midshipman Aisy" is one such challenging reference.

67 Clerk was a convert to Catholicism from Protestantism and took a very strong ultramontanist line with McGee in his newspaper. He did not hesitate to use "inflammatory and intolerant language" in making his judgments (Wilson, *Thomas D'Arcy McGee*, 2: 113). McGee had himself been a firm unltramontanist a few years previously (Wilson, *Thomas D'Arcy McGee*, 2: 111). Terry Finnegan judged Clerk accurately as "a Scotch interloper" who had belatedly become a Catholic of severe views: "Bein in doubt himself, he has always to put on a face of brass, and give as twinty ounces for a pound of bather, for fear he'd be suspected." See Letter 5 (9 May 1861). Wilson describes Clerk as McGee's "old enemy" (204).

68 Letter 8 (28 June 1851).

69 Isadore Gordon Ascher (1835–1933) was a Glasgow-born poet and novelist who had been raised in Montreal and earned a law degree from McGill. His first book, *Voices from the Hearth*, received a warm reception from not only Henry Youle Hinds but also Edward Dewart who included a few of Ascher's poems in his *Selections from Canadian Poets* (1864).

70 Henry Youle Hinds (1823–1908) was a well-educated, English-born young man when he arrived in Canada in 1846 (vol. 13, DCB). Known for his work as a teacher, professor, journalist, geologist, and explorer, he was living in Toronto in 1863 when he became the editor (1863–64) of the *British American Magazine*.

71 There is a certain irony in McCarroll's view that a scientist was constitution-ally unsuited to be a critic of the arts. He himself had significant scientific pretensions and sought publicity on occasion for his own experiments and "discoveries." Underlying his disdain for poets like Ascher lay his personal frus-trations (perhaps rooted in part in his own procrastination) in not yet having published his own book of poetry.

72 "Peggy Morin" is not found in *Madeline and Other Poems*. Another of the
poems (untitled) that Terry sent to McGee – attributed by Terry to a friend
named Boxty Mulloy – appears as "Hunted Down" in *Madeline* (293–5).

73 The letter is dated 20 August 1863. In describing the outdoor concert, Terry
noted that

> besides Madame Anna, there was Mr Humphrey's who sung wid her and
> wid himself splendidly; and Mr De Speiss that played the piana as if he
> was continually dhrawin the curtains of heaven aside wid his fingers; and
> Mr Sedgwick who made the Concertina warble like a linnet, and the
> audience roar wid his comic songs; and there was the Band of the 30th
> Regiment discoorsin eloquently undher the able baton of Zeigler, their
> Masther; and there were thousands and thousands of ladies and gintlemin
> passin to and fro benathe the colored lamps and sudden fireworks that,
> like a sort of soft, flushed faymale lightenin wove endless bright devices
> in the air; while the odher from countless aromatic shrubs and fragrant
> buds stole on you now and then as the gentle breezes sunk and rose, till
> begorra you could scarcely toll where you were, if you even had the City
> Diructhory in your pocket.

As a musician and an experienced music reviewer, McCarroll had here the
opportunity to praise some of his musical colleagues like Humphreys and
Sedgwick, and to wax effusive in describing the sensory pleasures to be enjoyed
on such a warm and "wondherful" Toronto evening.

74 McCarroll was a *Grumbler* contributor from its first year of operation. He
specialized in comic letter writing and comedic sketches (short plays and
dialogues) involving public figures like George Brown, John Sandfield
Macdonald, and D'Arcy McGee. However, because these contributions are
unsigned, they cannot be specifically linked to a particular writer.

75 Letter 16 (18 February 1863)

76 Letter 17 (27 February 1863)

77 The 1861 census made it clear that the population of Canada West had grown
larger than that of Canada East; moreover, among Canadians of British stock,
the largest number had emigrated from Ireland. Thus the dynamics of political
representation shifted. Indeed, the question of "rep by pop" became a major
issue in Canada West given the change in numbers.

78 Alexander McLachlan (1818–1896) had by this time published four collections
of poems in Toronto, including *Lyrics* (1858) and *The Emigrant and Other
Poems* (1861). It bothered McCarroll that he had not been able to bring out
a volume of his own poems, despite his conviction that his poetry was far
superior in form, purpose, and quality to McLachlan's.

79 Under the heading "Quebec Correspondence," McCarroll offered comic
letters written in a kind of "franglais" from "Pierre LaFontaine" in Quebec to

"De Hon. Mr Le Brun – de Brown, redacteur of de vorld – de Globe." They appeared in both the *Grumbler* and the *Latch-Key* (see 17 and 24 October 1863); on occasion they were deemed amusing enough to be reprinted in the *Daily Leader*. Their appearance in the *Grumbler* makes it clear that McCarroll was a contributor to that magazine before his Terry Finnegan letters began to appear there in 1862.

80 McCarroll to John A. Macdonald, 29 April 1864, Macdonald Papers, #136691–92, LAC. The *nom de plume* is of course Terry Finnegan.

81 As part of their cost-cutting plans, Worthington and Brunel set out to turn Collingwood into "an out port" of Toronto, thus eliminating the collector position. They had begun the changes on the basis of their analysis of the weak revenue of the Port of Collingwood and the evident intemperance of John McWatt and one or two of his helpers.

82 McCarroll liked to emphasize the extent to which the customs commissioners were overpaid. At one point he cited Brunel's salary as a startling 3,600 pounds; he also claimed Worthington was paid 2,000 pounds annually.

83 Only three issues of the *Latch-Key* for 1863 have survived. It began in early August and it appears that only one issue was published in September, the traumatic month in which McCarroll's customs position was terminated. Issues 1 through 4 (22 August) appeared in August, while issues 5 through 8 likely appeared consecutively from late September (24 September) into October (#7 on 17 October and #8 on 24 October). The paper was four pages in length.

84 Henry Martin had emerged as a leading voice in music in Toronto. He was the organist for St George's Church and taught courses in music and drawing. While he conducted various Toronto concerts in these years, he also wrote the series of columns about music and poetry that appeared in the *Daily Leader* in 1862–63. McCarroll saw him as a rival critic; when so inclined, he questioned Martin's authority and ability in print.

85 Monday, 26 October 1863. The *Leader* editor was still Charles Lindsey. Daniel Morrison, who later replaced McCarroll as the *Daily Leader*'s theatre reviewer, had not yet joined the *Leader* staff. He became the editor of the newspaper in 1855. Responding to a "rather severe" review of a Henry Martin column in McCarroll's *Latch-Key* (24 September 1863), the *Leader* praised Martin as a writer of much originality and "spiciness." In a deft riposte, the editor suggested that the principal writer of the *Latch-Key* should acknowledge his own plagiarisms from Artemus Ward in Terry Finnegan's letters. Ward had recently lectured in Toronto.

86 In *Madeline* (69), McCarroll added a footnote: "The Dalgais were the favorite troops of Brain Borrombhe, or Boru, who, when wounded in a fight and unable to stand, requested that they should be lashed to a stake and planted by the side of a sound man, so as they might still do battle."

87 For the full text of "O Sainted Shannon," see chapter 1.

88 See Sale's "Toronto's Pre-Confederation Music Societies, 1845–67." Sale provides a year-by-year list of concerts in Toronto. This is the most detailed record currently available. See also the advertisement in the *Daily Leader* (16 January 1863) for Mrs Stevenson's Grand Concert and Ball. Amateur performers other than the McCarrolls included Kate Macdonald and Dr O'Dea. One wonders if there was a family connection between Toronto's "Dr O'Dea" and Buffalo's "Patrick O'Day" (or O'Dea).

89 Likely Jean-Paul-Égide Martini (1741–1816) whose "Plaisir d'amour" became a favourite concert piece.

90 The *Daily Leader* review (31 October 1863) is unsigned but is consistent with his ongoing writing for the newspaper and with Terry Finnegan's dismissive remarks earlier in the year. Here McCarroll writes from a lofty, critical perspective and defines his sense of what constitutes "true poesy."

91 The *Daily Leader*, 8 April 1864; see the *British American Magazine*, vol. 2, 1864, 578. This poem was occasionally anthologized years after McCarroll's departure from Canada and was often regarded as an excellent representation of the beauties of a Canadian winter.

92 See "Kate Rooney" (1:3), "A Kiss" (1:3), "The First Kiss" (1:3), "Not an Original" (1:4), and "Autumn – Song" (1:4). Others like "The Quill" (1:1), "Summer" (1:1), "A Reverie" (1:2), and "Titular" (1:2) are not in *Madeline*.

93 Heretofore the *Growler* has not been attributed to James McCarroll as editor and primary contributor.

94 The issues of 22 August and 17 and 24 October include six McCarroll poems and three Terry Finnegan letters to D'Arcy McGee (#31, #34, and #35 in *The Letters of Terry Finnegan*). Having publishing control over these popular letters in the *Latch-Key* may have been important to McCarroll at the time, but he would later reconnect with the *Grumbler* to print Terry's later letters. Other comic letters (usually parts of an ongoing series) in these two issues are written by Matilda to Dear Jemimah (about Toronto social life and their love affairs); J.S. Macdonald to William Logan; and T.D. McGee to Michael Foley.

95 This was a response to Letter 14 that appeared on 28 October 1864. Both issues of the *Latch Key* containing Letters 13 and 14 are missing (21 and 18 October, 1864). It was about this time that McCarroll's frustration and anger with McGee began to become heated.

96 The *Growler* lasted only four issues in August 1864. The *Latch-Key* (2nd series) lasted into November 1864.

97 McCarroll to John A. Macdonald (16 February 1865), vol. 298, #136721. "Three Loaded Dice" was a nasty personal attack on Sandfield Macdonald. It first appeared in the *Latch-Key* and then was reprinted in the *Daily Leader* (14 October 1863).

98 See the *Latch-Key* (8 October 1864), 1. The five surviving issues, two from 1863 and three from 1864, provide interesting glimpses of McCarroll in his various literary guises – poet, prose writer, humorist, comedic letter writer, and editorialist.

99 "The House That Jack Built" is an English nursery rhyme written in the sixteenth century. Over time the phrase had come to mean an ill-constructed house. McCarroll used its popularity and imagery to comment on inadequacies in the English construction of its Canadian colony.

100 John A. Macdonald Papers, #136719, LAC.

101 The phrase comes from a public letter to George Brown (14 December 1866, *Montreal Gazette*). See Wilson, *Thomas D'Arcy McGee*, 2: 219.

102 McCarroll to John A. Macdonald, 13 April 1864, Macdonald Papers, #1366687–88.

103 In a letter written three days earlier (13 February 1865) he told Macdonald, "my status and influence amongst my countrymen in Upper Canada are not to be knocked on the head by Tom Worthington."

104 See Mulvany, *Toronto: Past and Present*, 189; and Wilson, *Thomas D'Arcy McGee*, 2: 124.

105 McCarroll to Macdonald, 19 January 1866, #136725–27, LAC. McCarroll corresponded with both Holmes and Longfellow in Boston and had written poems dedicated to their work as poets and writers. See *Madeline* for poems and letters. Holmes was a particular favourite.

Chapter Seven

1 *Buffalo Courier*, 8 March 1866. The review did not mention Mary McCarroll's participation.

2 In a late Terry Finnegan letter in *Pick*. The *Toronto Daily Leader* (20 May 1865) reported that Terry seems "quite ardent for annexation" and opposed to Confederation.

3 John O'Donohoe's brother Bernard (Barney) was living in Buffalo and may have helped McCarroll make Fenian connections there. See Jenkins, *Between Raid and Rebellion*, 184.

4 Likely he had sent Ann and their daughters to live with Ann's family in Peterborough.

5 The *Peterborough Review* (20 July 1866) reported that Ann McCarroll died at the residence of her mother on 14 July. The St James Cemetery records note that she died on 13 July at the age of forty-eight.

6 Details are found in the 1871 census. Fred Menet married Kate McCarroll in St Catharines on 10 January 1871. It is likely that the marriage involved the family of James Lamb, McCarroll's old friend from St Catharines, though by

then Lamb was likely alienated by McCarroll's outspoken Fenian voice and his decamping to Buffalo while leaving his family in Toronto. An Englishman by birth, Frederick Menet was listed as bookkeeper with a Church of England affiliation. Kate (Catherine) was reported to be twenty-eight years old; Mary was twenty-six. Both were listed as Irish. By then Mary was working as a music teacher in Toronto. In Peterborough, Emma McCarroll (twenty) and Clara McCarroll (seventeen) were also listed as music teachers; they lived with Emma Haslehurst, the widowed wife of James McCarroll's former printer for his Peterborough newspaper, the *Chronicle*, and later the editor/printer of the *Peterborough Despatch*.

7 By the time of Kate's wedding McCarroll would have been living in New York City; thus he did not attend the event, nor was he likely invited.

8 Jenkins, *Between Raid and Rebellion*, 26.

9 McCarroll to Macdonald, 15 February 1865. Written from Toronto. See also the Macdonald Papers #155022.

10 An active Fenian centre might have as many as 300 sworn members.

11 One of the prongs of attack would be launched from the Buffalo area.

12 Terry Finnegan often advised "cousin" D'Arcy Mc Gee to keep one foot on the floor while in government sessions but always to be ready to move the other quickly in another direction.

13 McCarroll to Macdonald, Macdonald Papers, 155022.

14 McCarroll to Macdonald, Macdonald Papers (21 February 1866), 155024.

15 The nine-page letter is repetitive in its complaints but steadily purposeful, conveying various vague threats to Macdonald and Galt as well as to their government. It was not, as McCarroll admitted, a letter that anticipated a reply.

16 None of these affirmative notes has survived in the John A. Macdonald Papers or elsewhere, though McCarroll reportedly kept one with him, in part to verify his story of having become a Fenian convert.

17 Michael (Mike) Murphy also wrote a scathing letter criticizing Worthington. See McCarroll to Macdonald, Macdonald Papers (18 March 1866), 155044.

18 McCarroll's relationship to his wife and daughters during these months remains a mystery. It would be interesting to know whether Mary came to Buffalo to perform with her father in March and how much he communicated with Ann and their girls once he crossed the border. It is possible that he followed Julia Dolmage and her family to Buffalo or that she followed him from Toronto.

19 McCarroll to Macdonald, Macdonald Papers (18 March 1866), 155044.

20 The image of the knife led directly to "Scian Dubh," the penname he chose in writing *Ridgeway* (1868). Scian Dubh means "black knife" in Gaelic. David Doolin has interpreted it to mean "concealed weapon."

21 The report is found in the Macdonald papers. Its recipient may have been Gilbert McMicken. Macdonald was the attorney general at the time.

Patrick O'Dea's auction house was a known Fenian Centre in Buffalo's First
Ward; O'Dea and Frank B. Gallagher were likely Mcarroll's two most import-
ant Fenian connections. Gallagher was a Civil War veteran and a well-known
First Ward resident; he was "a man of the people, and very popular with the
working class." He fought at Ridgeway but died in an industrial accident in
Buffalo in 1870 (Jenkins, *Between Raid and Rebellion*, 87).

22 Ibid. McCarroll doesn't mention the printing press in this letter; rather he
implies that he is waiting for a means to become engaged with Buffalo's
Fenian press. That "connection" would be developed once his printing press
arrived.

23 Jenkins, *Between Raid and Rebellion*, 184.

24 Bohen, *Against the Grain*, 6.

25 Jenkins, *Between Raid and Rebellion*, 83.

26 Saloons were "the most familiar commercial establishment in the First Ward."
They could also function as grocery stores, boarding houses, or meeting places.
Jenkins, *Between Raid and Rebellion*, 88.

27 These locations were a little to the north of the more densely populated,
labour-intensive streets of the First Ward.

28 Treble was an Englishman who worked for the government in Ottawa.
Thomas Worthington may well have been seeking specific information about
McCarroll's Buffalo activities; doubtless he was eager to pass on any negative
information he could find to the Canadian authorities.

29 Letter from Charles Treble to Thomas Worthington, passed on to John A.
Macdonald, 11 April 1866, vol. 57, John A. Macdonald Papers. The general
was Colonel John O'Neill, the commander of the Fenian forces that invaded
Canada on 2 June 1866.

30 The *Buffalo Courier* was a well-established, large-circulation city newspaper
that kept close tabs on the Fenians and their objectives. It also published several news items about McCarroll's activities in town.

31 McCarroll & Company, Publishers, had its office at the corner of Swan and
Pearl streets in Buffalo's First Ward in 1868. The novel was "stereotyped and
printed" for McCarroll & Company by Sage, Sons & Co. of Buffalo.

32 Canada launched its own secret service operation in 1864; its first chief was
Gerald McMicken.

33 Peter Vronsky mentioned to me in a telephone conversation that he found
McCarroll's description of the invasion in *Ridgeway* so accurate that he wondered if he had in fact accompanied the troops across the Niagara River.

34 No issues of the *Buffalo Globe* have survived. Patrick O'Dea in fact financed
three Fenian papers in Buffalo in quick succession. The short-lived *Globe*
(autumn 1866) was followed by the *Fenian Volunteer* (summer 1867–68), which
McCarroll edited in its early months, and finally the *United Irishman* (1869).

The first two newspapers may have been printed by McCarroll himself on his own press.

35 Patrick Boyle (1832–1901) began the *Irish Canadian* in January 1863 and employed James McCarroll as a writer and editor on occasion. Though he never advocated an invasion of Canada by the American Brotherhood (the Fenians), Boyle was strongly at odds with D'Arcy McGee and most moderate Irish Catholics in Canada West. In 1864 James Moylan of the *Canadian Freeman* publicly denounced Boyle's newspaper as a Fenian organ and, in April 1868, with fears of Fenians running high in Canada, Boyle was arrested by Canadian officials and imprisoned for three months, during which time the *Irish Canadian* had to cease publication.

36 The poem entitled "The Irish Wolf" appeared in an earlier edition of the *Buffalo Globe*. McCarroll included it in *Ridgeway* (1868) itself (116–17) and in his collected poetry, *Madeline and Other Poems* (1889). It has been anthologized numerous times, notably in Stoppard and Rolleston, eds, *A Treasury of Irish Poetry*, 180–1, and most recently in the *Penguin Book of Irish Verse* (2012).

37 Judging from surviving issues of the *Latch-Key* and the *Growler*, McCarroll was a master of laying out and typesetting an attractive and readable weekly newspaper when he had the time, money, and opportunity. He had his own printing press in Toronto, which he used on occasion to print his personalized magazines but also for job printing for local businesses. It is possible that he had somehow reclaimed the Washington Press he had originally used in Peterborough in the early 1840s; otherwise he may have bought a smaller unit once he settled in Toronto. He did not identify its make.

38 See the *Latch-Key* in its two incarnations (1863, 1864) and the *Growler* (1864).

39 "National Music" is included in *Madeline*, 229–30.

40 There is no evidence or likelihood that McCarroll was present at the actual raid into Canada. Still, he was emotionally invested in its events and possibilities and turned himself into a kind of informed witness in order to write *Ridgeway*.

41 See issues of the *St Catharines Evening Journal* for 28 April, 8 May, and 11 May.

42 SACERDOS is the Latin word for "priest." The author of the supportive letter has not been identified, though he clearly felt strong empathy with McCarroll. SACERDOS may have missed certain ironies involved in the *Toronto Daily Leader*'s comments, for the *Leader* often published wry appreciations of Terry Finnegan's letters: "He will be a good one for 'blowing,' – an accomplishment highly popular among the Fenians; and as for his English, the more impure it is, the more highly ought he to be appreciated by the Saxon-hating brotherhood."

43 A simultaneous story was in circulation in several newspapers concerning the arrest and prosecution of McMahon for his Fenian activities.

44 On 19 July 1867 the *Buffalo Evening Post* reported that Mr McCarroll, a noted newspaperman, was (still) collecting "biographies of leading self-made men in Buffalo for a leading New York weekly."

45 One issue of the *Fenian Volunteer* is held by the Library of Congress and is available on microfilm. However, it belongs to the period after McCarroll stepped down as its founding editor.

46 The *Buffalo City Directory* reported that in 1867 the *Fenian Volunteer* was located at No. 3 East Seneca Street. In 1868 it moved to "Terrace, corner of Main." O'Dea's third Fenian paper, the *United Irishman*, was also published at the Terrace address in 1869. No residence is recorded for McCarroll until 1869 when he was listed as an editor living at 343 Ninth Street. *Ridgeway* (1868) lists its publisher as the "J. McCarroll Company, Publishers, corner of Swan and Pearl Streets."

47 The *St Catharines Evening Journal* reported on 3 and 9 September 1868 that representatives of the "*Fenian Volunteer* had applied to Buffalo City Council for a grant of $1000 in support of the newspaper. The motion was defeated by a vote of 11–6." There is a likely connection between the failed attempt to access city money and McCarroll's retirement as editor a few weeks later.

48 I have not found that particular editorial.

49 The loss of the Terry Finnegan letters in the *Pick* (Toronto) in 1865 limits the available print evidence of his changing evaluation of D'Arcy McGee in 1865. However, by contrast to earlier letters, he became severe in his judgments.

50 Doolin, "Exploring Textures of Irish America," 159–61. Doolin's misrepresentation of McCarroll's name as O'Carroll (he also describes him as an "anonymous scribe") suggests the extent to which his time and work in Buffalo on behalf of Fenianism has been largely ignored or misunderstood to date.

51 Neither the Catholic bishop of Toronto, John Joseph Lynch, nor the bishop of Buffalo, John Timon, supported the Fenian campaigns.

52 Introduction, xiii.

53 *Ridgeway*, 66.

54 Similar arguments were part of Cahill's popular history, *How the Irish Saved Civilization*. An Irish-American with a Catholic education and an academic career, Cahill and his book stayed on the *New York Times* best seller list for two years, though a number of its arguments were challenged in reviews and opinion pieces.

55 "The chivalry of a stupendous past was upon them … and they shrank from the treacherous and dastardly acts of assassination introduced by the ignoble and cowardly Saxon" (vi).

56 Cahill places the blame for destructiveness on the Huns and Germanic tribes. The Saxons were but one of the warlike pagan peoples who cared nothing for the documents and volumes being preserved by the Irish monks.

57 James Moylan expressed outrage in the *Canadian Freeman* at "this late wickedness of Fenianism" enacted upon "a happy and contented people." To Moylan, the Fenians were little better than loudmouths and crooks engaged in mostly petty crimes until they took the outrageous step of trying to invade Canada (7 June 1866).

58 No authorship is listed for the report.

59 Gilbert McMicken (1813–91) was appointed by John A. Macdonald in 1864 to create Canada's "first undercover security force" and in that capacity his detectives watched the border closely for evidence of Fenian military preparation and activity (Wilson, *Thomas D'Arcy McGee*, 2: 262). In 1853 Francis Hincks appointed him to replace McCarroll as collector at Port Stamford. See DCB, vol. 12.

60 "Centres" were the primary organizational unit for the secretive operations of the Fenians. In *Ridgeway* Big Tom O'Brien is said to have 300 armed men at his command should he have occasion to call upon them (140).

61 McCarroll advertised the novel as "A BEAUTIFUL STORY. Every TRUE IRISHMAN will have it. Every AMERICAN should read it." The book was sold in "a People's Edition" for 50 cents and a Library Edition (bound in green and gold) for $1.50. McCarroll deliberately altered the spelling of his name to M'Carroll as in "M'Carroll & Co., Publishers," as he often did in his later years. Perhaps he wished to assure readers of his Catholic identity.

62 The notice appeared in the *Buffalo Courier*. It described McCarroll as "known throughout the Canadas and the United States as a poet of considerable merit and one of the oldest writers for the press in the country." The poem is eight stanzas in length. See also *Madeline and Other Poems*, 130–1.

63 The Museum and Opera House later became the Adelphi Theatre. Mrs English's tenure at the theatre was short-lived; she went on to perform with distinction in other American cities.

64 *Buffalo Daily Courier*, 8 August 1866. The brevity of Mrs English's tenure no doubt limited McCarroll's actual involvement as a musician and lecturer.

65 Payne was the author of the much-loved song "Home, Sweet Home," which had proved popular both on the stage and with soldiers during the Civil War. Equally well known as an actor and playwright, he became the American consul to Tunis (Tunisia) in 1842; in 1850 he was back in Washington lobbying for a renewal of his post. While there he saw several of his plays in new productions and began to court one of the company's leading actresses, Miss (M.A.) Tyrrell; he tried by means of letters to convince her to become his mistress. See "In Search of a Mistress," *American Magazine and Historical Chronicle* 4, no. 2 (Autumn/Winter, 1988–89): 43–6. It appears that nothing came of Payne's pursuit of Miss Tyrrell, except for the five surviving letters that form the basis of the aforementioned article.

66 The 1861 Canadian census lists the Dolmage family with Julia as its head. Henry Sr, who was five years older than Julia, was listed as deaf and blind. It is odd to find a census entry where the eldest male is not listed at the top of the family list, but Henry's condition clearly warranted such a change.

67 The US Census for 1870 listed Henry Dolmage as printer (age twenty-two), Florence (twenty-one) as "Keeping house," Jessie (nineteen), and Allen (fourteen) "at home."

68 The volume was included as part of a package of McCarroll memorabilia advertised for auction in 2014 by Sophie Dupre. In an email (30 December 2014) Ms Dupre told me that she had acquired the material about twenty years earlier from a San Francisco dealer. She did not put it on the market for many years. Nor could she recall the details of her original purchase.

69 1905 census.

Chapter Eight

1 "Madame Mina Geary Fitzpatrick" in the *Irish American Weekly*, 10 April 1869.

2 Madame Mina Geary Fitzpatrick was a soprano and the daughter of the very popular tenor, teacher, composer, and conductor, Gustavus Geary. Originally from Dublin, where he had performed regularly, conducted oratorios, and led the Dublin Madrigal Society, Geary had come to New York on tour in 1859 but had stayed on and established a series of yearly concerts featuring the ballads of Thomas Moore, as he had done in Dublin. His daughter Mina, who began to perform with him in the early 1860s, took over his yearly concert series in New York while he busied himself with other musical matters. A curious dimension of the Gearys' musical life in New York was their contract with P.T. Barnum to sing a selection of pieces as part of General Tom Thumb's appearances at Barnum's Hall.

3 Randolph Fitzpatrick had aroused great "Celtic enthusiasm" at a recent recitation at the Cooper Institute. John Savage lived from 1828 to 1888.

4 James and Julia had moved to New York City by the winter of 1868–69. The 1870 American census for New York reported that McCarroll was fifty-three and Julia Ellen was forty-one. It is likely that Julia immigrated to Toronto from England in the early 1860s with her family. The eldest son, Henry W. Dolmage (b. 1847), stayed on as a printer in Buffalo, where he had been trained by McCarroll himself. Allen continued to live in Henry's household, but later joined McCarroll and his mother in New York. Allen died while living with his mother and stepfather at the McCarroll flat in 1879 (*New York Herald*, 2 August 1879).

5 See his poem, "The Waif" (23 July), *Madeline*, 53. It begins, "Oh! poor little barefooted, hollow-cheeked thing, / How early dost thou and thy destiny meet."

6 During his Canadian years, McCarroll was often critical of American values and popular culture. Aggressive materialism, the influx of pulp writing, and the minstrel music that flooded into Canada were among his regular targets. He began to alter those views with his move to Buffalo, now feeling more attuned to the idea and opportunity of American democracy.

7 Called "the great wizard of the north" in the 16 April issue of WAJ, Bull was further described as "the great violinist, over whom time seems to have resigned all influence" (23 April). Only Paganini was viewed as a more dexterous and tonally diverse violinist.

8 "We passed two or three hours with Madame and her good husband a short time since" (22 January 1870). Anna Bishop was living at 205 West 11th Street where she received her students. The reference to "we" suggests that McCarroll and Watson visited together. McCarroll had attended several of Bishop's concerts in Toronto in the 1850s and at the Horticultural Gardens there in the early 1860s; he glowingly reported on the latter in his Terry Finnegan letters.

9 Charles Lotin Hildreth supplied this list of musician friends in his introduction to McCarroll's selected poems, *Madeline and Other Poems* (1889), vi. I have added the Irish soprano Catherine (Kate) Hayes whom he so much admired in the early 1850s. Anna Bishop was a particular favourite of McCarroll. *The Dictionary of American Biography*, vol. 6 (1933), 569, notes that "In the course of [his] travels, he met most of the celebrities in the concert field."

10 McCarroll may well have written squibs in *Frank Leslie's Illustrated Newspaper* on Henri Vieuxtemps and H. Wieniawski (18 February 1871). Both were among his musical acquaintances (see Hildreth's list). McCarroll later composed a piece integrating various Vieuxtemps' compositions.

11 Information about other concerts he appeared in is currently lacking.

12 McCarroll wrote three (unsigned) columns in a series for *Watson's Art Journal* entitled "A Glance at Ancient Music and Musical Instruments" (21 May, 28 May, and 4 June 1870). Records indicate that he was also involved with the Conservatory of New York as "a Professor" and lecturer in 1875.

13 The author here notes that, while there is some debate about where "The Messiah" was first performed, he believes that it took place in Dublin, not London. His case for the importance of a warm and informed Irish response to Handel hangs in part upon this assertion and on the very positive reception Handel received in Dublin.

14 "The Pepper-Pot Letters, No. IX" (24 September 1870).

15 Robert Belford was the youngest son of an Irish family from County Kerry that immigrated to Toronto in the early 1860s. They were related to James Beaty, the owner of the *Daily Leader*. See Maclaren's *Dominion and Agency*, chapter 3.

16 McCarroll's employment at *Watson's Art Journal* was unknown to me until 2016. See note 19.

17 Watson had also worked as art critic for the *New York Albion* and the *New York Tribune* at various points in his lengthy journalistic career.

18 McCarroll wrote a fine poem about Edgar Allen Poe (*Madeline*, 9). I have found no date for its initial appearance in print. Watson's connections with and his high opinion of Frank Leslie must have whetted McCarroll's interest in the firm as did his work in Buffalo as a stringer for Leslie.

19 Nowhere in biographical sketches or obituaries is McCarroll's work for Henry Watson mentioned. The connection came to my attention in 2015 when several letters from Oliver Wendell Holmes to McCarroll were put up for auction. Two of these were sent by Holmes to McCarroll, care of *Watson's Art Journal*, 746 Broadway. Several repositories, including the New York Public Library, have bound volumes of the magazine.

20 See volumes 12 and 13 of *Watson's Art Journal* at the New York Public Library (Lincoln Centre Fine Arts Library). In the wake of Watson's death (c. 1876), the weekly journal was renamed the *American Art Journal*. More of McCarroll's writing and editorials appeared in vol. 14. Most of the run of the magazine is available on microfilm.

21 Before J.M. Barrie's popular play of the same title, "the admirable Crichton" was a much-used phrase referring back to James Crichton (1560–1585?), a Scottish nobleman and scholar who was admired for his great range of talents and his scholarly achievements. McCarroll was impressive in so many ways that men like Henry Watson and James Lamb could not restrain themselves in praising him.

22 Three pieces entitled "A Glance at Ancient Music and Musical Instruments: From a Cosmopolitan Point of View" (21 May, 28 May, 4 June) echo other such articles written by McCarroll. The penname "Gradgrind" might well be another McCarroll pseudonym, borrowed from Charles Dickens's *Hard Times*. Dickens died while McCarroll was working at waj. McCarroll may even have contributed to the several pieces that reported on Dickens's death and eulogized the popular author. Several reviews about literary matters also bear a McCarroll stamp, especially those commending the poetry of Thomas Moore and Oliver Wendell Holmes.

23 "Capsicum" is the name of a genus of plants that includes spices, vegetables, and drugs, most notably in this instance the piquant pepper and chili family.

24 In waj a signed poem would often be directly followed by an unsigned story, or vice versa; the implication may have been that the announced authorship of the one applied to other.

25 The Pepper-Pot Papers #2 included "Dawn" (6 July 1870) and #7 contained "The Rainbow" (27 August 1870). On 15 October McCarroll's poem entitled "Mirage" appeared under N.K. Capiscum's name. He would also use Capsicum's name as author of "To the Son of My Oldest Friend" on 11 February 1871; see "Early Joys," in *Madeline*, 290–1.

26 "Dawn" is included in *Madeline* (112), but "Cede Majori" is not. Rather it is attributed to Capiscum's uncle, Arthur Grainger. Holmes's poetic "genius" stood out for McCarroll among their American contemporaries. While he also praised Longfellow and William Cullen Bryant (see 11 June, under the pseudonym "A Golden Grasshopper"), he does not mention Emerson or Whitman. McCarroll ranked Holmes with Thomas Moore as a melodic poet of the first order.

27 An irony that follows is that McCarroll himself would copyright several of his plays and prose works in the 1870s. None of these manuscripts has survived.

28 31 December 1870. The sixteen-verse poem is unusually long for McCarroll. He did not choose to include it in *Madeline*.

29 Andrew Carpenter Wheeler (1835–1903) wrote for the *New York World* in the early 1870s. Like McCarroll, he was a career journalist who delighted in using pseudonyms (like Nym Crickle); he also wrote plays.

30 The Lotus Club critique was long over when McCarroll left the magazine. It is possible that McCarroll's insistence on high poetic standards may have rubbed Watson, himself a poet, the wrong way. McCarroll mocked him passingly in one of the PPP sketches. Whatever their disagreements, the more likely explanation is that Frank Leslie offered him a better-paying position. Nevertheless, Watson's utter silence on losing his "Managing Editor" requires an explanation.

31 Leslie bought the *New York Journal of Romance* in 1854.

32 See George Everett and Frank Leslie in Garraty and Carnes, *American National Biography*, 518.

33 Watson wrote that he had been connected with Frank Leslie's newspaper for "several years" and had "ample opportunity of knowing the magnitude of the undertaking [Leslie] has made [and] so many sacrifices to bring it to its present point of brilliant success."

34 Leslie included stories by a few name writers like Louisa May Alcott, but his stable of writers was far from the first rank. For her part Alcott was scornful of his offers but appreciated the money that he promptly sent to her. See *The Journals of Louisa May Alcott*, passim.

35 For instance, the lead article in *Frank Leslie's Popular Monthly* for August 1883 (129–39) was entitled "The Home of Illustrated Literature." It is typical of the self-promoting pieces that describe and praise Leslie's publishing operations as well as the variety of his various magazines and the extent of his audience. By this time McCarroll had left the company's employ.

36 The letterhead reads "Frank Leslie's Publishing House / 537 Pearl Street, corner of Elm St / one Block from Broadway, / New York." Historian Chris Raible led me to McCarroll's letter to Lindsey in the Mackenzie/Lindsey Papers at the Archives of Ontario. Lindsey and McCarroll had been fellow journalists

and supporters of the Reform movement in Canada West in the 1840s. In 1853, while McCarroll was living in Port Credit, Lindsey had hired him to write occasional columns and poems for James Beaty's new newspaper, the *Toronto Leader*, of which he was the founding editor.

37 McCarroll had been working for several years on the "portrait gallery" of self-made men that appeared weekly in *Frank Leslie's Chimney Corner*. He had begun this work in Buffalo in 1867, according to a report in the *Buffalo Courier*. In this important letter he apologizes to Lindsey because the biography and portrait of a Hamilton politician named "Whillon" (actually Whitton) had appeared before his own (see 7 May 1873), but then he adds that "I should like to get a few more Canadian self-made men" into the journal: he then asks Lindsey to "Name me some worthy persons with whom you would like to be associated."

38 By "here" McCarroll could mean Buffalo or New York City. Certainly his financial situation was woeful when he decamped to Buffalo from Toronto in March 1866.

39 McCarroll also neglected to mention his work with *Watson's Art Journal*.

40 Brown, *Beyond the Lines*, 150.

41 Ibid., 26.

42 *The Journals of Louisa May Alcott*, 130, 139.

43 Ibid., 140. The story was "A Double Tragedy: An Actor's Story" in the *Chimney Corner* (3 June 1865).

44 Among the Buffalo men were Samuel G. Cornell (30 November 1872) of the Cornell White Lead Company and Charles B. Stuart (8 February 1873). Stuart was only briefly a Buffalo man; he was a well-known civil engineer who built railroads and boat docks during his career in New York State; he also served as a general in the Union Navy. McCarroll may have known him because of his spectacular work in creating the suspension bridge across the Niagara River.

45 The Witton profile appeared about a month before Lindsey's; its dating suggests that McCarroll deliberately staggered the Canadian profiles he placed before his American readers.

46 McCarroll rehearses here his life as a fervent Reformer in Upper Canada (Canada West) and his distress at what he saw as Canada's apathy in contrast to American energy and initiative. He may have meant the Jarvises rather than the Joneses as a leading Family Compact family in Toronto, though both names were relevant.

47 Crawford was born in Dublin but raised in Paisley, Ontario. In the late 1860s she was living with her family; her father, Stephen, had become the doctor in the village of Lakefield, north of Peterborough. In Lakefield Crawford met Catharine Parr Traill and may also have met and befriended her daughter Mary Muchall, who was herself an aspiring writer (see *I Bless You in My Heart*),

151, 166. The Crawfords moved to Peterborough about 1870 where her father had a larger clientele which somewhat compensated for his drinking problem.

48 All five poems had appeared in the *Toronto Daily Leader* and would later be included in *Madeline*.

49 Some wording in this poem was changed from the *Illustrated Newspaper* version to its appearance in *Madeline* (145–6). I have used the *Madeline* wording as likely McCarroll's preferred version of the poem.

50 The first issue of the *Favorite* also included a Crawford story, "The Silvers' Christmas Eve."

51 The first Muchall story in *Frank Leslie's Illustrated Newspaper* was her reworking of a story written up but never published by her mother, Catharine Parr Traill. It is found in Traill's papers for 1836 and was tentatively entitled "A Night of Terror. A True Story"; it appeared in the issue for 11 December 1869. See *Forest and Other Gleanings: The Fugitive Stories of Catharine Parr Traill* (1994) where it is entitled "My Irish Maid Isabella – A Night of Peril" (99–110). A shortened version appeared under Muchall's name in the *Canadian Monthly and National Review* 1 (February 1872) under the title "A Night of Terror in the Backwoods of Canada: A True Story." The second Muchall story appeared in the *Chimney Corner* on 24 August 1872 under the title "The Professor Outwitted." It was a shortened version of Traill's story "Cousin Kate; or, the Professor Outwitted," which had appeared in the *Anglo-American Magazine* (Toronto), 2 (1853), 510–14. The elderly Mrs Traill was trying to help her daughter get started with her own writing career; in both cases she provided her with stories from her own archives that Mary revised and sent out to publishers. Traill and McCarroll were friends from their Peterborough days.

52 Surprisingly, the poem is not included in *Madeline*. Neither did it appear in *Watson's Art Journal*.

53 For example, "Handel and the Irish."

54 In a number of biographical sketches he is described as having been the theatre critic for the *Toronto Leader* and the *Colonist* in the late 1850s and 60s. Since theatre reviews in both papers were unsigned, it is difficult to pinpoint even a small selection of his contributions.

55 The biographical entry on McCarroll in *Appleton's Cyclopedia* was written during this period; it reads, "In 1866 he removed to Buffalo, N.Y., and after a few years to New York, where he has since engaged as a musical and dramatic critic, and as a writer of general literature." McCarroll worked in various capacities for Appleton's Publishing House during the late 1870s and early 1880s; his personal contribution to this biographical description gives it particular reliability.

56 In biographical sketches (likely provided in this and other instances by McCarroll himself) he described the plays he wrote as belonging to the tradition of Scribe and Dumas, though, given Dumas *fils's* greater interest in

being realistic in his representations, that comparison seems more wishful than accurate. Scribe (1791–1861) was a very productive playwright who was reputedly the first Frenchman to get rich writing plays. His strict rules about structure and action were followed closely by the likes of Wilkie Collins, Strindberg, and Chekhov, but were much satirized by later playwrights like G.B. Shaw and Oscar Wilde.

57 Krause, ed., *The Dolmen Boucicault*, 13. This volume includes Boucicault's three best-known Irish plays, the third being *The Shaughraun* (1874), along with Krause's introductory essay "The Theatre of Dion Boucicault."

58 Ibid., 13.

59 The evidence available in the Leslie periodicals in which McCarroll was involved suggests that the company expected or even insisted that their editors not include their own writing in issues that they were editing. McCarroll's linking of a few of his unsigned poems with Crawford's chapters of "Wrecked" in the *Illustrated Newspaper* may have been a quiet breach of house protocol.

60 It is possible that McCarroll's old friend James Lamb of St Catharines, Ontario, exercised his continuing influence with the *Evening Journal*, the newspaper he formerly edited, in placing this story for publication.

61 "The Poor Scholar," "The Ruby Cross of Oulart," and "The Two Spies."

62 19 January 1866. It is difficult to track down the writing and publication of such tales by McCarroll over his career. He suggested to John A. that he had a number of them on hand at his desk in Toronto in 1866. Toronto readers would likely have known "Adventures of a Night" and "The New Life Boat," which were republished several times. The biggest burst of such publications on record are the seven stories published in *Frank Leslie's Chimney Corner*, although his several stories in *Watson's Art Journal* (1870–71) are also noteworthy.

63 Brown, *Beyond the Lines*, 63. The *Popular Monthly* became the *American Magazine* after 1905.

64 McCarroll's poems included "Grand Sequences" (February 1877), "The Magic Mirror" (April 1877), "Why Dost Thou Tarry?" (April 1877), "A Royal Race" (May 1877), "God Help Her!" (June 1877), "The Great Iron Cyclops" (August 1877), "Gold" (September 1877), "Old Homes" (October 1877), "To a Husbandman" (October 1877), "To a Butterfly" (March 1878), "February" (February 1878), "Clouds" (April 1878).

65 This darkly vivid New York poem first appeared in Toronto. It was also in *Watson's Art Journal* under the title "Winter" (26 November 1870). McCarroll included it in *Madeline* using the title "February" (138–9).

66 William Hanna (1808–1882) wrote *The Life of Christ* in several volumes. The American Tract Society published it in 1871.

67 Dr William McClure Thomson (1806–1894) was a Protestant missionary who

worked in Syria and Lebanon for most of his life. His *The Land and the Book* (1859) was a best seller for decades, second only to *Uncle Tom's Cabin*.

68 McCarroll's only signed contribution to the 1879 revised version of *Appleton's Encyclopedia* was an entry on William Lyon Mackenzie, 794–6. The Montreal connection is difficult to unlock. Various biographical dictionaries noted that he edited for a brief time the *Quebec Morning Chronicle*, but that connection was likely in the 1840s.

69 *The Cyclopedia of American Biography* lists his work for these two cyclopedias.

70 In writing about and debating the mysteries of the gyroscope, McCarroll proposed "a new law of motion." However, his theory was debunked in an article in the *New York Herald* on 29 January 1879.

71 *American National Biography*, vol. 9, 374.

72 *The Heritage Encyclopedia of Band Music* lists forty-seven pieces for bands and twenty-seven quicksteps for piano by Grafulla, among them "Captain Shepherd's Quickstep," "Nightingale Waltzes," and "Washington Greys."

73 Quoting Clark in *The History of the 7th Regiment 1806–1889* (1890), see ANB, 9: 374.

74 Other residents of the Grafulla house were Harry and Claude Connor, both bachelor musicians working in the city.

75 I have found no first name for Mrs Belford, but am struck in reading the poem by her "perfect loveliness," her "silvery laugh," her "regal mien and sweetness," and her sympathetic nature.

76 *Belford's Magazine* was edited by Robert Belford's lawyer, Colonel Dan Piatt.

77 "Obituary," *Belford's Magazine* (June 1892), 137–8. The author was either Robert Belford or Charles Lotin Hindreth.

78 McLaren, *Dominion and Agency*, 72,

79 In Robert Belford's obituary in *Publishers' Weekly* (18 May 1920), it was noted that he was "born in Canada about 60 years ago." His date of birth was not provided, but was likely 1858 or 1859. He was described as "one of the brilliant and enterprising group of Canadians who came to the States for wider fields to conquer in the seventies."

80 Obituary, *Belford's Magazine*, 137.

81 A prominent Torontonian of Irish birth, James Beaty (1798–1892) was the great uncle of the Belford brothers. He was quick to offer a job on his newspaper to Charles, the eldest, and likely found jobs for Aleck and Robert as they came of age.

82 Robert's parents both died in 1863, leaving him and his younger brothers to make their own way as best they could.

83 See McCarroll's letter to Foster (chapter 1, p. 14).

84 The exploits of the Belford Brothers made plenty of news in the publishing and legal worlds of Canada in the 1870s. See Parker, *The Beginnings of the*

Book Trade in Canada, 187–8 and McLaren, *Dominion and Agency*, 69–101. McLaren's book offers the most comprehensive treatment of what George Doran, a contemporary of the Belfords, called "one of the most romantic adventures in Canadian publishing" (*Chronicles of Barabbas*, 97).

85 Belford, Clarke & Company became a successful New York publisher, though the enterprise was often underfunded and propped up by loans. The company successfully undertook new ways of marketing books (using stalls in department stores) before, under James Clarke's direction, they began selling the *Encyclopedia Britannica* by instalment in Britain and the United States. By 1878 Charles Belford had left the company for health reasons while Robert stayed in Toronto to oversee their interests there, including the monthly publication of *Rose-Belford's Magazine*.

86 Ella Jennings had studied medicine in New York and later married the sculptor John Wilson Macdonald. They separated after the death of their only child. She took up the cause of the poor, and women in particular, seeking ways to provide reliable medical services for struggling women and their children in the city. Her dispensary was funded by donations from wealthy individuals including Peter Cooper. She died in 1908.

87 Dr Jennings was one of six sisters; remarkably, three of them became doctors. They were born in Norwich, Upper Canada to Quaker parents who had followed Pieter Lossing and his wife north from New York State to Norwich where he established an agricultural settlement. Ella's medical sisters included the famous Dr Emily Jennings Stowe (1831–1903), who became one of the first Canadian women to earn a medical degree (following her classmate Jennie Trott). She achieved considerable praise for her medical work, especially in homeopathy; later, under the influence by Susan B. Anthony, she became one of the leading suffragettes in Canada, arguing influentially for equal rights for women.

88 The dispensary or clinic was originally located at 42 Washington Place. Reportedly there were two such dispensaries.

89 Belle Hunt, as she sometimes called herself, was a novelist and story writer who came to New York from Terrell, Texas in 1890 to expand the opportunities available to her as a writer. Among her New York friends were McCarroll, Mrs Frank Leslie, and the novelist Ella Wheeler. Her father, Colonel William Hunt, came from New York but established himself as a leading pioneer and soldier in what became Wise County, Texas; his farm became one of the prototypes for large-scale ranching in the state. Belle Hunt Shortridge, considered the first white child born in Wise County, was admired for her gentle sketches of rural Texas life, especially "A Texas Thanksgiving." Her sister Kate Hunt Craddock and cousin Helen Hunt Jackson also became writers. Her two novels were both published in 1892. *Lone-Star Lights* was her only book of poems.

90 *Humanity and Health* (May 1892), 33.

91 James McCarroll's death certificate lists the cause of death as "pneumonia, heart failure and previous attack of the grippe."

92 He was buried on 12 April in Summit Lot 42 of Maple Grove Cemetery; however, the grave was unmarked, leading to confusion in the present day.

93 The 1905 census reports that Julia was living in Buffalo with her son Henry Dolmage (a printer) and his family.

Appendix B

1 Moylan lists three Fenian newspapers before focusing on the *Fenian Volunteer*.

2 The "Gauger" reference refers both to McCarroll's former position as a customs inspector in Canada and his serialized novel, "Jack Trainer's Story; or, The New Gauger," published in 1856–57 in Toronto.

3 See chapter 7, pp. 250–2.

Bibliography

Manuscript Sources

Archives of Ontario

William Foster Papers (two McCarroll letters)
William Lyon MacKenzie Papers (including Charles Lindsey papers)
(two McCarroll letters)

National Archives

Customs and Revenue Department Fonds, RG 16, Series A, vol. 50 (Cobourg);
vol. 56 (Collingwood); vol. 236 (Niagara); vol. 64 (Port Credit); vol. 335 (Port
Stamford); vol. 312 (St Catharines); vol. 374, 375, 376, 377 (Toronto).
John A. Macdonald Papers (sixteen McCarroll letters)
Upper Canada Sundries, RG 5 AI

Newspapers and Magazines

Anglo-American Magazine (Toronto) (1852–57)
Appleton's Cyclopedia (rev. ed. 1874)
Backwoodsman and Sentinel (Peterborough) (1837–41)
Belford's Magazine (New York) (1887–92)
British American Magazine (Toronto) (1863–64)
Canadian Freeman (Toronto) (1858–70)

Canadian Gem and Family Visitor (Cobourg, Toronto) (1850–51)

Christian Guardian (Cobourg, Toronto) (1840–70)

Cobourg Sentinel (1862–63)

Cobourg Star (1832–56)

Courier (Buffalo) (1866–70) [see also the *Evening Courier and Republic*]

Daily Leader (Toronto) (1853–1870) [initially the *Leader* was a weekly]

Dublin Warder (Dublin) (1840–57)

The Favorite (Montreal) (1873–74)

Fenian Volunteer (Buffalo) (1867–68)

Frank Leslie's Chimney Corner (New York) (1865–92)

Frank Leslie's Illustrated Newspaper (New York) (1867–92)

Frank Leslie's Lady's Magazine (New York) (1867–92)

Frank Leslie's Pleasant Hours (New York) (1880–96)

Frank Leslie's Popular Magazine (New York) (1880–1905)

Frank Leslie's Sunday Magazine (New York) (1876–80)

Gazette (Montreal) (1866–70)

Globe (Buffalo) (1866) [no issues extant]

Globe (Toronto) (1850–70)

Graham's Monthly Magazine (Philadelphia) (1851–52)

Growler (Toronto) (1864)

Grumbler (Toronto) (1859, 1860–65, 1869)

Hamilton Canadian (1865–66)

Hamilton Gazette (1856)

Hearthstone (Montreal) (1872)

Home Journal (Toronto) (1860–61)

Irish Canadian (Toronto) (1863–92)

Journalist (New York) (1884–92)

Literary Garland (Montreal) (1838–52)

Momus (Toronto) (1861) (no issues extant)

Montreal Herald (1860–70)

Newcastle Courier (Cobourg) (1847–48) (two issues extant)

New Era (Montreal) (1857–58)

Niagara Mail (Newark, Canada West) (1845–60)

Patriot (Toronto) (1857–64)

Peterboro Chronicle (1843–46)

Peterborough Examiner (1863–64, 1891–92)

Peterborough Gazette (1844–48)

Peterborough Review (1866)

Peterborough Weekly Despatch (1846–56)

Pick (Toronto) (1865) (no issues extant)

Roscommon & Leitrim Gazette (1818–32)

St Catharines Constitutional (1851–54)

St Catharines Evening Journal (1851–72)
St Catharines Semi-Weekly Post (1858)
Streetsville (Weekly) Review (1855–64)
Victoria Magazine (Belleville) (1847–48)
Watson's Art Journal (New York) (1868–73)

Printed Sources

Akenson, Donald Harman. *The Irish in Ontario: A Study in Rural History*. Montreal & Kingston: McGill-Queen's University Press, 1984.
– *The Orangeman: The Life and Times of Ogle Gowan*. Toronto: J. Lorimer, 1986.
Alcott, Louisa May. *The Journals of Louisa May Alcott*. Edited by Joel Myerson and Daniel Shealy. New York: Little Brown, 1989.
Aoki, Jodi, ed. *Revisiting "Our Forest Home": The Immigrant Letters of Frances Stewart*. Toronto: Dundurn Press, 2011.
Ascher, Isadore G. *Voices from the Hearth*. Montreal: Lovell, 1863.
Ballstadt, Carl, Elizabeth Hopkins, and Michael A. Peterman, eds. *I Bless You in My Heart: Selected Correspondence of Catharine Parr Traill*. Toronto: University of Toronto Press, 1997.
– *Letters of Love and Duty: The Correspondence of John and Susanna Moodie*. Toronto: University of Toronto Press, 1993.
– *Susanna Moodie: Letters of a Lifetime*. Toronto: University of Toronto Press, 1985.
Bellen, Rubin C. Alexander, "Gilbert McMicken." In *Dictionary of Canadian Biography online*. http://www.biographi.ca.
Benson, Eugene, and William Toye, eds. *The Oxford Companion of Canadian Literature*. 2nd ed. Toronto: Oxford University Press, 1997.
Berger, Carl. *The Sense of Power: Studies in the Ideas of Canadian Imperialism, 1867–1914*. Toronto: University of Toronto Press, 1970.
Bohen, Timothy. *Against the Grain: The History of Buffalo's First Ward*. Buffalo: Western New York Wares, 2012.
Bonenfant, J.-C. "George-Étienne Cartier." In *Dictionary of Canadian Biography online*. http://www.biographi.ca.
Brady, Alexander. *Thomas D'Arcy McGee*. Toronto: Macmillan, 1925.
Brown, Joshua. *Beyond the Lines: Pictorial Reporting, Everyday Life, and the Crisis in Gilded Age America*. Los Angeles: University of California Press, 2006.
Brown, Mary Markham. *An Index to* The Literary Garland *(Montreal 1838–1851)*. Toronto: Bibliographical Society of Canada, 1962.
Bulman, Joan. *Jenny Lind: A Biography*. London: James Barrie, 1956.
Burns, Robin B. "Thomas D'Arcy McGee." In *Dictionary of Canadian Biography online*. http://www.biographi.ca.
Burpee, Laurence J., ed. *Humour of the North*. Toronto: Musson, 1912.

Cahill, Thomas. *How the Irish Saved Civilization.* New York: Doubleday, 1995.

Careless, J.M.S. *Brown of the Globe.* Vol. 1, *The Voice of Upper Canada, 1818–1859.* Toronto: Macmillan, 1959.

– *Brown of the Globe.* Vol. 2, *Statesman of Confederation, 1860–1880.* Toronto: Macmillan, 1963.

– ed. *The Pre-Confederation Premiers: Ontario's Government Leaders, 1841–67.* Toronto: University of Toronto Press, 1980.

Carter-Edwards, Dennis. "Promoting a 'Unity of Feeling': The Rebellions of 1837/38 and the Peterborough Region." *Ontario History* 101, no. 2 (2009): 165–86.

Cavanah, Frances. *Jenny Lind's America.* Philadelphia: Chelton, 1969.

Clarkson, Betty. *At the Mouth of the Credit.* Erin, ON: Boston Mills Press, 1977.

– *Credit Valley Gateway: The Story of Port Credit.* Port Credit: Port Credit Public Library, 1967.

Climo, Percy. *Early Cobourg.* Cobourg: Haynes Printing Co., 1985.

Cole, Jean. "Peterborough in the Hutchison-Fleming Era, 1845–46." Peterborough Historical Society, Occasional Paper 5, 1984.

Connor, D. "'The Irish Canadian': Image and Self-Image, 1847–1870." PhD diss., University of British Columbia, 1976.

Connors, Linda E., and Mary Lu MacDonald. *National Identity in Great Britain and North America, 1815–1851: The Role of Nineteenth-Century Periodicals.* Farnham, Surrey and Burlington, VT: Ashgate Publishing Limited, 2011.

Cooper, Dorothy Rachel. "Opera in Montreal and Toronto: A Study of Performance Traditions and Repertoire, 1783–1980." PhD diss., University of Toronto, 1983.

Corkery, John. "Some Forgotten Longford Exiles." *Teathbho* 1, no. 3 (1973): 206–21.

Cottrell, Michael. "Irish Catholic Politics in Ontario." In Robert O'Driscoll and Lorna Reynolds, eds, *The Untold Story: The Irish in Canada,* 2; 791–810. Toronto: University of Toronto Press, 1988.

Creighton, Donald Grant. *John A. Macdonald.* Vol. 1, *The Young Lion.* Toronto: Macmillan, 1952.

– *Road to Confederation: The Emergence of Canada, 1863–1867.* Toronto: Macmillan 1966.

Crotty, Patrick, ed. *The Penguin Book of Irish Poetry.* London: Penguin, 2010.

Davin, Nicholas Flood. *The Irishman in Canada.* London: Samson Low and Marston; Toronto: Maclear [1877].

Davis, Richard. *Anna Bishop: The Adventures of an Intrepid Prima Donna.* Sydney: Currency Press, 1997.

de la Fosse, Frederick. *Centennial History of St John's Church, Peterborough, 1827–1927.* Peterborough, 1927.

de Nie, Michael. *The Eternal Paddy: Irish Identity and the British Press, 1798–1882.* Madison: University of Wisconsin Press, 2004.

Dent, John Charles. *The Last Forty Years: Canada since the Union of 1841*. 2 vols. Toronto, 1881. Abridged edition, edited by Donald Swainson. Toronto: McClelland and Stewart, 1972.

Dewart, Edward Hartley. *Selections from Canadian Poets*. Montreal: John Lovell, 1864.

Dictionary of American Biography. Vol. 6. New York: Charles Scribner's Sons, 1933.

Doolin, D.M. "Exploring Textures of Irish America: A New Perspective on the Fenian Invasion of Canada." *Irish Studies Review* 23, no. 2 (2015): 159–61.

Doran, George H. *Chronicles of Barabbas, 1884–1934*. New York: Harcourt Brace, 1935.

Dubinsky, Karen. *The Second Greatest Disappointment: Honeymooning and Tourism at Niagara Falls*. Toronto: Between the Lines Press, 1995.

Dzwonkoski, Peter, ed. *American Literary Publishing Houses, 1638–1899*. Vol. 49, *Dictionary of Literary Biography*. Detroit: Gale Research, 1986.

Edmonds, John W., and George T. Dexter. *Spiritualism*. New York Partridge and Britian, Publishers.1853.

Edwards, Mary Jane. "Alexander McLachlan." In *Dictionary of Canadian Biography online*. http://www.biographi.ca.

Filteau, Huguette. "Henry J. Morgan." *Dictionary of Canadian Biography online*. http://www.biographi.ca.

– "Henry J. Morgan." In Francess Halpenny, ed., *Dictionary of Canadian Biography*. Vol. 12. Toronto: University of Toronto Press, 1990.

Flynn, T.M.O. *History of Leitrim*. Dublin: C.J. Fallon, 1937.

Foster, William A. *Canada First; or, Our New Nationality: An Address*. Toronto: Adams, Stevenson, 1871.

Gagan, David. "William A. Foster." In *Dictionary of Canadian Biography online*. http://www. biographi.ca.

Galarneau, Claude. "George-Édouard Desbarats." In *Dictionary of Canadian Biography online*. http://www.biographi.ca.

Garraty, John A., and Mark C. Carnes, eds. *American National Biography*. New York: Oxford University Press, 1999.

Gatenby, Greg. *Toronto: A Literary Guide*. Toronto: McArthur & Company, 1999.

Gibbons, Stephen Randolph. *Captain Rock, Night Errant: The Threatening Letters of Pre-Famine Ireland, 1801–1845*. Dublin: Four Courts Press, 2004.

Grand Conservatory of the City of New York, 21 East 14th Street. Annual Reports. New York: Lincoln Centre Library and Archives.

Gray, Charlotte. "George-Étienne Cartier." In *The Promise of Canada: 150 Years – People and Ideas That Have Shaped Our Country*. Toronto: Simon & Schuster, 2016.

– *Mrs. King: The Life & Times of Isabel Mackenzie King*. Toronto: Viking, Allen Lane, 1997.

Guiguet, Kristina Marie. *The Ideal World of Mrs. Widder's Soirée Musicale: Social*

Identity and Musical Life in Nineteenth-Century Ontario. Gatineau, QC: Canadian Museum of Civilization, 2004.

Guillet, Edwin C. *Cobourg, 1798–1948.* Oshawa: Goodfellow Printing, 1948.

– ed. *The Valley of the Trent.* Toronto: Champlain Society, 1957.

Gwyn, Richard. *John A.: The Man Who Made Us: The Life and Times of John A. Macdonald.* Vol. 1, 1815–1867. Toronto: Random House Canada, 2007.

– *Nation Maker: Sir John A. Macdonald: His Life, Our Times.* Vol. 2, 1867–1891. Toronto: Random House Canada, 2011.

Hicks, Kathleen A. *Port Credit: Past to Present.* Mississauga: Mississauga Library System, 2007.

Hodgetts, J.E. "Alfred Brunel." In *Dictionary of Canadian Biography online.* http://www.biographi.ca.

Hodgins, Bruce W. *John Sandfield Macdonald, 1812–1872.* Toronto: University of Toronto Press, 1971.

– "John Sandfield Macdonald." In *Dictionary of Canadian Biography online.* http://www.biographi.ca.

– "Michael Hamilton Foley." In *Dictionary of Canadian Biography online.* http://www.biographi.ca.

Holmes, Oliver Wendell. *Humorous Poems.* Boston: Ticknor, Fields, 1867.

Holmgren, Michele J. "Native Muses and National Poetry: Nineteenth-Century Irish Canadian Poets." PhD dissertation, University of Western Ontario, 1997.

– "Ossian Abroad: James MacPherson and Canadian Literary Nationalism, 1830–1994." *Canadian Poetry* 50 (Spring/Summer 2002): 51–81.

Houston, Cecil J., and William J. Smyth. *The Sash Canada Wore: A Historical Geography of the Orange Order in Canada.* Toronto: University of Toronto Press, 1980.

Humphreys, Charles W. "John Joseph Lynch." In *Dictionary of Canadian Biography online.* http://www.biographi.ca.

Jenkins, William. *Between Raid and Rebellion: The Irish in Buffalo and Toronto, 1867–1916.* Montreal & Kingston: McGill-Queen's University Press, 2013.

– "Poverty and Place: Documenting and Representing Toronto's Catholic Irish, 1845–1890." In *At the Anvil: Essays in Honour of William S. Smyth,* edited by Patrick J. Duffy and William Nolan, 477–511. Dublin: Geography Publications, 2012.

The John MacKay Shaw Collection of Childhood in Poetry. Tallahassee: Florida State University Library, Gale Research Co., 1976.

Johnson, J.K. "Samuel Zimmerman." In *Dictionary of Canadian Biography online.* http://www.biographi.ca.

Jones, Elwood H. "Daniel Morrison." In *Dictionary of Canadian Biography online.* http://www.biographi.ca.

– *Peterborough: The Electric City.* Burlington, ON: Windsor Publications, 1987.

– *St John's Church: The Sesquicentennial History of an Anglican Parish, 1826–1976.* Peterborough: Maxwell Press, 1976.

Kallmann, Helmut. "Frederick Griebel." In *Dictionary of Canadian Biography online*. http://www.biographi.ca.

– *A History of Music in Canada, 1534–1914*. Toronto: University of Toronto Press, 1960.

Killan, Gerald. "C. Pelham Mulvany." In *Dictionary of Canadian Biography online*. http://www.biographi.ca.

Krause, David, ed. *The Dolmen Boucicault*. Dublin: Dolmen Press, 1965.

Kunitz, Stanley Jasspon, and Howard Haycraft, eds. *American Authors, 1600-1900: A Biographical Dictionary of American Literature*. New York: The H.W. Wilson Company, 1938.

Lever, Charles. *Charles O'Malley, The Irish Dragoon* (1841). *Selected Novels of Charles Lever*. London: George Routledge & Sons, 1880.

Longley, Ronald Stewart. *Sir Francis Hincks: A Study of Canadian Politics, Railways, and Finance in the Nineteenth Century*. Toronto: University of Toronto Press, 1943.

MacLaren, Eli. *Dominion and Agency: Copyright and the Structuring of the Canadian Book Trade, 1867–1918*. Toronto: University of Toronto Press, 2011.

Macmillan Dictionary of Canadian Biography. Edited by W. Stewart Wallace. London: Macmillan, 1963.

MacMurchy, Archibald. *Handbook of Canadian Literature*. Toronto: William Briggs, 1906.

Martin, Ged. *Britain and the Origins of Canadian Confederation, 1837–1864*. Vancouver: University of British Columbia Press, 1995.

McAllister, Bernard. "Reminiscences of Cobourg," Cobourg, 1918. CIHM/ICMH #87705 (Canadian Institute for Historical Microreproductions).

McCalla, Douglas. "James Beaty." In *Dictionary of Canadian Biography online*. http://www.biographi.ca.

McCarroll, James. *The Letters of Terry Finnegan, Author of Several Imaginary Works*. Volume 1, first series. Toronto: 1863.

– second series (twelve or more uncollected letters by Terry Finnegan in 1864–65). *Grumbler* (1864) and *Pick* (1865).

– *Madeline and Other Poems*. New York: Belford, Clarke & Company; London: J.H. Drane, 1889.

– *Nearly a Tragedy: A Comedy*. New York: John F. Trow & Son., 1874.

– "The New Gauger; or, Jack Trainer's Story." *Anglo-American Magazine*. Toronto, 1855–56.

– (Scian Dubh) *Ridgeway: An Historical Romance of the Fenian Invasion of Canada*. Buffalo: McCarroll & Company, 1868.

McGahern, John. *Love of the World: Essays*. London: Faber & Faber, 2009.

McGee, Thomas D'Arcy. *Canadian Ballads, and Occasional Verses*. Montreal: Lovell, 1858.

– *Popular History of Ireland: From the Earliest Period to the Emancipation of the Catholics*. Montreal: D. & J. Sadlier, 1861.

– *Speeches and Addresses on the Subject of British-American Union*. London: Chapman and Hall, 1865.

McGoogan, Ken. *Celtic Lightning: How the Scots and the Irish Created a Canadian Nation*. Toronto: Patrick Crean Editions, Harper Collins, 2015.

McGowan, Mark. "Patrick Boyle." In *Dictionary of Canadian Biography online*. http://www.biographi.ca.

Moodie, Susanna. *Roughing It in the Bush: or, Life in Canada*. Toronto: McClelland and Stewart, 1990.

Moore, Thomas. *Letters and Journals of Lord Byron, with Notices of his Life*. 2 vols. London, 1830.

– *Memoirs of Captain Rock: The Celebrated Irish Chieftain*. London, 1824.

– *Odes of Anacreon* [1800]. Translated into English verse with notes by Thomas Moore. In *The Collected Works of Thomas Moore*. Boston: Phillips and Sampson, 1853.

– *Poetical Works of Thomas Moore, Collected by Himself*. 10 vols. 1841 (including earlier volumes of poetry like *Irish Melodies* and *National Songs*).

Morgan, Henry J., *Sketches of Celebrated Canadians*. Toronto: Hunter Rose & Co., 1862.

– *Bibliotheca Canadensis*. Ottawa: Printed by G.E. Desbarats, 1867.

Mott, Frank Luther. *A History of American Magazines, 1805–1905*. Cambridge: Belknap, 1957.

Mount, Nick. *When Canadian Literature Moved to New York*. Toronto: University of Toronto Press, 2005.

Mulvany, C. Pelham. *History of the County of Peterborough*. Toronto: C.B. Robinson, 1884.

– *Toronto: Past and Present: A Handbook of the City until 1882*. Toronto: W.E. Caiger, 1884.

The National Cyclopaedia of American Biography. Vol. 4. New York: The Press Association Compilers, 1915.

Neidhardt, W.S. *Fenianism in North America*. State College: Penn State University, 1975.

– "Michael Murphy." In *Dictionary of Canadian Biography online*. http://www. biographi.ca.

O'Dell, George C.D. *Annals of the New York Stage*. 15 vols. New York: Columbia University Press, 1927–49.

O'Donoghue, D.J. *The Poets of Ireland: A Biographical and Bibliographical Dictionary of Irish Writers of English Verse*. Dublin: Hodges and Figgis, 1912.

O'Driscoll, Robert, and Lorna Reynolds, eds. *The Untold Story: The Irish in Canada*. Toronto: Celtic Arts of Canada, 1988.

O'Neill, Patrick B. "From Puffery to Criticism: William Lyon Mackenzie, Joseph

Howe and Daniel Morrison: Theatre Criticism in Halifax and Toronto." In Anton Wagner, ed., *Establishing Our Borders: English Theatre Criticism*. Toronto: University of Toronto Press, 2010.

– "Thomas Pope Besnard: Less than Enshrinement." *Theatre Research in Canada* 14, no. 2 (Fall 1993): 144–64.

Ormsby, William G. "Francis Hincks." In J.M.S. Careless, ed., *The Pre-Confederation Premiers: Ontario Government Leaders, 1841–1867*. Toronto: University of Toronto Press, 1980.

Page, Rhoda Ann (RAP). "Wild Notes from the Backwoods." Cobourg, 1850.

Parker, George. *The Beginnings of the Book Trade in Canada*. Toronto: University of Toronto Press, 1965.

Performing Arts Biography Master Index. Edited by Barbara McNeil and Miriam C. Herbert. Detroit: Gale Research Co., 1979.

Peterman, Michael A. "Case Study: Lost from View: James McCarroll, Journalist, Poet, and Satirist." In Fiona Black, Patricia Lockhart, and Yvan Lamonde, eds, *The History of the Book in Canada*. Vol. 2. 1840–1918, 134–6. Toronto: University of Toronto Press, 2005.

– "From Terry Finnegan to Terry Fenian: The Truncated Literary Career of James McCarroll." In Wilson, *Irish Nationalism in Canada*, 140–59.

– *James McCarroll, alias Terry Finnegan: Newspapers, Controversy and Literature in Victorian Canada*. Peterborough, ON: Peterborough Historical Society, Occasional Paper #17, 1996.

– "Literary Cultures and Popular Reading in Upper Canada." In Patricia Lockhart Fleming, Gilles Gallichan, and Yvan Lamonde, eds, *The History of the Book in Canada*. Vol. 1, *Beginnings to 1840*, 395–408 Toronto: University of Toronto Press, 2004.

– "Writing for the Illustrated Story Papers in the 1870's: Individuality and Conformity in the Short Stories of Isabella Valancy Crawford." *Short Story*, New Series 13, no. 1 (spring 2005): 73–87.

– ed., Susanna Moodie, *Roughing It in the Bush*. New York: W.W. Norton, 2007.

– ed., with Len Early. *Collected Stories of Isabella Valancy Crawford*. London, ON: Canadian Poetry Press, 2009.

– ed., with Len Early. Isabella Valancy Crawford, *Winona; or The Foster Sisters*. Peterborough: Broadview Press, 2007.

Poole, Thomas. *Early Settlement of Peterborough County*. 1846, Peterborough: Peterborough Printing Company, 1967.

Rutherford, Paul. *A Victorian Authority: The Daily Press in Late Nineteenth-Century Canada*. Toronto: University of Toronto Press, 1982.

Sadie, Stanley, and John Tyrell, eds. *The New Grove Dictionary of Music and Musicians*, 29 vols. London: Oxford University Press, 2004. See also editions of the earlier *Grove Dictionary of Music and Musicians*, edited by George Grove, 1879–89.

Sadlier, Mary Ann, ed. *The Poems of Thomas D'Arcy McGee*. New York: D. & J. Sadlier, 1869.

Sale, John David. "Toronto's Pre-Confederation Music Societies, 1845–67." Master's thesis, University of Toronto, 1968.

Senior, Hereward. *The Fenians and Canada*. Toronto: Macmillan, 1978.

– *The Last Invasion of Canada: The Fenian Raids, 1866–1870*. Toronto and Oxford: Dundurn Press in collaboration with the Canadian War Museum, Canadian Museum of Civilization, 1991.

– "Ogle R. Gowan." In *Dictionary of Canadian Biography online*. http://www.biographi.ca.

Shortridge, Belle Hunt. *Lone-Star Nights*. New York: Clarke, Belford, 1890.

Shultz, Gladys Denny. *Jenny Lind: The Swedish Nightingale*. New York, Philadelphia: J.B. Lippincott, 1962.

Slattery, T.P. *The Assassination of Thomas D'Arcy McGee*. Toronto: Doubleday Canada, 1968.

Smich, Mortimer. *The Life of Ole Bull*. New York: Princeton University Press, 1943.

Sotiron, Mike. "John Ross Robertson." In *Dictionary of Canadian Biography online*. http://www.biographi.ca.

Stacey, C.P. "A Fenian Interlude: The Story of Michael Murphy." *Canadian Historical Review* 15, no. 2 (1934): 133–54.

Stagg, Ronald. "J. Joseph Gold." In *Dictionary of Canadian Biography online*. http://www.biographi.ca.

Stern, Madeleine B. *Purple Passage: The Life of Mrs. Frank Leslie*. Norman: University of Oklahoma Press, 1953.

Stoppard, A. Brooke, and T.W. Rolleston, eds. *A Treasury of Irish Poetry*. London: Smith, Elder, 1900.

Storey, Graham, et al, eds. *The Letters of Charles Dickens*, vol. 10 (1862–64). Oxford: Clarendon Press, 1998.

Story, Norah, ed. *The Oxford Companion to Canadian History and Literature*. Toronto: Oxford University Press, 1967.

Strickland, Samuel. *Twenty-Seven Years in Canada West*. 2 vols. London: Richard Bentley, 1854.

Swainson, Donald. "John Hillyard Cameron." In *Dictionary of Canadian Biography online*. http://www.biographi.ca.

Talmadge, Nathaniel, *The Healing of Nations*. New York, 1855.

Toner, Peter M. "The Fanatic Heart of the North." In Wilson, *Irish Nationalism in Canada*, 34–51.

Upton, George P. *Musical Memories: My Recollection of Celebrities of a Half Century, 1850–1900*. Chicago: A.C. McClung, 1908.

Urschel, Katrin. "Surfacing Again: Ethnic Identity in Irish-Canadian Literature." PhD diss., University of Galway, 2010.

Virgo, Sean. *Selected Verse of Thomas D'Arcy McGee*. Toronto: Exile Editions, 2000.

Vronsky, Peter, *Ridgeway: The American Fenian Invasion and the 1866 Battle That Made Canada*. Toronto: University of Toronto Press, 2011.

Walsh, Basil. *Catharine Hayes: The Hibernian Prima Donna*. Dublin: Irish Academic Press, 2000.

Ware, W. Porter, and Thaddeus C. Lockard Jr. *The Lost Letters of Jenny Lind*. London: Victor Gollancz, 1966.

Waters, Maureen. *The Comic Irishman*. New York: SUNY Press, Excelsior Editions, 1984.

Wilson, David A. "'Orange Influences of the Right Kind': Thomas D'Arcy McGee, the Orange Order and the New Nationality." In *The Orange Order in Canada*, edited by David A. Wilson, 89–108. Dublin: Four Courts Press, 2007.

– *Thomas D'Arcy McGee*. Vol. 1, *Passion, Reason, and Politics, 1825–57*. Montreal & Kingston: McGill-Queen's University Press, 2008.

– *Thomas D'Arcy McGee*. Vol. 2, *The Extreme Moderate, 1857–1868*. Montreal & Kingston: McGill-Queen's University Press, 2011.

– ed. *Irish Nationalism in Canada*. Montreal & Kingston: McGill-Queen's University Press, 2009.

World Biographical Index of Music (the American volumes). New Providence, NJ: K.G. Saur, 1995.

Wright, Joseph, ed. *The English Dialect Dictionary*. 6 vols. Oxford: Oxford University Press, 1900.

Index

A page reference in italics indicates
the partial or complete text of a poem
by James McCarroll. A page reference
followed by an italic *f* indicates an
illustration. The abbreviation "JM" has
been used for "James McCarroll" in
subheadings.